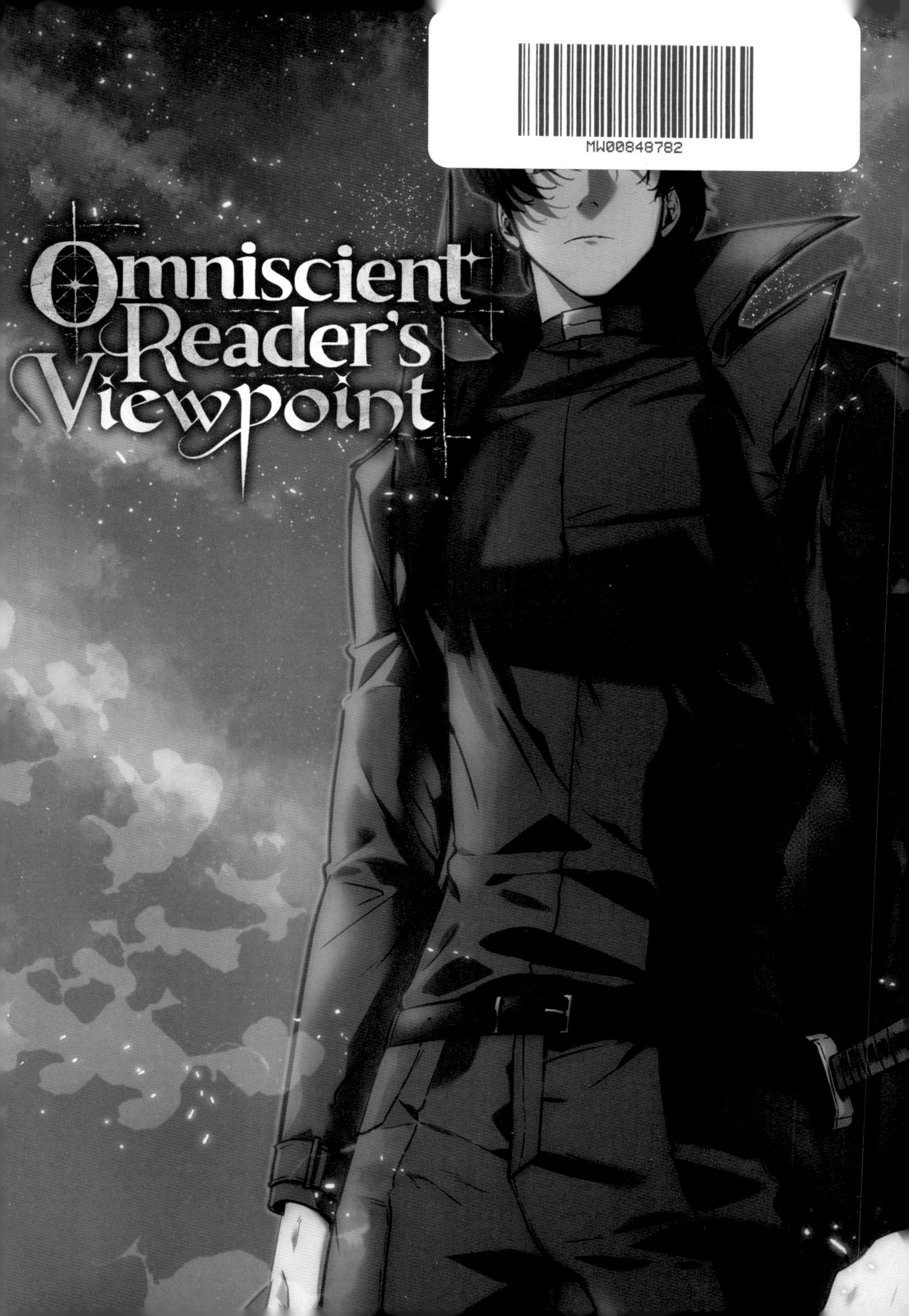
Omniscient Reader's Viewpoint

Omniscient Reader's Viewpoint

CONTENTS

CHARACTERS

DOKJA KIM

The only reader of

TWSA

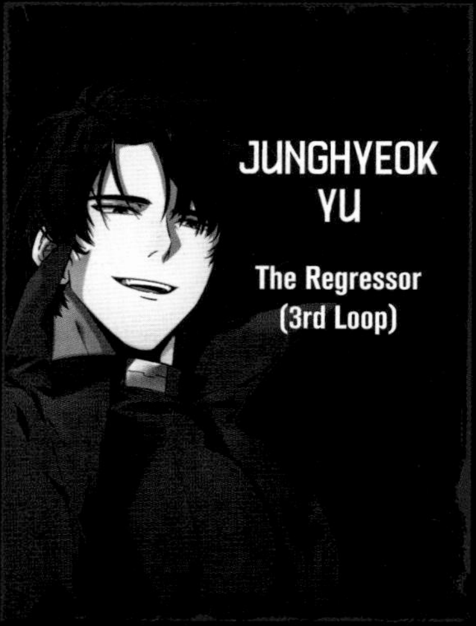

JUNGHYEOK YU

The Regressor (3rd Loop)

GILYEONG LEE

Insect Collector

HUIWON JEONG

Crouching Figure

EP. 02

MAIN CHARACTER

EP. 02

Omniscient
Reader's
Viewpoint

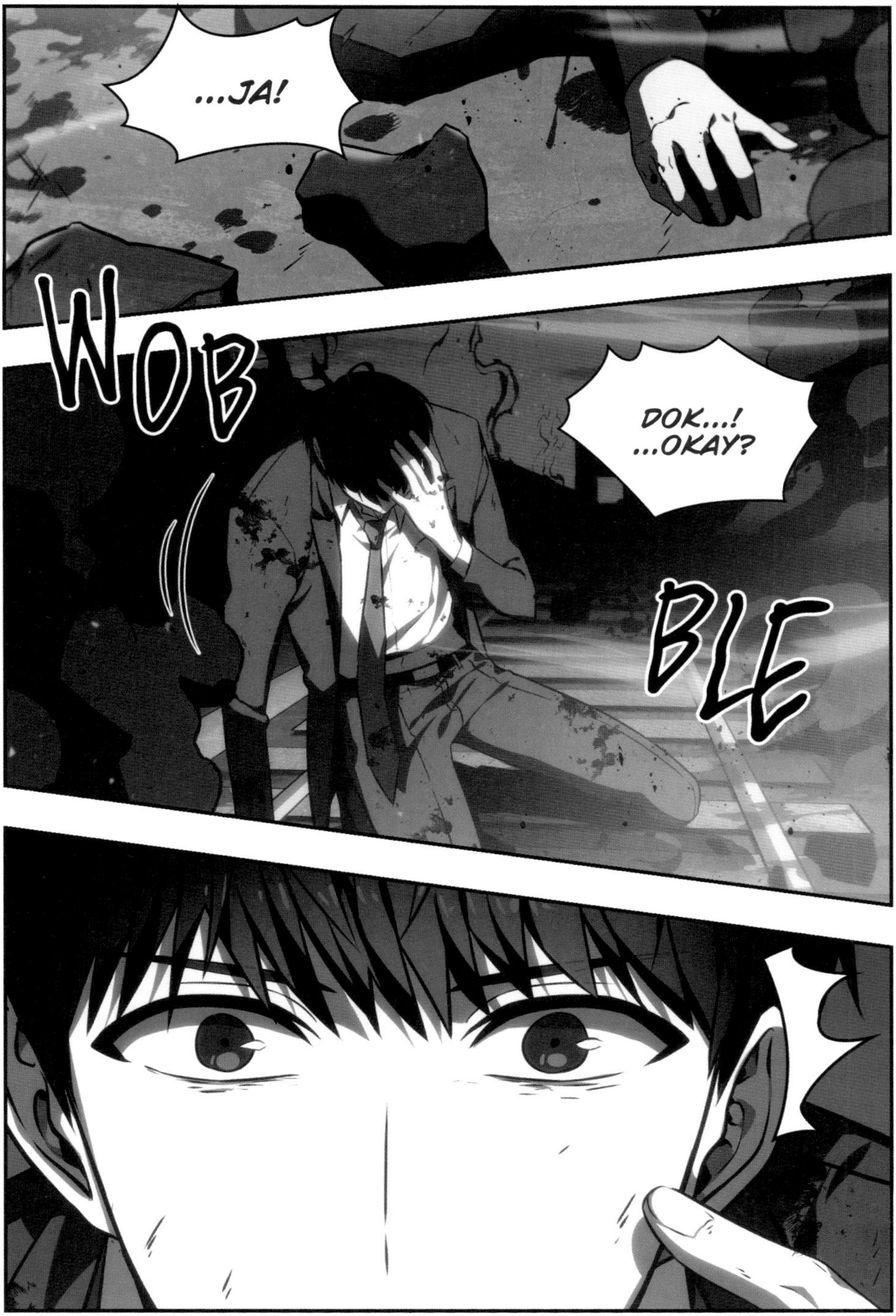
...JA!
WOB
DOK...! ...OKAY?
BLE

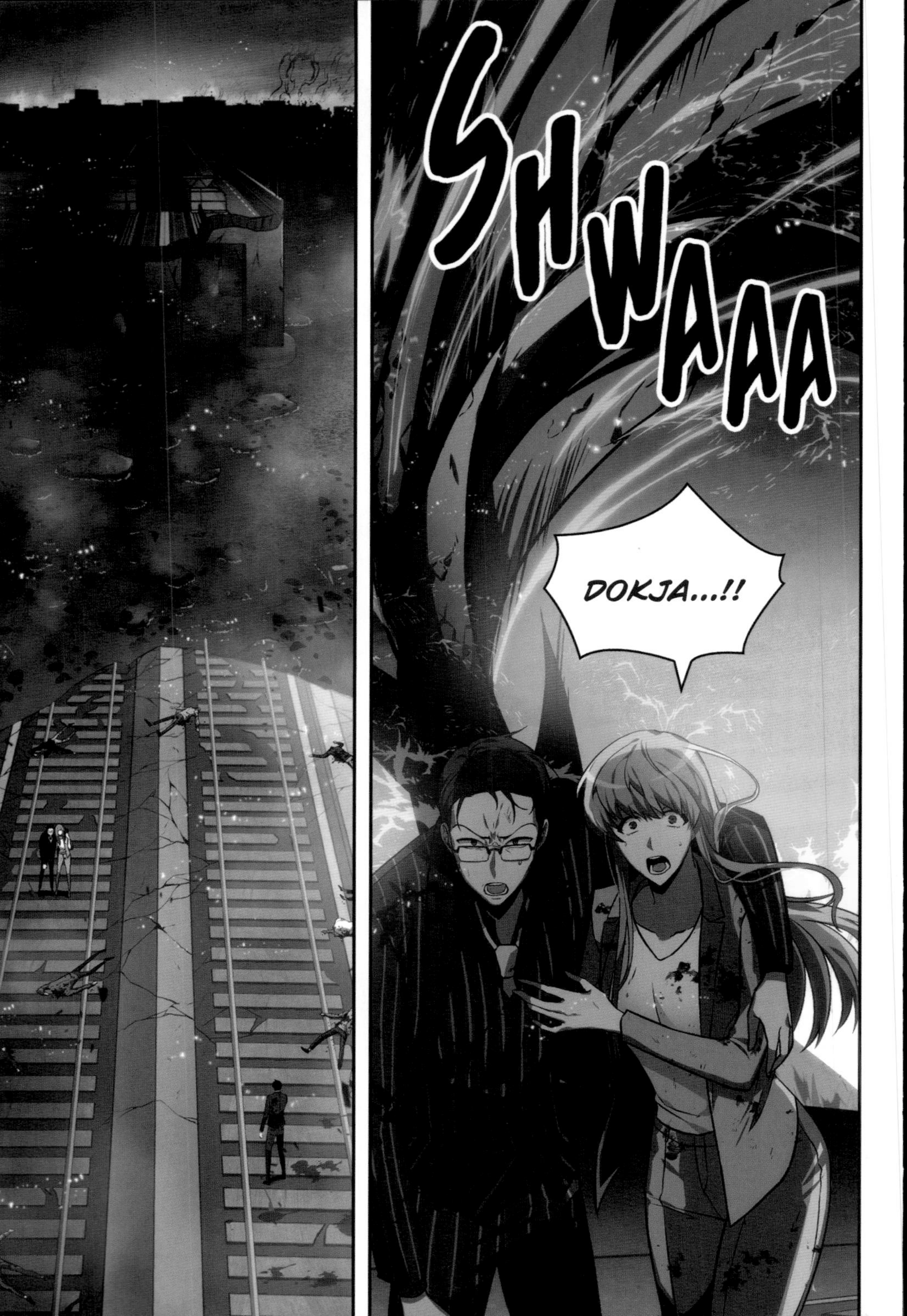
SHWAAA
DOKJA...!!

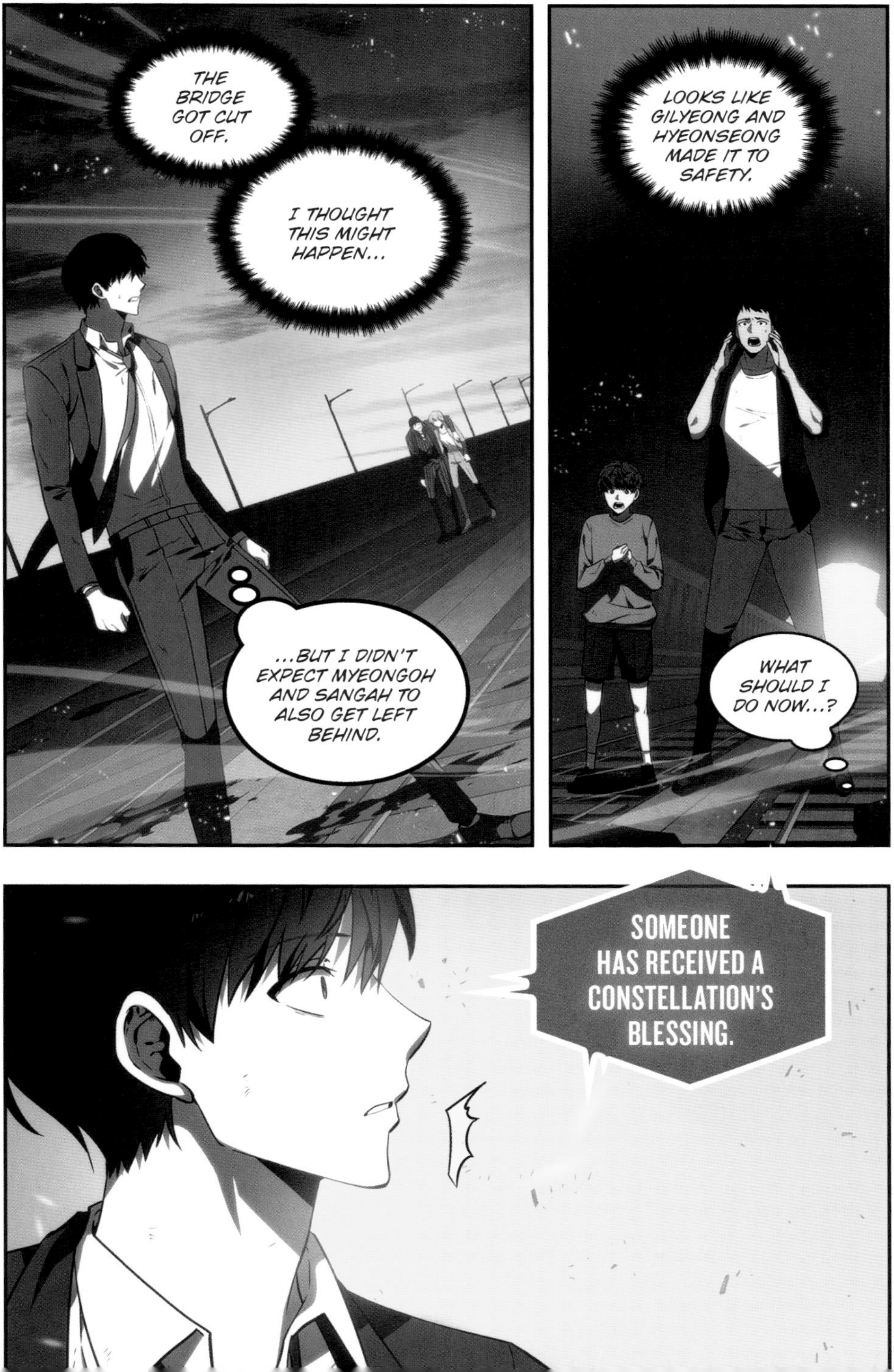
THE BRIDGE GOT CUT OFF.
I THOUGHT THIS MIGHT HAPPEN...
...BUT I DIDN'T EXPECT MYEONGOH AND SANGAH TO ALSO GET LEFT BEHIND.
LOOKS LIKE GILYEONG AND HYEONSEONG MADE IT TO SAFETY.
WHAT SHOULD I DO NOW...?
SOMEONE HAS RECEIVED A CONSTELLATION'S BLESSING.

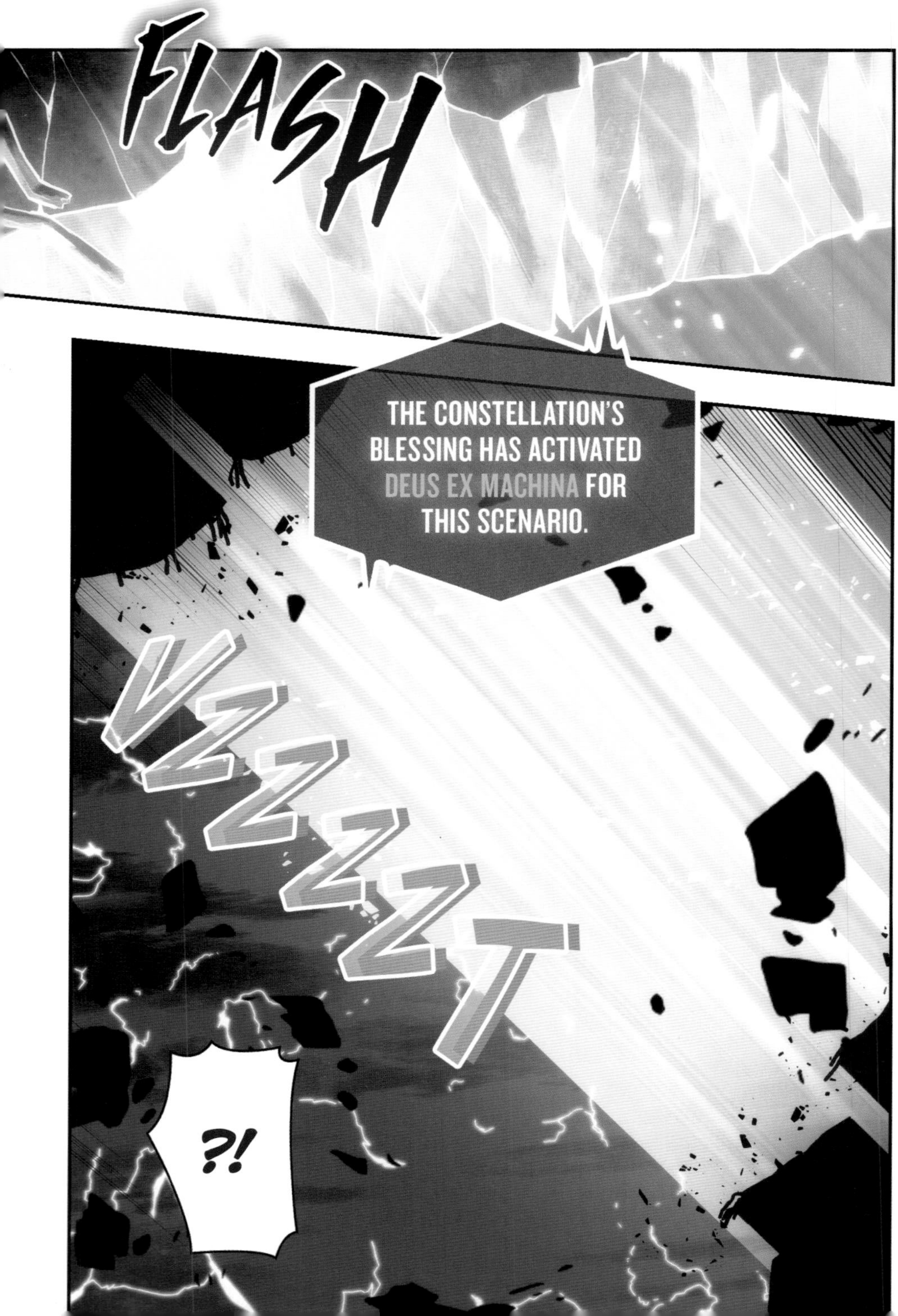
FLASH
THE CONSTELLATION'S BLESSING HAS ACTIVATED DEUS EX MACHINA FOR THIS SCENARIO.
VZZZZZT
?!

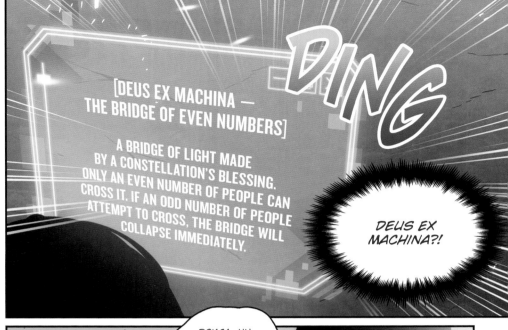

[DEUS EX MACHINA — THE BRIDGE OF EVEN NUMBERS]

A BRIDGE OF LIGHT MADE BY A CONSTELLATION'S BLESSING. ONLY AN EVEN NUMBER OF PEOPLE CAN CROSS IT. IF AN ODD NUMBER OF PEOPLE ATTEMPT TO CROSS, THE BRIDGE WILL COLLAPSE IMMEDIATELY.

DING

DEUS EX MACHINA?!

DOKJA, UH... IN MY HEAD, THIS THING SUDDENLY—

Deus Ex Machina

A power that can be used by constellations to directly intervene in a scenario, albeit at a massive cost.

DID SANGAH'S SPONSORING CONSTELLATION...

...INTERVENE IN THE SCENARIO TO SAVE HER...?!

DING

[THIS CHARACTER'S INFORMATION CANNOT BE VIEWED VIA "CHARACTER PROFILE."]

THIS RARELY HAPPENED IN ALL OF TWSA.

WHAT ON EARTH COULD HER SPONSOR BE?

ACTIVATE "CHARACTER PROFILE."

DING

[THIS CHARACTER'S INFORMATION CANNOT BE VIEWED VIA "CHARACTER PROFILE."]

!

I CAN'T SEE HER INFO WITH MY SKILL?

IS HER SPONSORING CONSTELLATION THAT SPECIAL?

[...ER'S INFORMATION CANNOT BE VIEWED VIA "CHARACTER PROFILE.":]

OR DOES SHE HAVE THE "MENTAL BARRIER" SKILL?

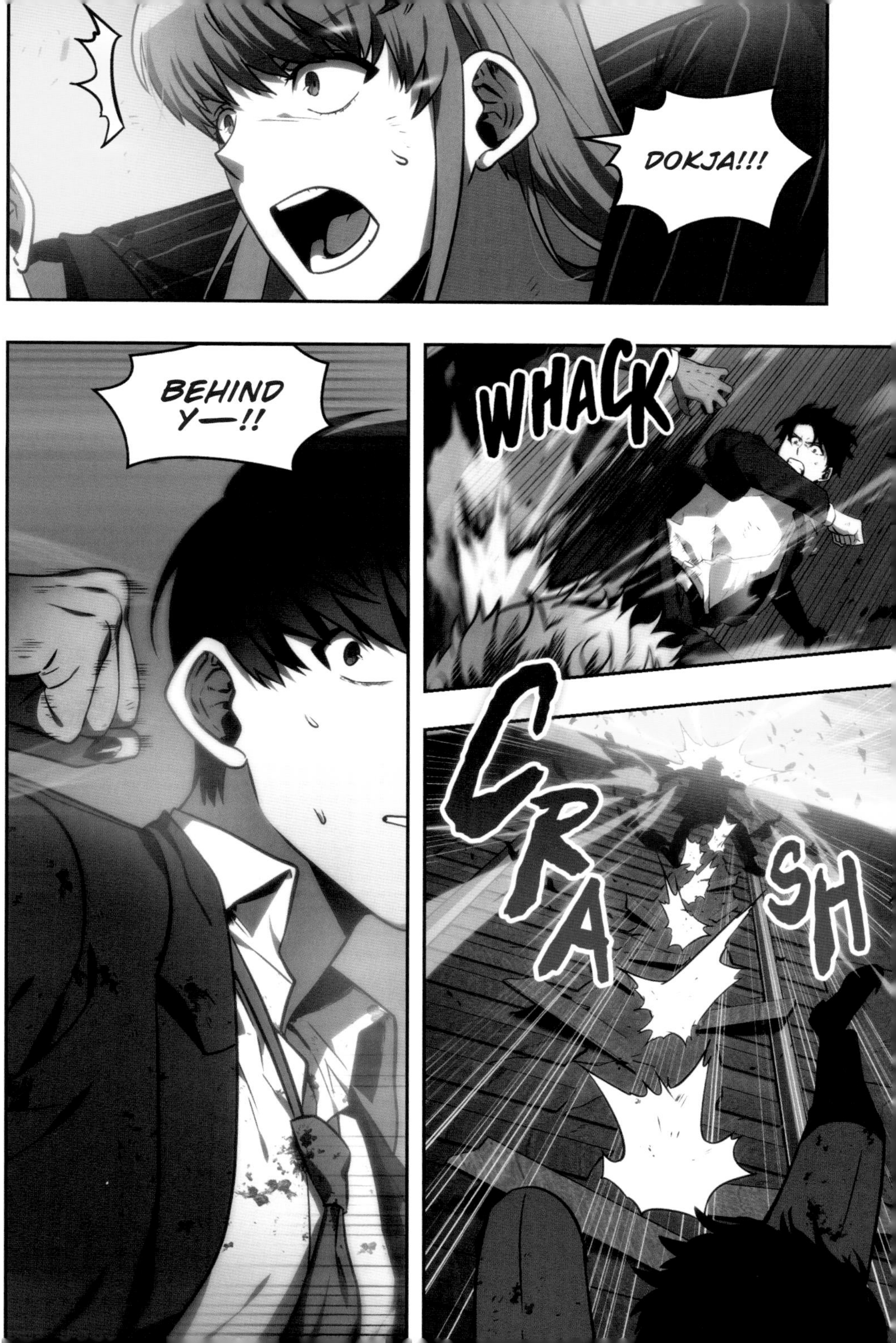
DOKJA!!!
BEHIND Y—!!
WHACK
CRASH

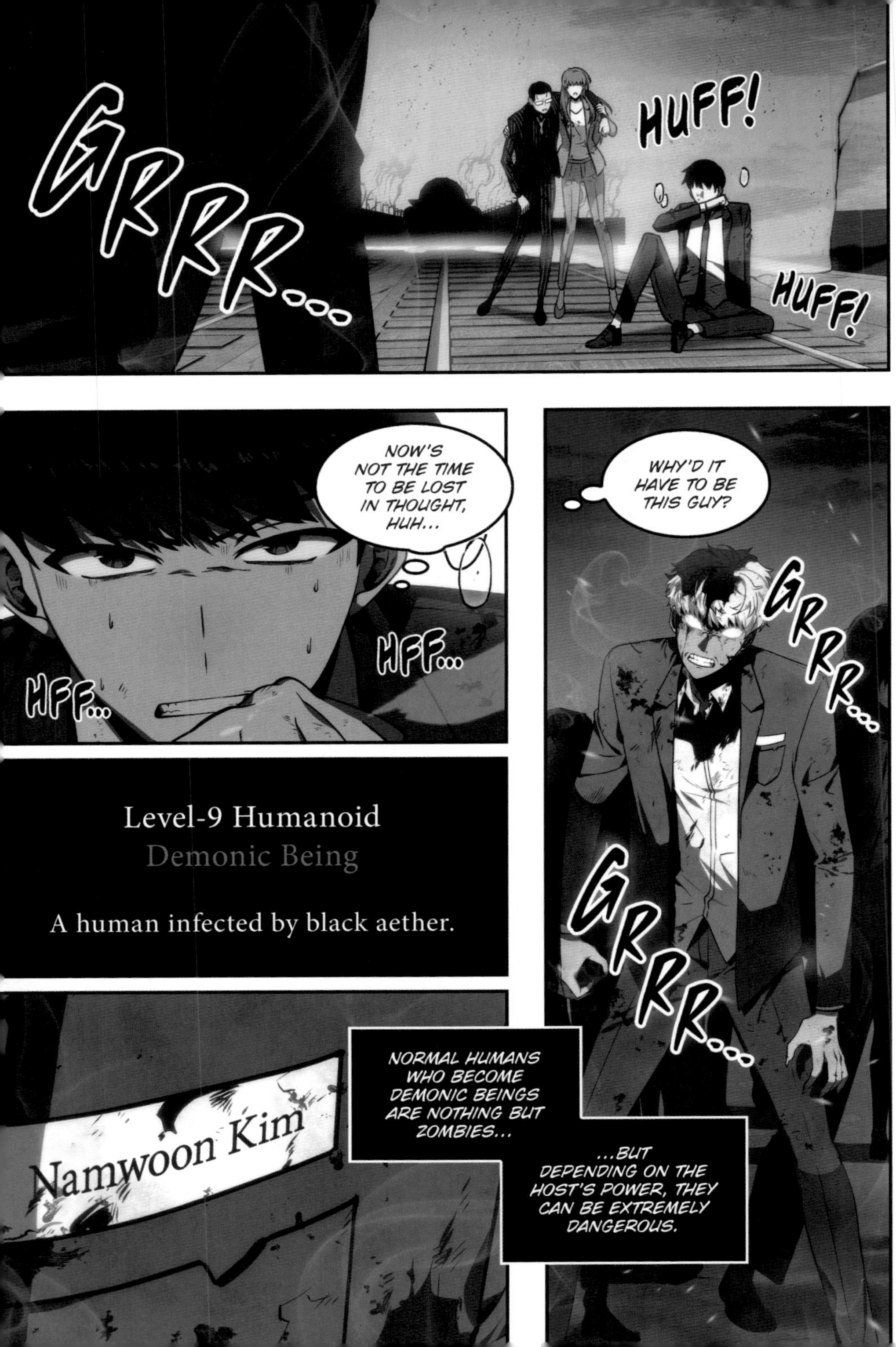
GRRR...
HUFF!
HUFF!
NOW'S NOT THE TIME TO BE LOST IN THOUGHT, HUH...
HFF...
HFF...
WHY'D IT HAVE TO BE THIS GUY?
GRRR...
Level-9 Humanoid
Demonic Being
A human infected by black aether.
GRRR...
Namwoon Kim
NORMAL HUMANS WHO BECOME DEMONIC BEINGS ARE NOTHING BUT ZOMBIES...
...BUT DEPENDING ON THE HOST'S POWER, THEY CAN BE EXTREMELY DANGEROUS.

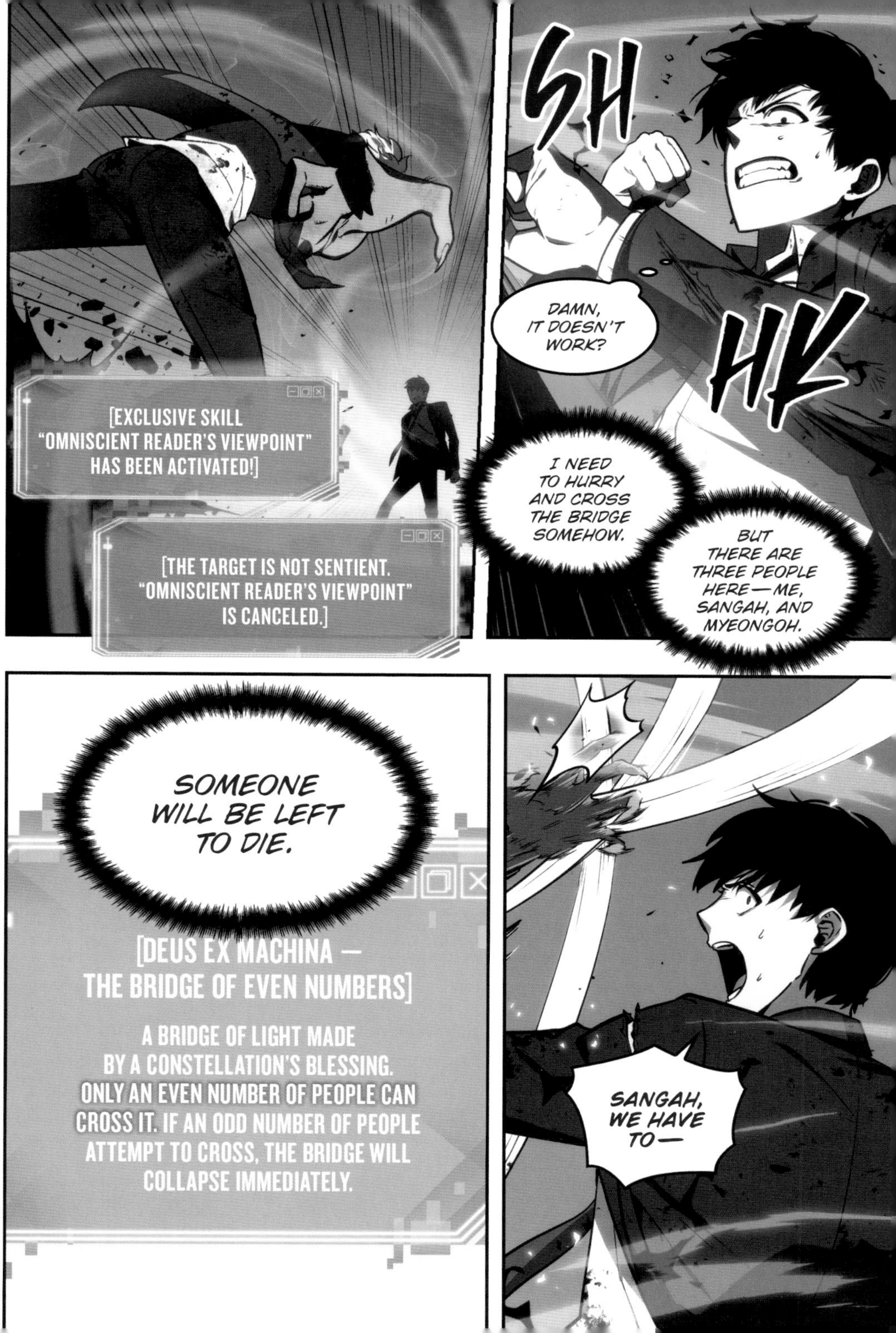
[EXCLUSIVE SKILL "OMNISCIENT READER'S VIEWPOINT" HAS BEEN ACTIVATED!]
[THE TARGET IS NOT SENTIENT. "OMNISCIENT READER'S VIEWPOINT" IS CANCELED.]
SH
DAMN, IT DOESN'T WORK?
HK
I NEED TO HURRY AND CROSS THE BRIDGE SOMEHOW.
BUT THERE ARE THREE PEOPLE HERE—ME, SANGAH, AND MYEONGOH.
SOMEONE WILL BE LEFT TO DIE.
[DEUS EX MACHINA — THE BRIDGE OF EVEN NUMBERS]
A BRIDGE OF LIGHT MADE BY A CONSTELLATION'S BLESSING. ONLY AN EVEN NUMBER OF PEOPLE CAN CROSS IT. IF AN ODD NUMBER OF PEOPLE ATTEMPT TO CROSS, THE BRIDGE WILL COLLAPSE IMMEDIATELY.
SANGAH, WE HAVE TO—

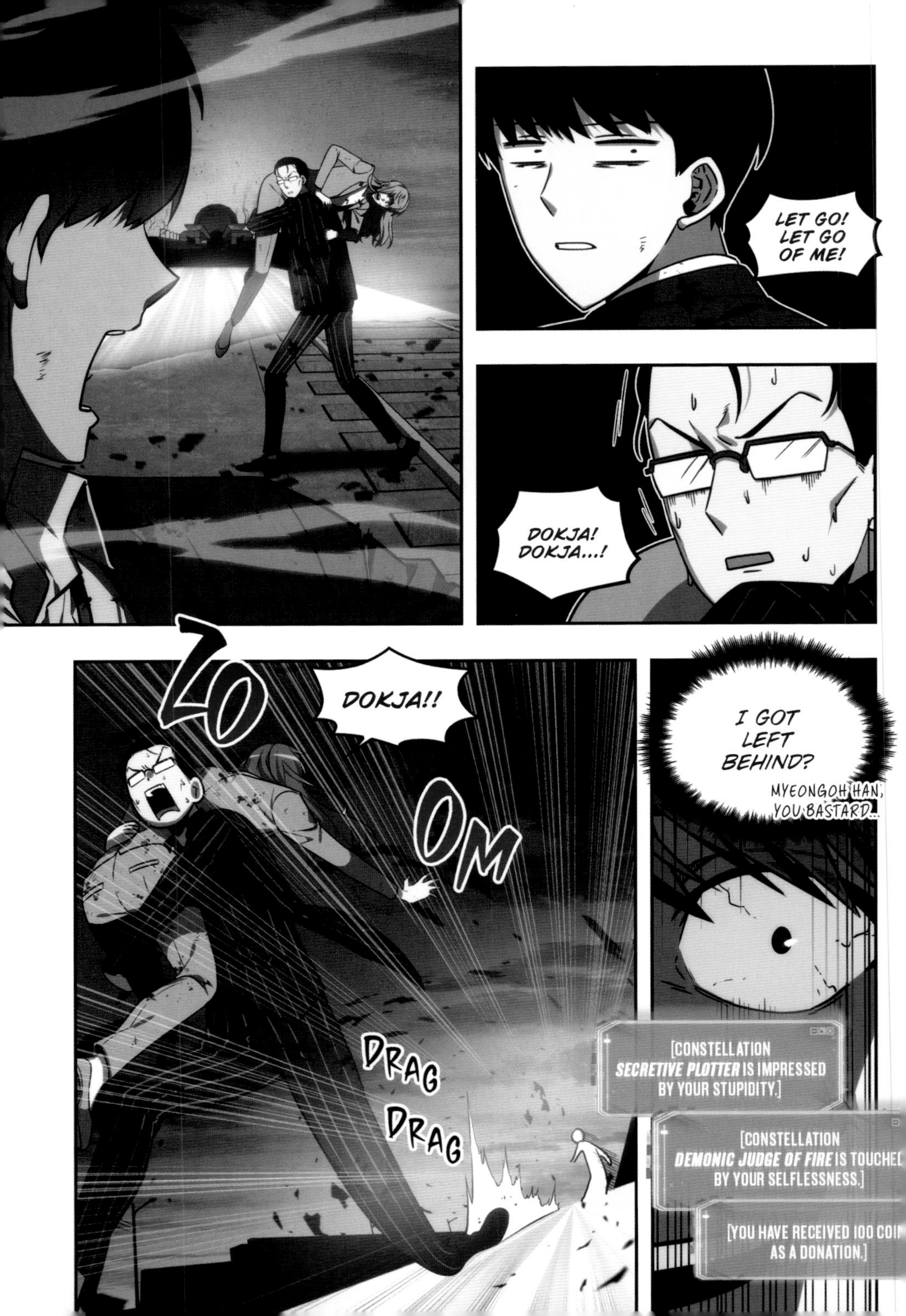
LET GO! LET GO OF ME!
DOKJA! DOKJA...!
ZOOM
DOKJA!!
I GOT LEFT BEHIND?
MYEONGOH HAN, YOU BASTARD...
DRAG DRAG
[CONSTELLATION SECRETIVE PLOTTER IS IMPRESSED BY YOUR STUPIDITY.]
[CONSTELLATION DEMONIC JUDGE OF FIRE IS TOUCHED BY YOUR SELFLESSNESS.]
[YOU HAVE RECEIVED 100 COI AS A DONATION.]

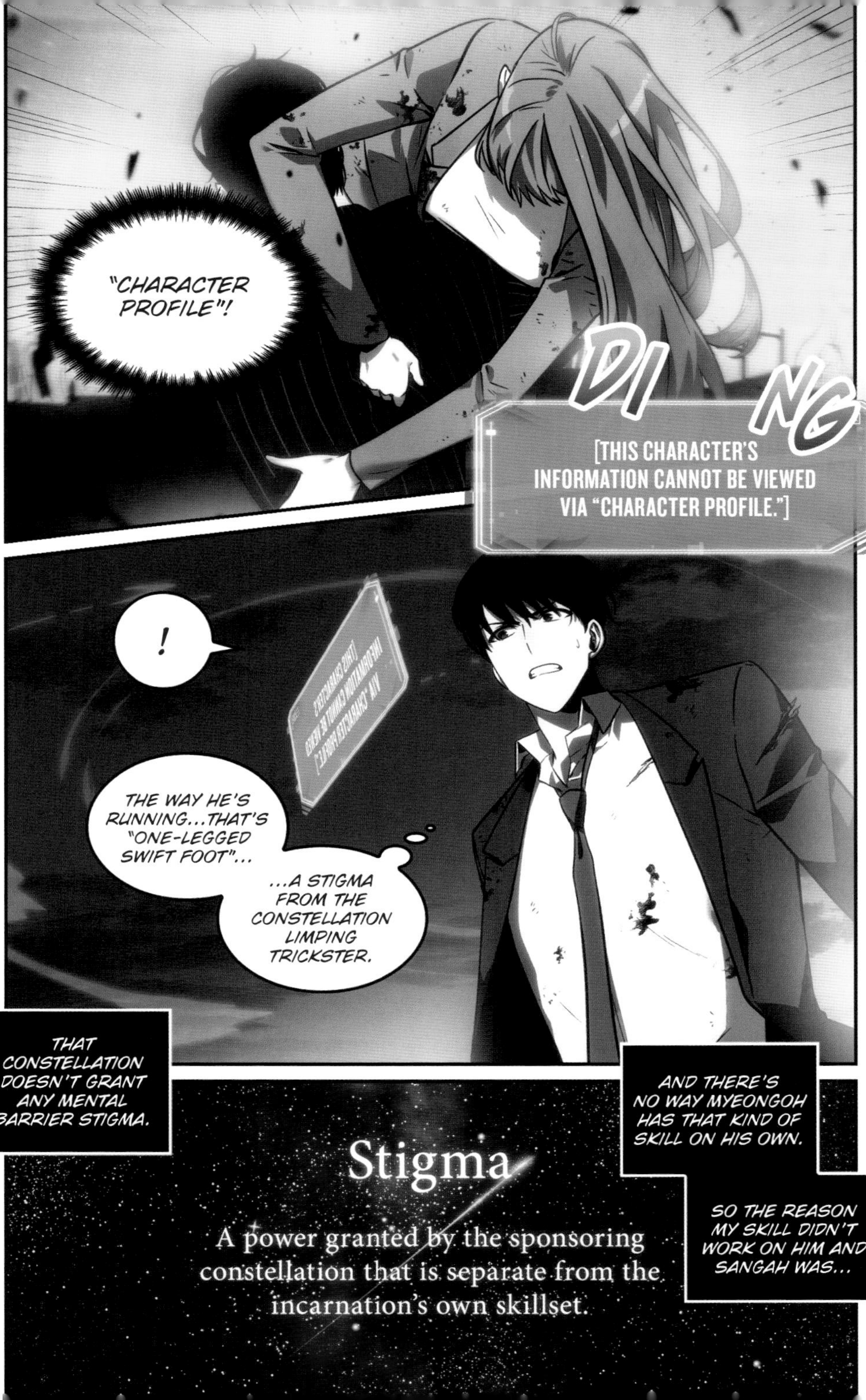
"CHARACTER PROFILE"!
DING
[THIS CHARACTER'S INFORMATION CANNOT BE VIEWED VIA "CHARACTER PROFILE."]
!
THE WAY HE'S RUNNING...THAT'S "ONE-LEGGED SWIFT FOOT"...
...A STIGMA FROM THE CONSTELLATION LIMPING TRICKSTER.
THAT CONSTELLATION DOESN'T GRANT ANY MENTAL BARRIER STIGMA.
AND THERE'S NO WAY MYEONGOH HAS THAT KIND OF SKILL ON HIS OWN.
Stigma
A power granted by the sponsoring constellation that is separate from the incarnation's own skillset.
SO THE REASON MY SKILL DIDN'T WORK ON HIM AND SANGAH WAS...

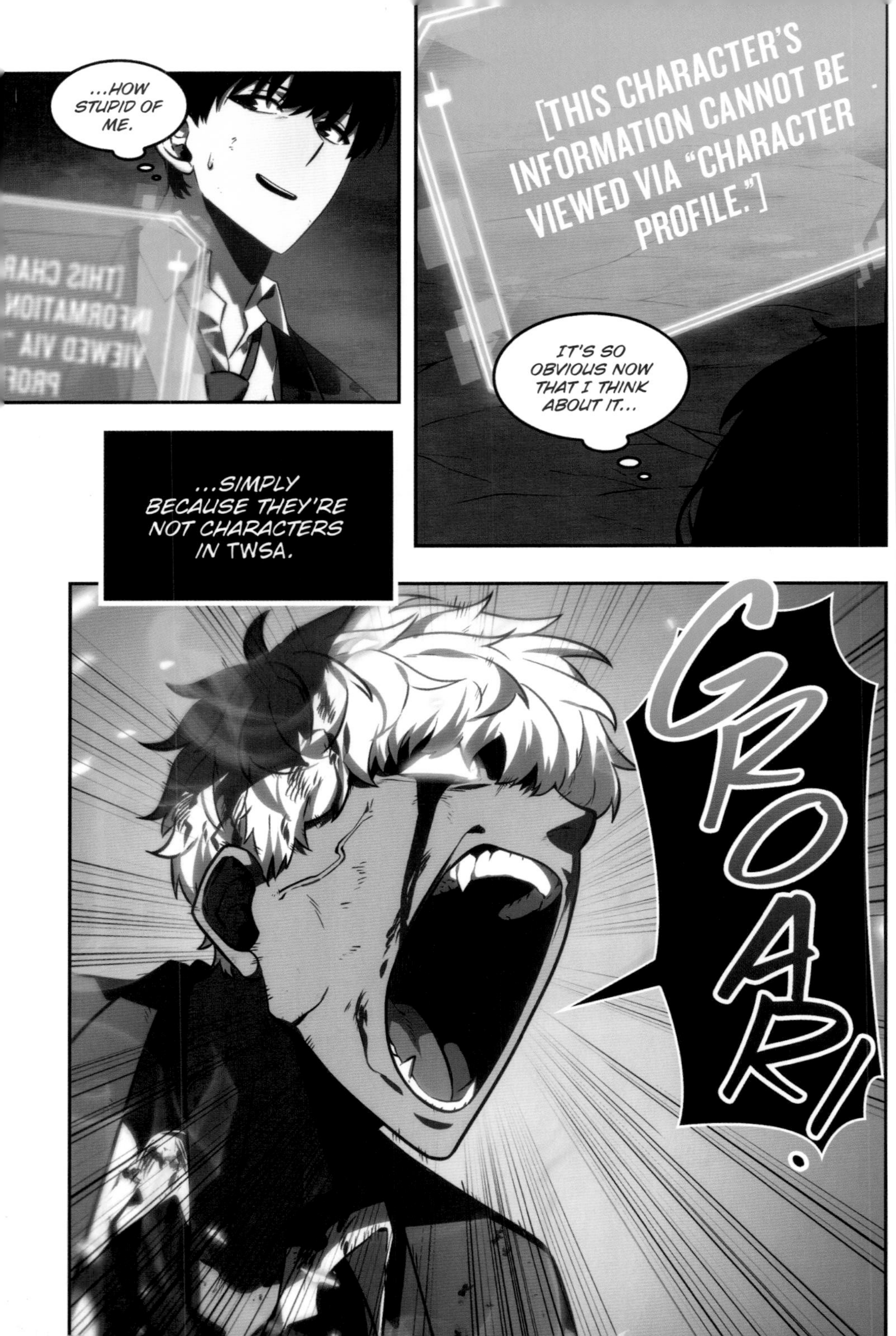
...HOW STUPID OF ME.
[THIS CHARACTER'S INFORMATION CANNOT BE VIEWED VIA "CHARACTER PROFILE."]
IT'S SO OBVIOUS NOW THAT I THINK ABOUT IT...
...SIMPLY BECAUSE THEY'RE NOT CHARACTERS IN TWSA.
GROAR!

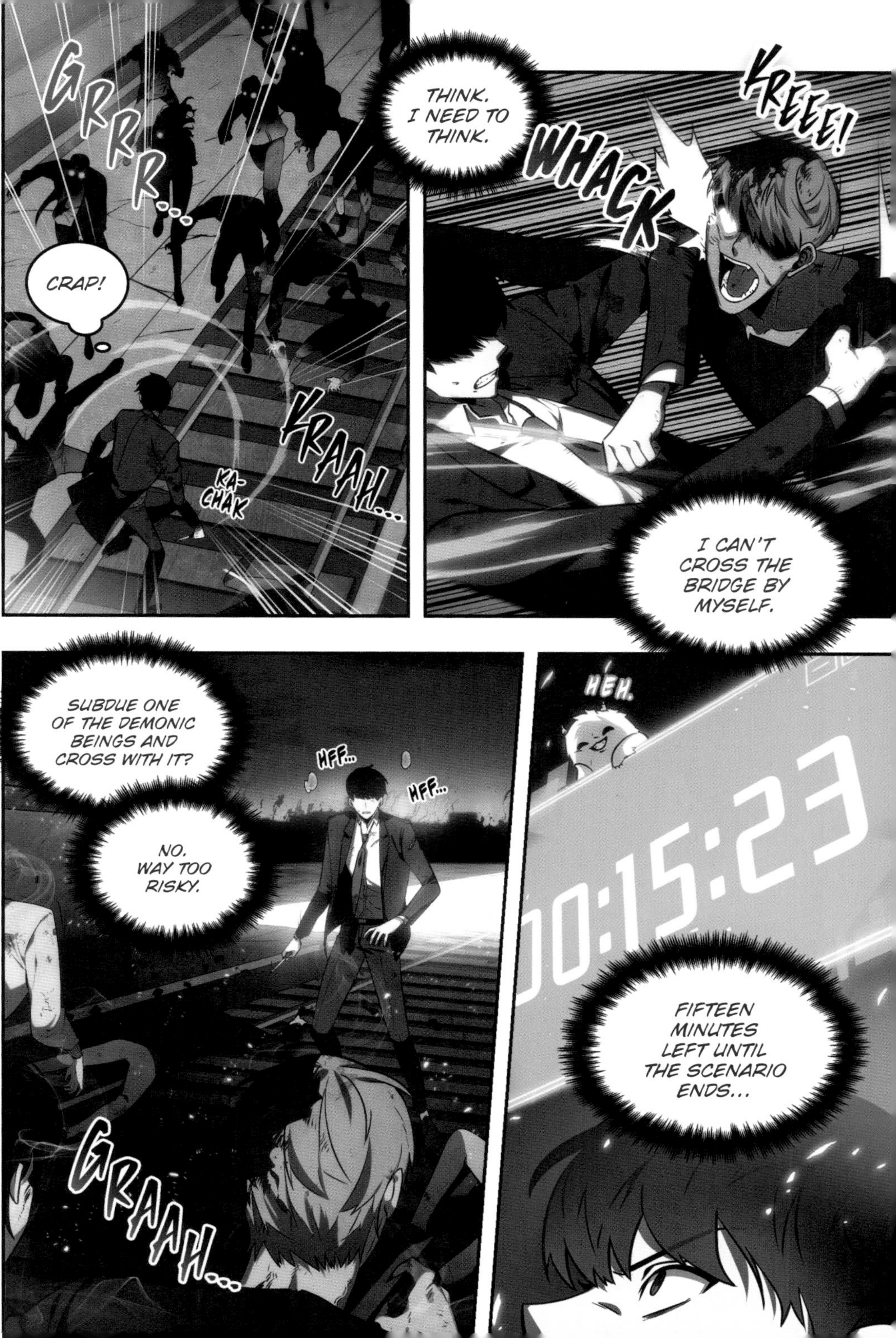
GRRRR...
CRAP!
KRAAH...
KA-CHAK
THINK. I NEED TO THINK.
WHACK
KREEE!
I CAN'T CROSS THE BRIDGE BY MYSELF.
SUBDUE ONE OF THE DEMONIC BEINGS AND CROSS WITH IT?
HFF...
HFF...
NO. WAY TOO RISKY.
GRAAAH...
HEH.
00:15:23
FIFTEEN MINUTES LEFT UNTIL THE SCENARIO ENDS...

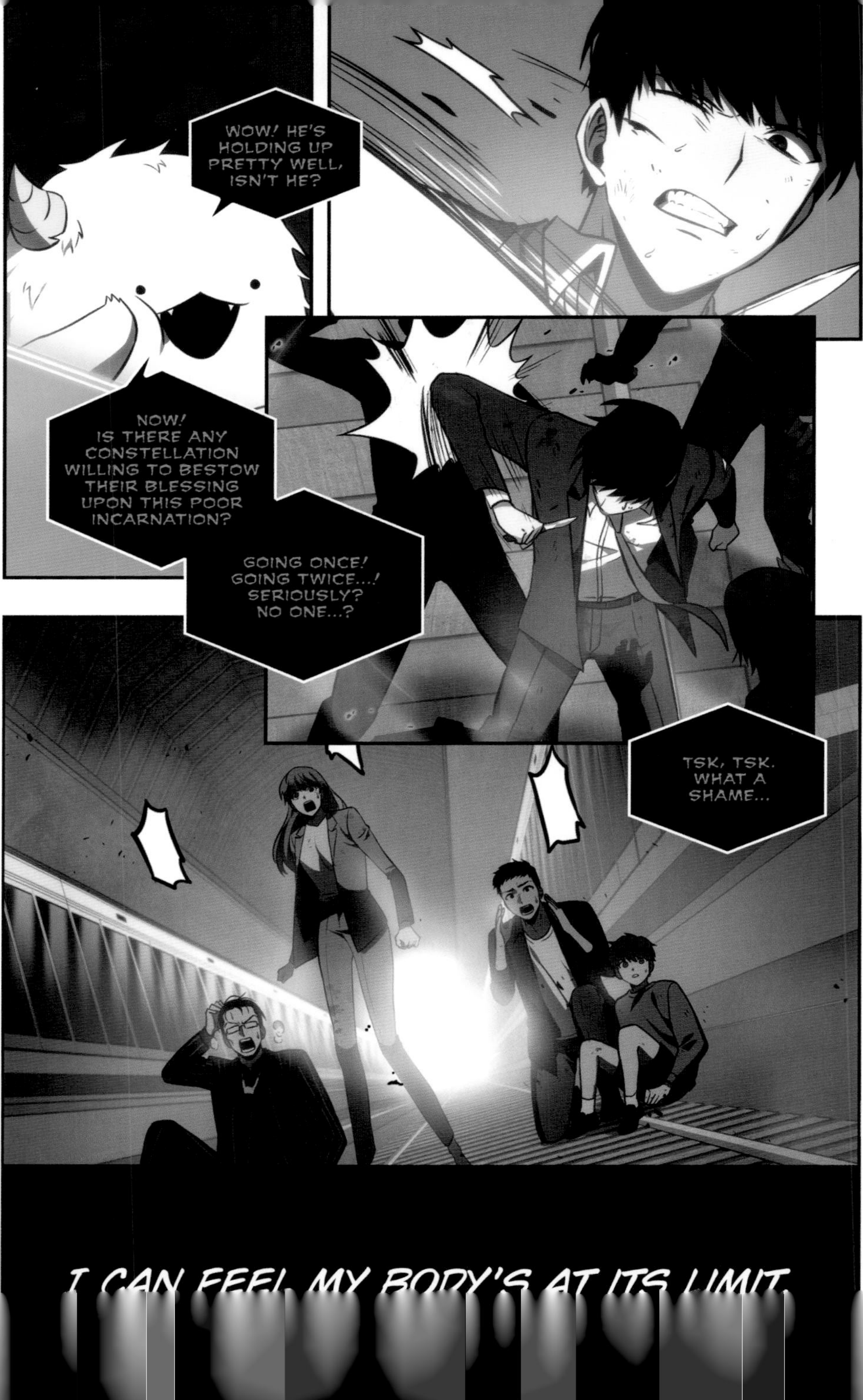
WOW! HE'S HOLDING UP PRETTY WELL, ISN'T HE?
NOW! IS THERE ANY CONSTELLATION WILLING TO BESTOW THEIR BLESSING UPON THIS POOR INCARNATION?
GOING ONCE! GOING TWICE...! SERIOUSLY? NO ONE...?
TSK, TSK. WHAT A SHAME...
I CAN FEEL MY BODY'S AT ITS LIMIT.

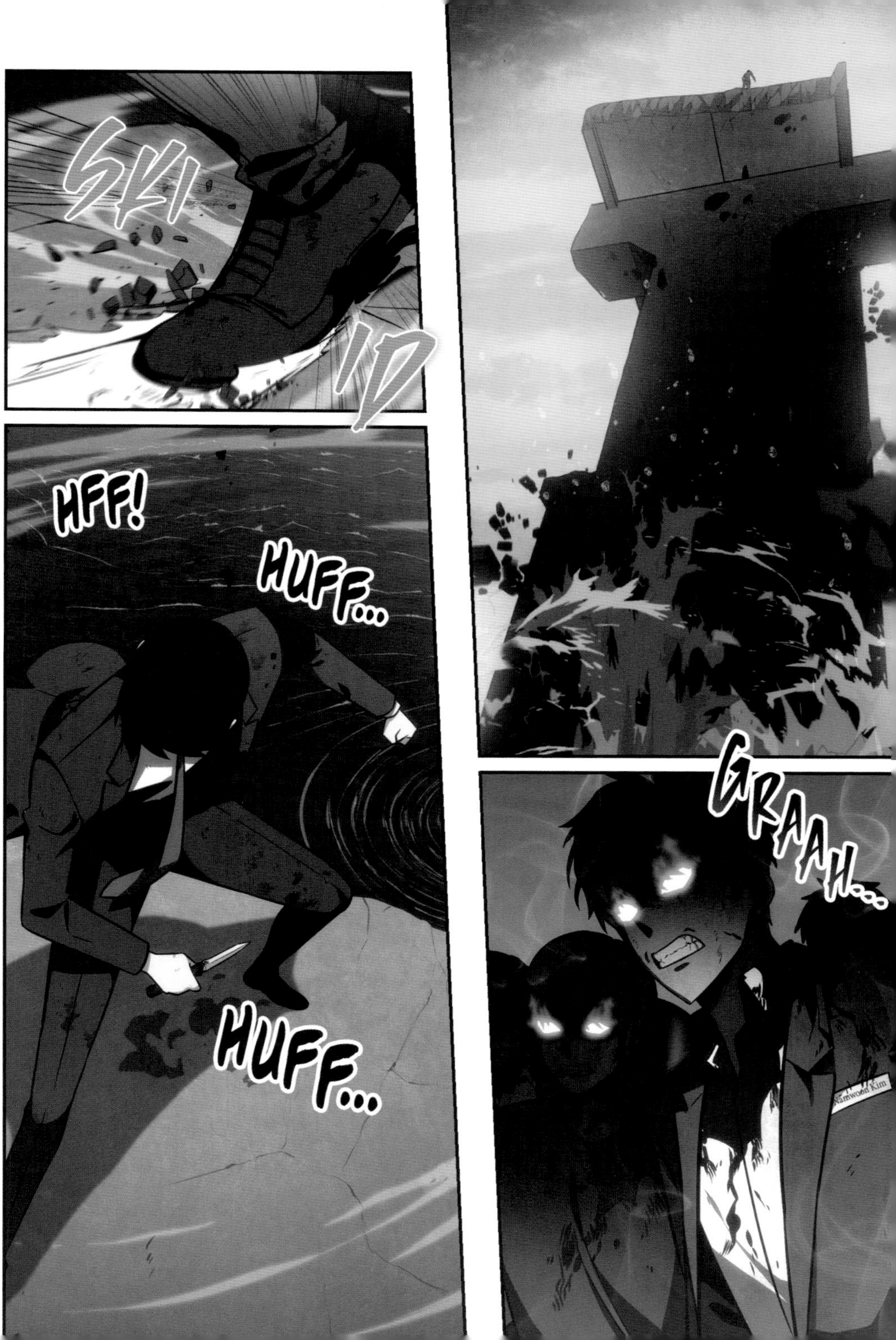
SKI
ID
HFF!
HUFF...
HUFF...
GRAAAH...
Namwoon Kim

I REALLY MIGHT DIE THIS TIME.
DAMN, IF I ONLY HAD A COMBAT SKILL...
...IT WOULDN'T HAVE BEEN THIS HARD.
SHWOOO

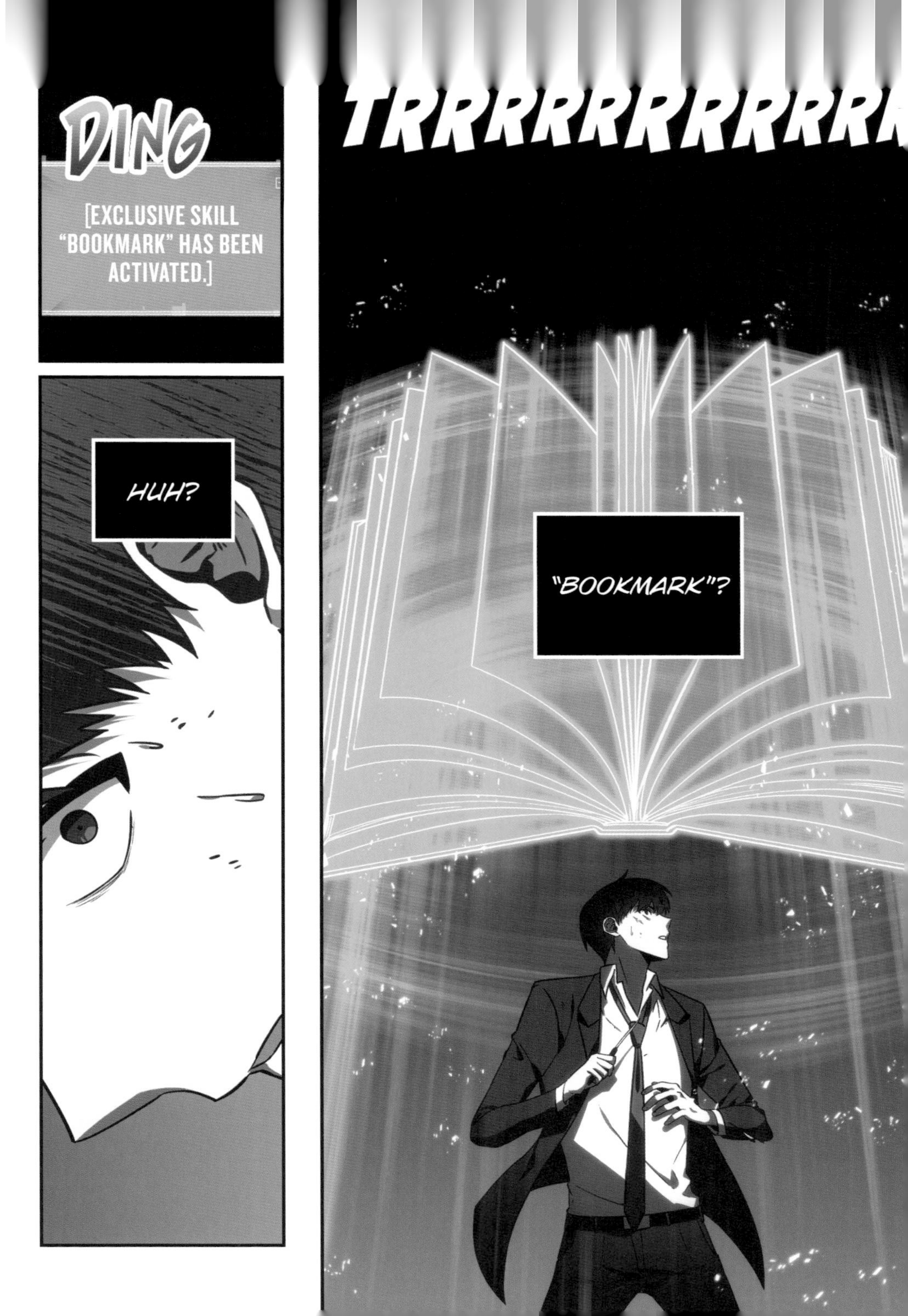
DING
[EXCLUSIVE SKILL "BOOKMARK" HAS BEEN ACTIVATED.]
HUH?
TRRRRRRRRRRR
"BOOKMARK"?

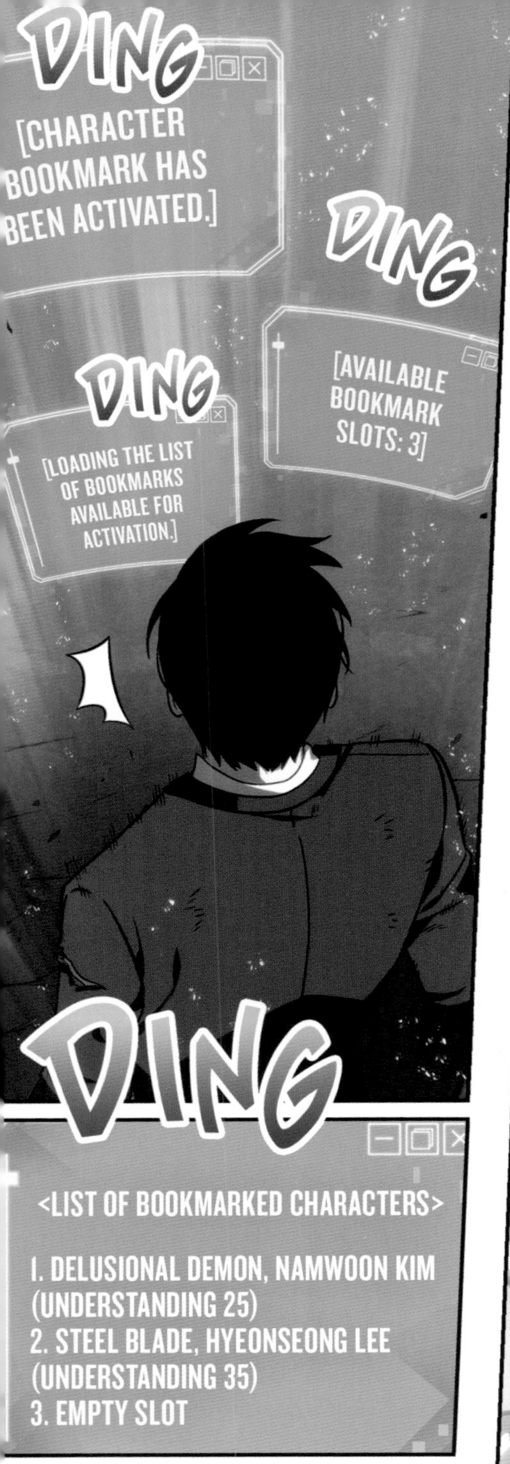
DING
[CHARACTER BOOKMARK HAS BEEN ACTIVATED.]
DING
DING
[AVAILABLE BOOKMARK SLOTS: 3]
[LOADING THE LIST OF BOOKMARKS AVAILABLE FOR ACTIVATION.]
DING
<LIST OF BOOKMARKED CHARACTERS>
1. DELUSIONAL DEMON, NAMWOON KIM (UNDERSTANDING 25)
2. STEEL BLADE, HYEONSEONG LEE (UNDERSTANDING 35)
3. EMPTY SLOT

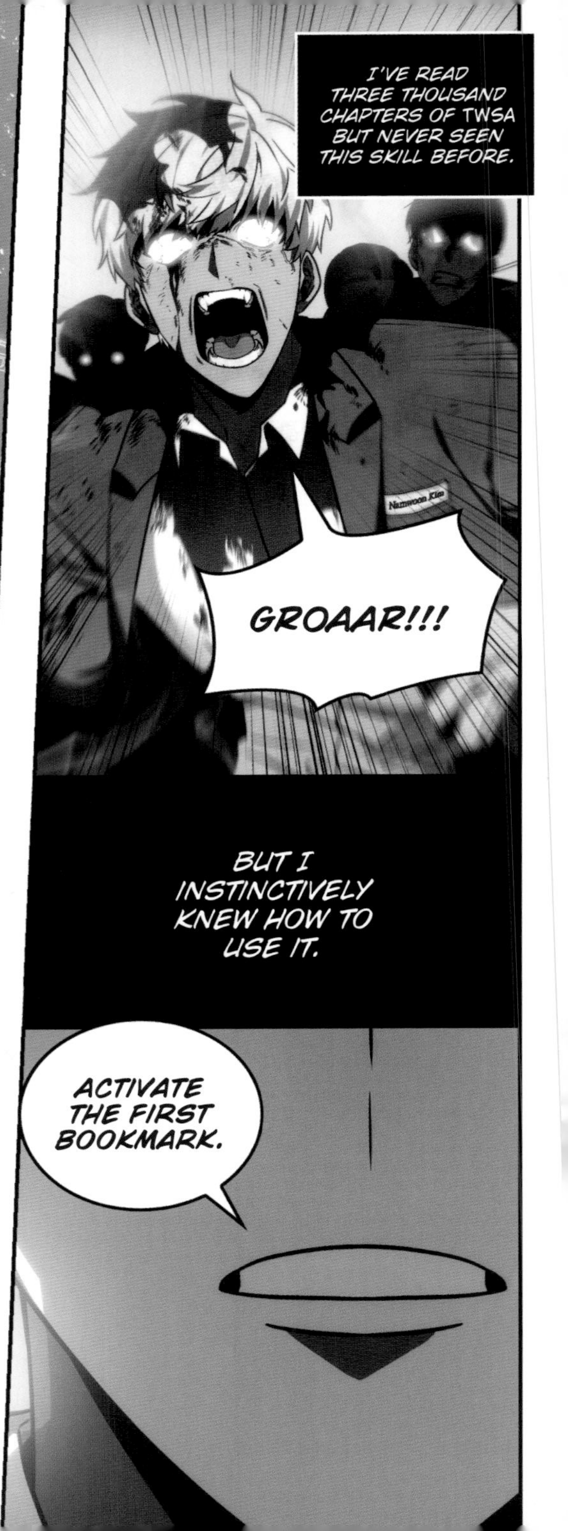
I'VE READ THREE THOUSAND CHAPTERS OF TWSA BUT NEVER SEEN THIS SKILL BEFORE.
GROAAR!!!
BUT I INSTINCTIVELY KNEW HOW TO USE IT.
ACTIVATE THE FIRST BOOKMARK.

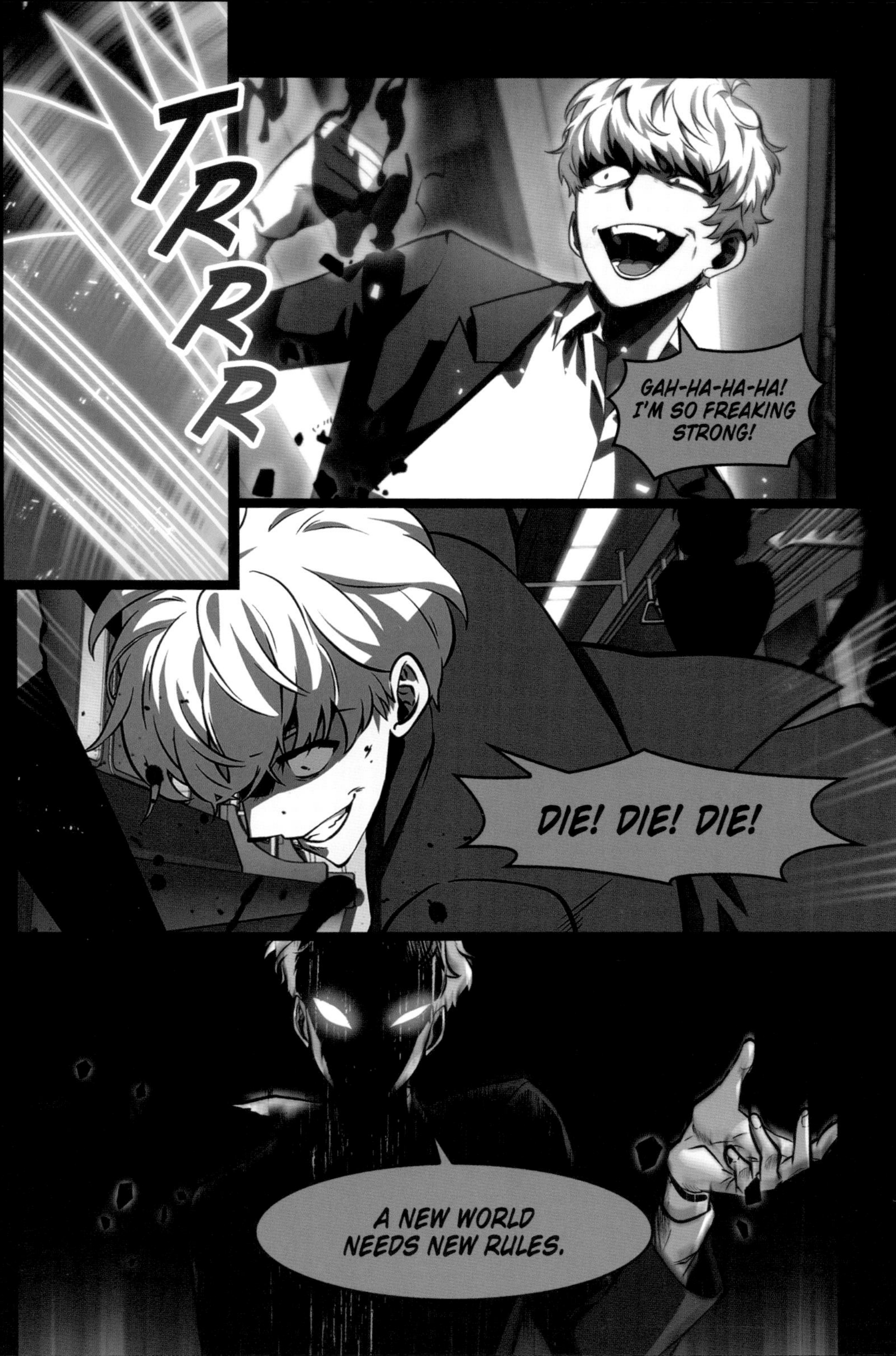
TRRRR
GAH-HA-HA-HA! I'M SO FREAKING STRONG!
DIE! DIE! DIE!
A NEW WORLD NEEDS NEW RULES.

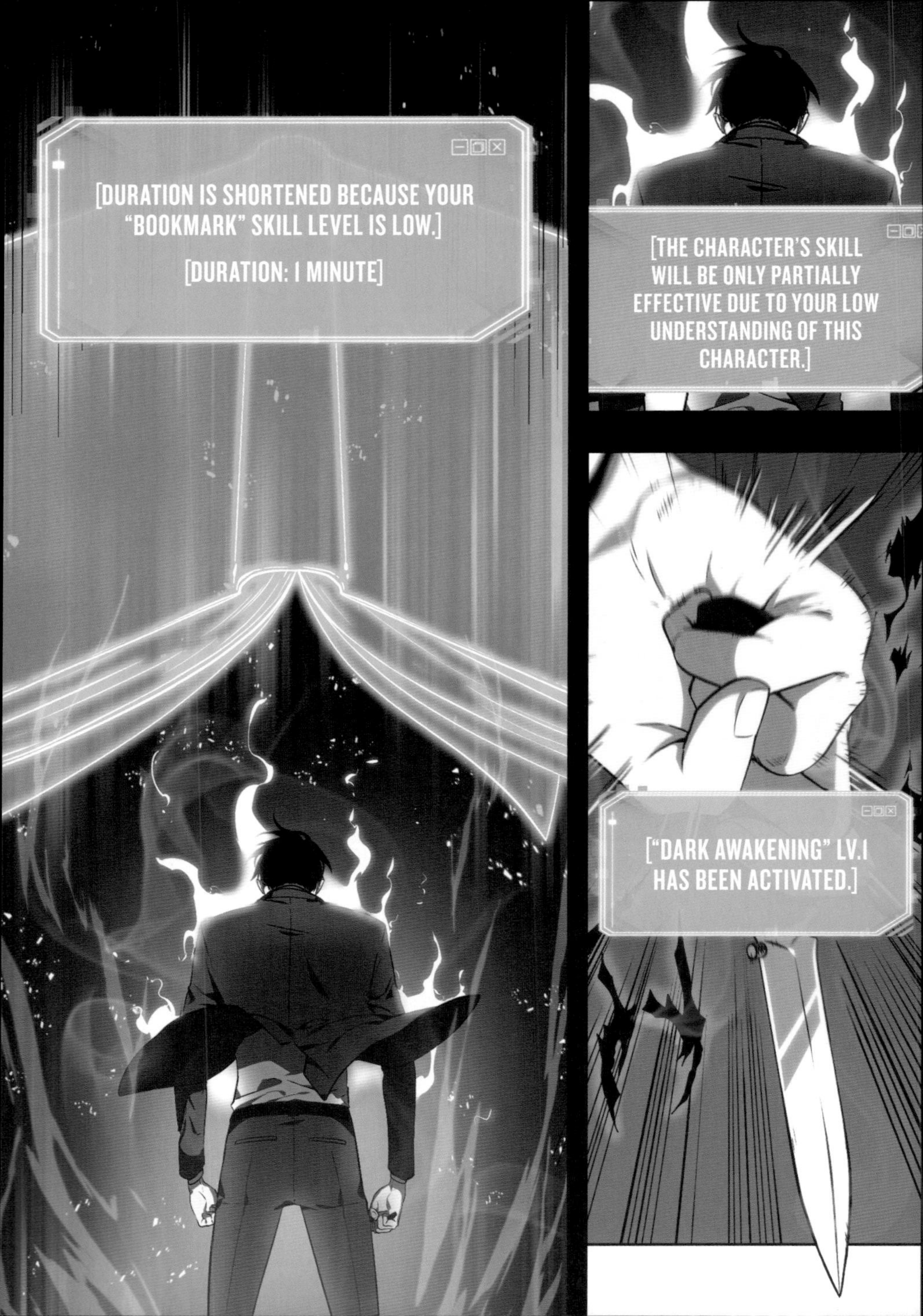
[DURATION IS SHORTENED BECAUSE YOUR "BOOKMARK" SKILL LEVEL IS LOW.]
[DURATION: 1 MINUTE]
[THE CHARACTER'S SKILL WILL BE ONLY PARTIALLY EFFECTIVE DUE TO YOUR LOW UNDERSTANDING OF THIS CHARACTER.]
["DARK AWAKENING" LV.1 HAS BEEN ACTIVATED.]

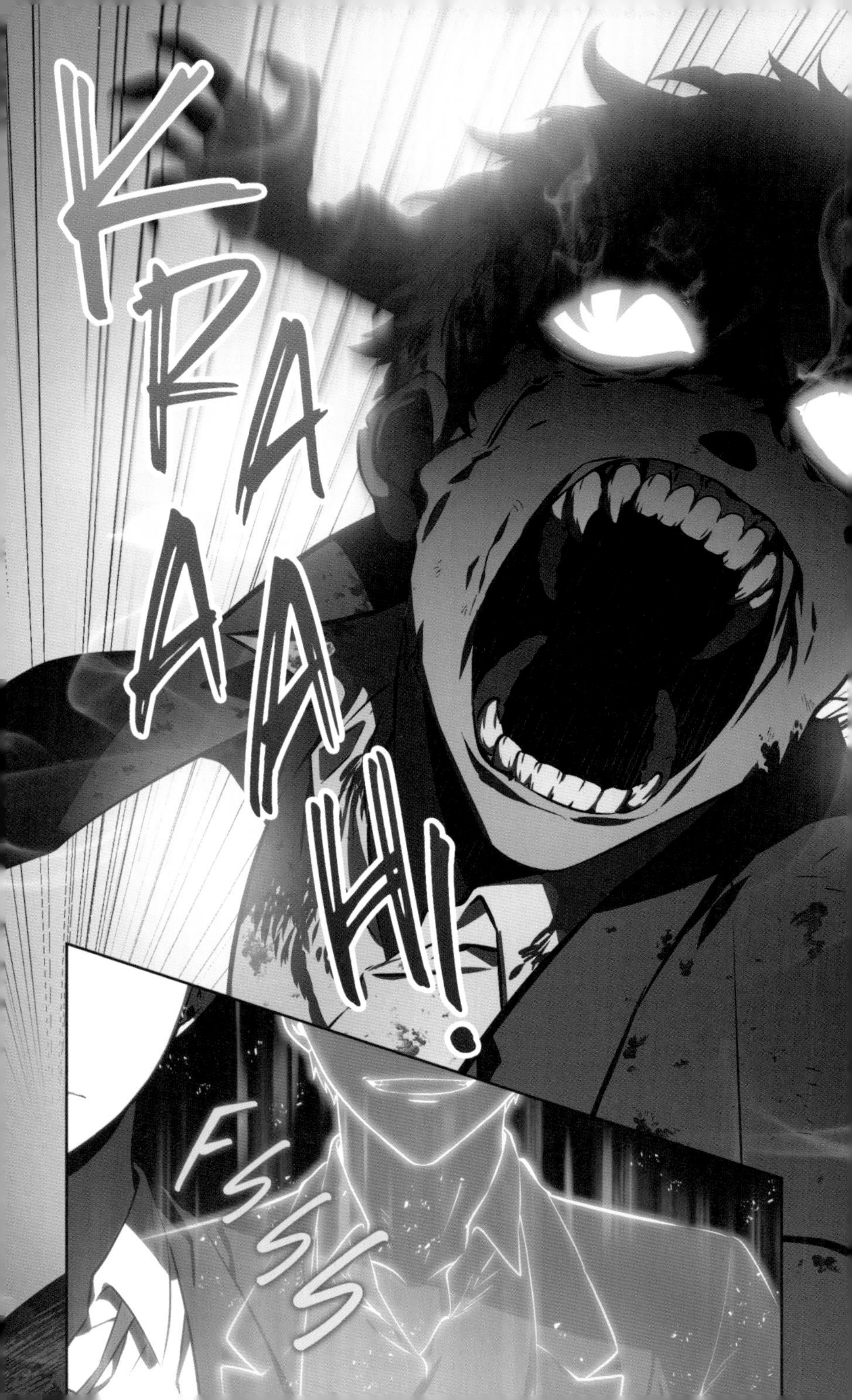
KRAAAH!
FSSSS

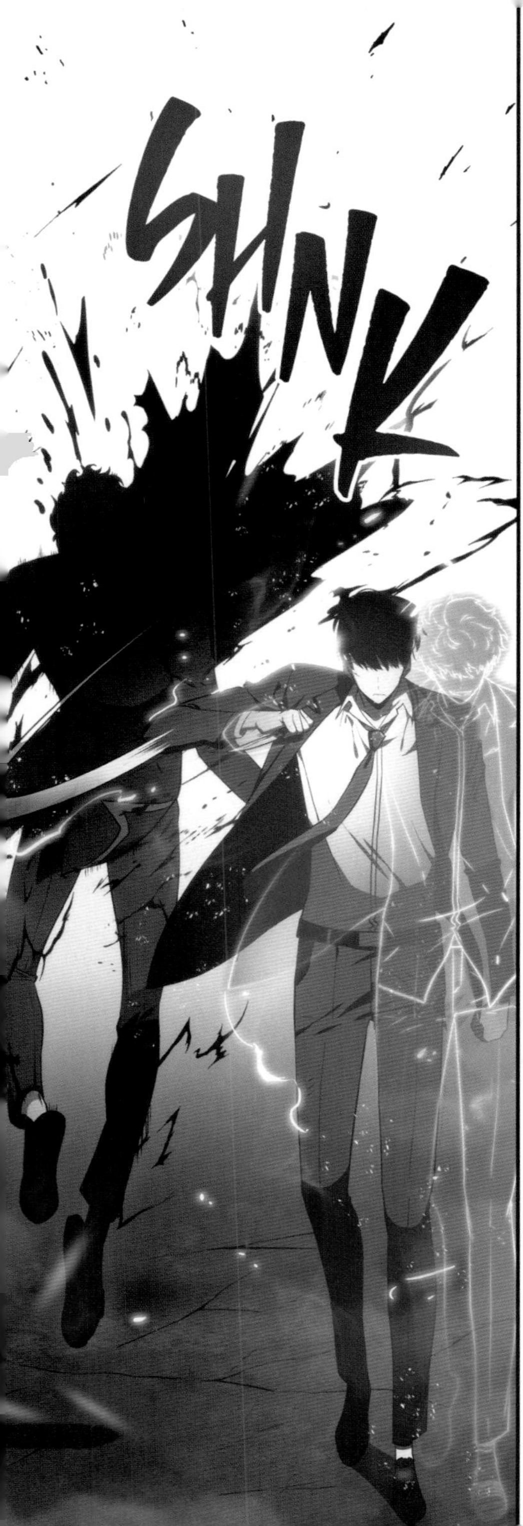
SHNK

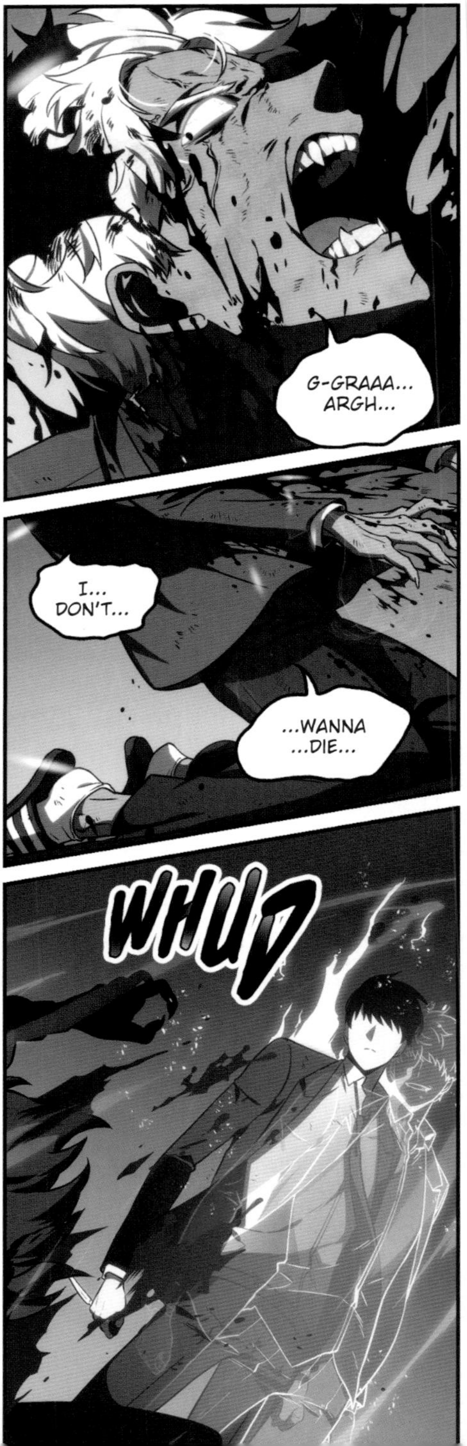
G-GRAAA...
ARGH...
I...
DON'T...
...WANNA
...DIE...
WHUD

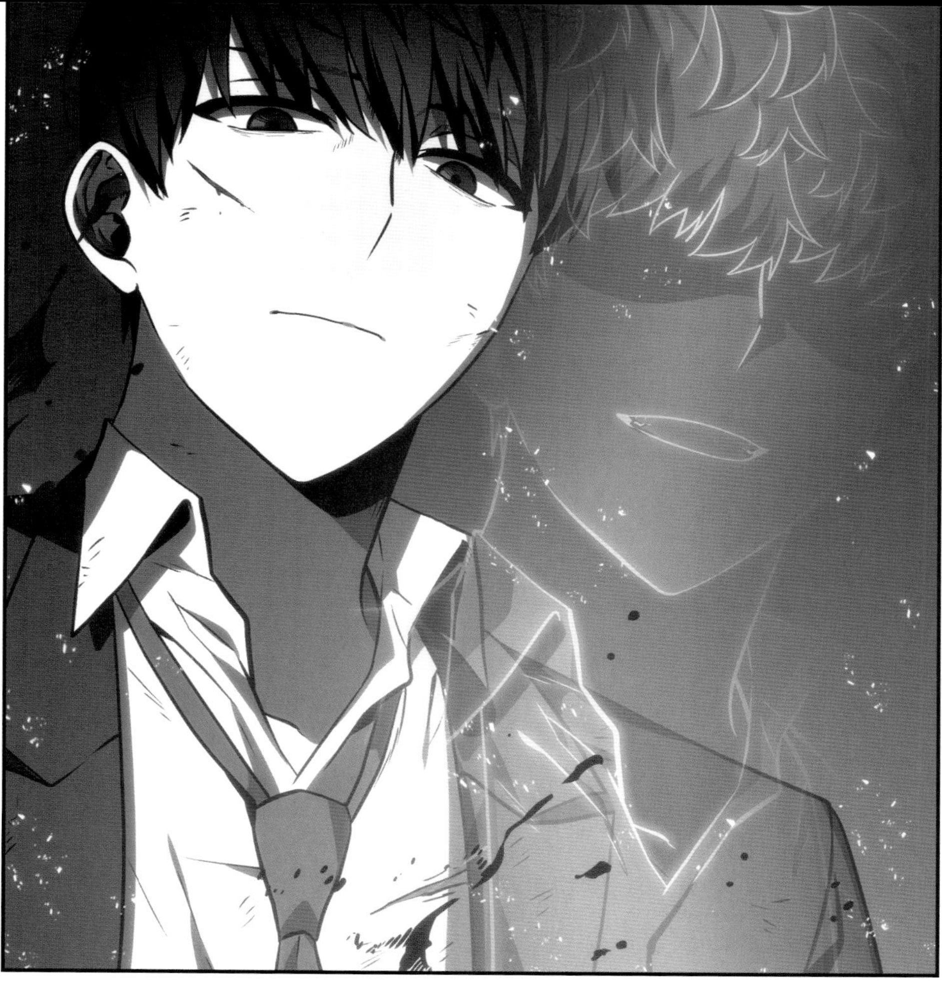

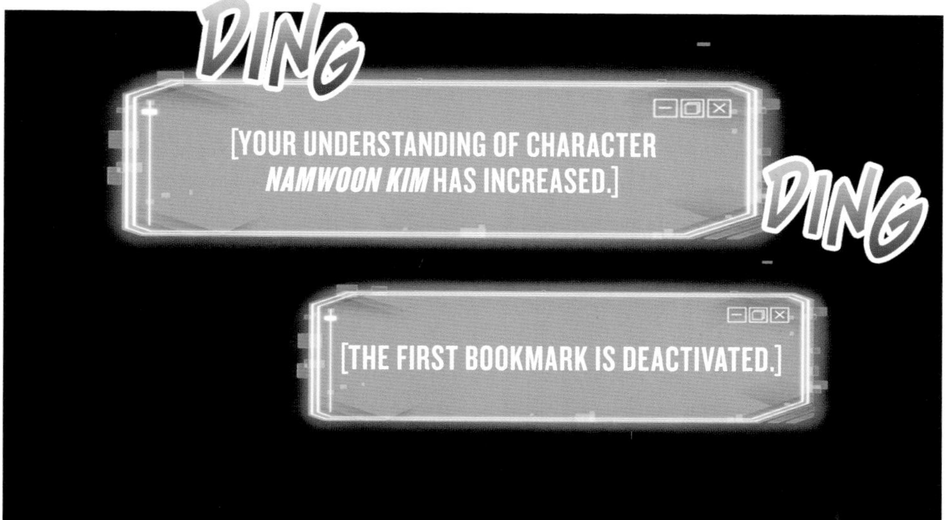
DING
[YOUR UNDERSTANDING OF CHARACTER
NAMWOON KIM HAS INCREASED.]
DING
[THE FIRST BOOKMARK IS DEACTIVATED.]

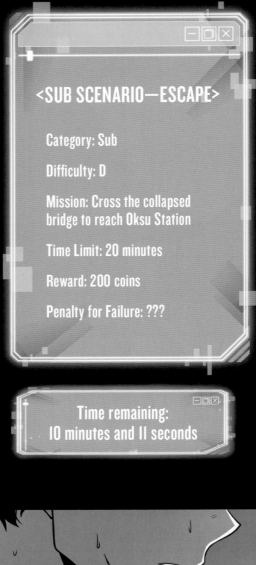

<SUB SCENARIO—ESCAPE>

Category: Sub

Difficulty: D

Mission: Cross the collapsed bridge to reach Oksu Station

Time Limit: 20 minutes

Reward: 200 coins

Penalty for Failure: ???

Time remaining:
10 minutes and 11 seconds

HUFF...

HUFF...

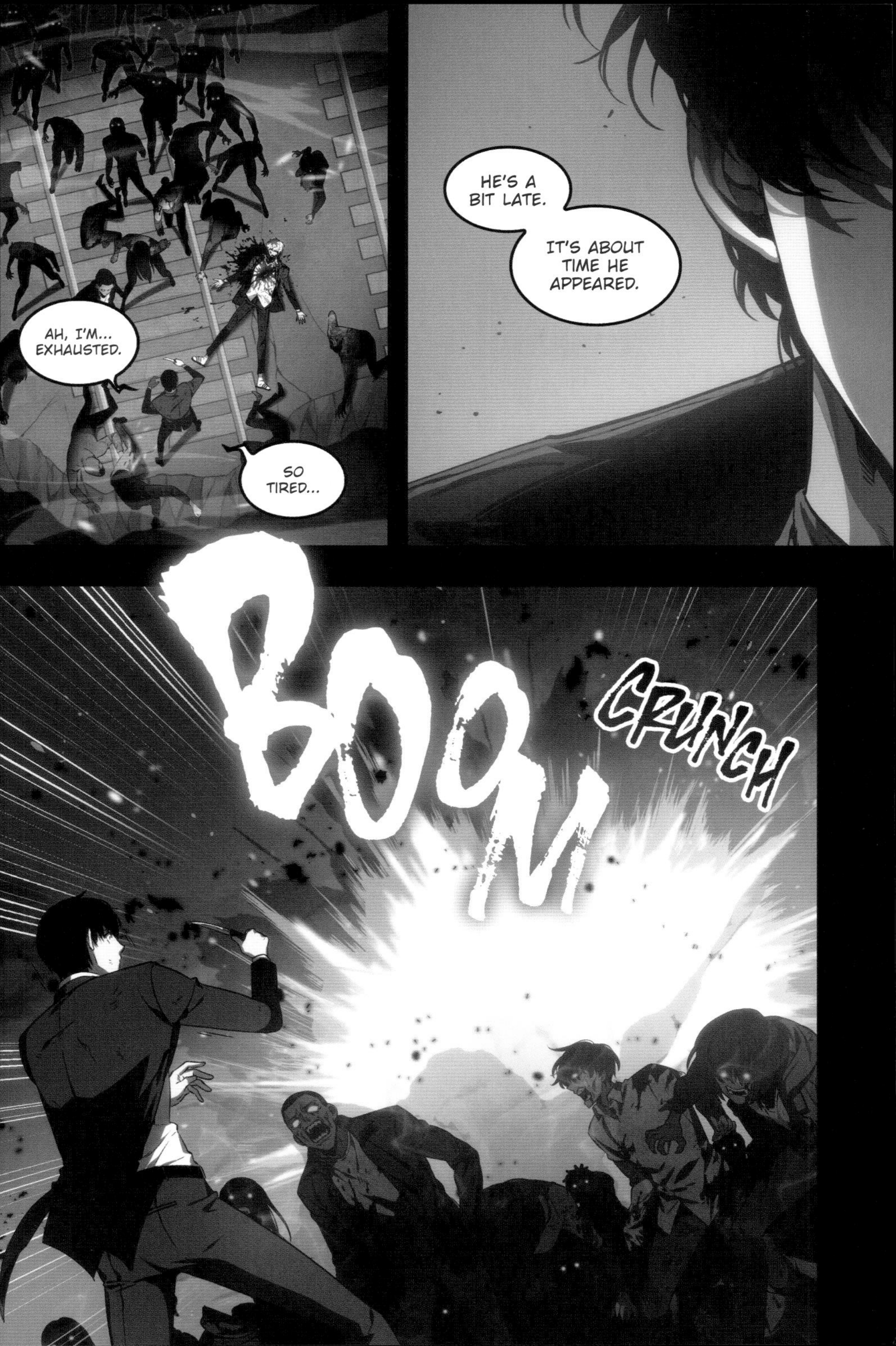
AH, I'M... EXHAUSTED.
SO TIRED...
HE'S A BIT LATE.
IT'S ABOUT TIME HE APPEARED.
BOOM
CRUNCH

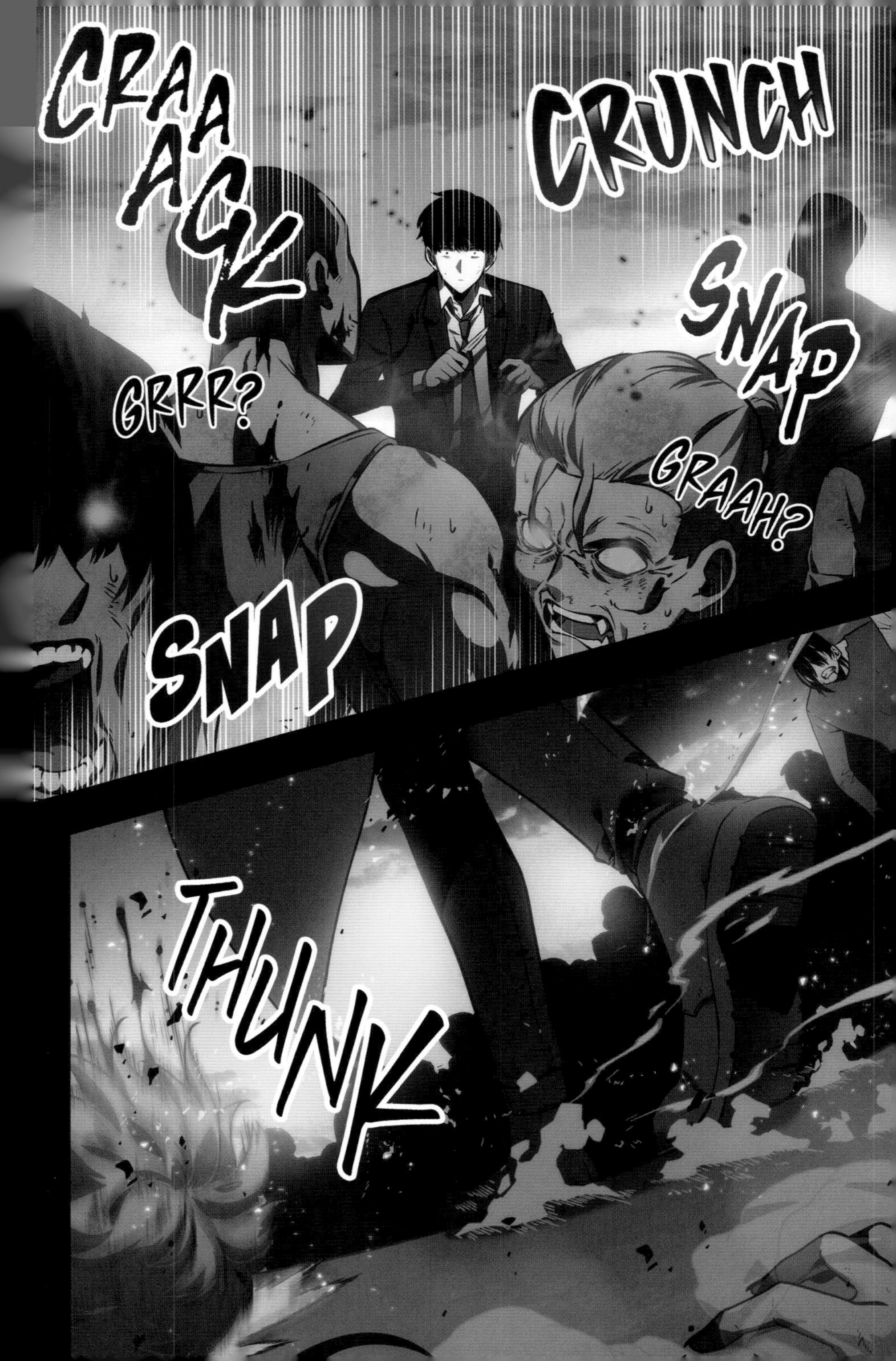
CRUNCH
SNAP
GRAAH?
CRAAAACK
GRRR?
SNAP
THUNK

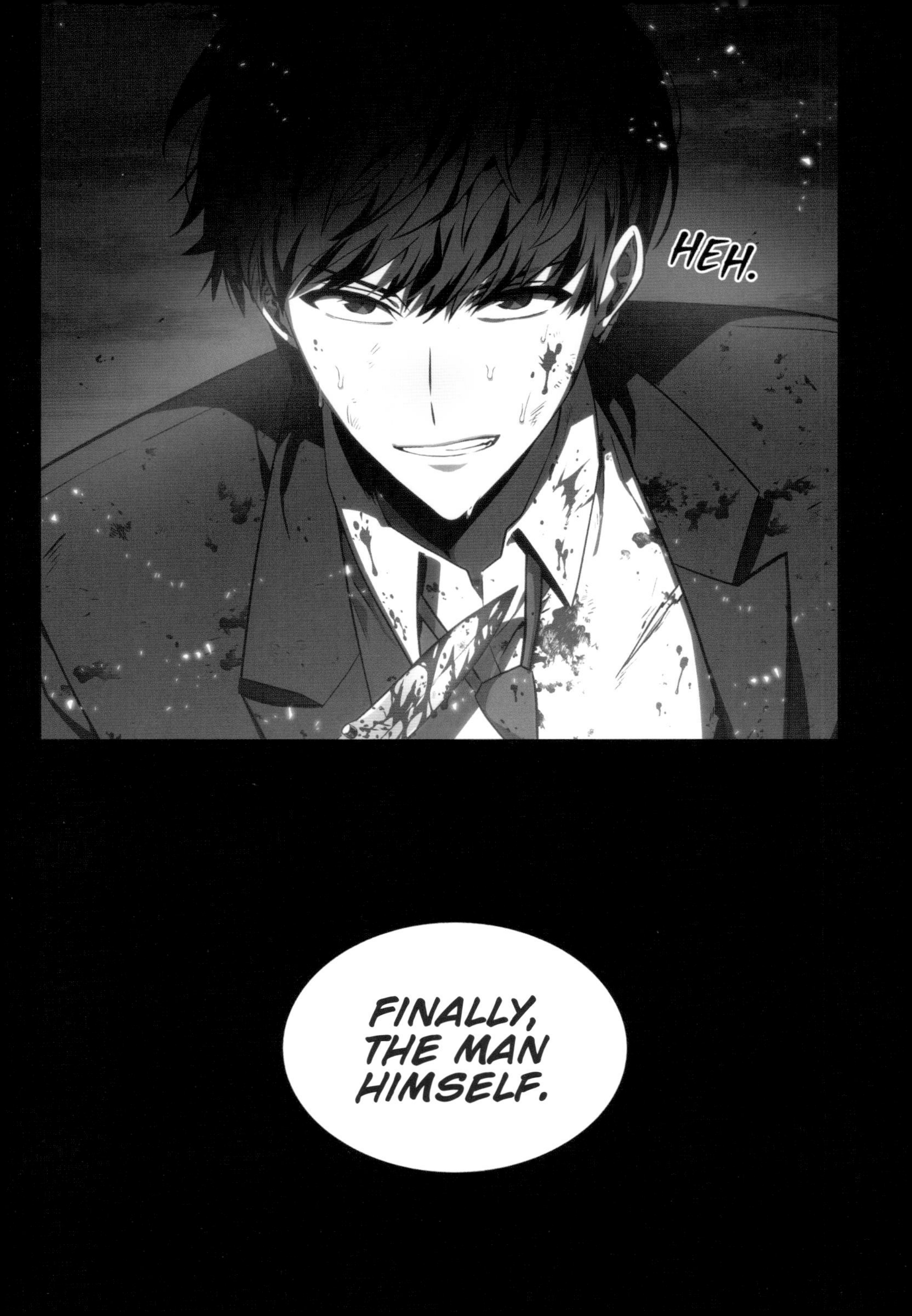
HEH.
FINALLY, THE MAN HIMSELF.

EP. 02

Omniscient
Reader's
Viewpoint

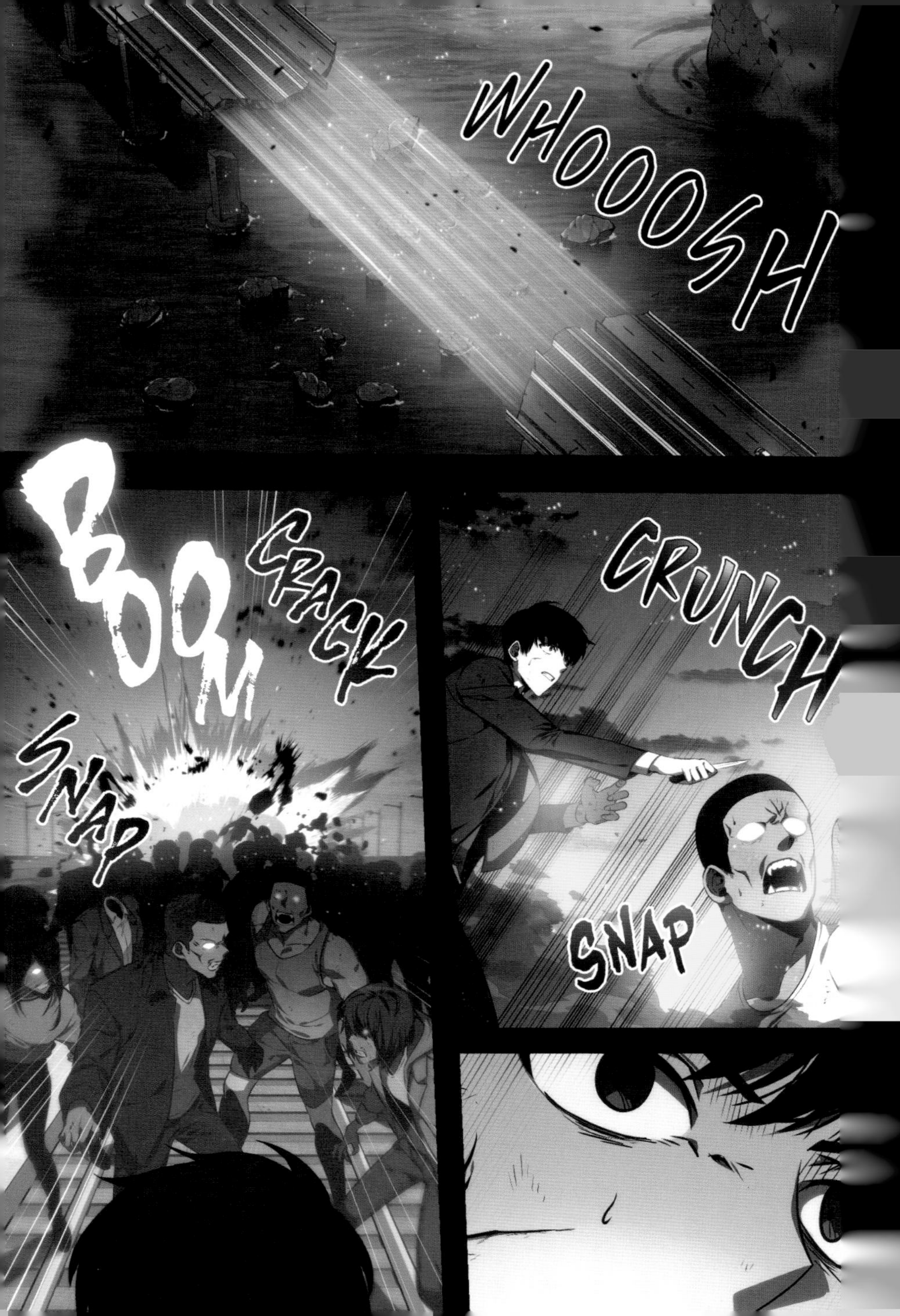
WHOOOSH
CRUNCH
CRACK
BOOM
SNAP
SNAP

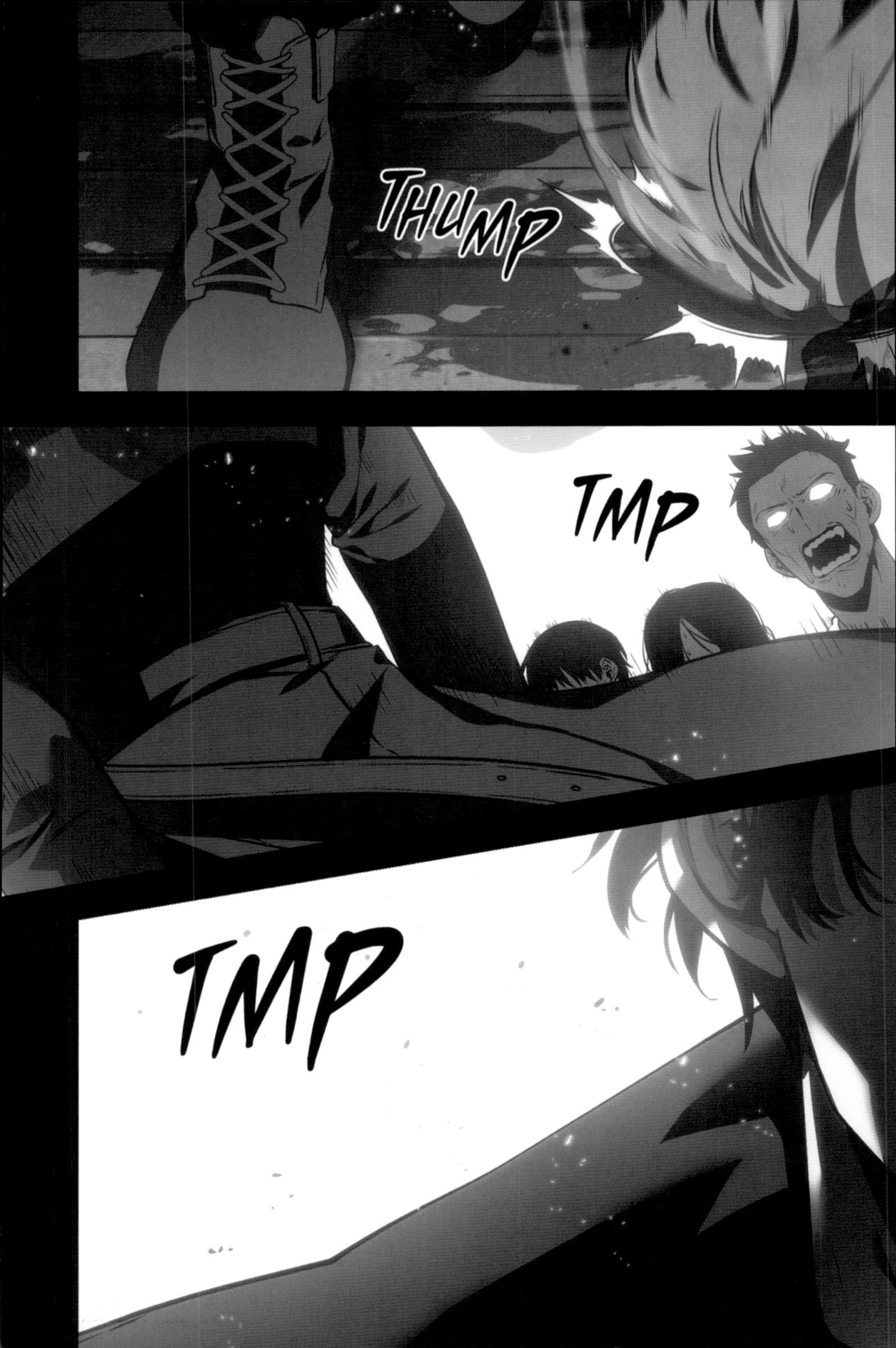
THUMP
TMP
TMP

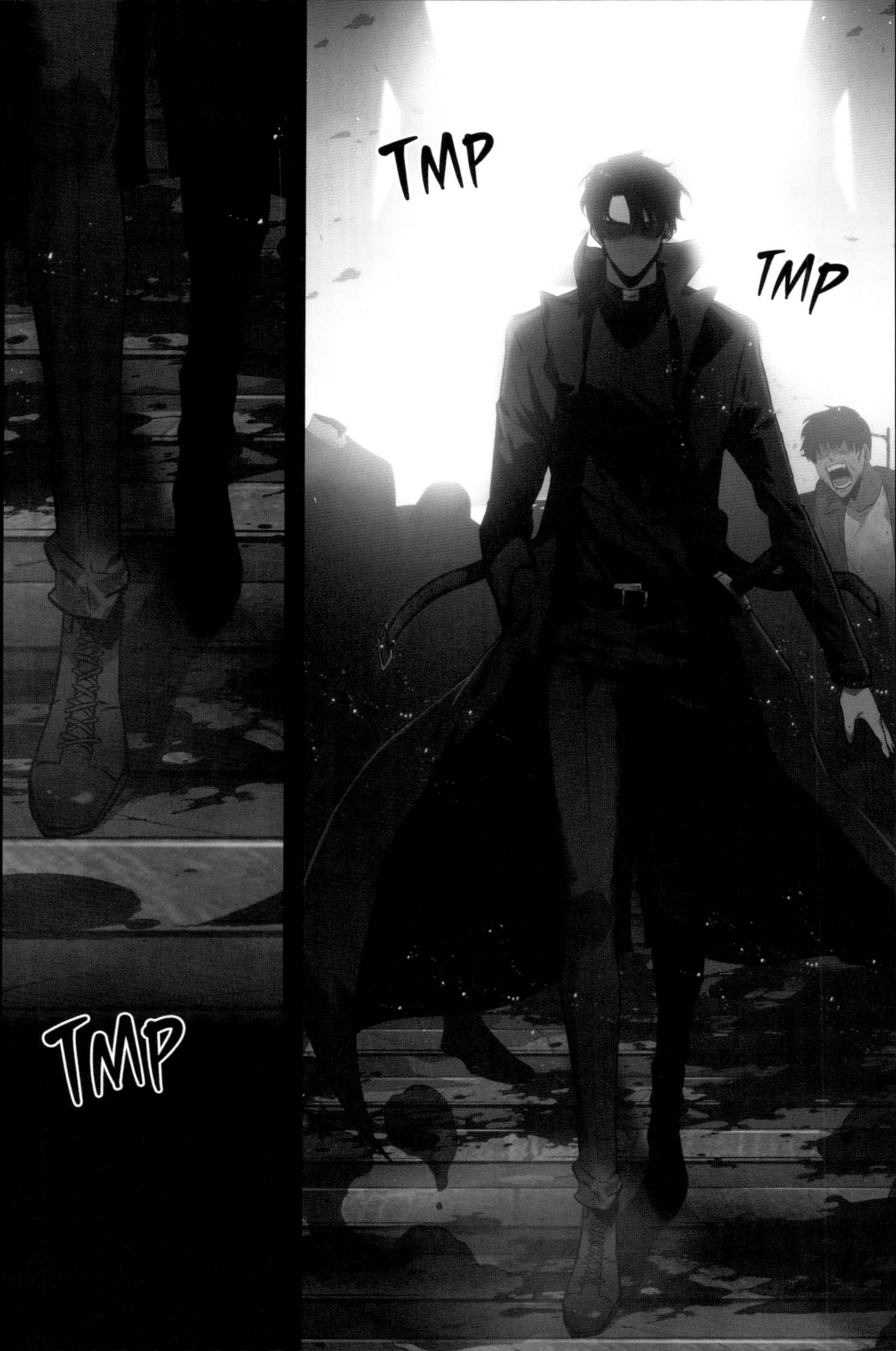
TMP
TMP
TMP

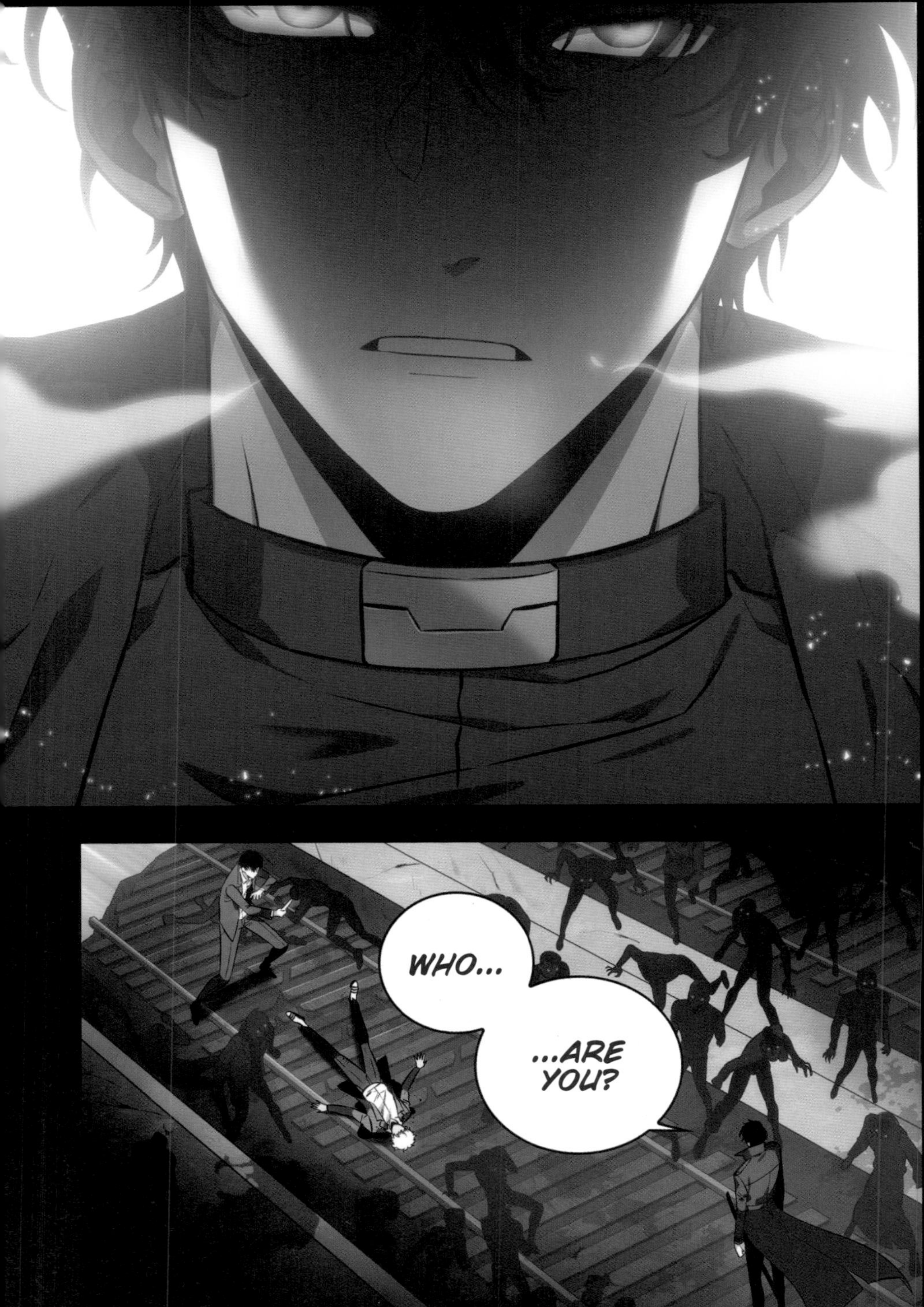
WHO...
...ARE YOU?

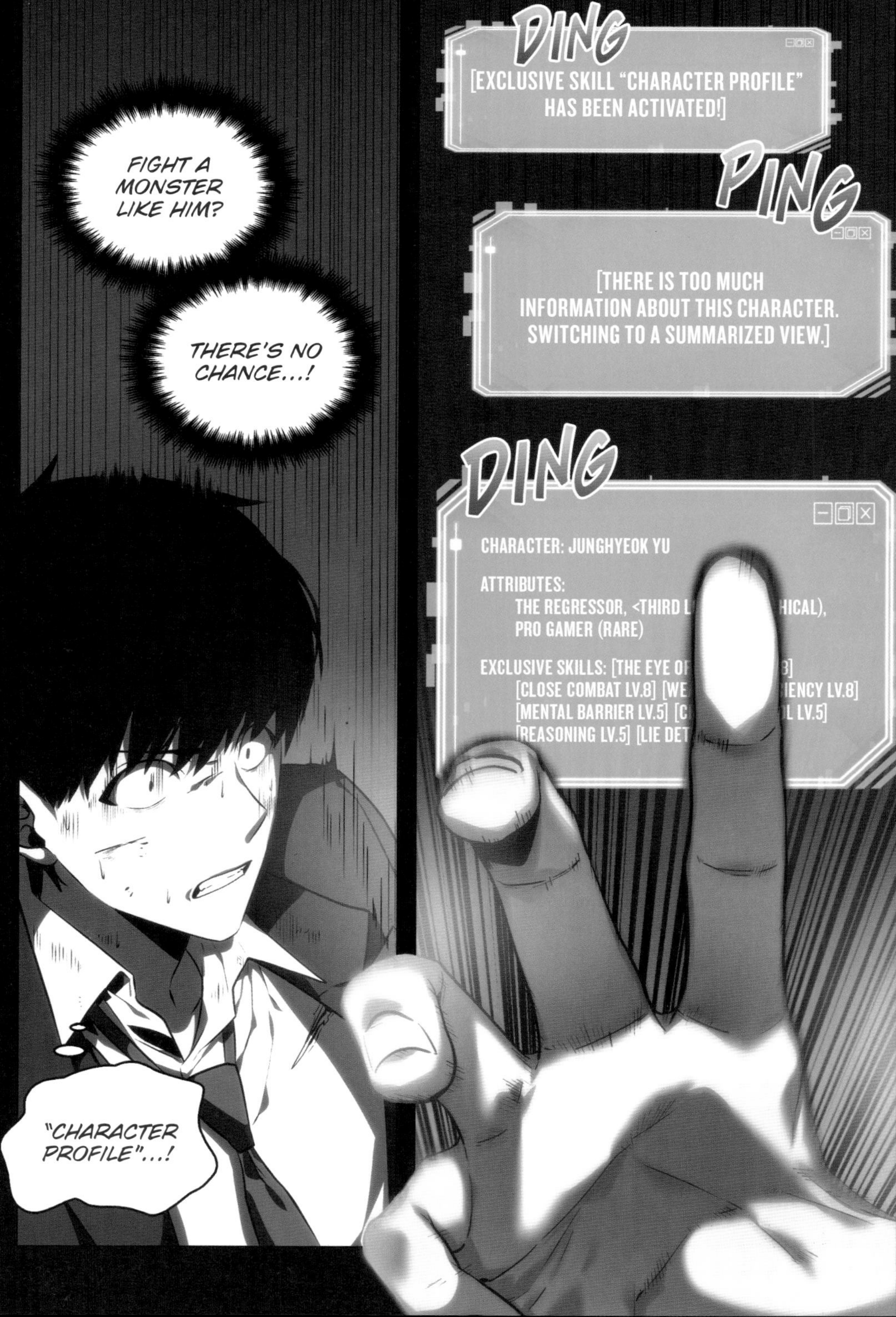

FIGHT A MONSTER LIKE HIM?
THERE'S NO CHANCE...!
"CHARACTER PROFILE"...!
DING
[EXCLUSIVE SKILL "CHARACTER PROFILE" HAS BEEN ACTIVATED!]
PING
[THERE IS TOO MUCH INFORMATION ABOUT THIS CHARACTER. SWITCHING TO A SUMMARIZED VIEW.]
DING
CHARACTER: JUNGHYEOK YU
ATTRIBUTES:
THE REGRESSOR, <THIRD L HICAL),
PRO GAMER (RARE)
EXCLUSIVE SKILLS: [THE EYE OF
[CLOSE COMBAT LV.8] [WE ENCY LV.8]
[MENTAL BARRIER LV.5] [C L LV.5]
[REASONING LV.5] [LIE DET

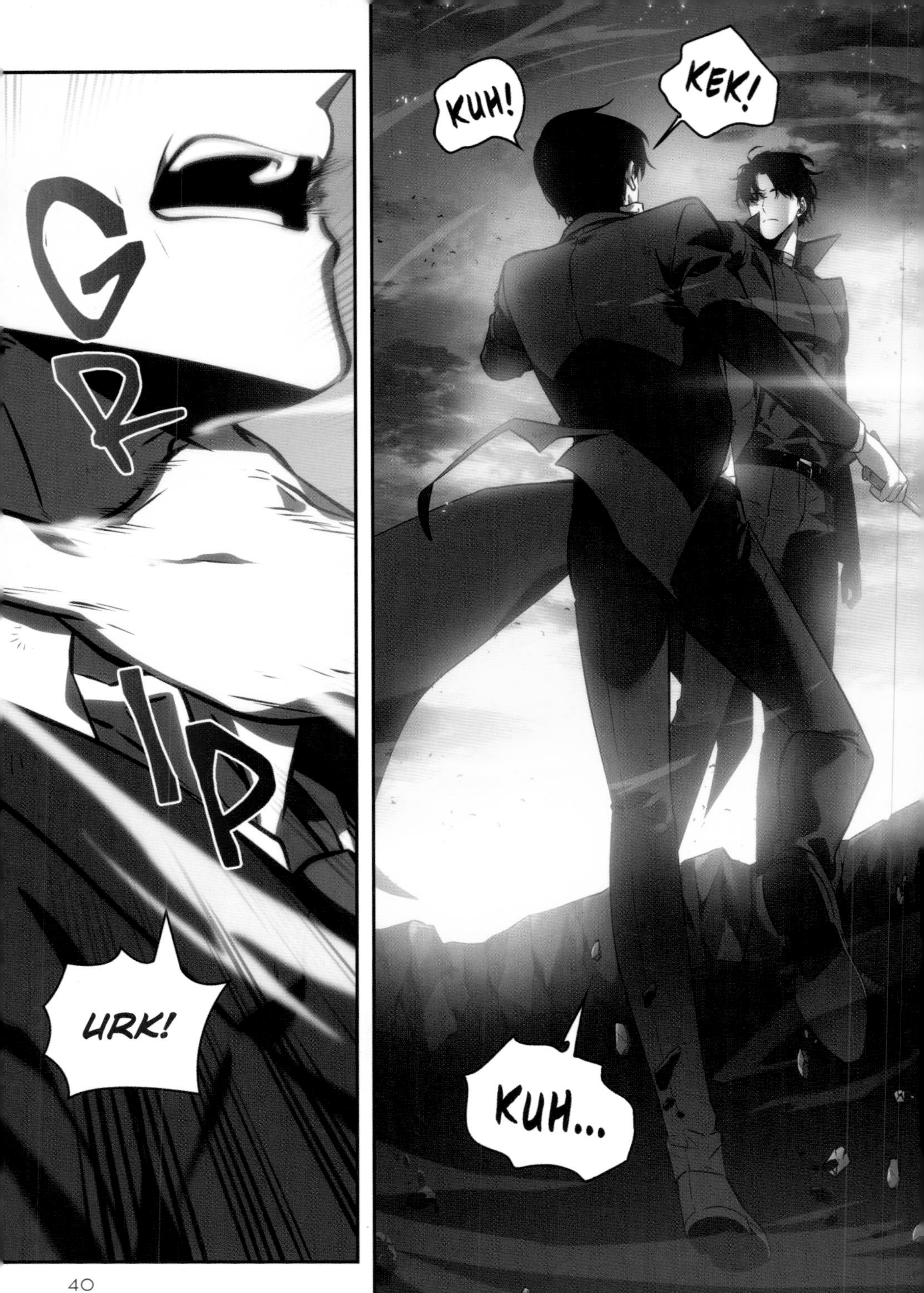
GRIP
URK!
KUH!
KEK!
KUH...

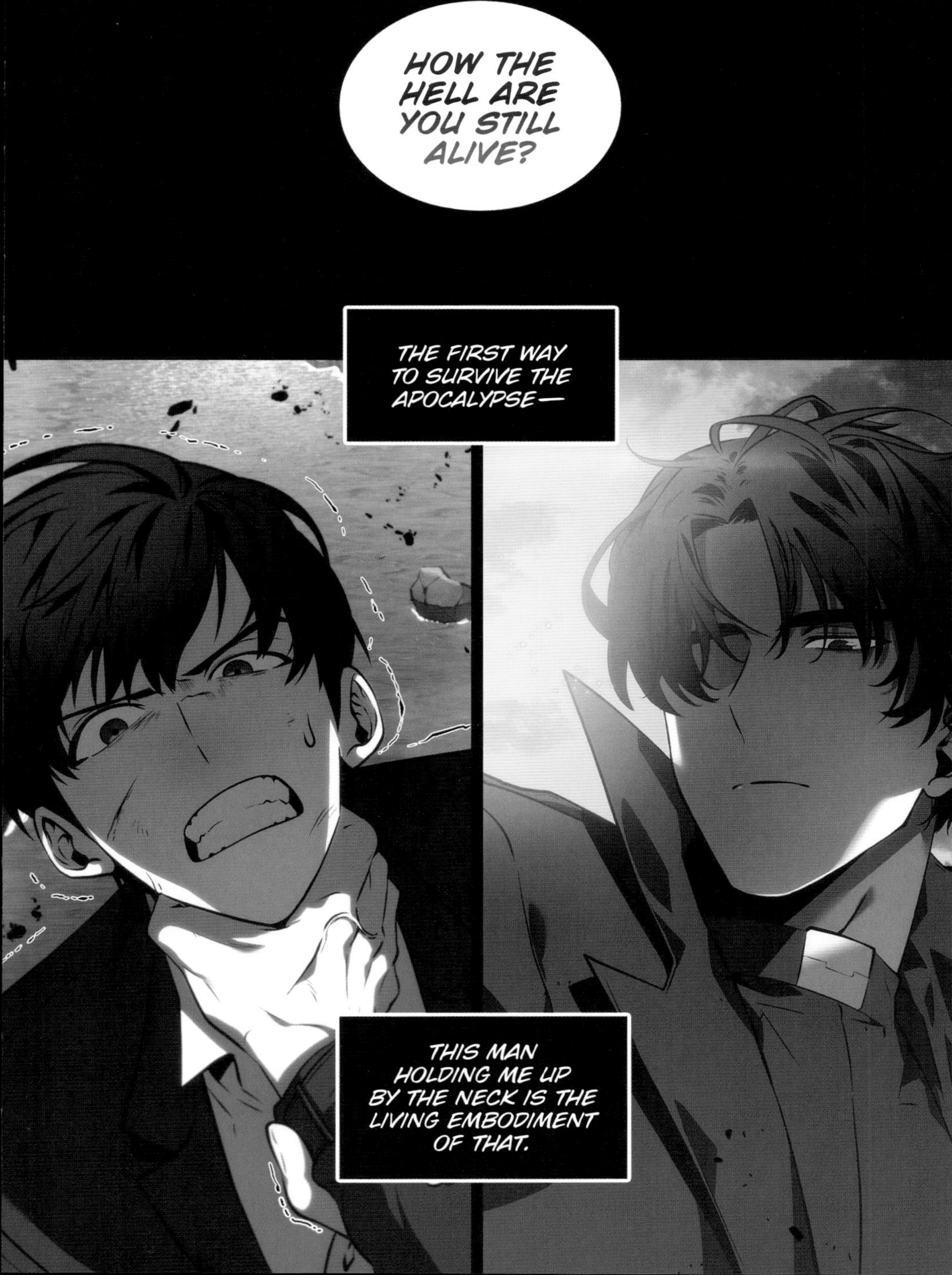
HOW THE HELL ARE YOU STILL ALIVE?
THE FIRST WAY TO SURVIVE THE APOCALYPSE—
THIS MAN HOLDING ME UP BY THE NECK IS THE LIVING EMBODIMENT OF THAT.

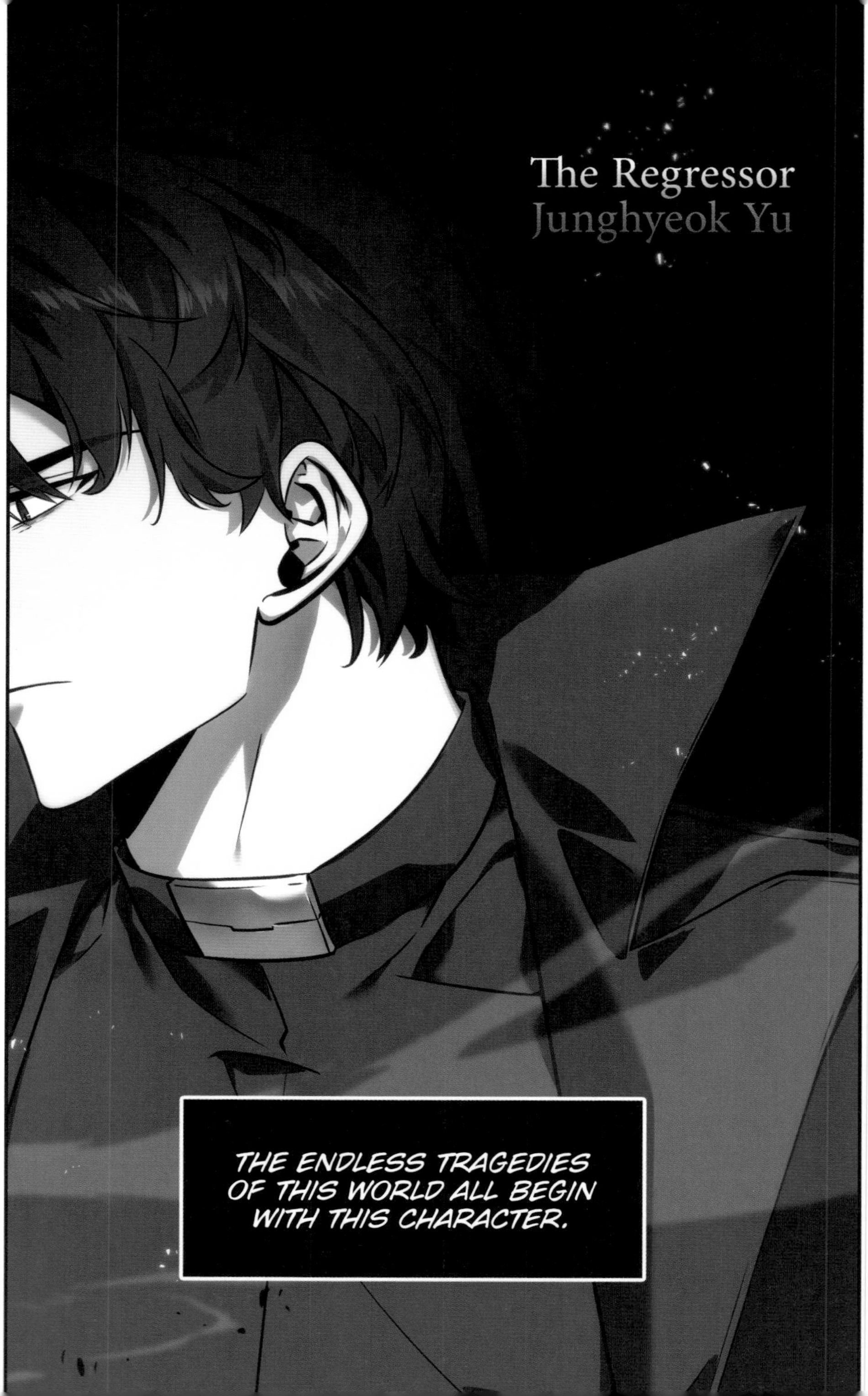
The Regressor
Junghyeok Yu
THE ENDLESS TRAGEDIES OF THIS WORLD ALL BEGIN WITH THIS CHARACTER.

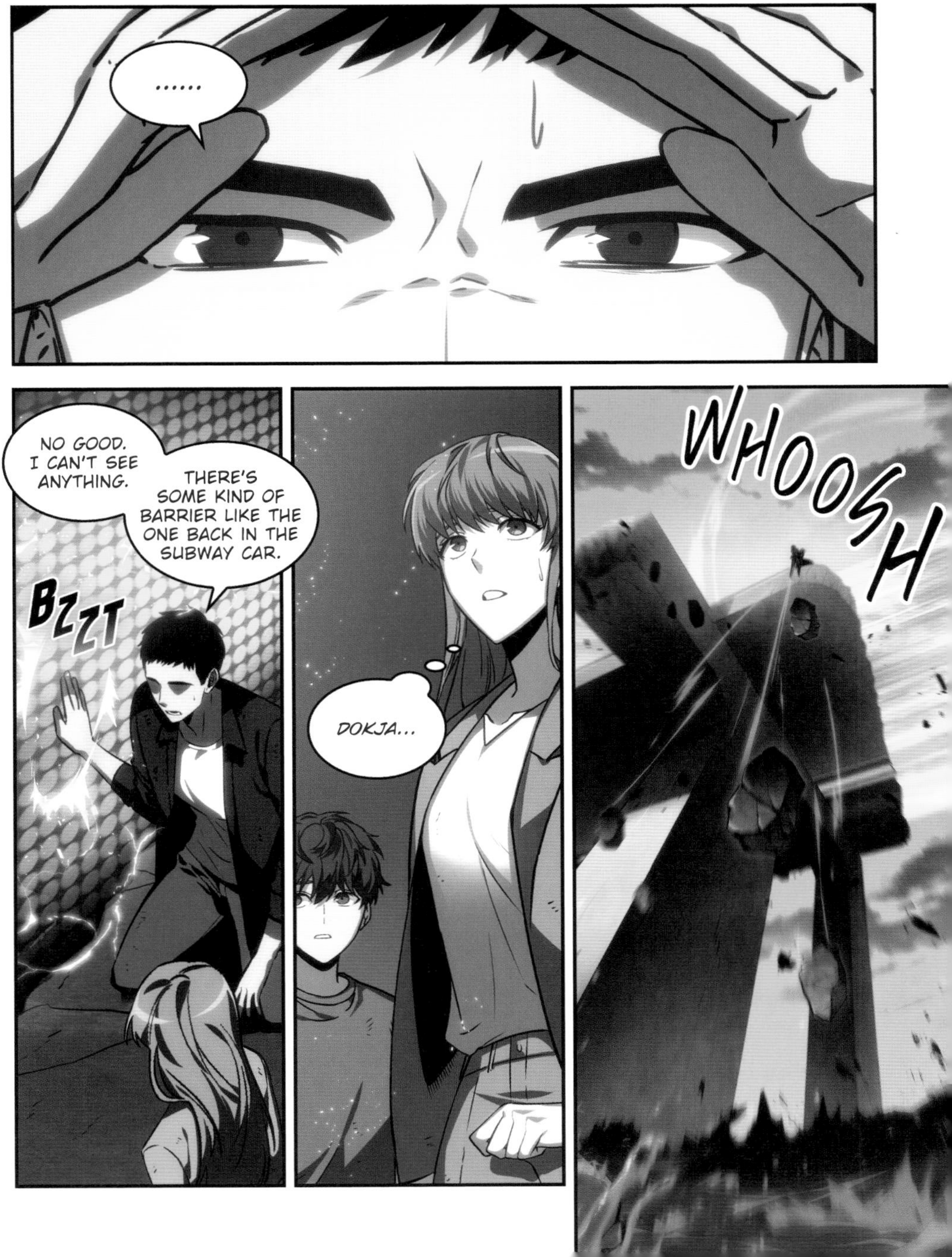
......
NO GOOD. I CAN'T SEE ANYTHING.
THERE'S SOME KIND OF BARRIER LIKE THE ONE BACK IN THE SUBWAY CAR.
BZZT
DOKJA...
WHOOSH

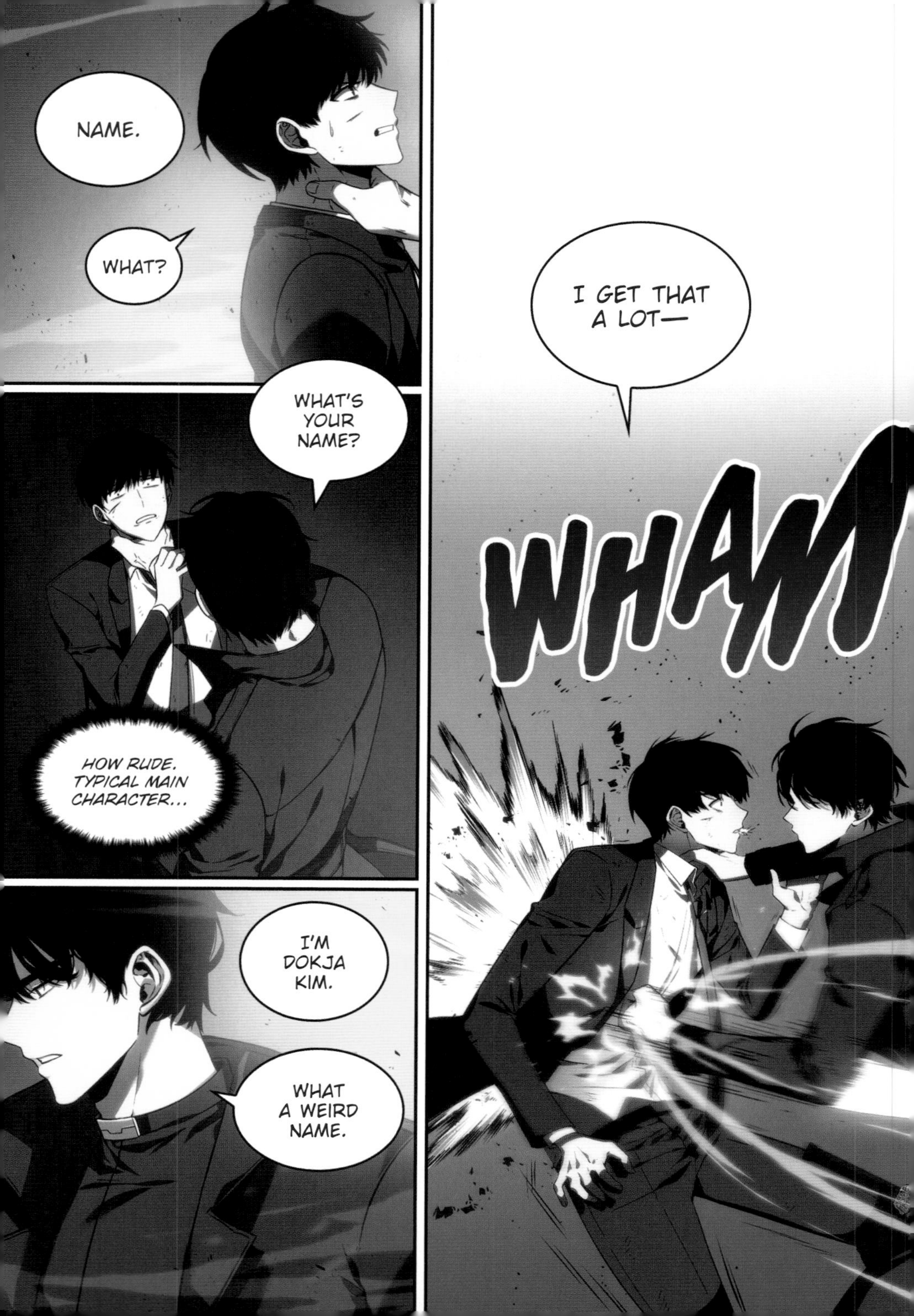
NAME.
WHAT?
WHAT'S YOUR NAME?
HOW RUDE. TYPICAL MAIN CHARACTER...
I'M DOKJA KIM.
WHAT A WEIRD NAME.
I GET THAT A LOT—
WHAM

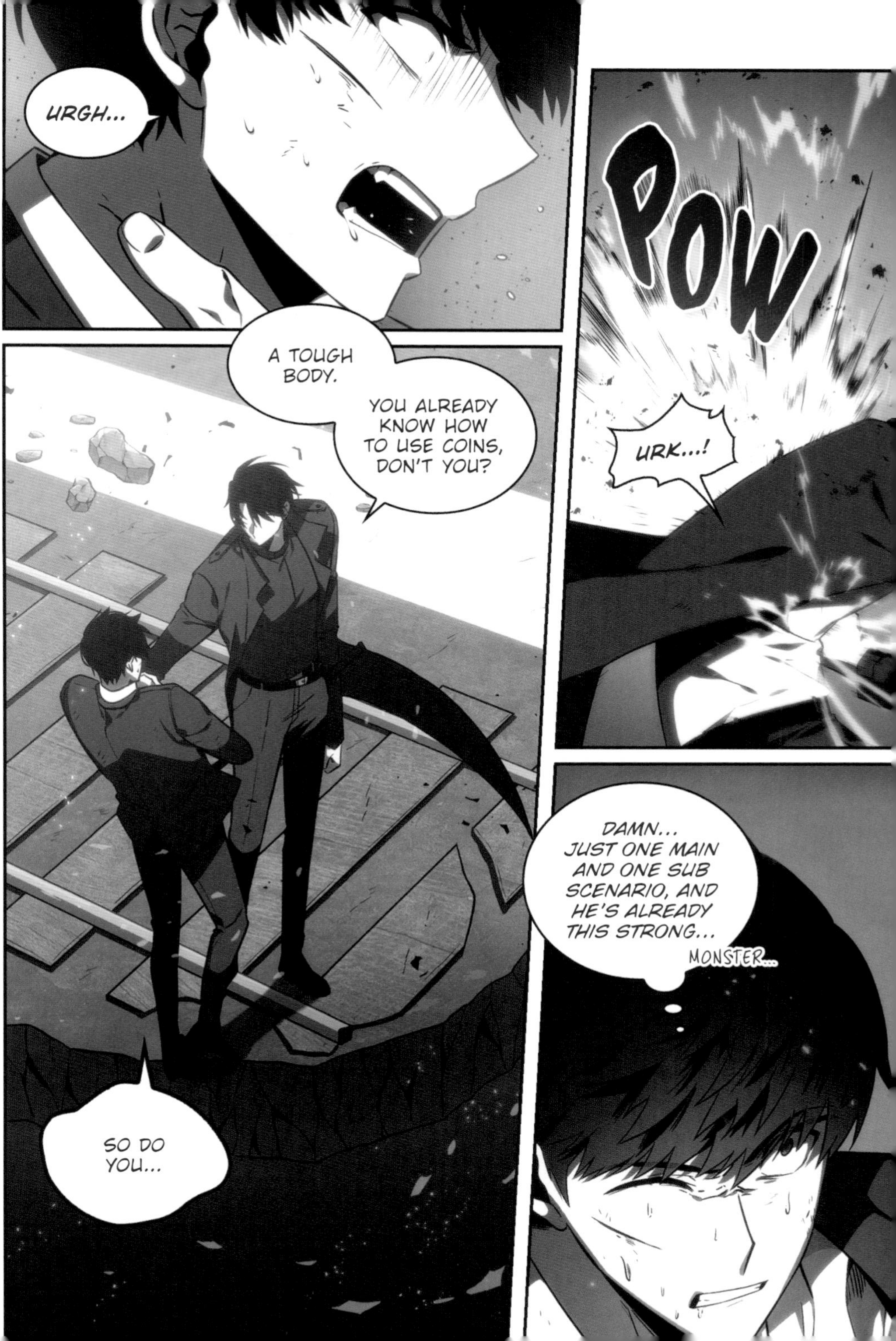
URGH...
POW
URK...!
A TOUGH BODY.
YOU ALREADY KNOW HOW TO USE COINS, DON'T YOU?
SO DO YOU...
DAMN... JUST ONE MAIN AND ONE SUB SCENARIO, AND HE'S ALREADY THIS STRONG...
MONSTER...

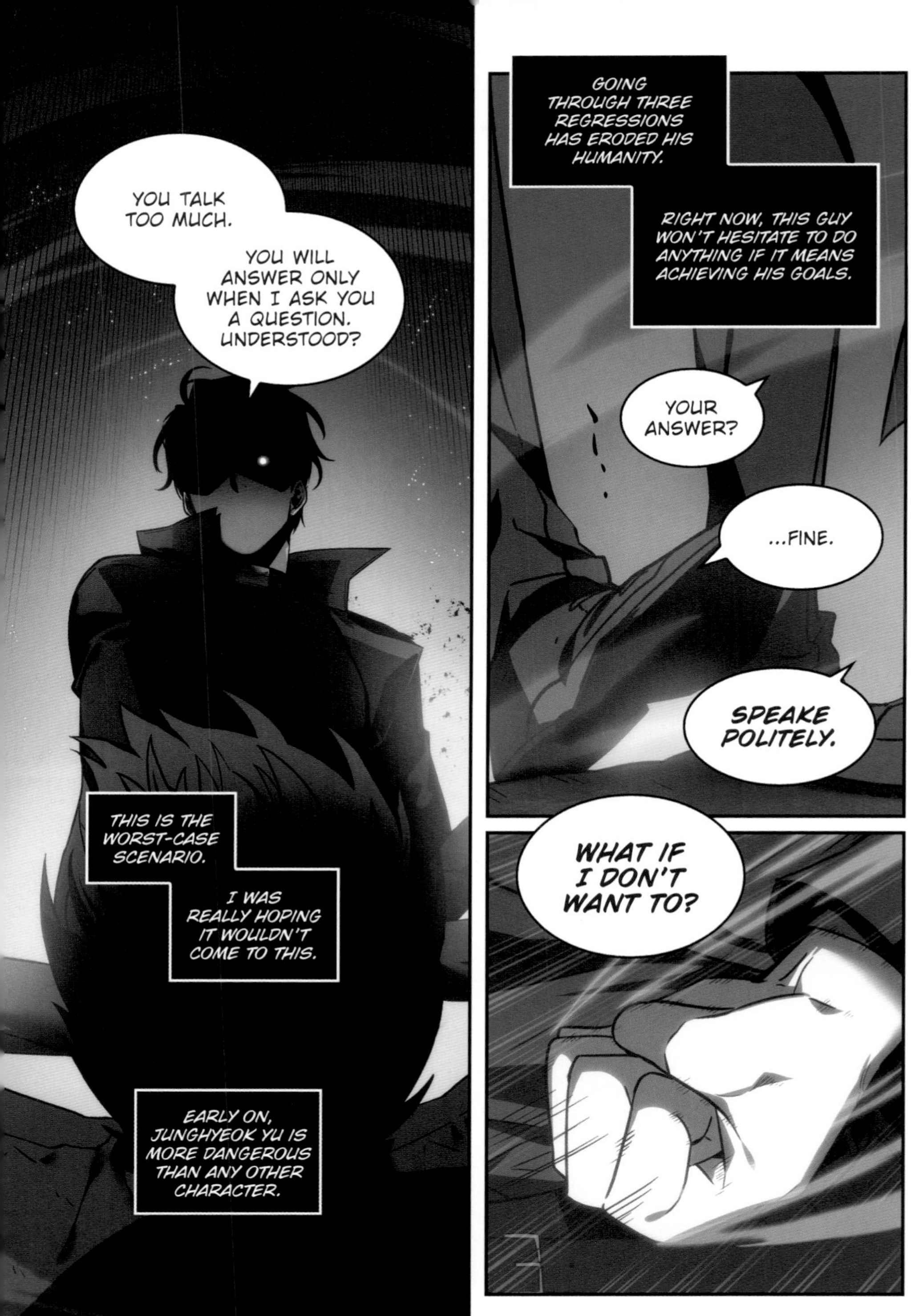

YOU TALK TOO MUCH.
YOU WILL ANSWER ONLY WHEN I ASK YOU A QUESTION. UNDERSTOOD?
THIS IS THE WORST-CASE SCENARIO.
I WAS REALLY HOPING IT WOULDN'T COME TO THIS.
EARLY ON, JUNGHYEOK YU IS MORE DANGEROUS THAN ANY OTHER CHARACTER.
GOING THROUGH THREE REGRESSIONS HAS ERODED HIS HUMANITY.
RIGHT NOW, THIS GUY WON'T HESITATE TO DO ANYTHING IF IT MEANS ACHIEVING HIS GOALS.
YOUR ANSWER?
...FINE.
SPEAKE POLITELY.
WHAT IF I DON'T WANT TO?

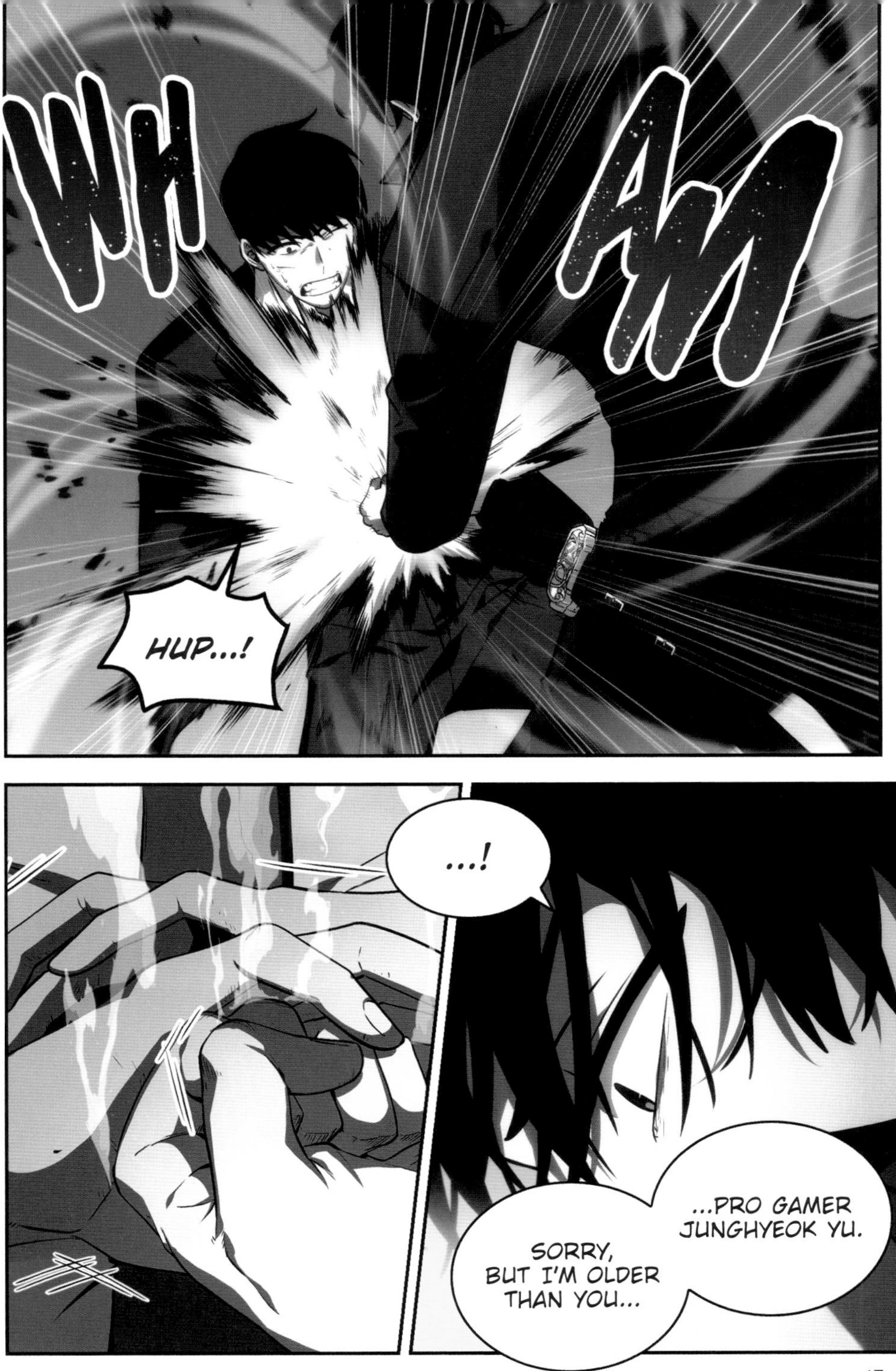
WHAM
HUP...!
...!
SORRY, BUT I'M OLDER THAN YOU...
...PRO GAMER JUNGHYEOK YU.

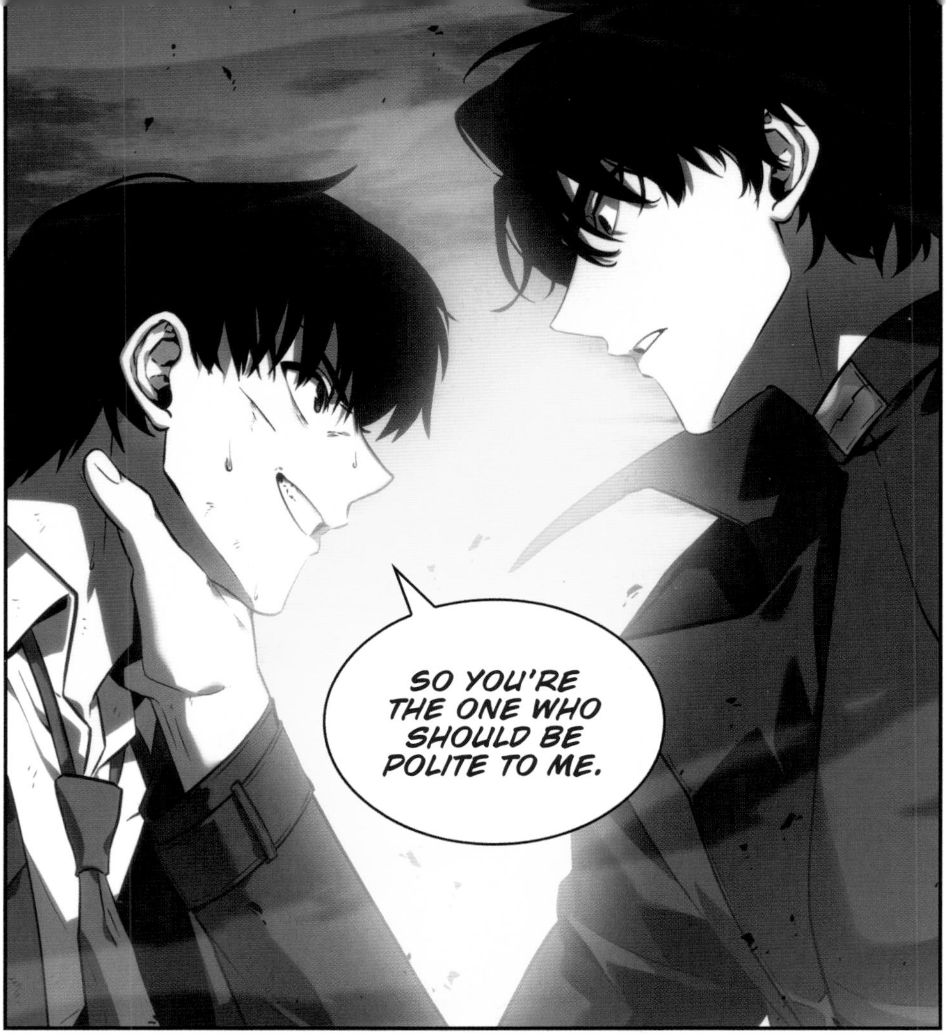
SO YOU'RE THE ONE WHO SHOULD BE POLITE TO ME.

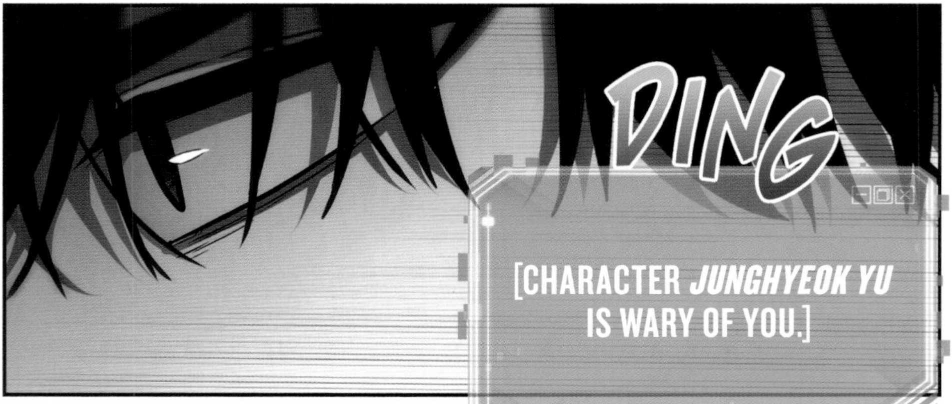
DING
[CHARACTER JUNGHYEOK YU IS WARY OF YOU.]

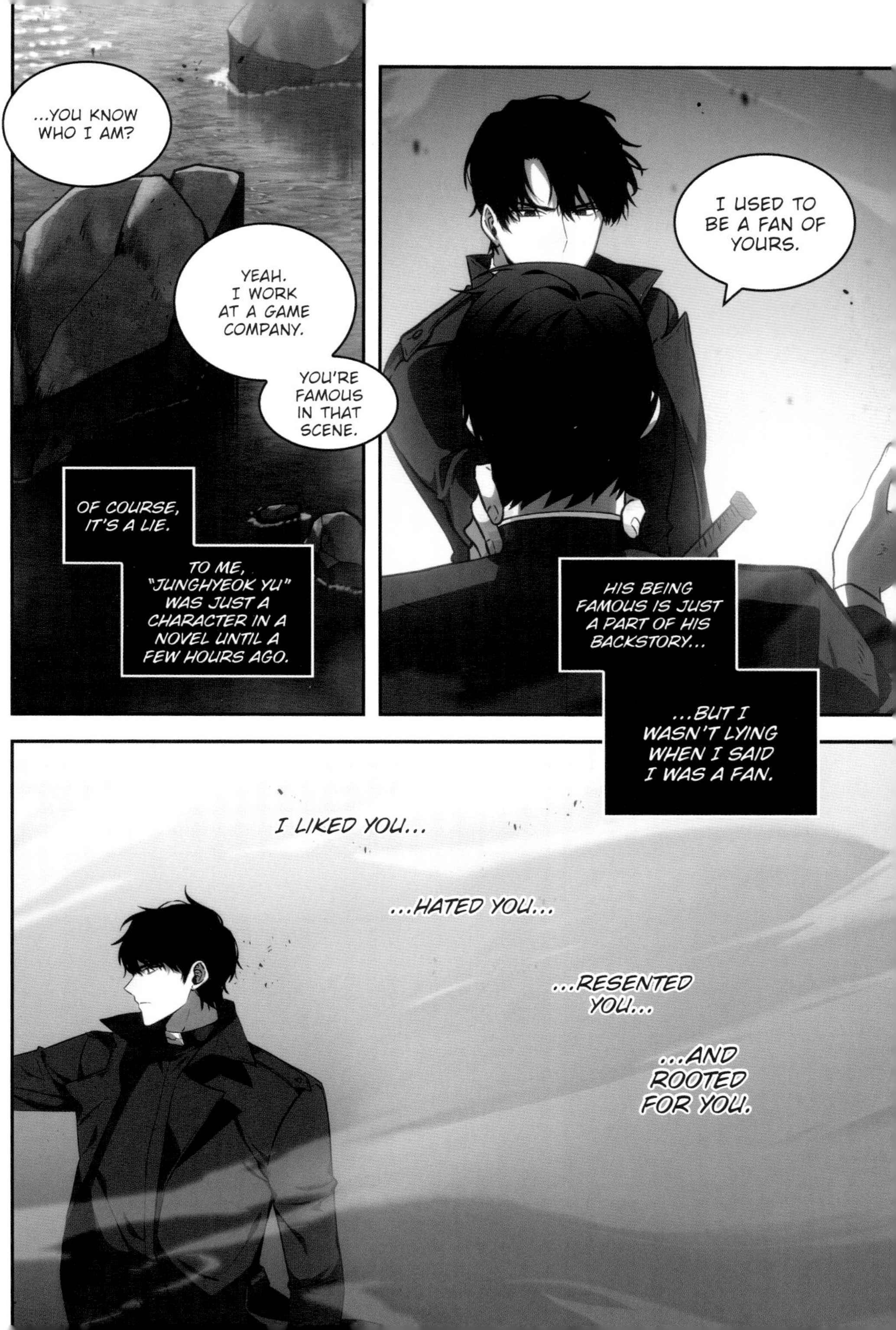
...YOU KNOW WHO I AM?
YEAH. I WORK AT A GAME COMPANY.
YOU'RE FAMOUS IN THAT SCENE.
OF COURSE, IT'S A LIE.
TO ME, "JUNGHYEOK YU" WAS JUST A CHARACTER IN A NOVEL UNTIL A FEW HOURS AGO.
I USED TO BE A FAN OF YOURS.
HIS BEING FAMOUS IS JUST A PART OF HIS BACKSTORY...
...BUT I WASN'T LYING WHEN I SAID I WAS A FAN.
I LIKED YOU...
...HATED YOU...
...RESENTED YOU...
...AND ROOTED FOR YOU.

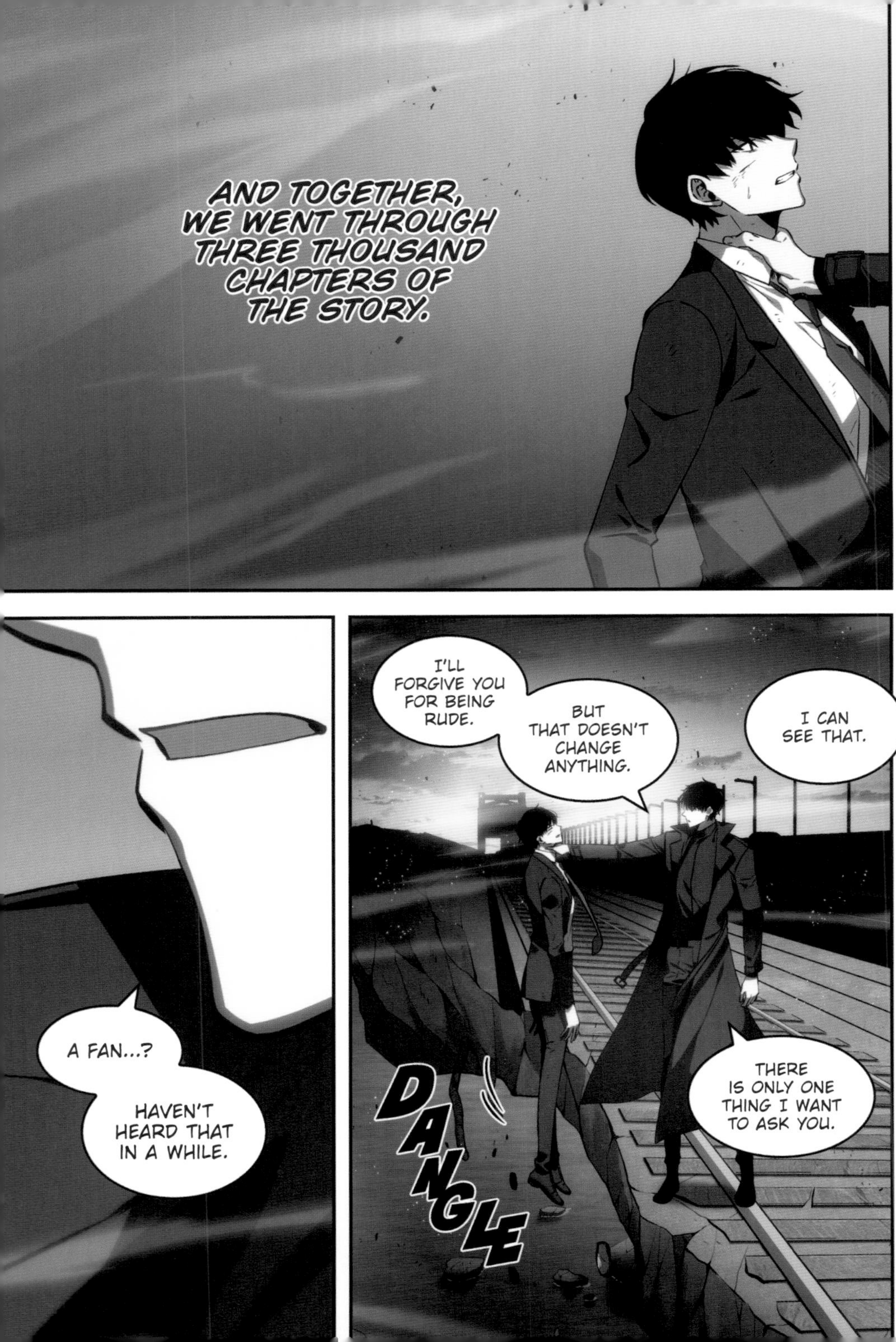
AND TOGETHER, WE WENT THROUGH THREE THOUSAND CHAPTERS OF THE STORY.
A FAN...?
HAVEN'T HEARD THAT IN A WHILE.
I'LL FORGIVE YOU FOR BEING RUDE.
BUT THAT DOESN'T CHANGE ANYTHING.
I CAN SEE THAT.
THERE IS ONLY ONE THING I WANT TO ASK YOU.
DANGLE

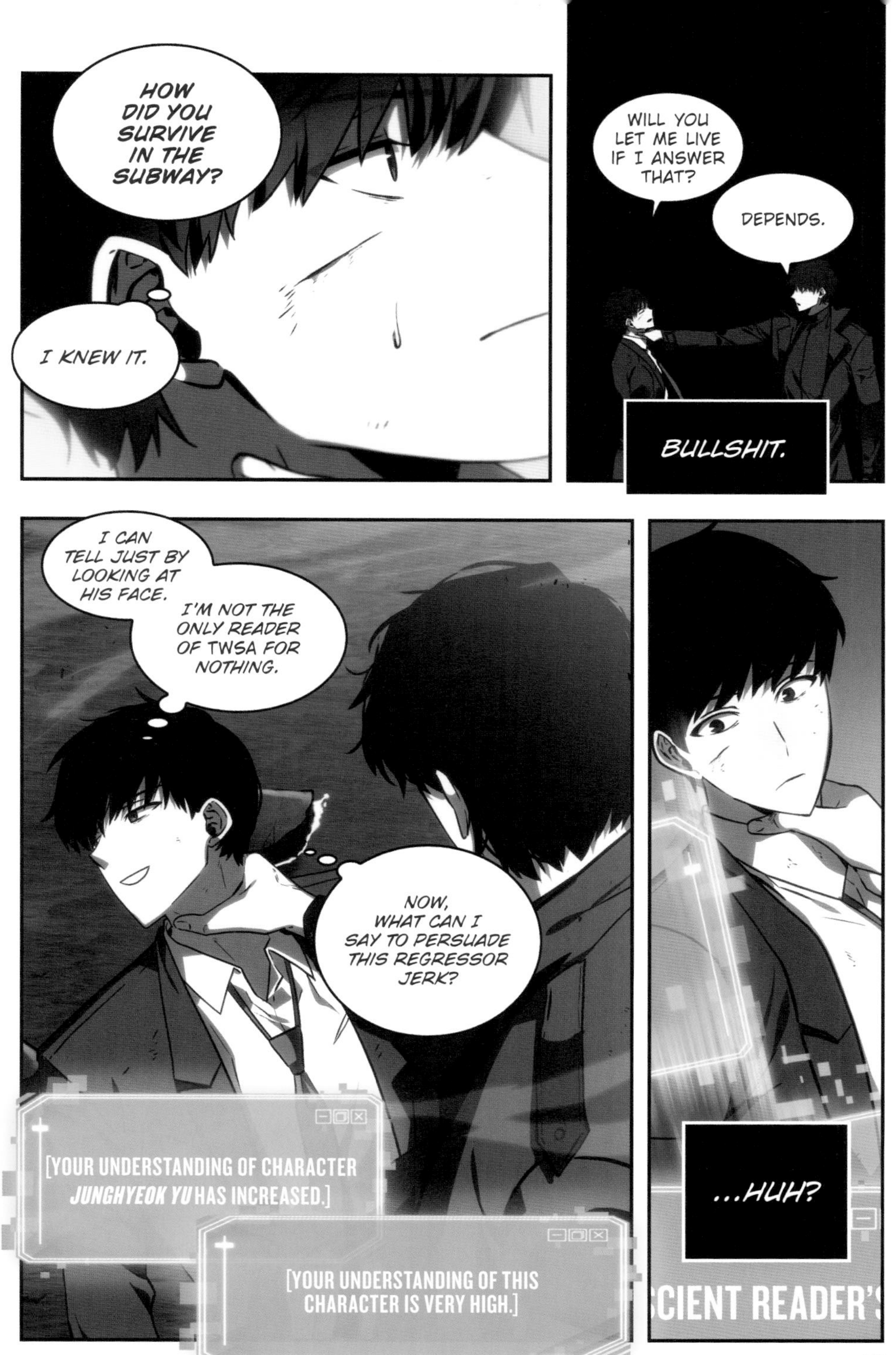

HOW DID YOU SURVIVE IN THE SUBWAY?
I KNEW IT.
WILL YOU LET ME LIVE IF I ANSWER THAT?
DEPENDS.
BULLSHIT.
I CAN TELL JUST BY LOOKING AT HIS FACE.
I'M NOT THE ONLY READER OF TWSA FOR NOTHING.
NOW, WHAT CAN I SAY TO PERSUADE THIS REGRESSOR JERK?
[YOUR UNDERSTANDING OF CHARACTER JUNGHYEOK YU HAS INCREASED.]
[YOUR UNDERSTANDING OF THIS CHARACTER IS VERY HIGH.]
...HUH?
SCIENT READER'S

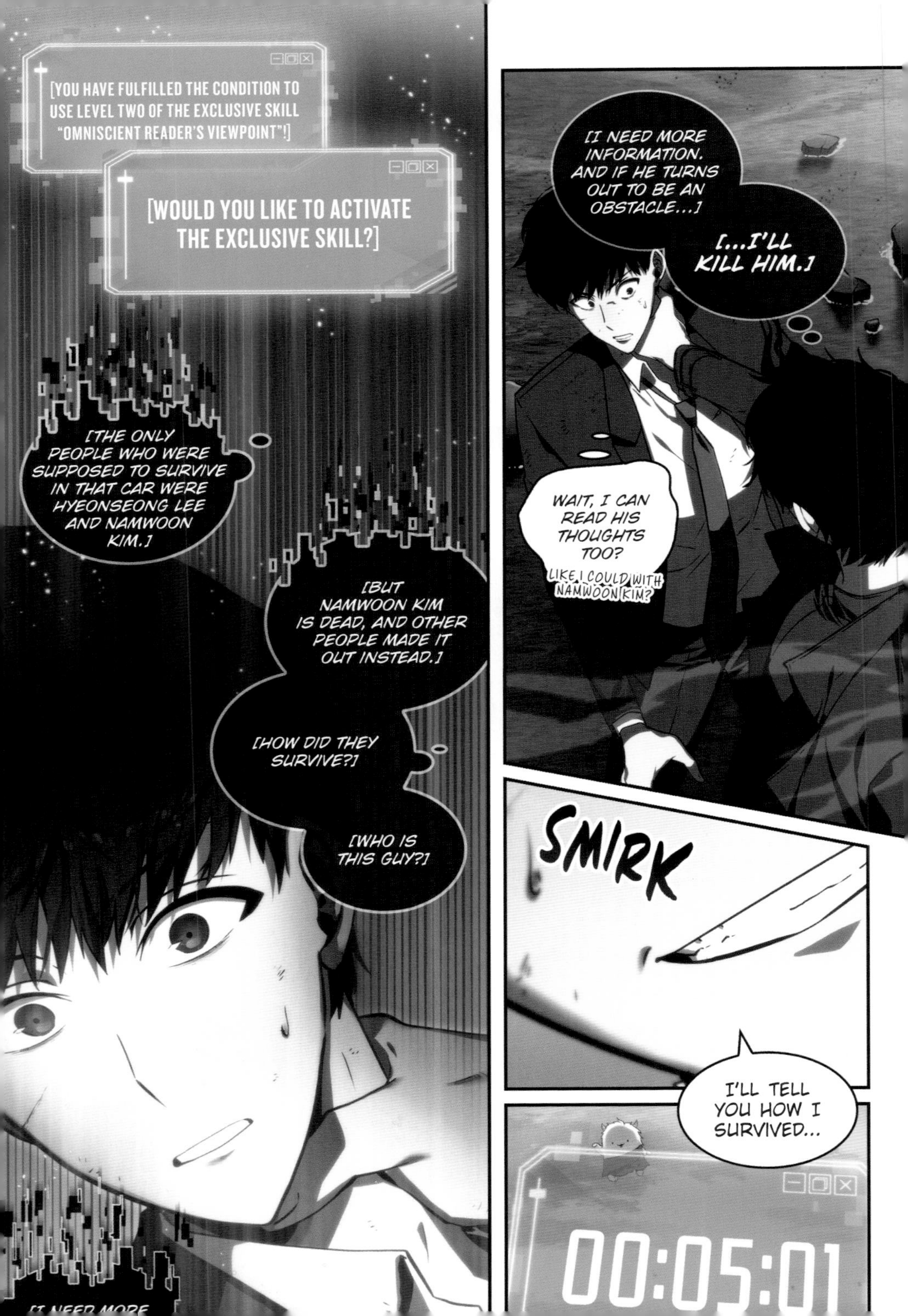
[YOU HAVE FULFILLED THE CONDITION TO USE LEVEL TWO OF THE EXCLUSIVE SKILL "OMNISCIENT READER'S VIEWPOINT"!]
[WOULD YOU LIKE TO ACTIVATE THE EXCLUSIVE SKILL?]
[THE ONLY PEOPLE WHO WERE SUPPOSED TO SURVIVE IN THAT CAR WERE HYEONSEONG LEE AND NAMWOON KIM.]
[BUT NAMWOON KIM IS DEAD, AND OTHER PEOPLE MADE IT OUT INSTEAD.]
[HOW DID THEY SURVIVE?]
[WHO IS THIS GUY?]
[I NEED MORE INFORMATION. AND IF HE TURNS OUT TO BE AN OBSTACLE...]
[...I'LL KILL HIM.]
WAIT, I CAN READ HIS THOUGHTS TOO?
LIKE I COULD WITH NAMWOON KIM?
SMIRK
I'LL TELL YOU HOW I SURVIVED...
00:05:01

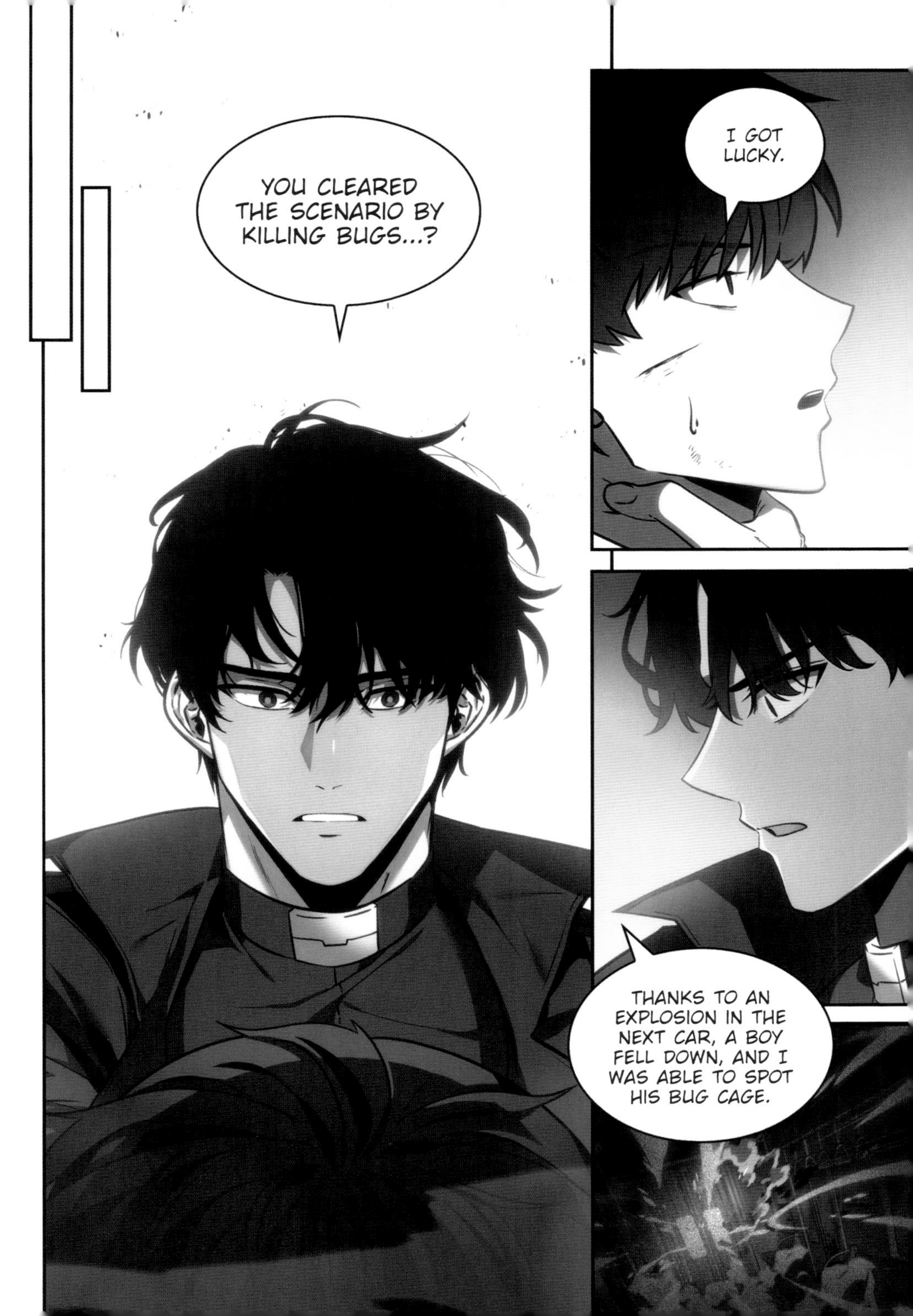

YOU CLEARED THE SCENARIO BY KILLING BUGS...?
I GOT LUCKY.
THANKS TO AN EXPLOSION IN THE NEXT CAR, A BOY FELL DOWN, AND I WAS ABLE TO SPOT HIS BUG CAGE.

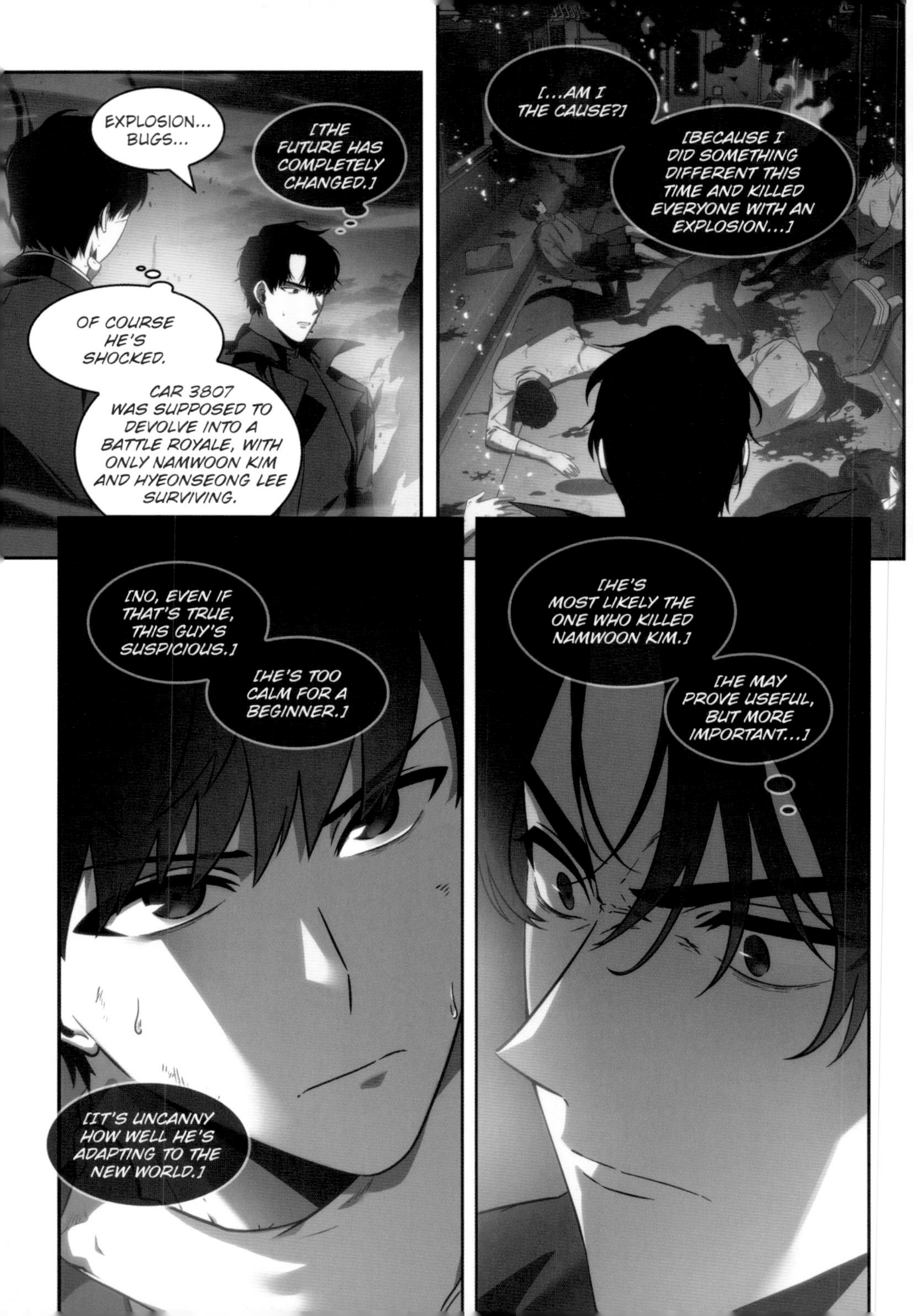
EXPLOSION... BUGS...
[THE FUTURE HAS COMPLETELY CHANGED.]
OF COURSE HE'S SHOCKED.
CAR 3807 WAS SUPPOSED TO DEVOLVE INTO A BATTLE ROYALE, WITH ONLY NAMWOON KIM AND HYEONSEONG LEE SURVIVING.
[...AM I THE CAUSE?]
[BECAUSE I DID SOMETHING DIFFERENT THIS TIME AND KILLED EVERYONE WITH AN EXPLOSION...]
[NO, EVEN IF THAT'S TRUE, THIS GUY'S SUSPICIOUS.]
[HE'S TOO CALM FOR A BEGINNER.]
[IT'S UNCANNY HOW WELL HE'S ADAPTING TO THE NEW WORLD.]
[HE'S MOST LIKELY THE ONE WHO KILLED NAMWOON KIM.]
[HE MAY PROVE USEFUL, BUT MORE IMPORTANT...]

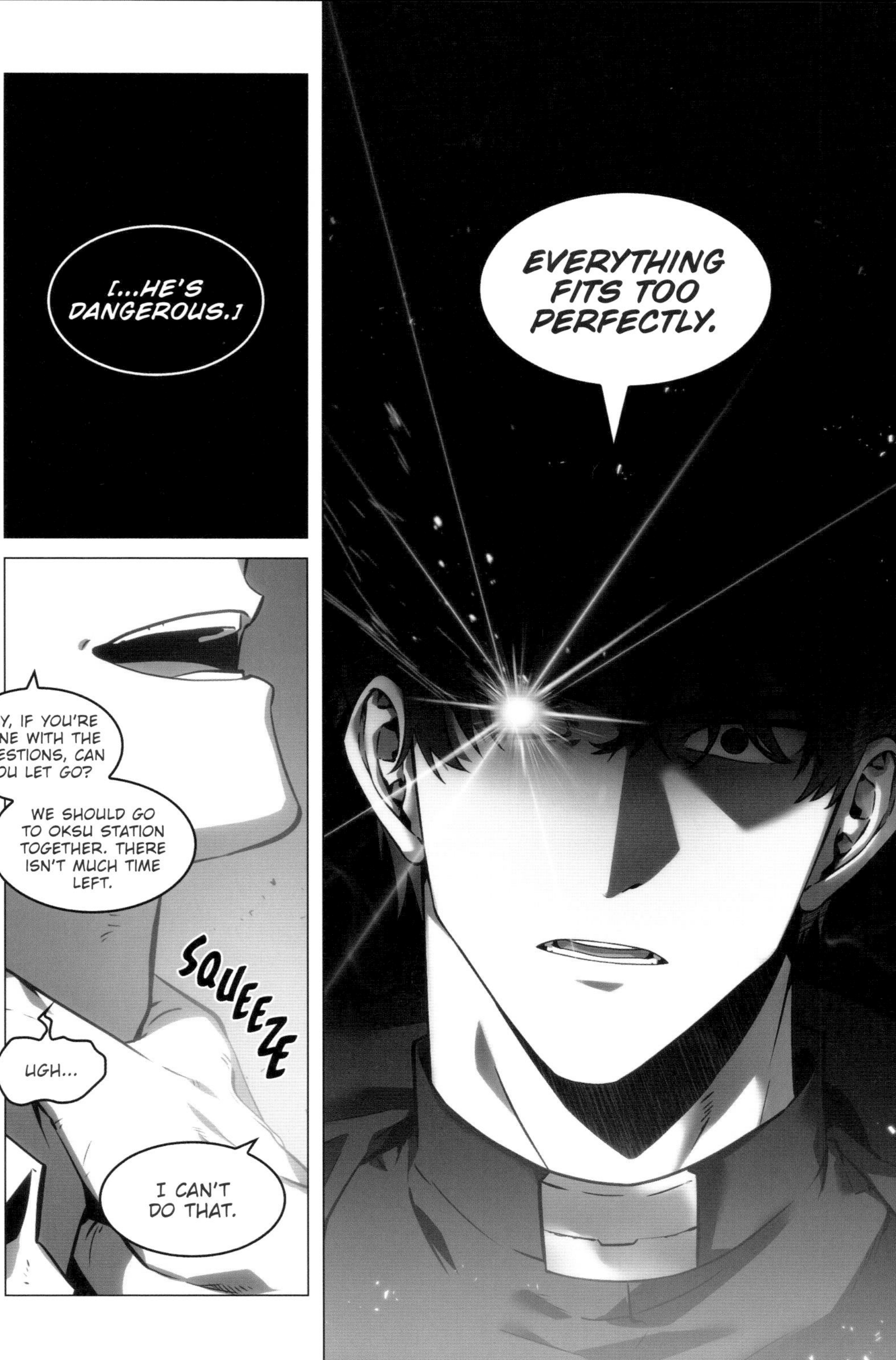
[...HE'S DANGEROUS.]
EVERYTHING FITS TOO PERFECTLY.
HEY, IF YOU'RE DONE WITH THE QUESTIONS, CAN YOU LET GO?
WE SHOULD GO TO OKSU STATION TOGETHER. THERE ISN'T MUCH TIME LEFT.
SQUEEZE
UGH...
I CAN'T DO THAT.

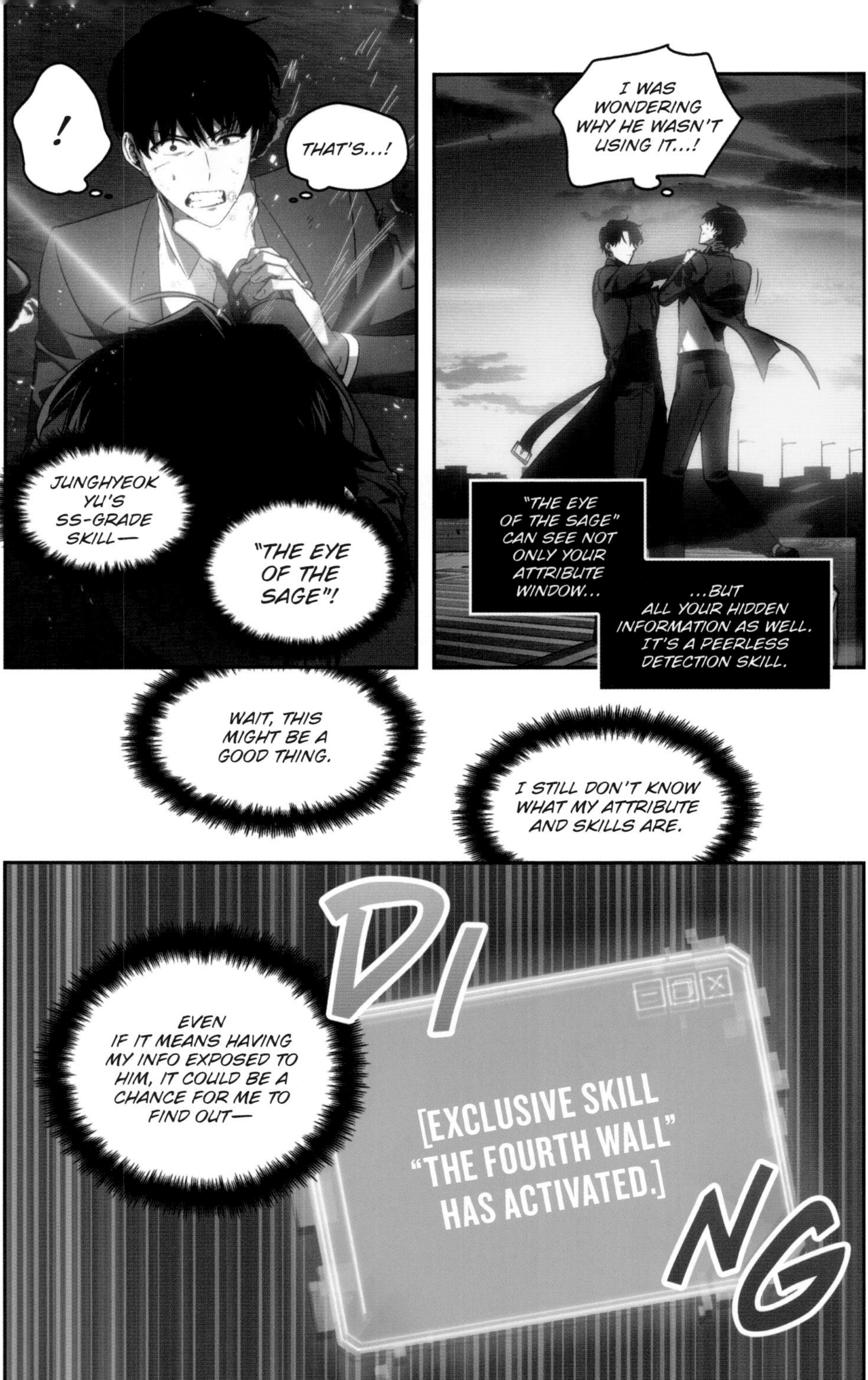
!
THAT'S...!
I WAS WONDERING WHY HE WASN'T USING IT...!
JUNGHYEOK YU'S SS-GRADE SKILL—
"THE EYE OF THE SAGE"!
"THE EYE OF THE SAGE" CAN SEE NOT ONLY YOUR ATTRIBUTE WINDOW...
...BUT ALL YOUR HIDDEN INFORMATION AS WELL. IT'S A PEERLESS DETECTION SKILL.
WAIT, THIS MIGHT BE A GOOD THING.
I STILL DON'T KNOW WHAT MY ATTRIBUTE AND SKILLS ARE.
EVEN IF IT MEANS HAVING MY INFO EXPOSED TO HIM, IT COULD BE A CHANCE FOR ME TO FIND OUT—
DING
[EXCLUSIVE SKILL "THE FOURTH WALL" HAS ACTIVATED.]

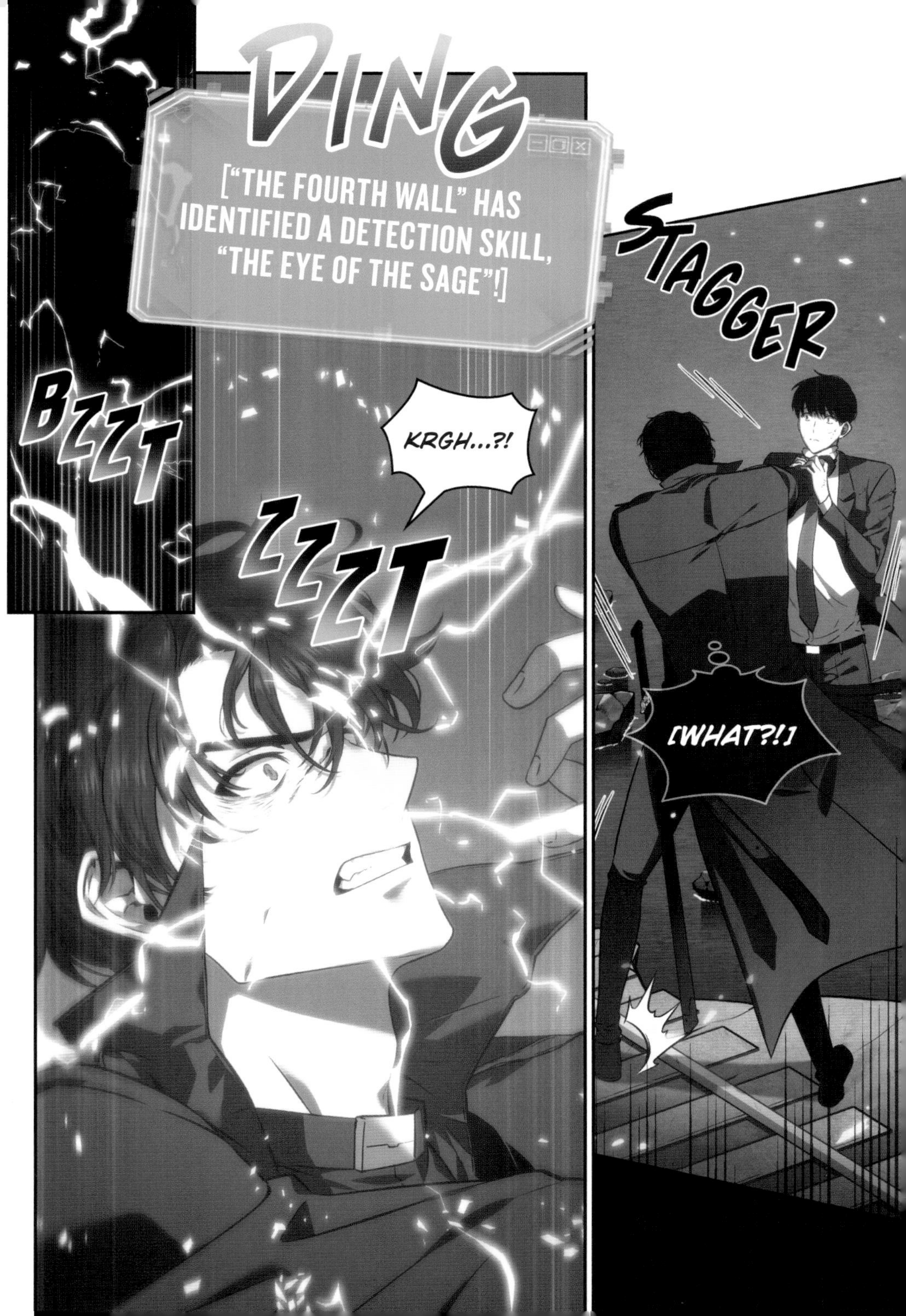
BZZZT
DING
["THE FOURTH WALL" HAS IDENTIFIED A DETECTION SKILL, "THE EYE OF THE SAGE"!]
KRGH...?!
ZZZZT
STAGGER
[WHAT?!]

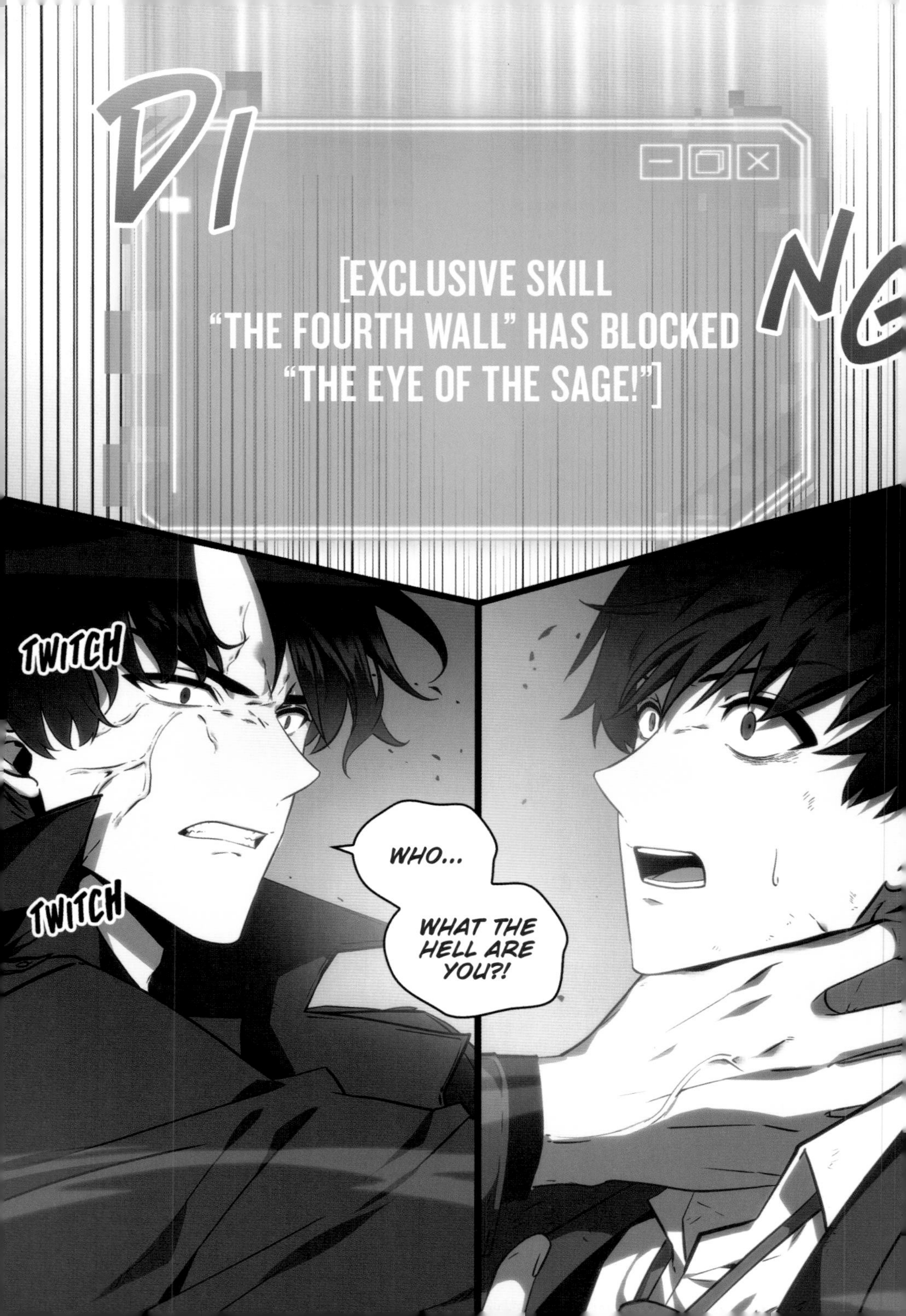
DING
[EXCLUSIVE SKILL
"THE FOURTH WALL" HAS BLOCKED
"THE EYE OF THE SAGE!"]
TWITCH
TWITCH
WHO...
WHAT THE HELL ARE YOU?!

\<SUB SCENARIO—ESCAPE\>

Category: Sub

Difficulty: D

Mission: Cross the collapsed bridge to reach Oksu Station

Time Limit: 20 minutes

Reward: 200 coins

Penalty for Failure: ???

Time Remaining:
2 minutes and 14 seconds

EP. 02

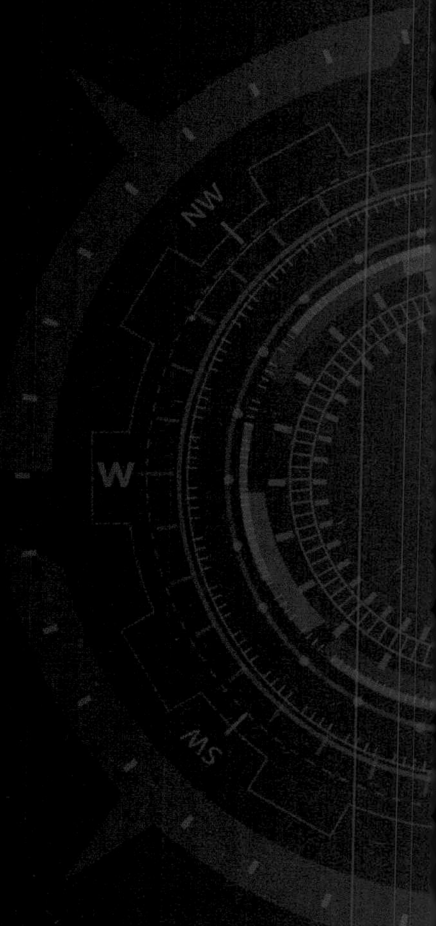
NW
W
SW

Omniscient Reader's Viewpoint

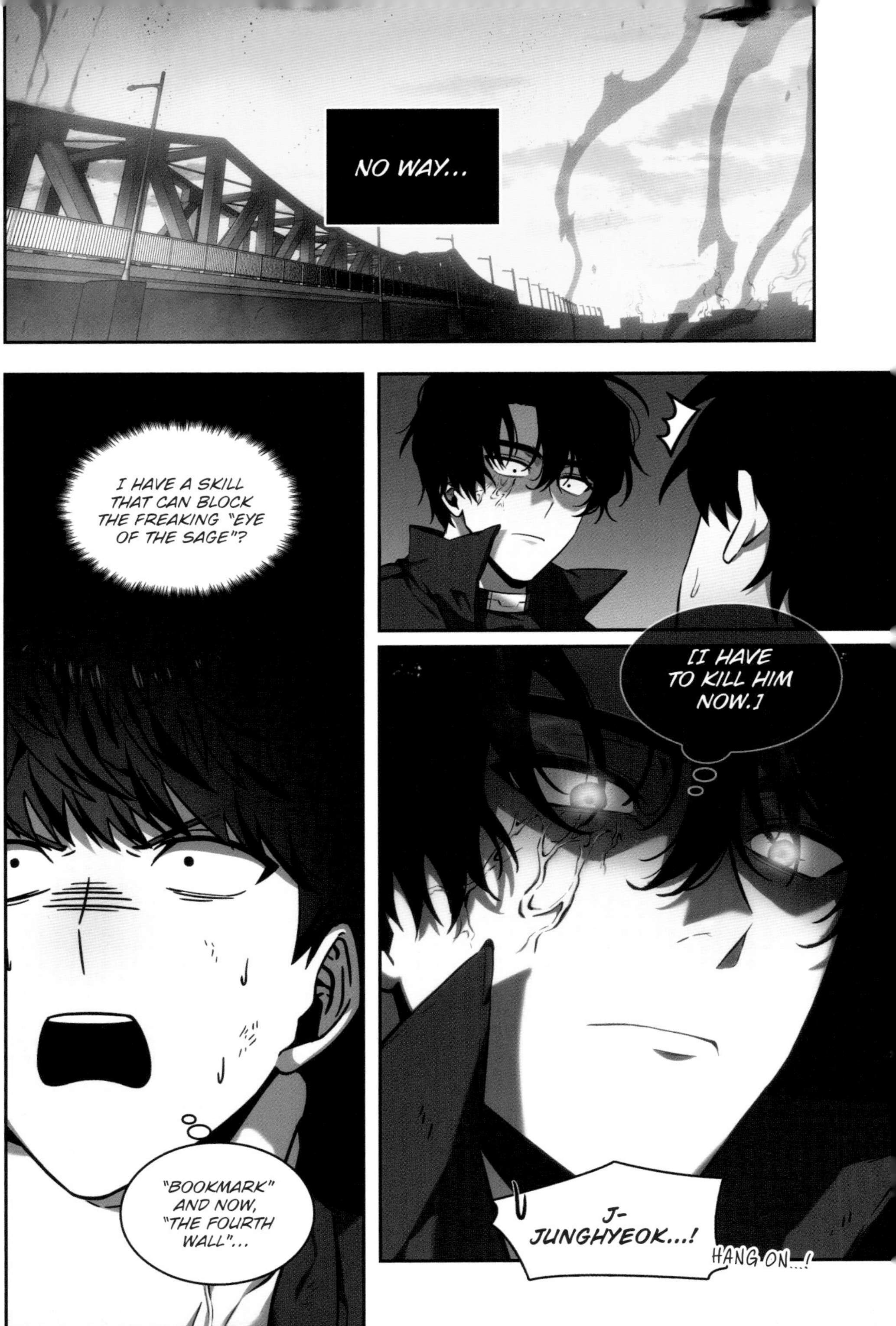
NO WAY...
I HAVE A SKILL THAT CAN BLOCK THE FREAKING "EYE OF THE SAGE"?
[I HAVE TO KILL HIM NOW.]
"BOOKMARK" AND NOW, "THE FOURTH WALL"...
J- JUNGHYEOK...!
HANG ON...!

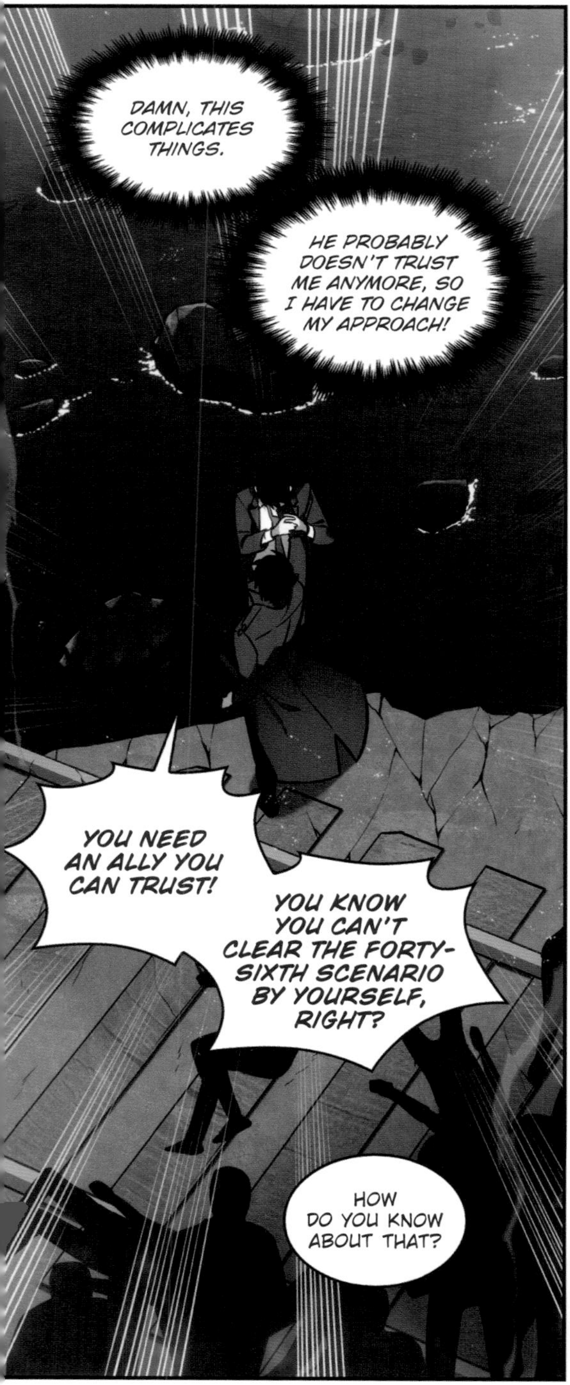
DAMN, THIS COMPLICATES THINGS.
HE PROBABLY DOESN'T TRUST ME ANYMORE, SO I HAVE TO CHANGE MY APPROACH!
YOU NEED AN ALLY YOU CAN TRUST!
YOU KNOW YOU CAN'T CLEAR THE FORTY-SIXTH SCENARIO BY YOURSELF, RIGHT?
HOW DO YOU KNOW ABOUT THAT?

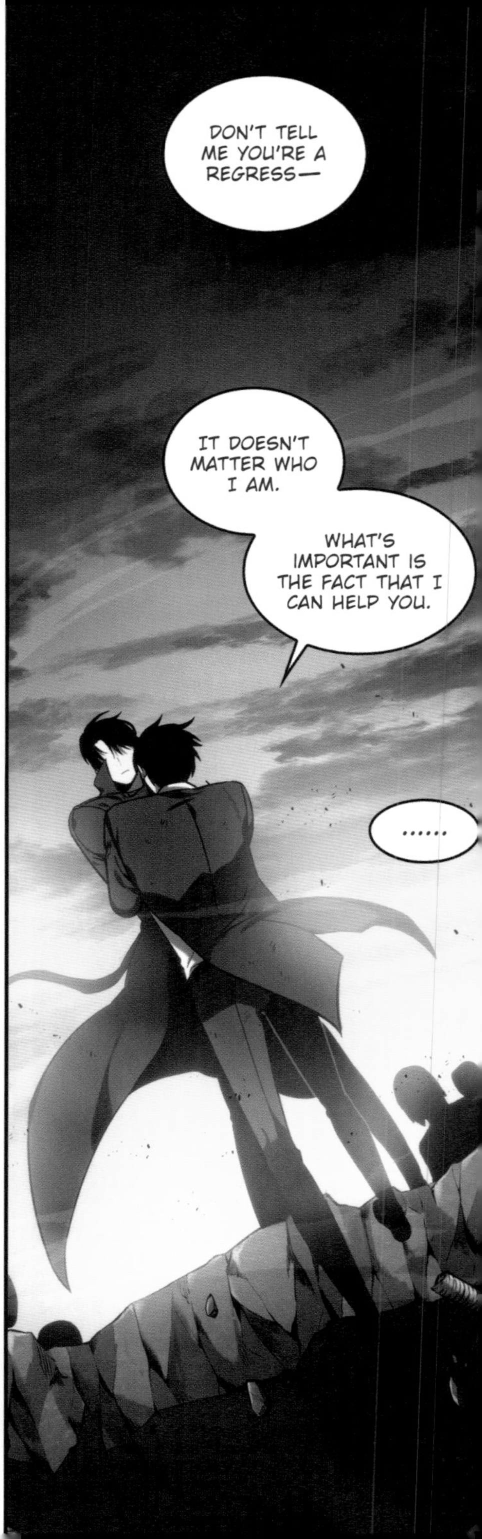
DON'T TELL ME YOU'RE A REGRESS—
IT DOESN'T MATTER WHO I AM.
WHAT'S IMPORTANT IS THE FACT THAT I CAN HELP YOU.
......

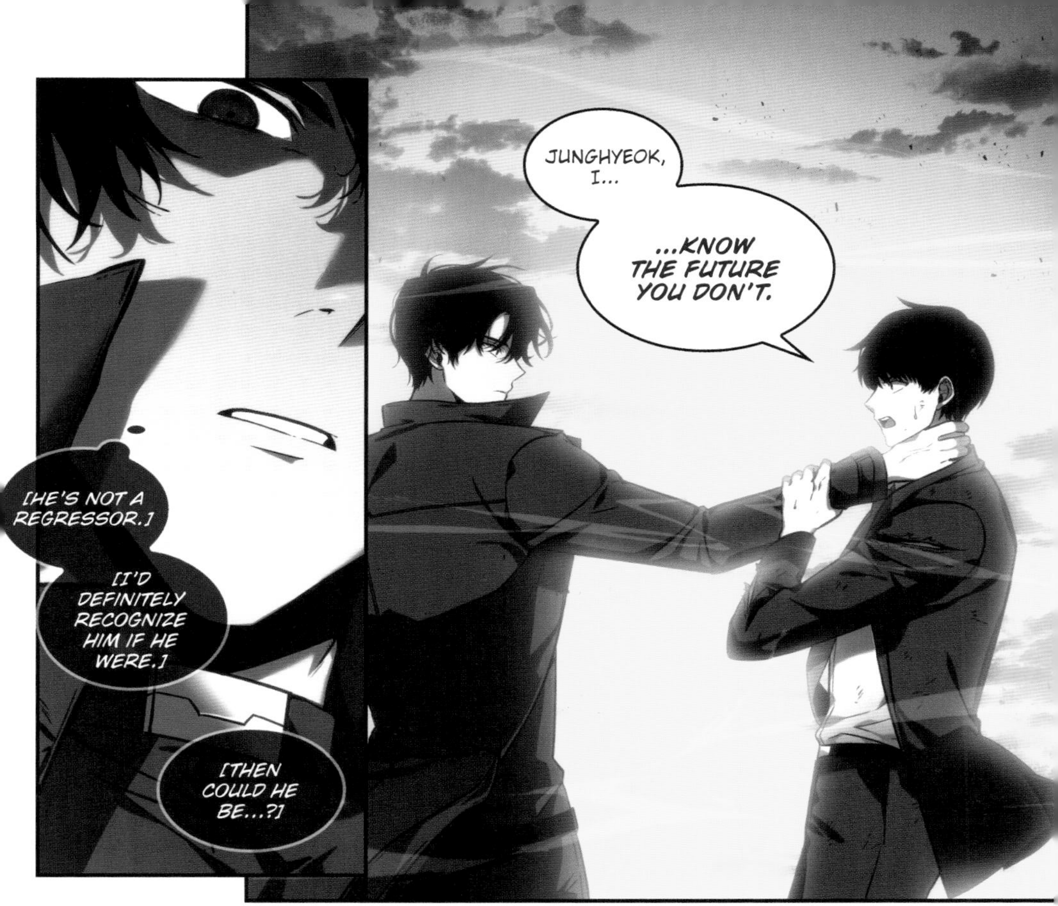
JUNGHYEOK, I...
...KNOW THE FUTURE YOU DON'T.
[HE'S NOT A REGRESSOR.]
[I'D DEFINITELY RECOGNIZE HIM IF HE WERE.]
[THEN COULD HE BE...?]

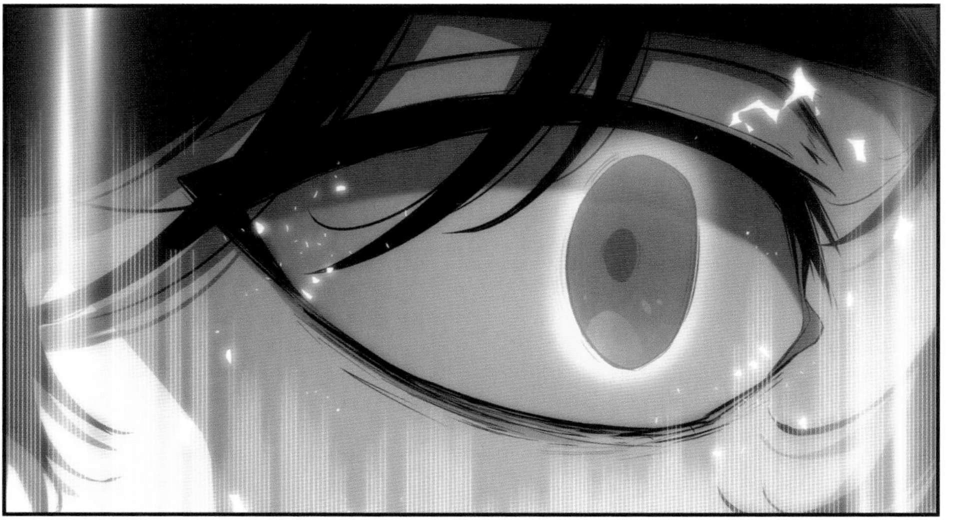

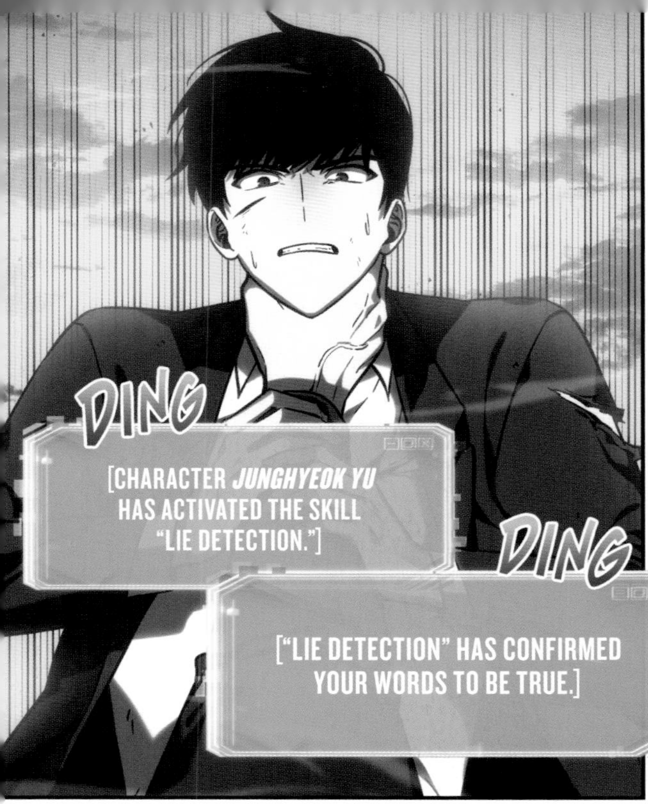
DING
[CHARACTER *JUNGHYEOK YU* HAS ACTIVATED THE SKILL "LIE DETECTION."]
DING
["LIE DETECTION" HAS CONFIRMED YOUR WORDS TO BE TRUE.]

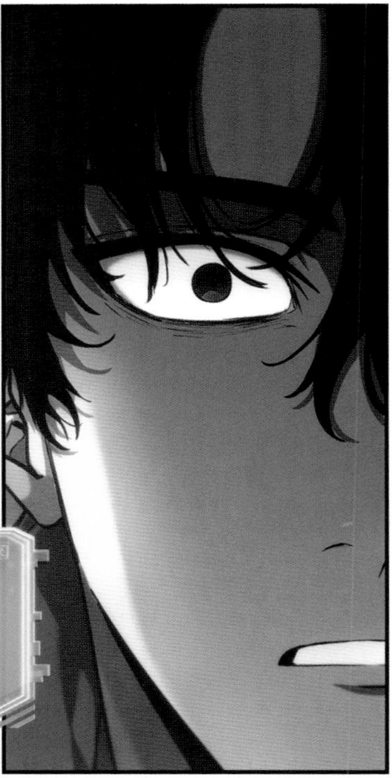

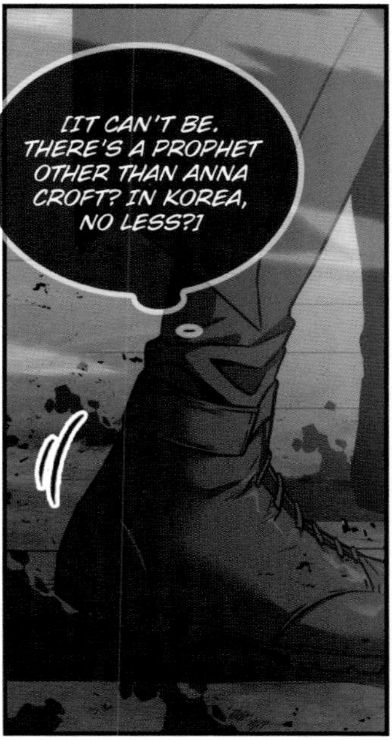
[IT CAN'T BE. THERE'S A PROPHET OTHER THAN ANNA CROFT? IN KOREA, NO LESS?]

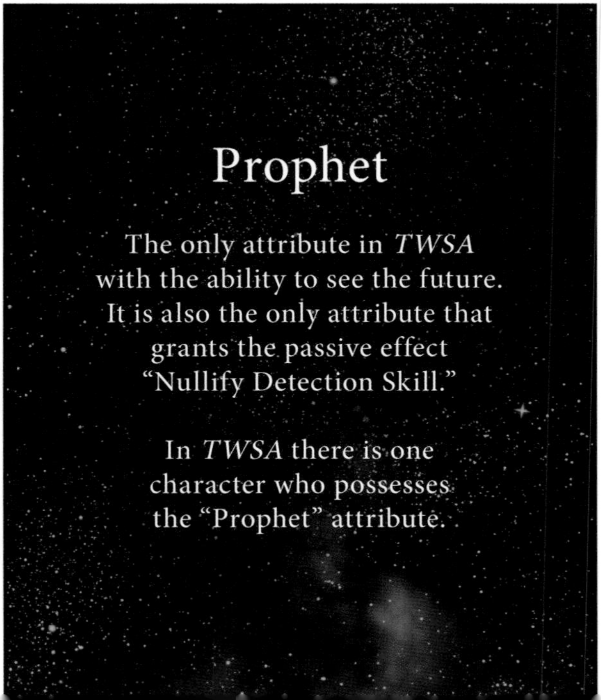
Prophet
The only attribute in *TWSA* with the ability to see the future. It is also the only attribute that grants the passive effect "Nullify Detection Skill."
In *TWSA* there is one character who possesses the "Prophet" attribute.

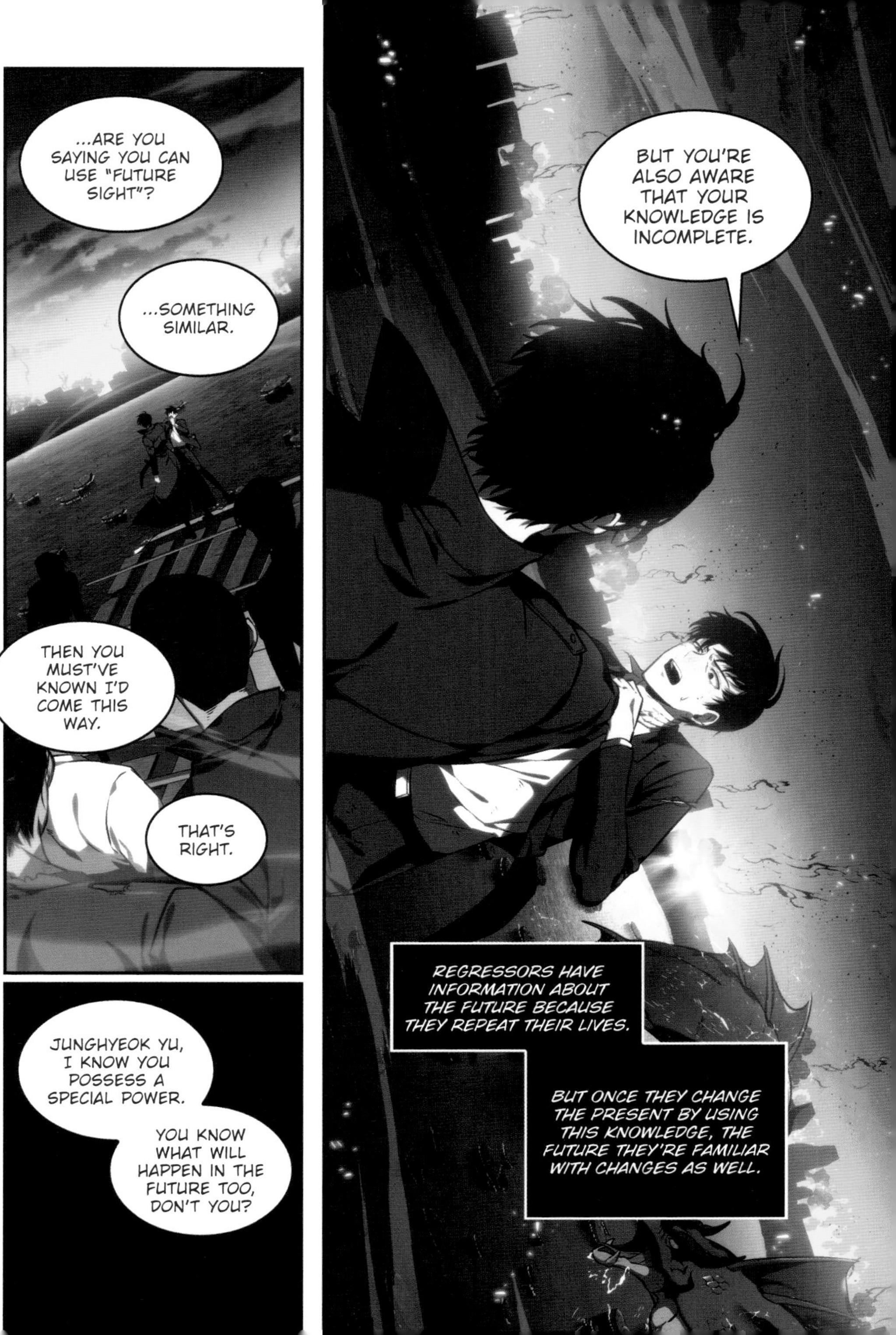
...ARE YOU SAYING YOU CAN USE "FUTURE SIGHT"?
...SOMETHING SIMILAR.
THEN YOU MUST'VE KNOWN I'D COME THIS WAY.
THAT'S RIGHT.
JUNGHYEOK YU, I KNOW YOU POSSESS A SPECIAL POWER.
YOU KNOW WHAT WILL HAPPEN IN THE FUTURE TOO, DON'T YOU?
BUT YOU'RE ALSO AWARE THAT YOUR KNOWLEDGE IS INCOMPLETE.
REGRESSORS HAVE INFORMATION ABOUT THE FUTURE BECAUSE THEY REPEAT THEIR LIVES.
BUT ONCE THEY CHANGE THE PRESENT BY USING THIS KNOWLEDGE, THE FUTURE THEY'RE FAMILIAR WITH CHANGES AS WELL.

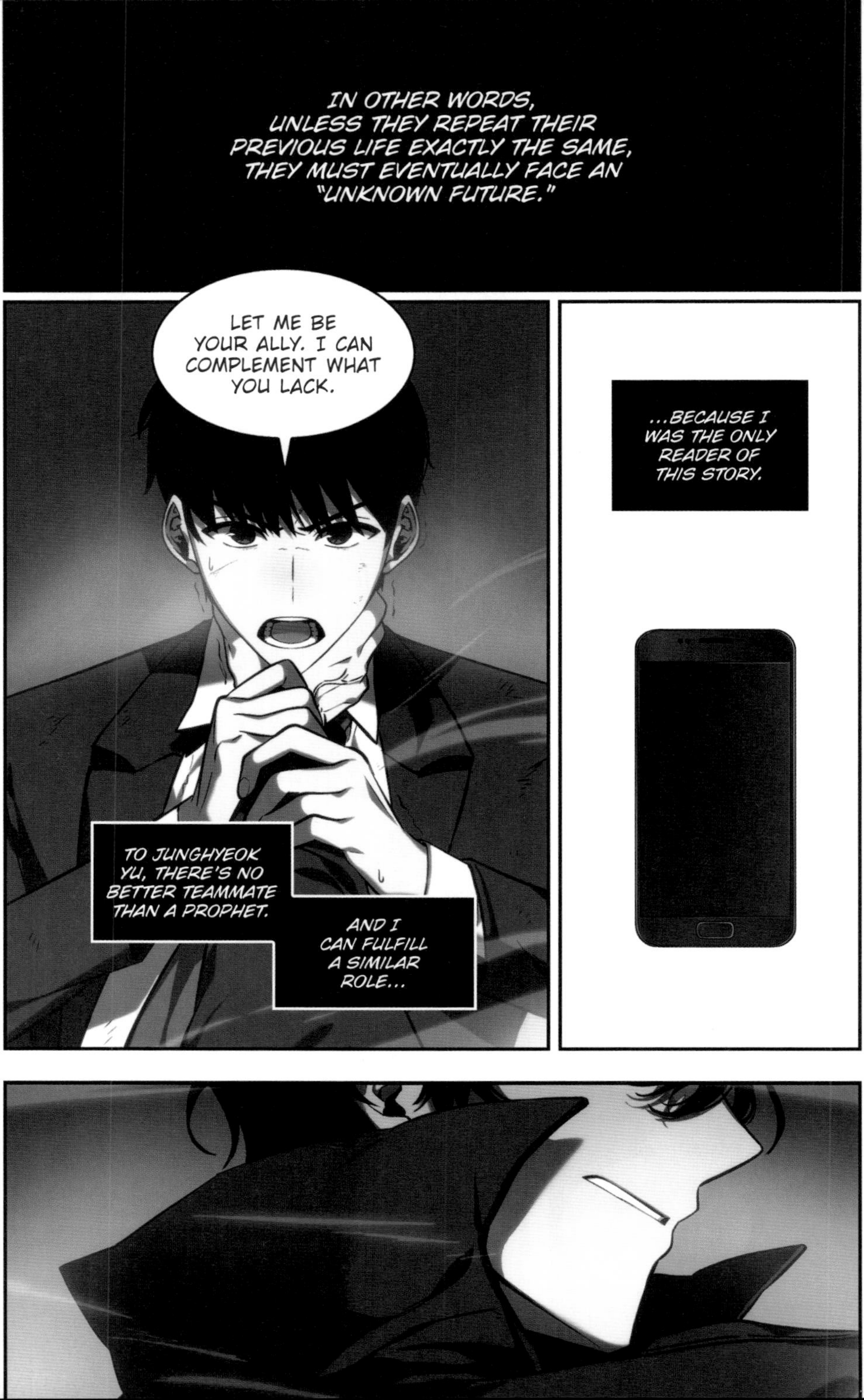
IN OTHER WORDS, UNLESS THEY REPEAT THEIR PREVIOUS LIFE EXACTLY THE SAME, THEY MUST EVENTUALLY FACE AN "UNKNOWN FUTURE."
LET ME BE YOUR ALLY. I CAN COMPLEMENT WHAT YOU LACK.
TO JUNGHYEOK YU, THERE'S NO BETTER TEAMMATE THAN A PROPHET.
AND I CAN FULFILL A SIMILAR ROLE...
...BECAUSE I WAS THE ONLY READER OF THIS STORY.

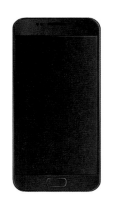

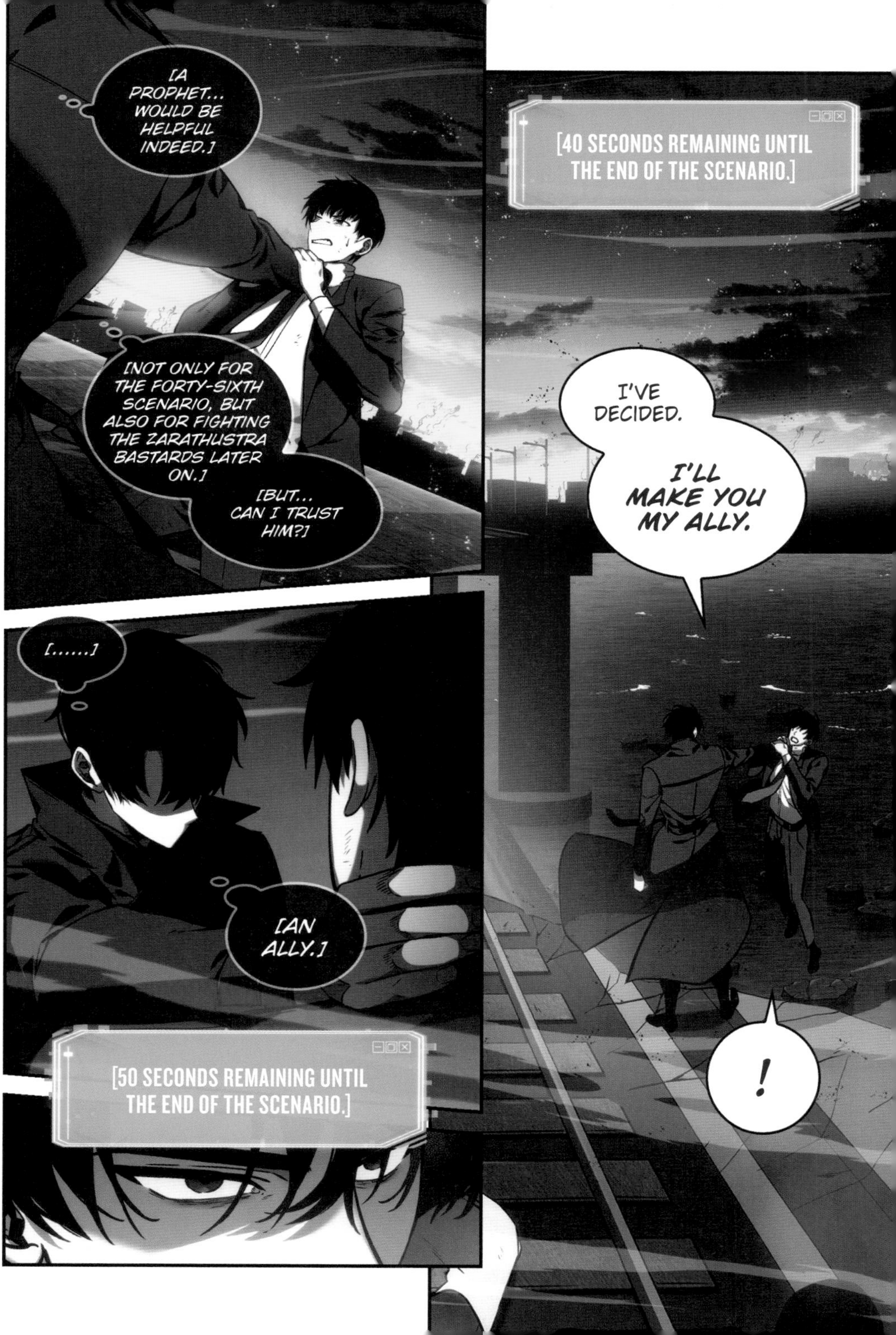
[A PROPHET... WOULD BE HELPFUL INDEED.]
[NOT ONLY FOR THE FORTY-SIXTH SCENARIO, BUT ALSO FOR FIGHTING THE ZARATHUSTRA BASTARDS LATER ON.]
[BUT... CAN I TRUST HIM?]
[......]
[AN ALLY.]
[50 SECONDS REMAINING UNTIL THE END OF THE SCENARIO.]
[40 SECONDS REMAINING UNTIL THE END OF THE SCENARIO.]
I'VE DECIDED.
I'LL MAKE YOU MY ALLY.
!

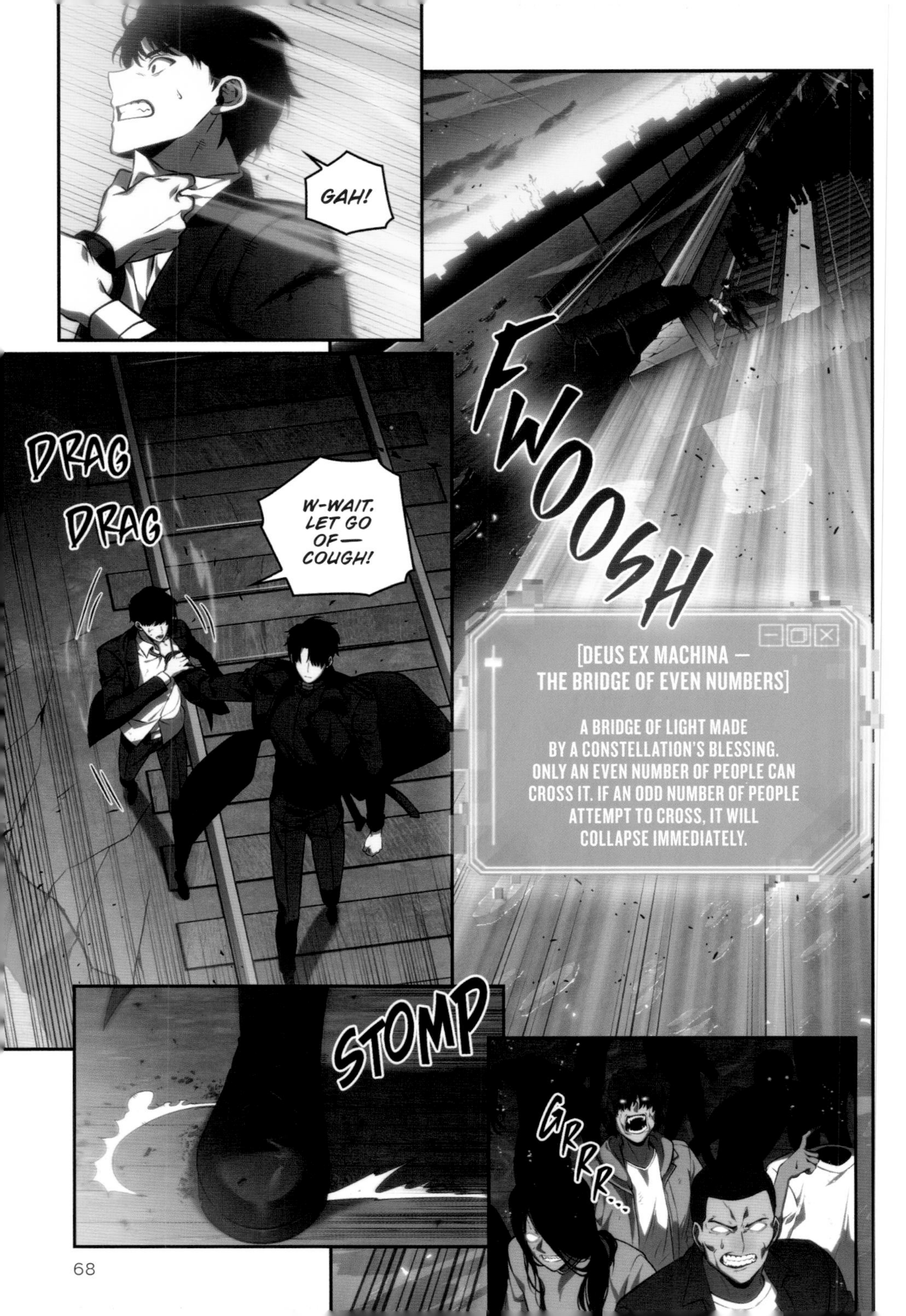
GAH!
DRAG
DRAG
W-WAIT. LET GO OF— COUGH!
FWOOSH
[DEUS EX MACHINA — THE BRIDGE OF EVEN NUMBERS]
A BRIDGE OF LIGHT MADE BY A CONSTELLATION'S BLESSING. ONLY AN EVEN NUMBER OF PEOPLE CAN CROSS IT. IF AN ODD NUMBER OF PEOPLE ATTEMPT TO CROSS, IT WILL COLLAPSE IMMEDIATELY.
STOMP
GRRR...

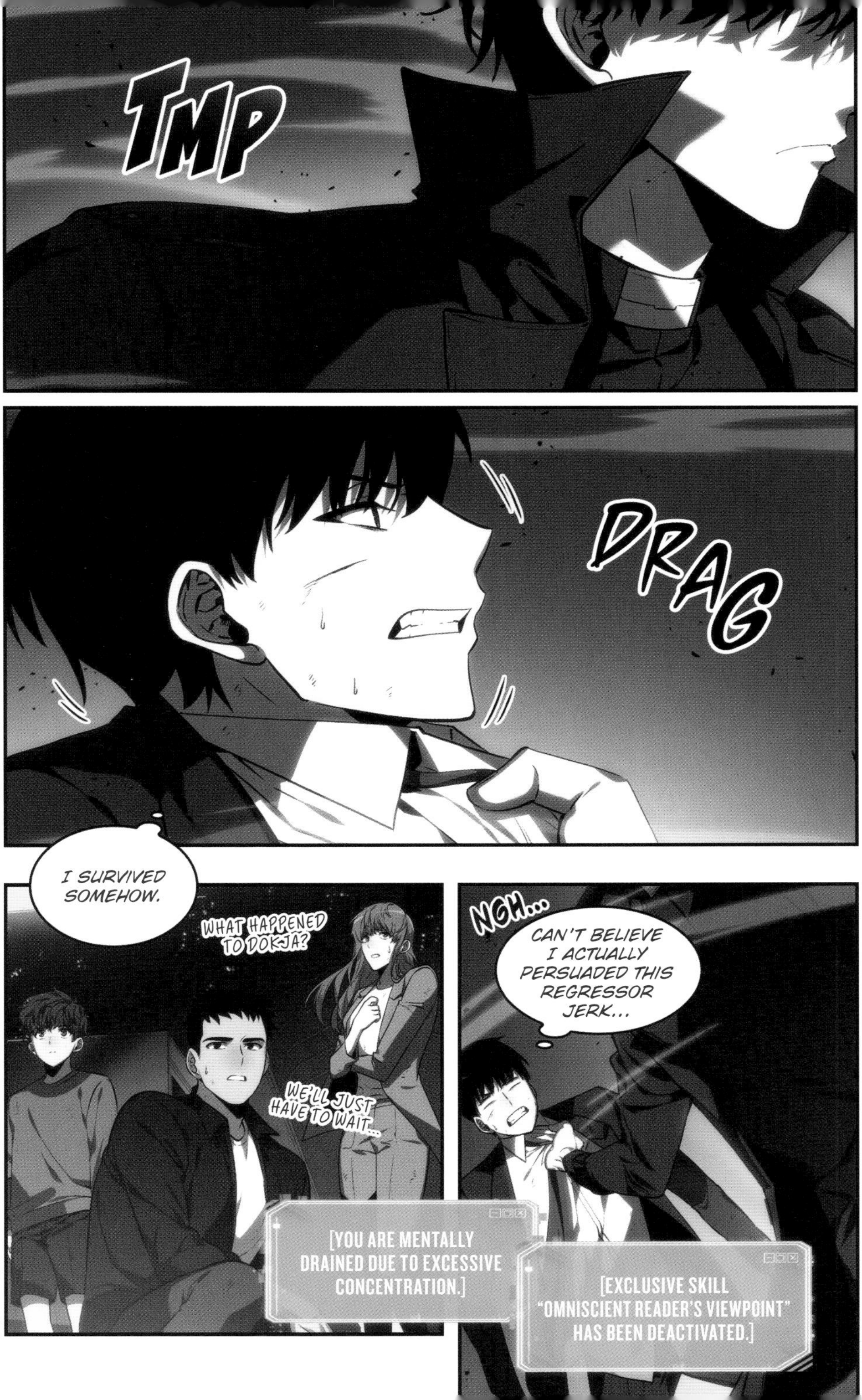
TMP
DRAG
I SURVIVED SOMEHOW.
WHAT HAPPENED TO DOKJA?
WE'LL JUST HAVE TO WAIT...
NGH...
CAN'T BELIEVE I ACTUALLY PERSUADED THIS REGRESSOR JERK...
[YOU ARE MENTALLY DRAINED DUE TO EXCESSIVE CONCENTRATION.]
[EXCLUSIVE SKILL "OMNISCIENT READER'S VIEWPOINT" HAS BEEN DEACTIVATED.]

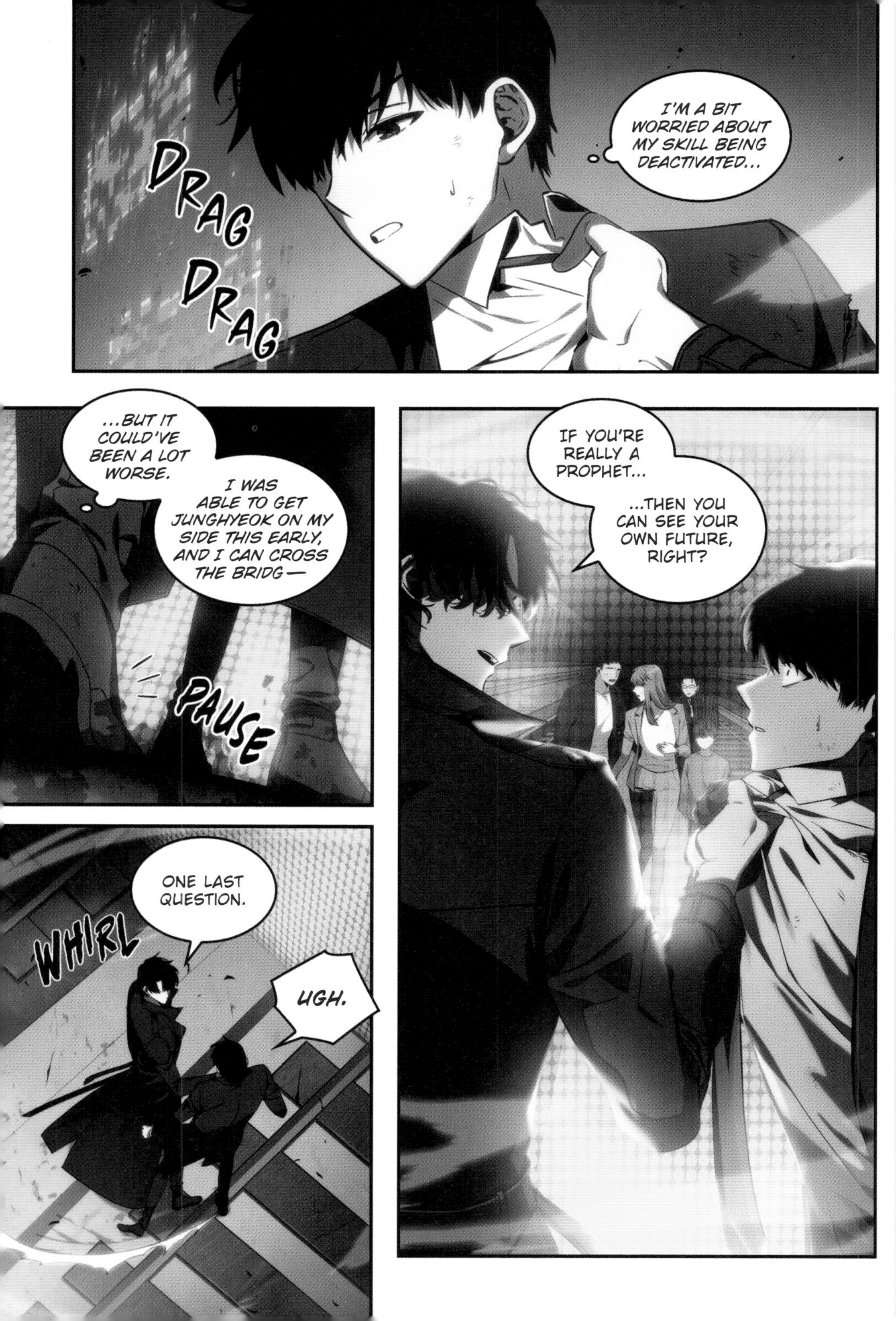
DRAG DRAG
I'M A BIT WORRIED ABOUT MY SKILL BEING DEACTIVATED...
...BUT IT COULD'VE BEEN A LOT WORSE.
I WAS ABLE TO GET JUNGHYEOK ON MY SIDE THIS EARLY, AND I CAN CROSS THE BRIDG—
PAUSE
IF YOU'RE REALLY A PROPHET...
...THEN YOU CAN SEE YOUR OWN FUTURE, RIGHT?
ONE LAST QUESTION.
WHIRL
UGH.

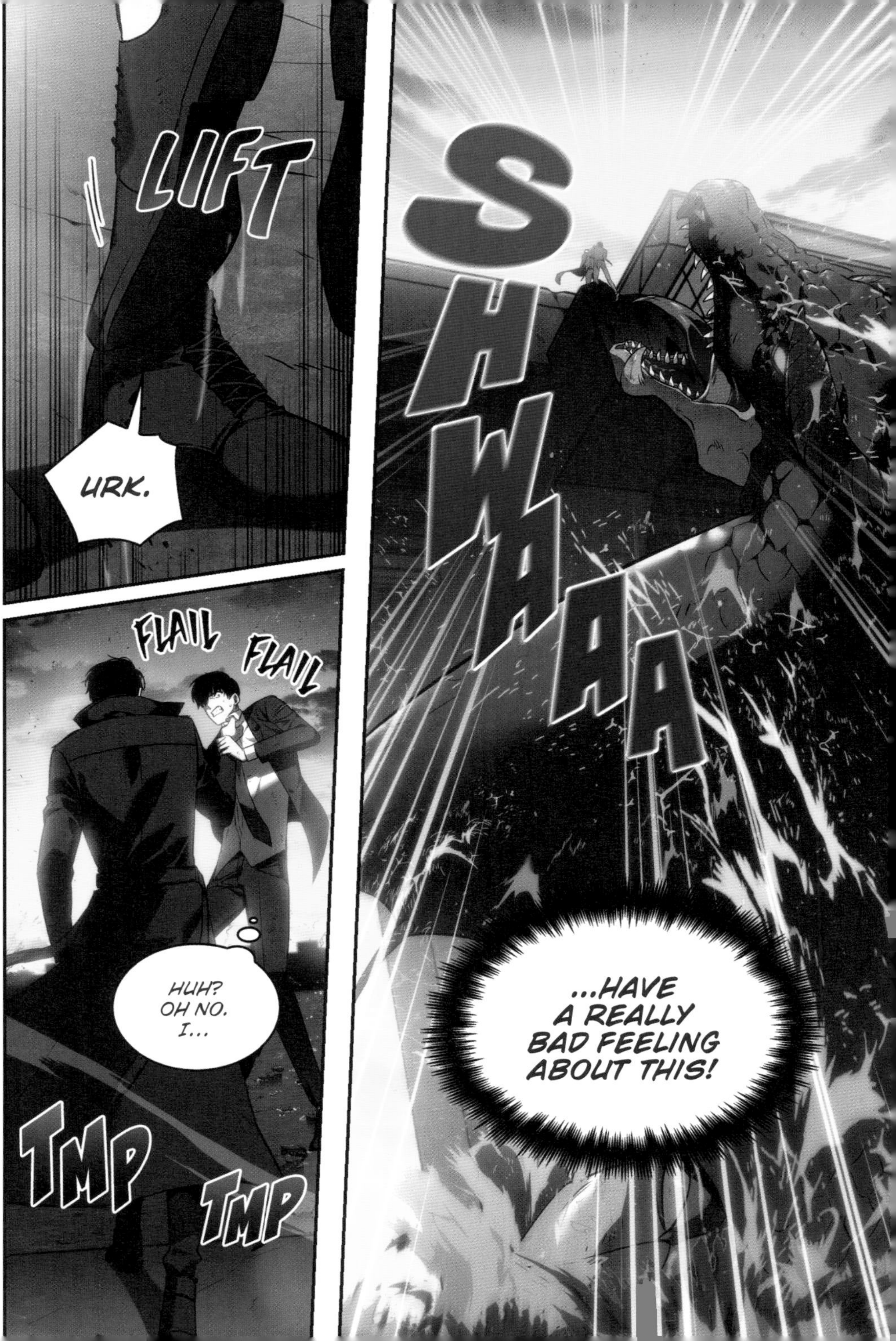
LIFT
URK.
FLAIL FLAIL
HUH? OH NO. I...
TMP TMP
SHWAAAA
...HAVE A REALLY BAD FEELING ABOUT THIS!

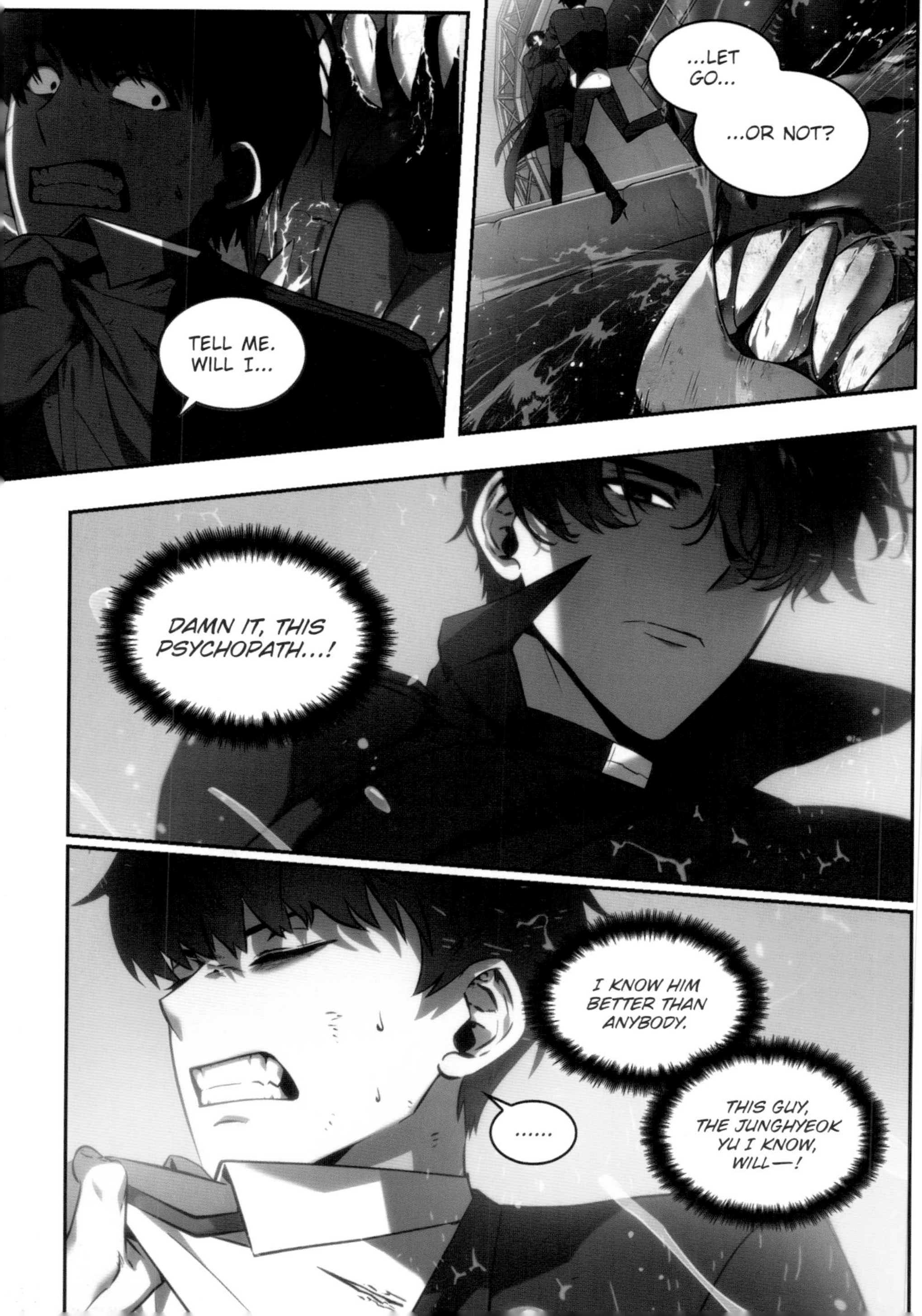
TELL ME. WILL I...
...LET GO...
...OR NOT?
DAMN IT, THIS PSYCHOPATH...!
I KNOW HIM BETTER THAN ANYBODY.
......
THIS GUY, THE JUNGHYEOK YU I KNOW, WILL—!

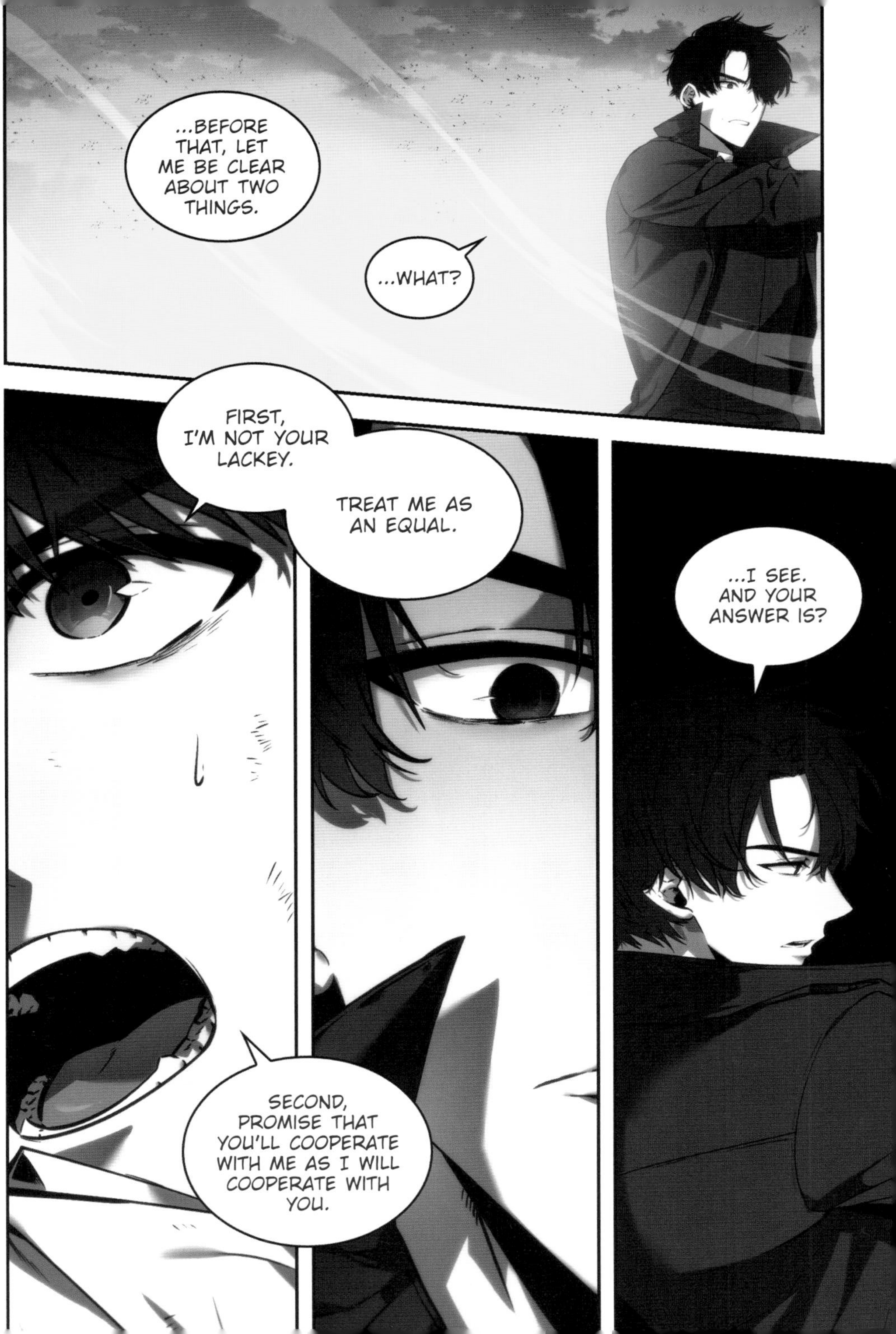
...BEFORE THAT, LET ME BE CLEAR ABOUT TWO THINGS.
...WHAT?
FIRST, I'M NOT YOUR LACKEY.
TREAT ME AS AN EQUAL.
...I SEE. AND YOUR ANSWER IS?
SECOND, PROMISE THAT YOU'LL COOPERATE WITH ME AS I WILL COOPERATE WITH YOU.

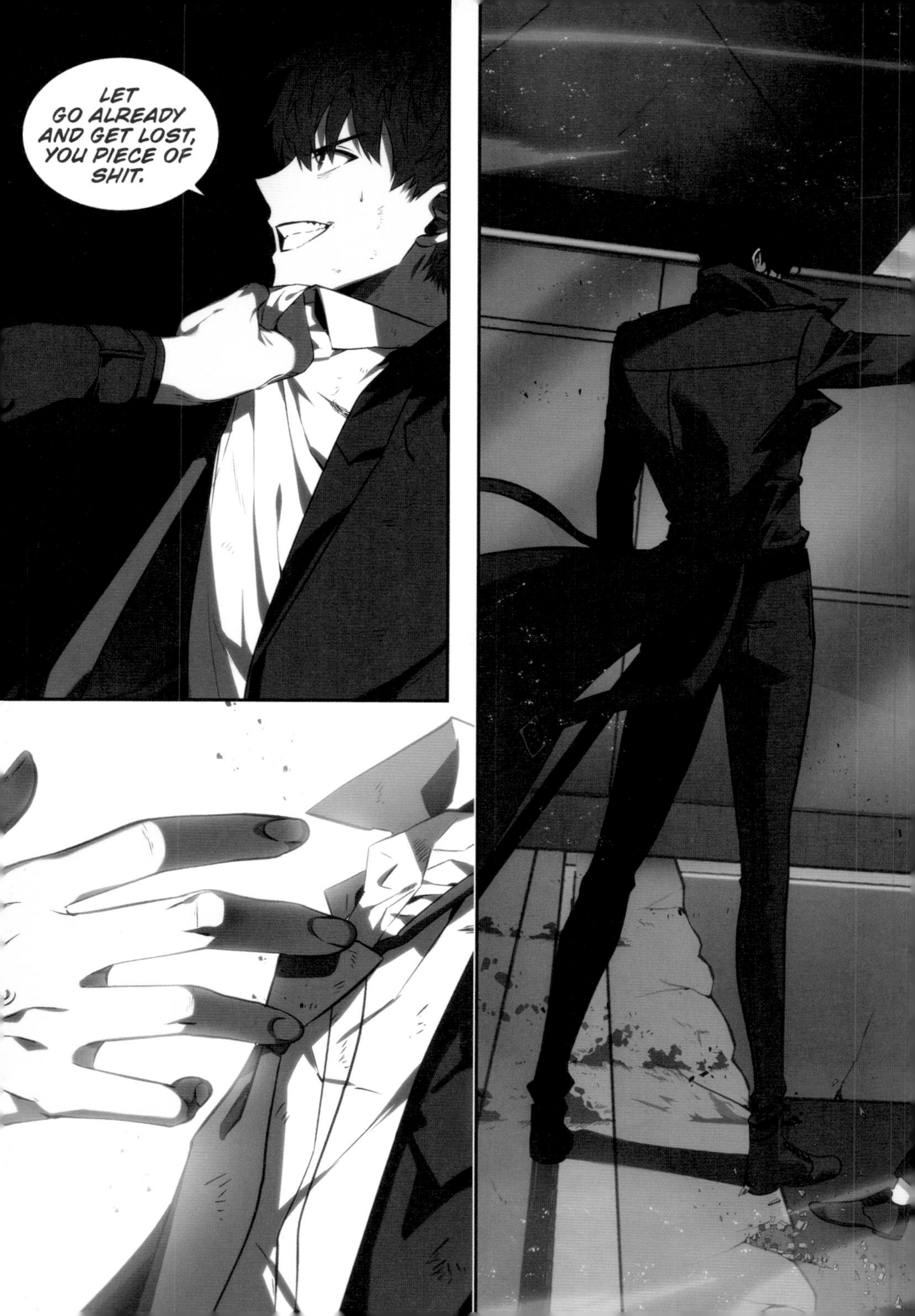
LET GO ALREADY AND GET LOST, YOU PIECE OF SHIT.

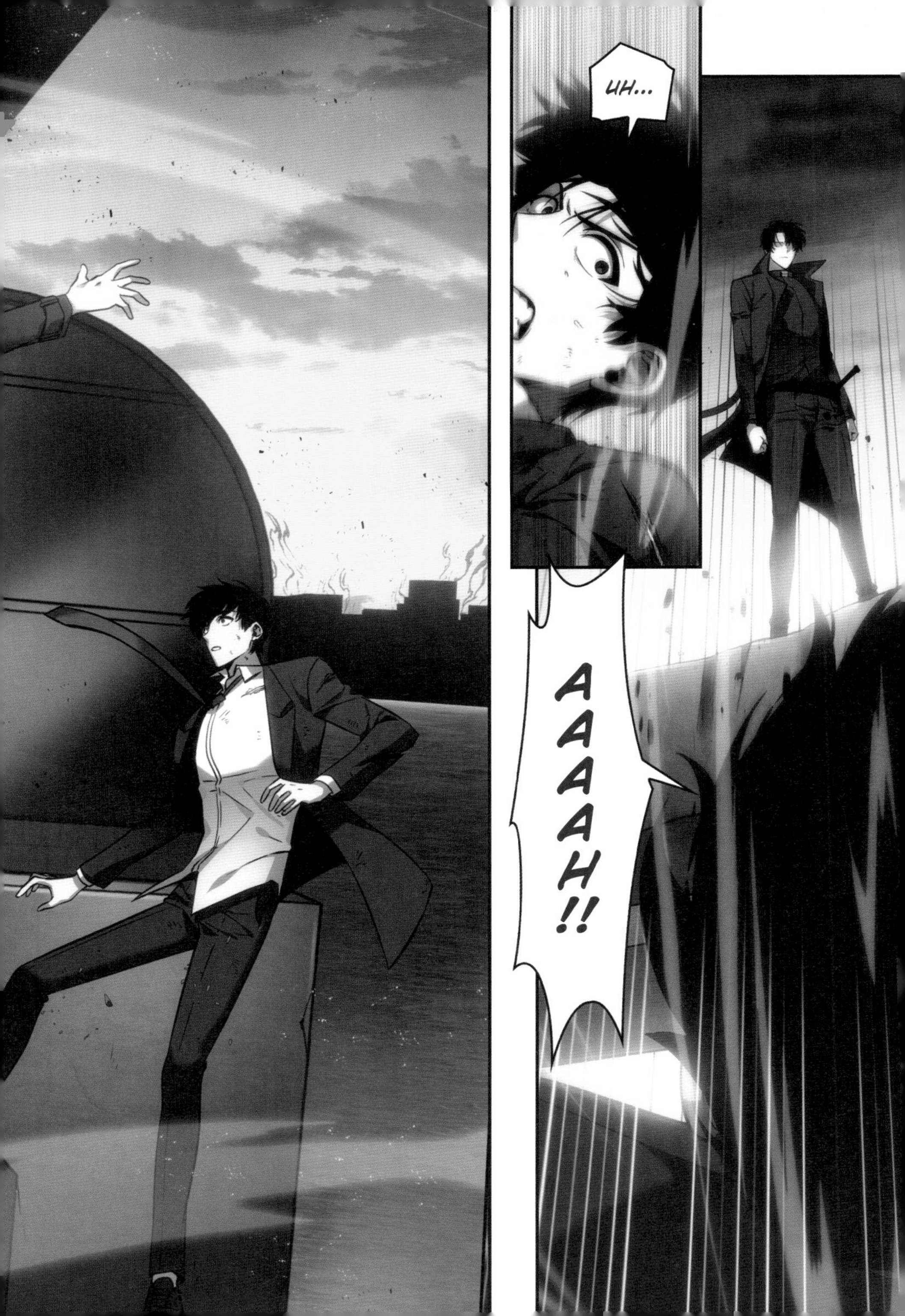
UH...
AAAAAH!!

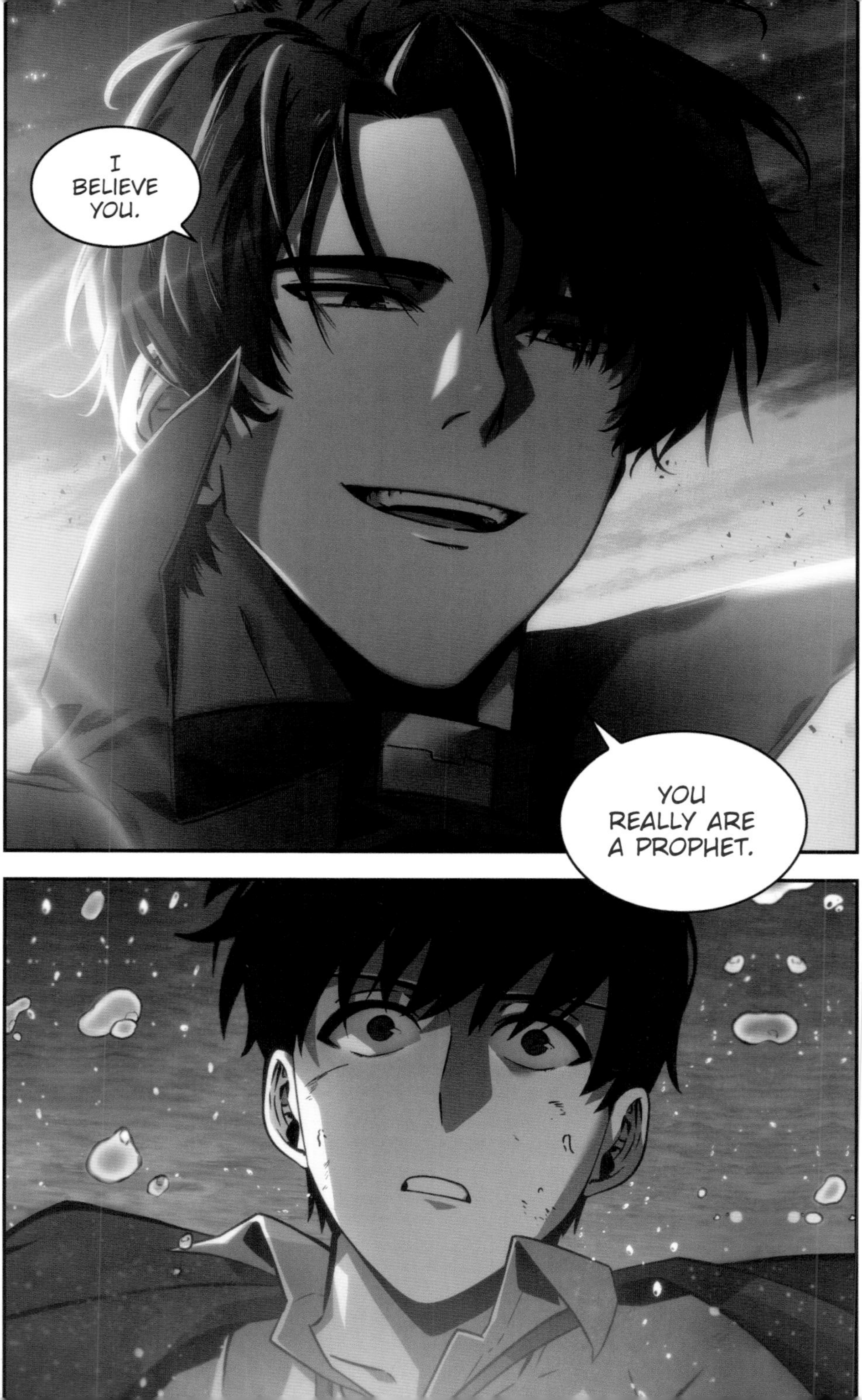
I BELIEVE YOU.
YOU REALLY ARE A PROPHET.

HAAH...

THAT SON OF A—

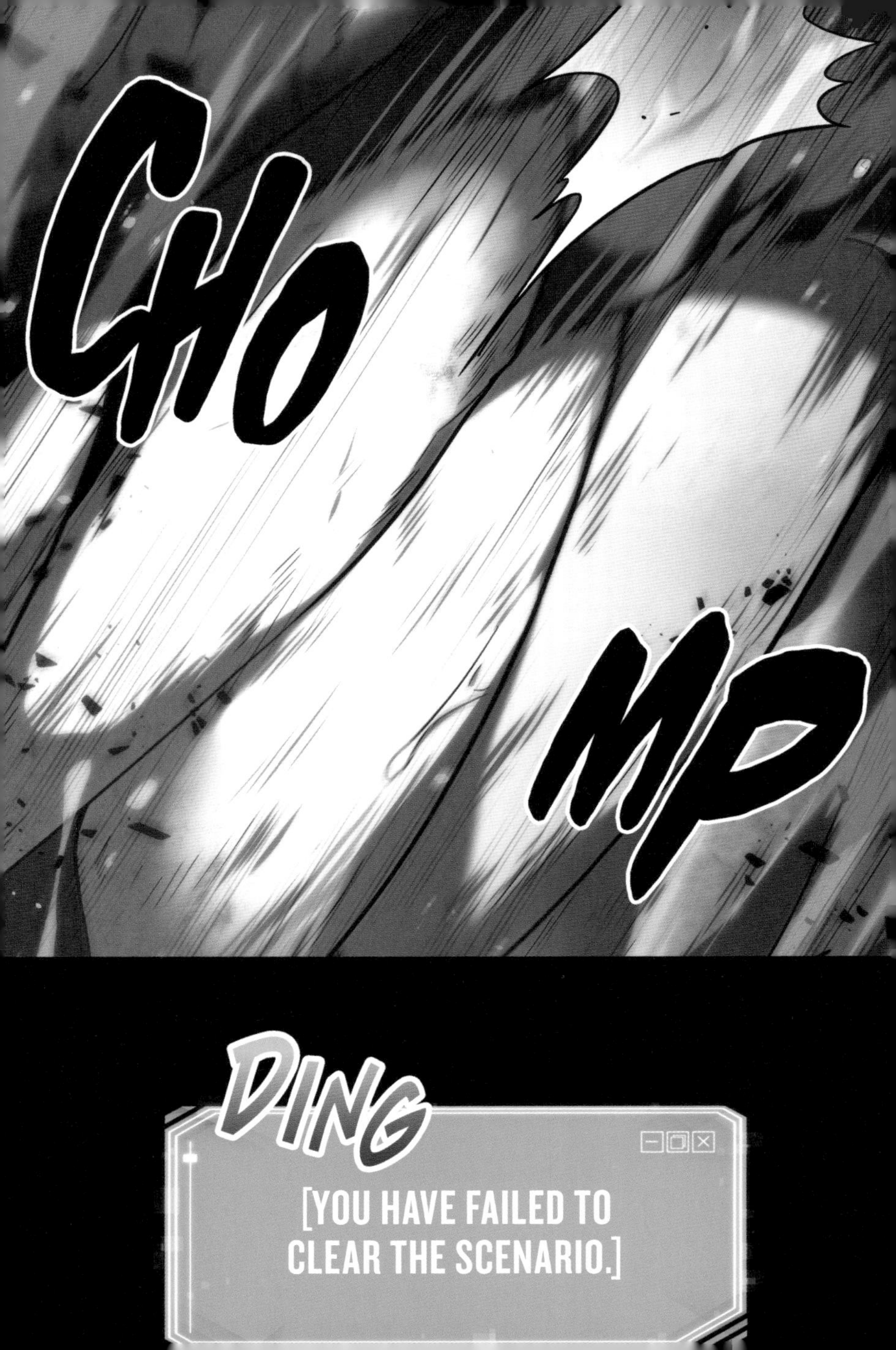
CHO
MP
DING
[YOU HAVE FAILED TO
CLEAR THE SCENARIO.]

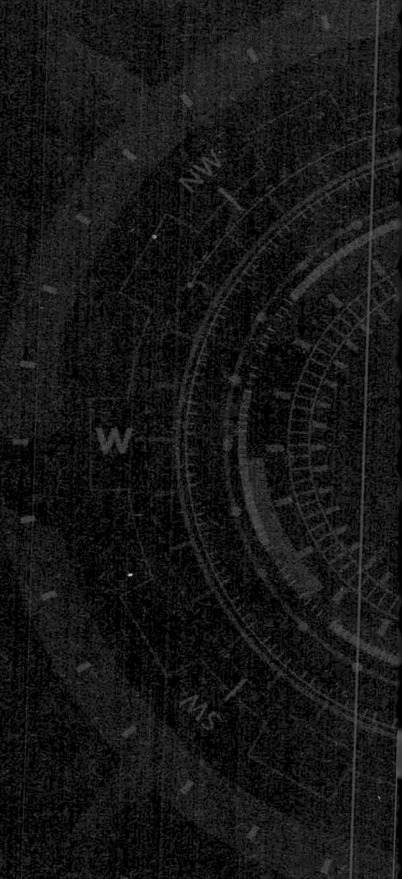
NW
W
SW

EP. 03

THE CONTRACT

EP. 03

Omniscient
Reader's
Viewpoint

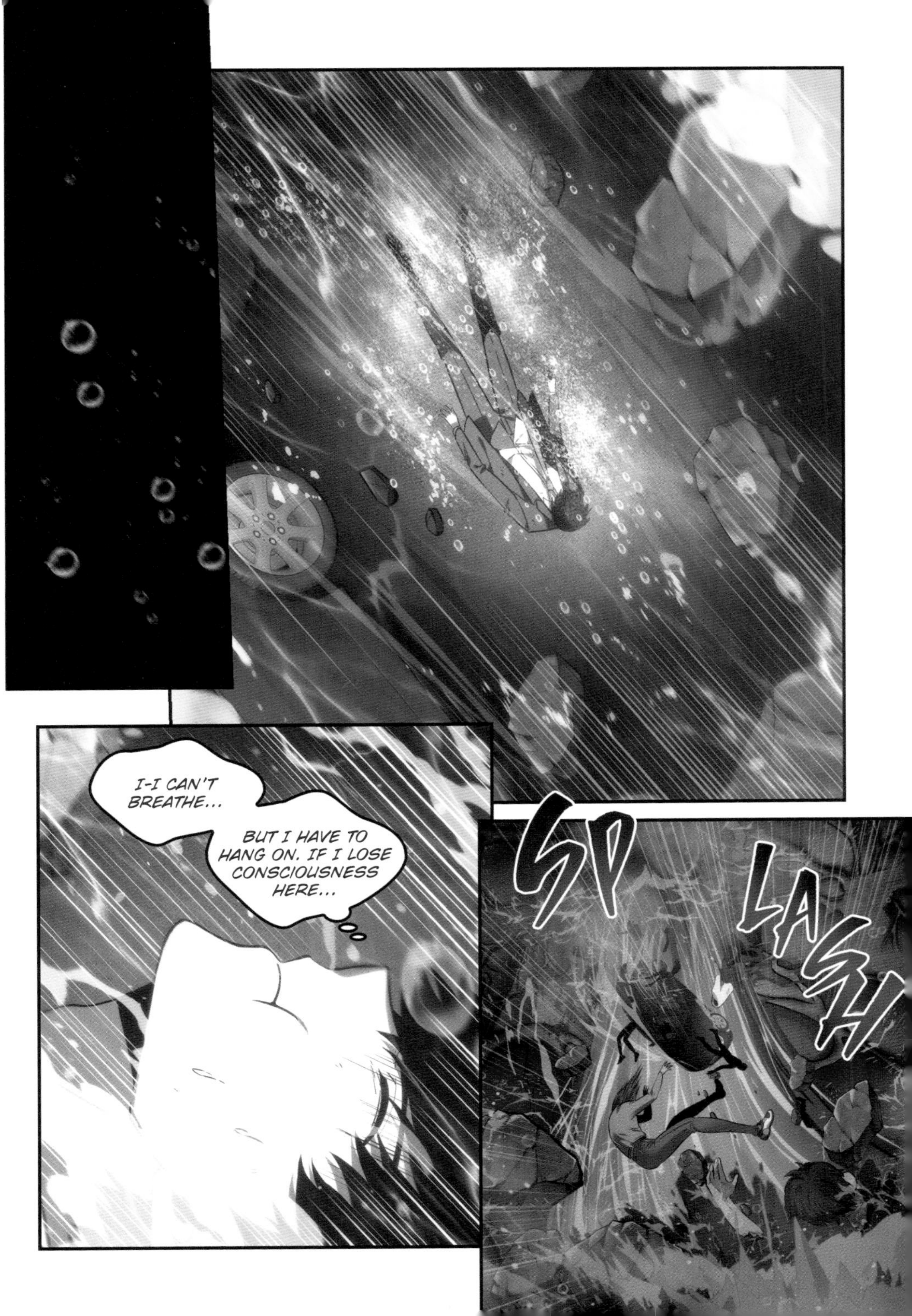
I-I CAN'T BREATHE...
BUT I HAVE TO HANG ON. IF I LOSE CONSCIOUSNESS HERE...
SPLASH

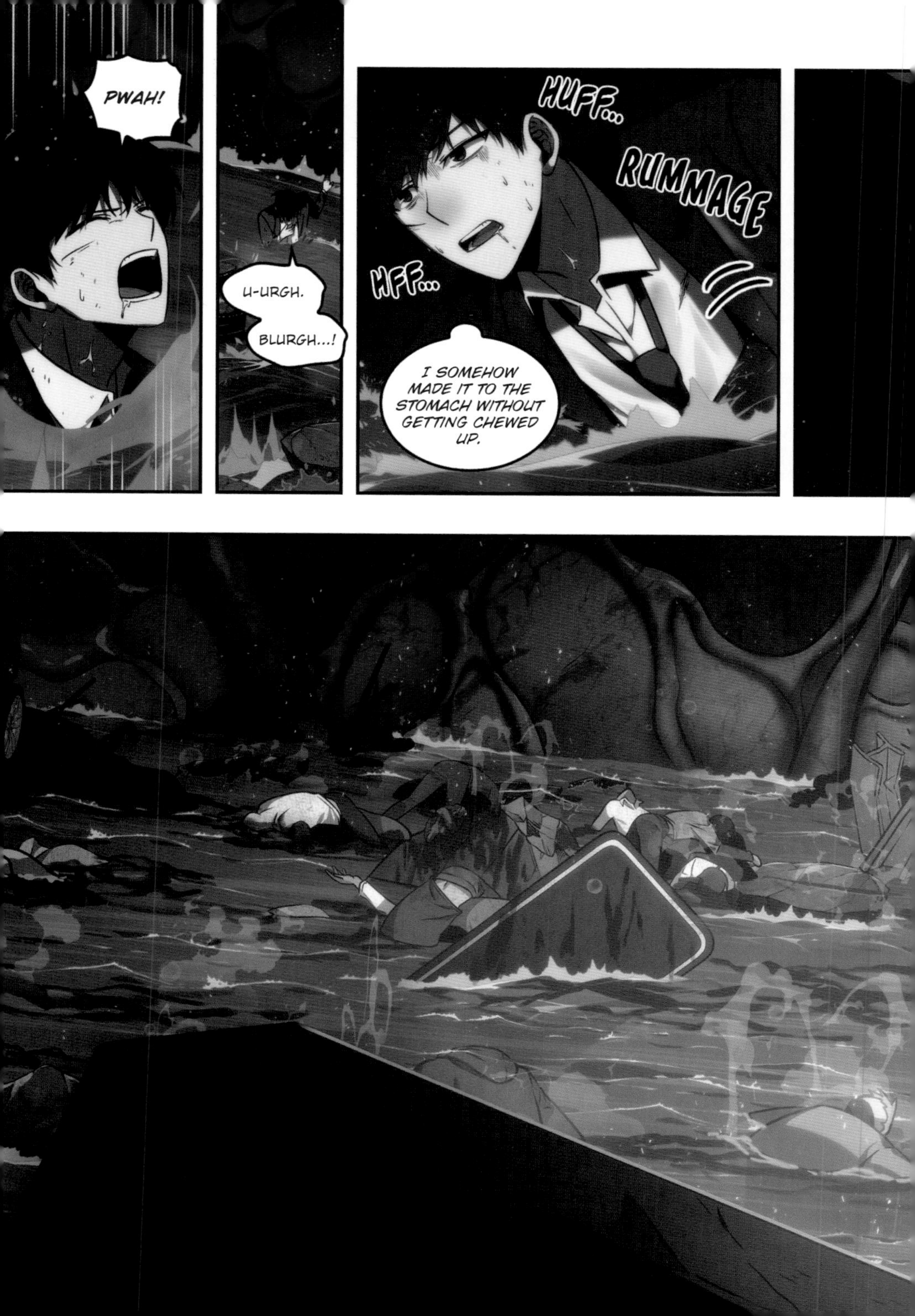

PWAH!
U-URGH.
BLURGH...!
HUFF...
RUMMAGE
HFF...
I SOMEHOW MADE IT TO THE STOMACH WITHOUT GETTING CHEWED UP.

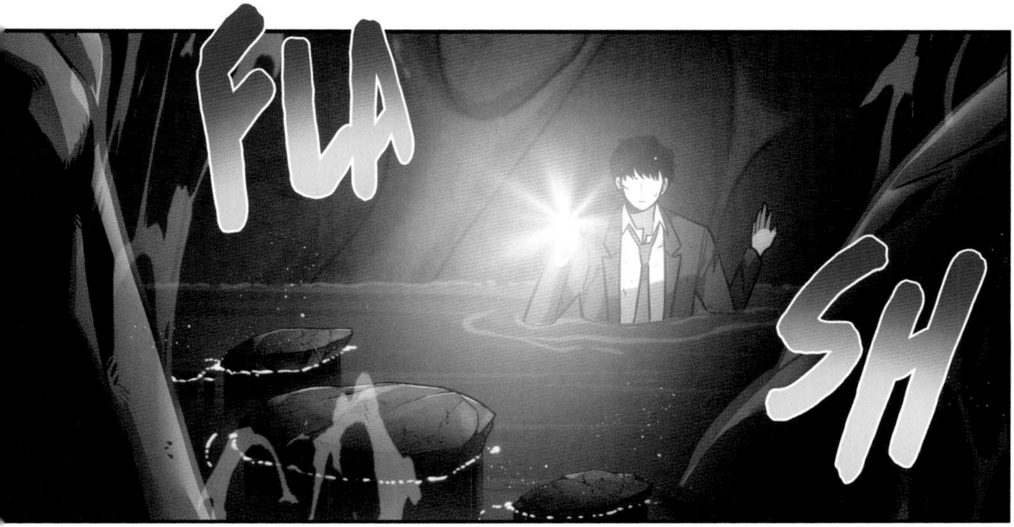
FLA
SH

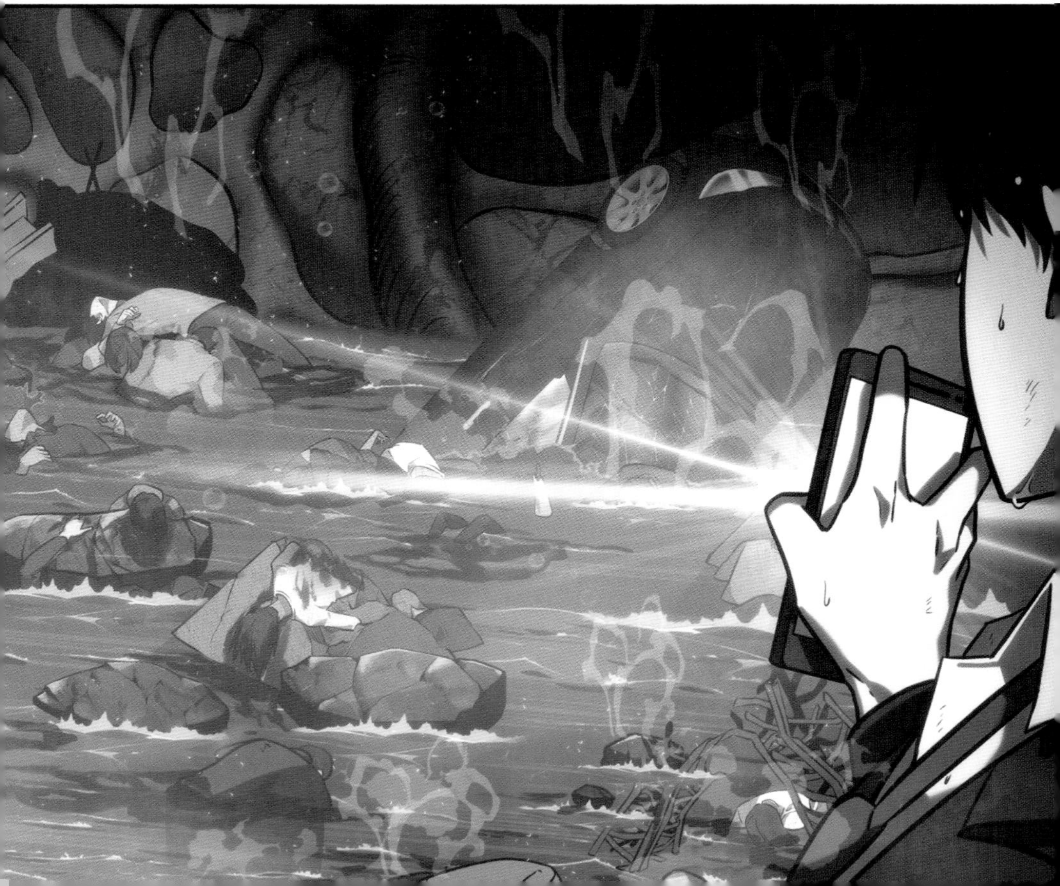

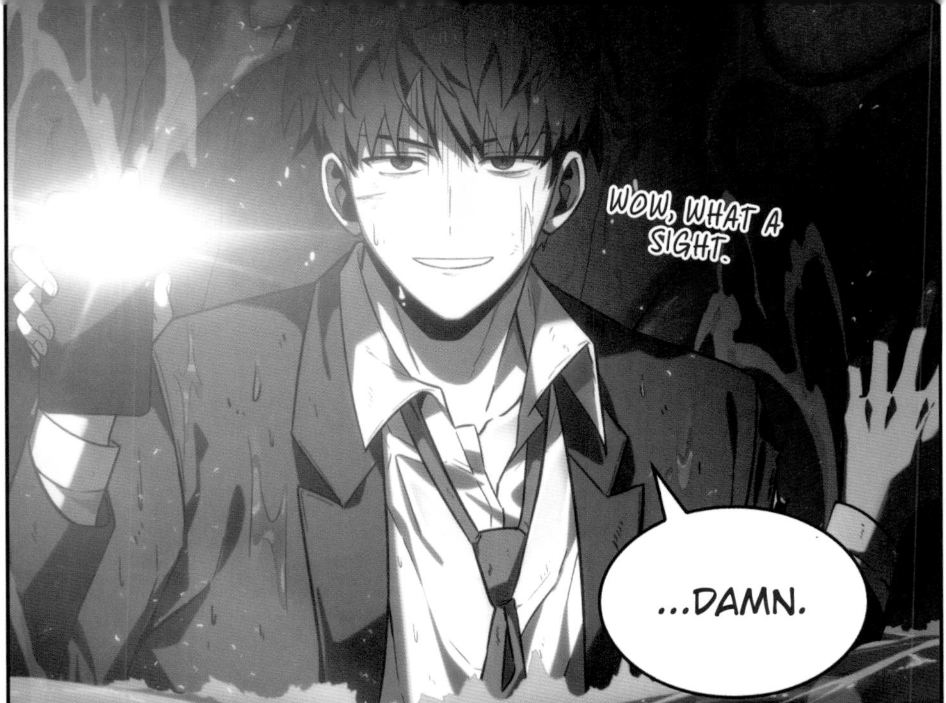
WOW, WHAT A SIGHT.
...DAMN.

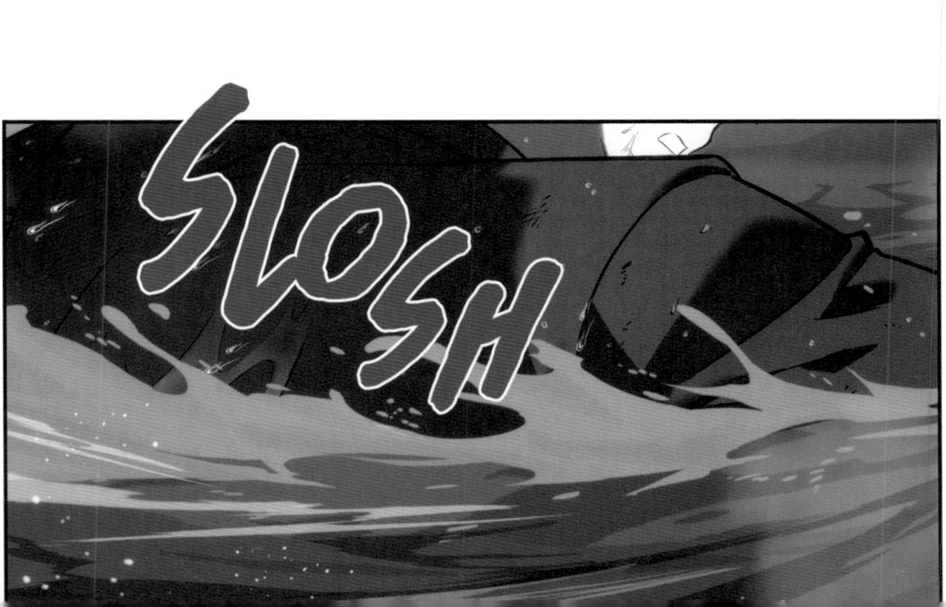
SLOSH

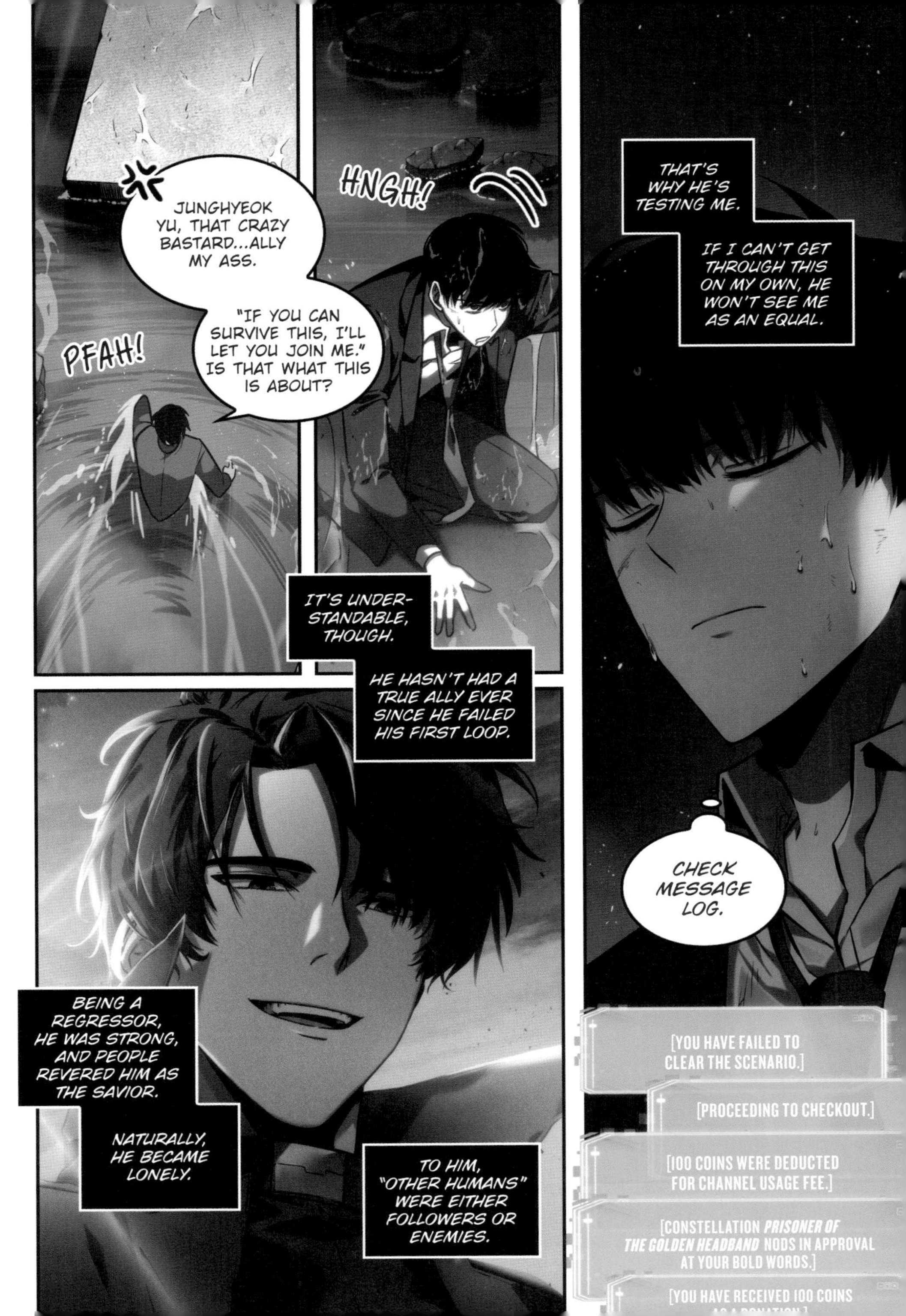
JUNGHYEOK YU, THAT CRAZY BASTARD...ALLY MY ASS.
PFAH!
"IF YOU CAN SURVIVE THIS, I'LL LET YOU JOIN ME." IS THAT WHAT THIS IS ABOUT?
HNGH!
IT'S UNDER-STANDABLE, THOUGH.
HE HASN'T HAD A TRUE ALLY EVER SINCE HE FAILED HIS FIRST LOOP.
BEING A REGRESSOR, HE WAS STRONG, AND PEOPLE REVERED HIM AS THE SAVIOR.
NATURALLY, HE BECAME LONELY.
TO HIM, "OTHER HUMANS" WERE EITHER FOLLOWERS OR ENEMIES.
THAT'S WHY HE'S TESTING ME.
IF I CAN'T GET THROUGH THIS ON MY OWN, HE WON'T SEE ME AS AN EQUAL.
CHECK MESSAGE LOG.
[YOU HAVE FAILED TO CLEAR THE SCENARIO.]
[PROCEEDING TO CHECKOUT.]
[100 COINS WERE DEDUCTED FOR CHANNEL USAGE FEE.]
[CONSTELLATION *PRISONER OF THE GOLDEN HEADBAND* NODS IN APPROVAL AT YOUR BOLD WORDS.]
[YOU HAVE RECEIVED 100 COINS

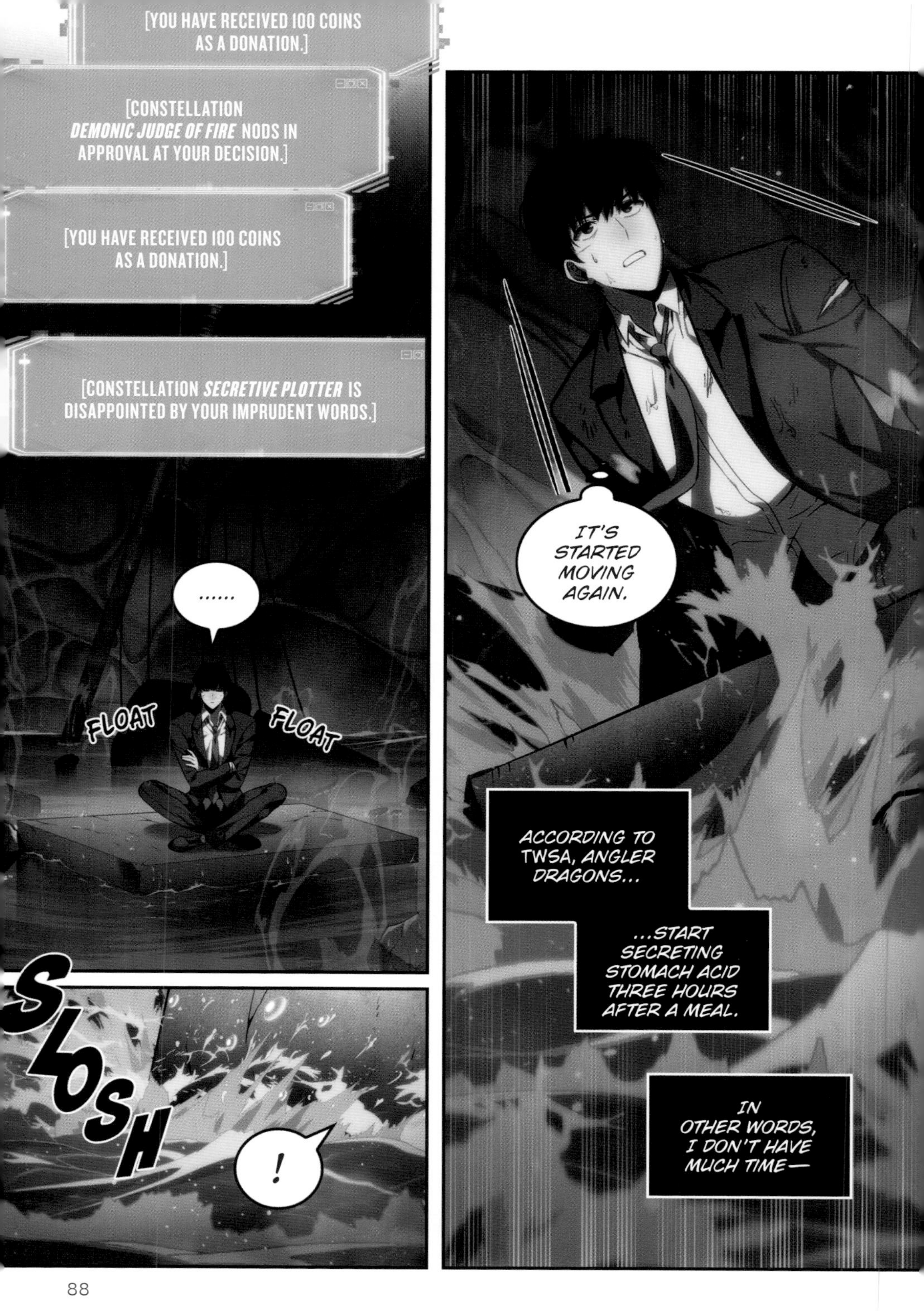
[YOU HAVE RECEIVED 100 COINS AS A DONATION.]
[CONSTELLATION *DEMONIC JUDGE OF FIRE* NODS IN APPROVAL AT YOUR DECISION.]
[YOU HAVE RECEIVED 100 COINS AS A DONATION.]
[CONSTELLATION *SECRETIVE PLOTTER* IS DISAPPOINTED BY YOUR IMPRUDENT WORDS.]
......
FLOAT
FLOAT
SLOSH
!
IT'S STARTED MOVING AGAIN.
ACCORDING TO TWSA, ANGLER DRAGONS...
...START SECRETING STOMACH ACID THREE HOURS AFTER A MEAL.
IN OTHER WORDS, I DON'T HAVE MUCH TIME—

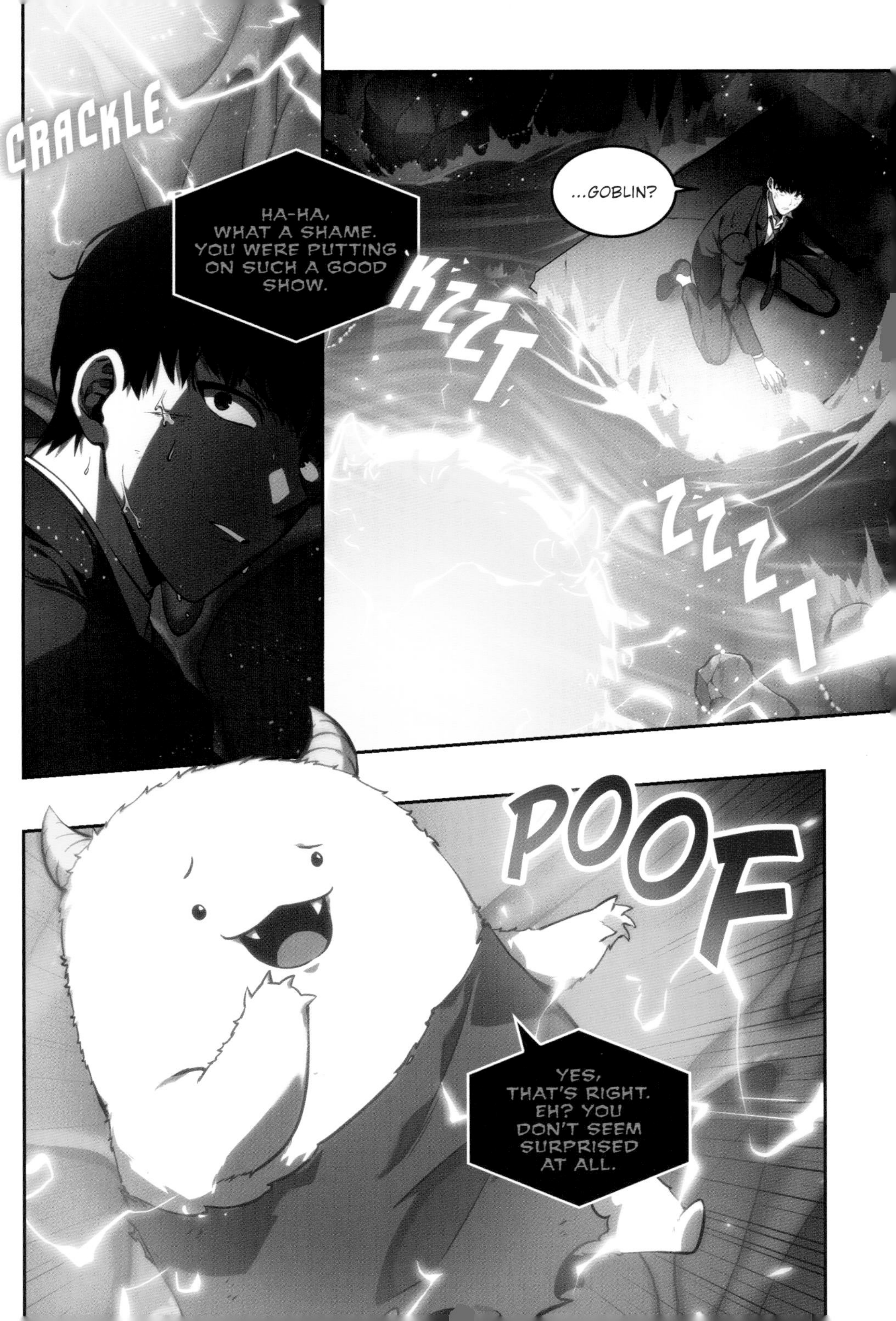
CRACKLE
HA-HA, WHAT A SHAME. YOU WERE PUTTING ON SUCH A GOOD SHOW.
...GOBLIN?
KZZT
ZZZZT
POOF
YES, THAT'S RIGHT. EH? YOU DON'T SEEM SURPRISED AT ALL.

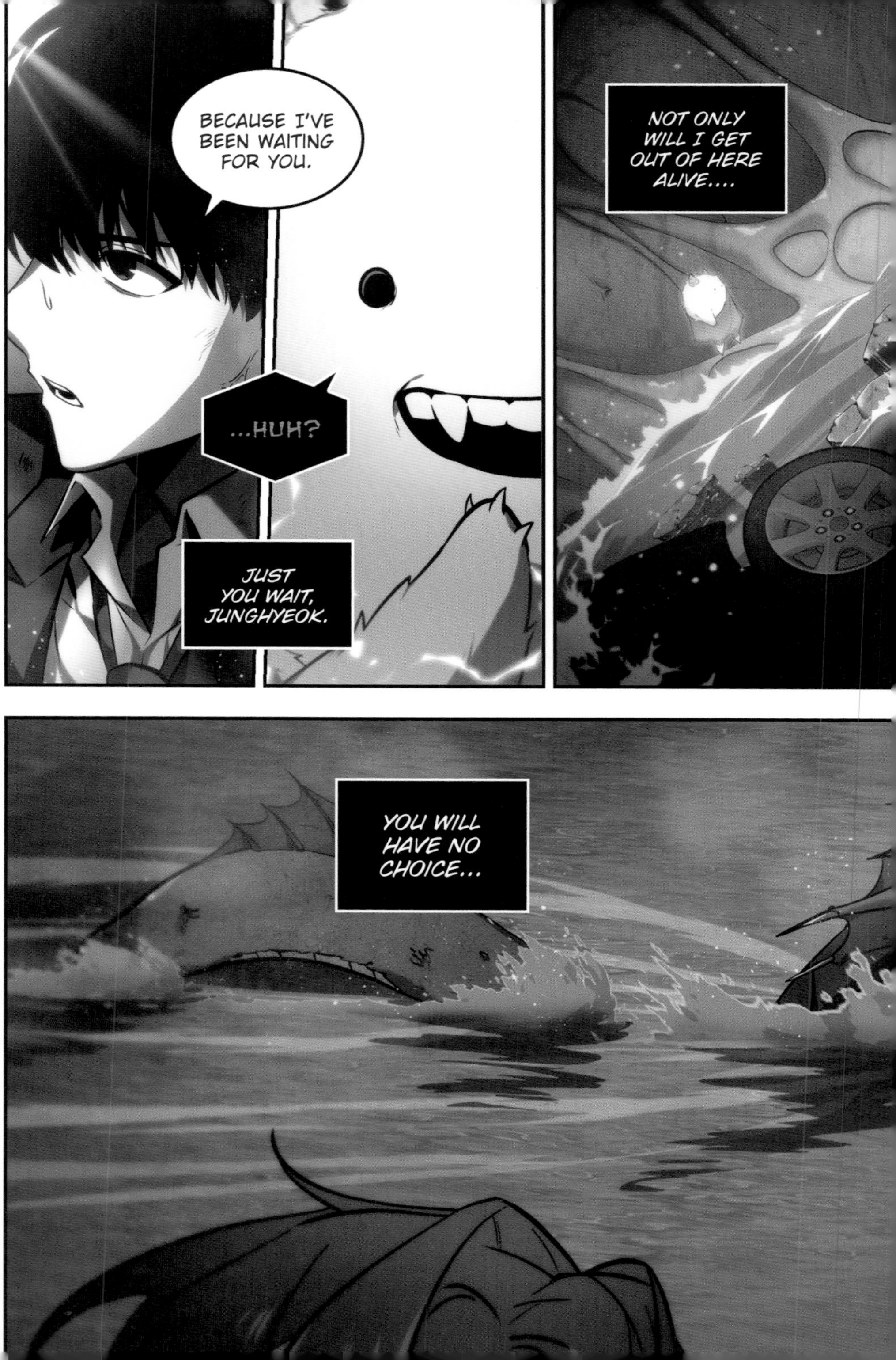
BECAUSE I'VE BEEN WAITING FOR YOU.
...HUH?
JUST YOU WAIT, JUNGHYEOK.
NOT ONLY WILL I GET OUT OF HERE ALIVE....
YOU WILL HAVE NO CHOICE...

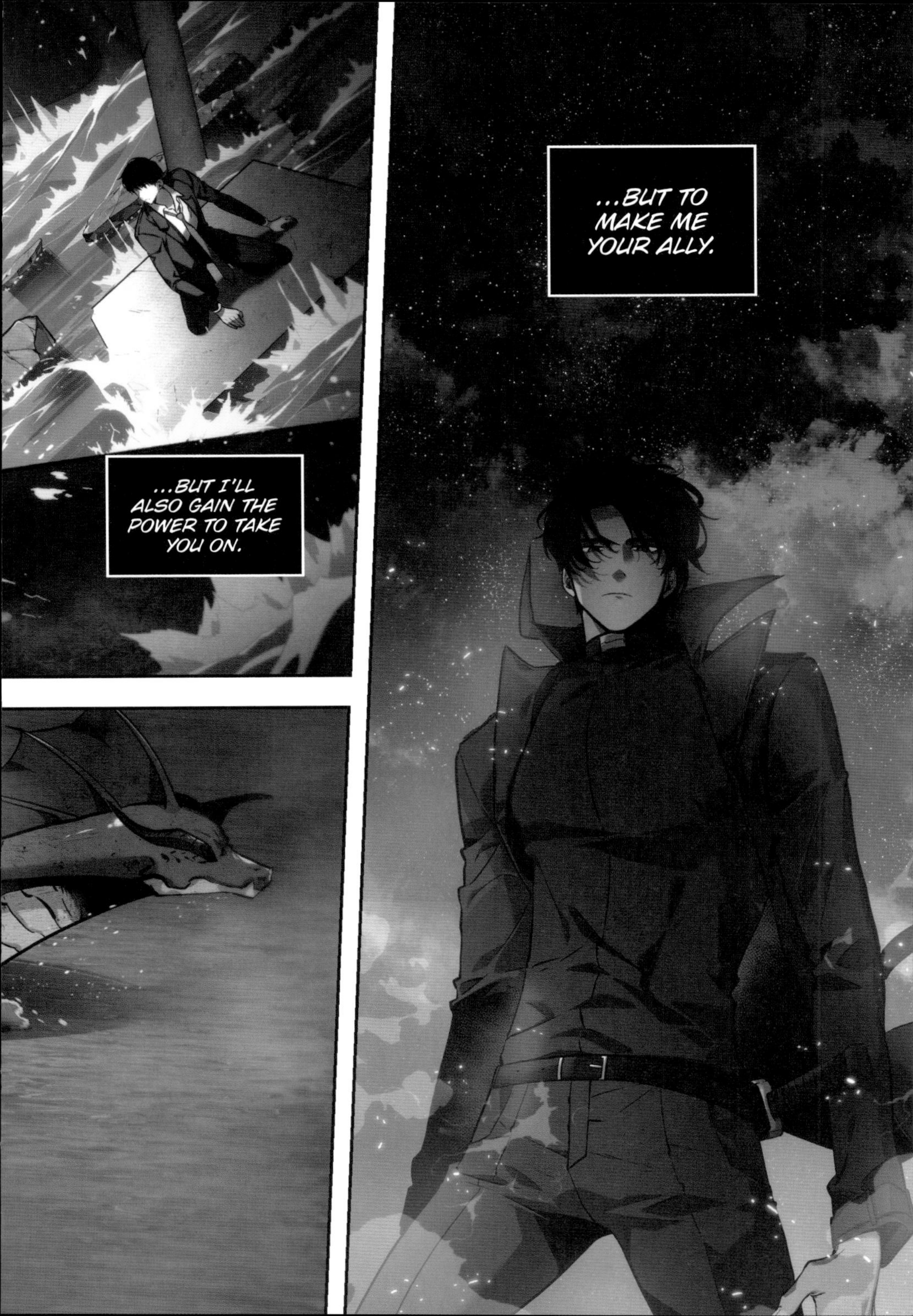
...BUT TO MAKE ME YOUR ALLY.
...BUT I'LL ALSO GAIN THE POWER TO TAKE YOU ON.

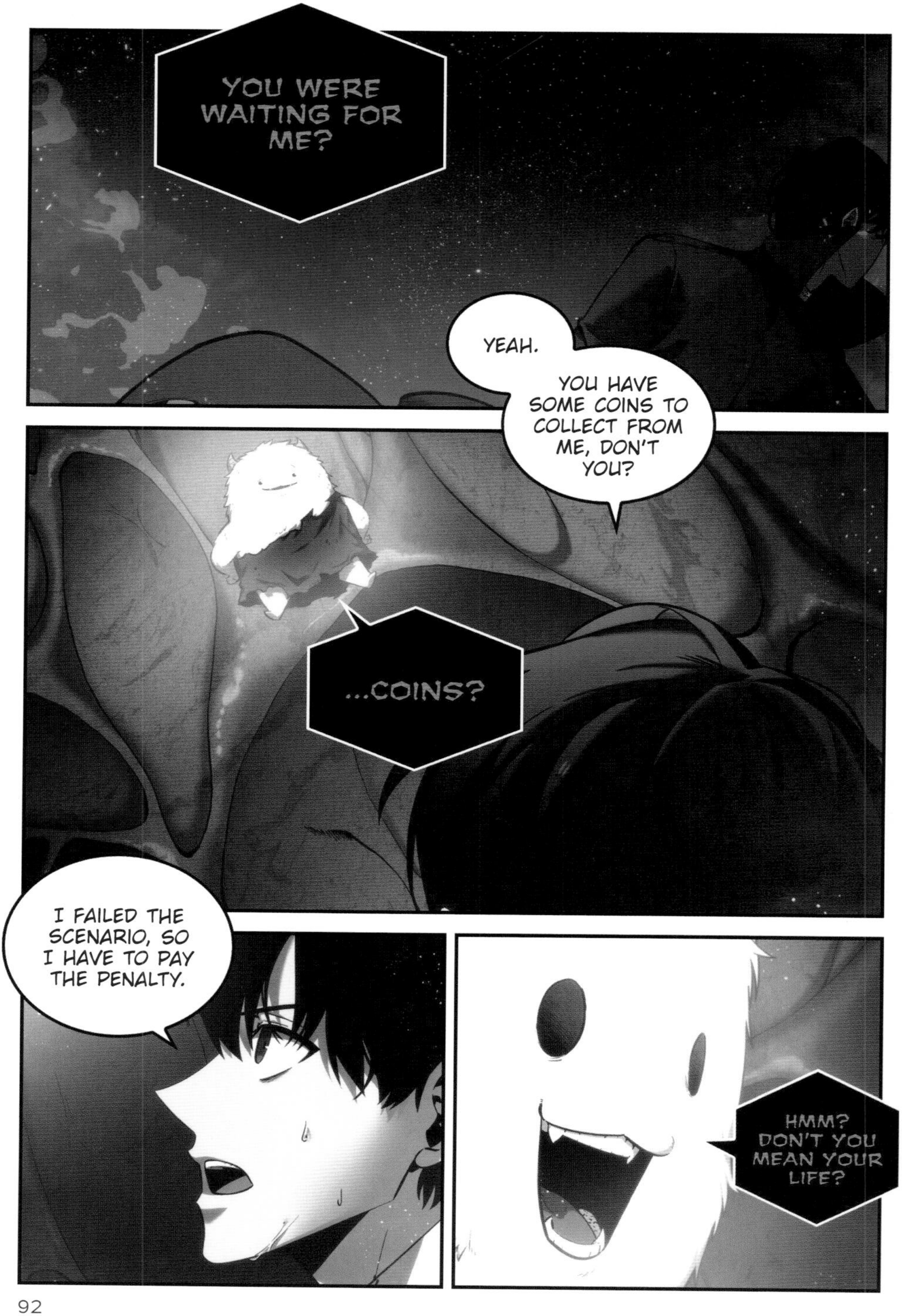
YOU WERE WAITING FOR ME?
YEAH.
YOU HAVE SOME COINS TO COLLECT FROM ME, DON'T YOU?
...COINS?
I FAILED THE SCENARIO, SO I HAVE TO PAY THE PENALTY.
HMM? DON'T YOU MEAN YOUR LIFE?

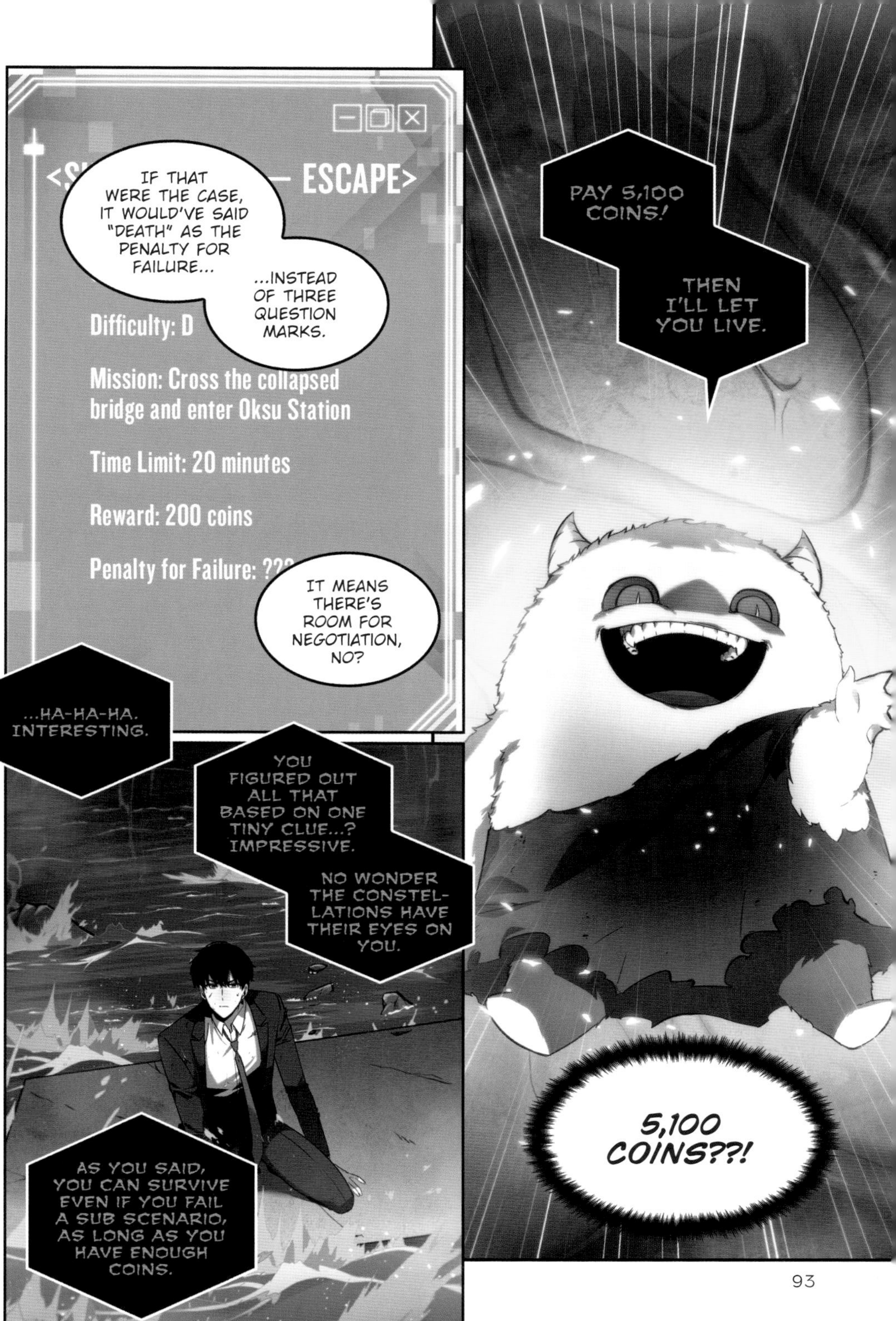
ESCAPE>
IF THAT WERE THE CASE, IT WOULD'VE SAID "DEATH" AS THE PENALTY FOR FAILURE...
...INSTEAD OF THREE QUESTION MARKS.
Difficulty: D
Mission: Cross the collapsed bridge and enter Oksu Station
Time Limit: 20 minutes
Reward: 200 coins
Penalty for Failure: ???
IT MEANS THERE'S ROOM FOR NEGOTIATION, NO?
...HA-HA-HA. INTERESTING.
YOU FIGURED OUT ALL THAT BASED ON ONE TINY CLUE...? IMPRESSIVE.
NO WONDER THE CONSTEL-LATIONS HAVE THEIR EYES ON YOU.
AS YOU SAID, YOU CAN SURVIVE EVEN IF YOU FAIL A SUB SCENARIO, AS LONG AS YOU HAVE ENOUGH COINS.
PAY 5,100 COINS!
THEN I'LL LET YOU LIVE.
5,100 COINS??!

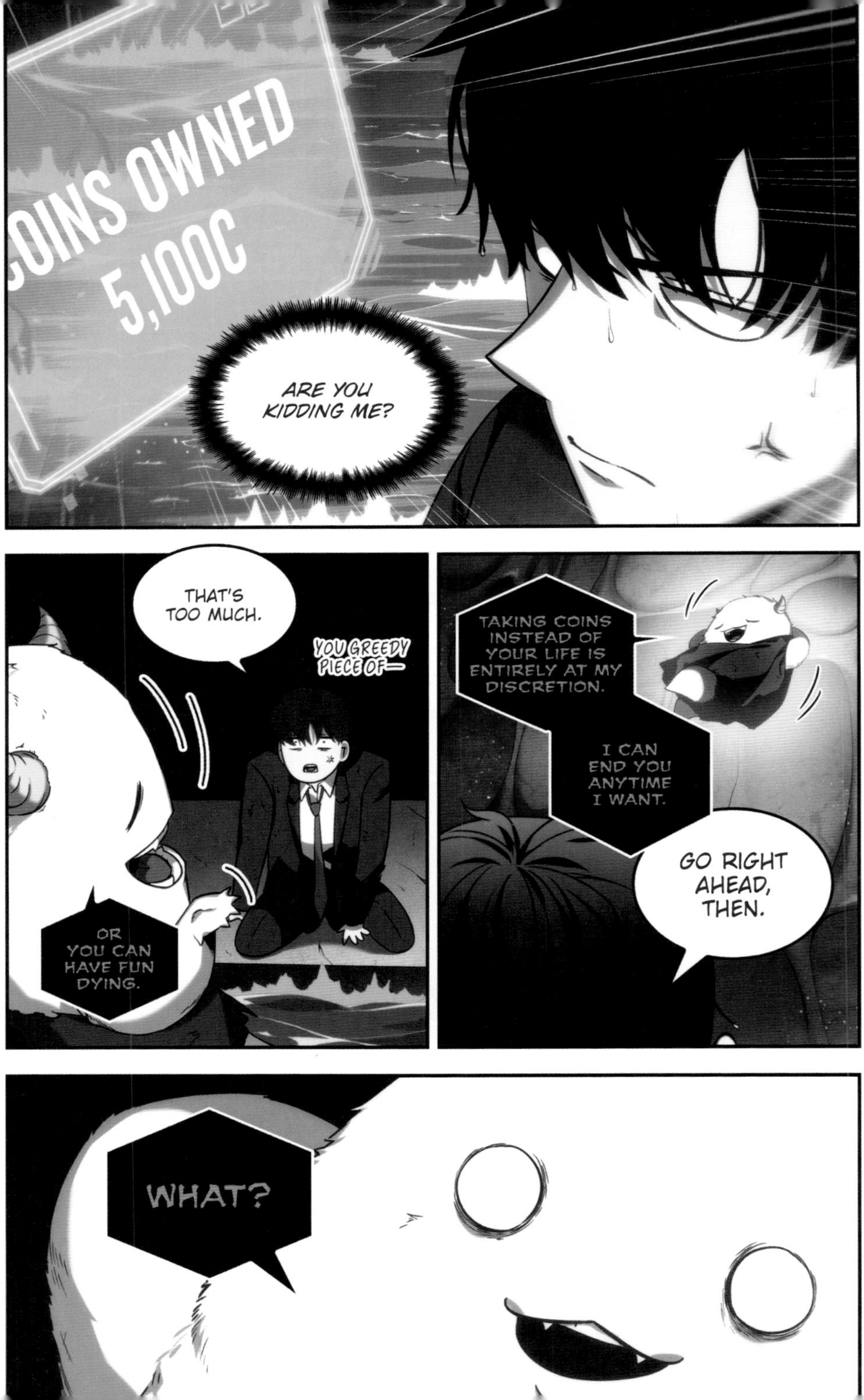

COINS OWNED
5,100C
ARE YOU KIDDING ME?
THAT'S TOO MUCH.
YOU GREEDY PIECE OF—
OR YOU CAN HAVE FUN DYING.
TAKING COINS INSTEAD OF YOUR LIFE IS ENTIRELY AT MY DISCRETION.
I CAN END YOU ANYTIME I WANT.
GO RIGHT AHEAD, THEN.
WHAT?

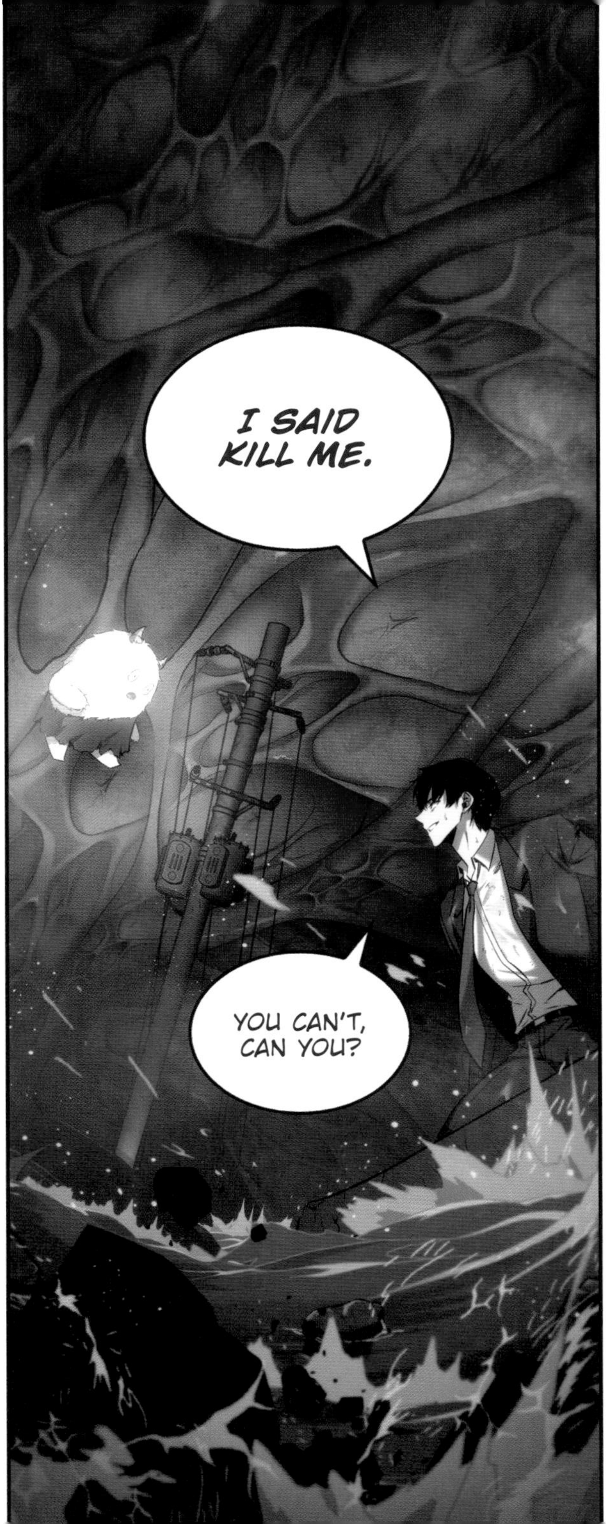

I SAID KILL ME.
YOU CAN'T, CAN YOU?

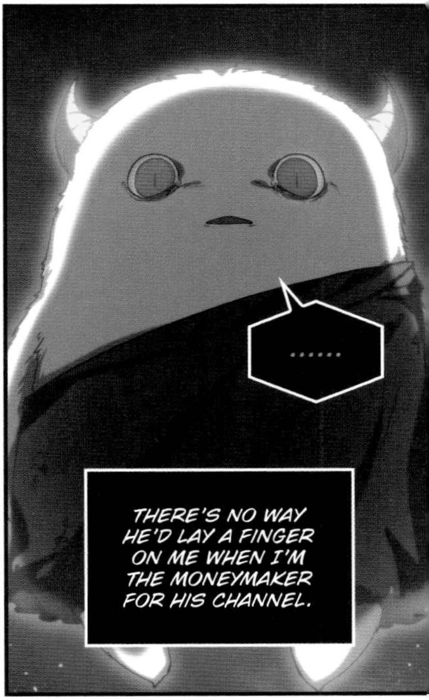

......
THERE'S NO WAY HE'D LAY A FINGER ON ME WHEN I'M THE MONEYMAKER FOR HIS CHANNEL.

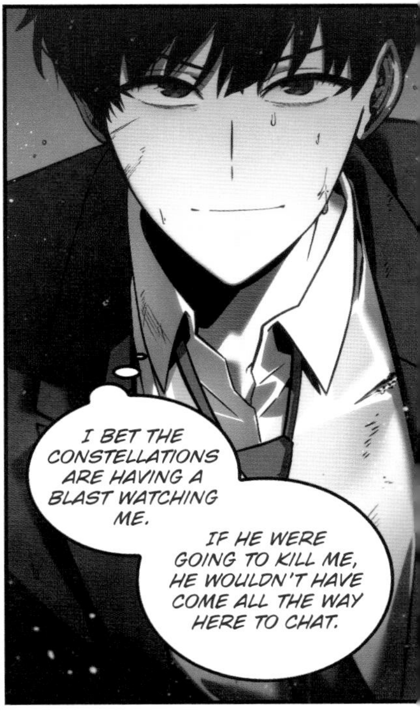

I BET THE CONSTELLATIONS ARE HAVING A BLAST WATCHING ME.
IF HE WERE GOING TO KILL ME, HE WOULDN'T HAVE COME ALL THE WAY HERE TO CHAT.

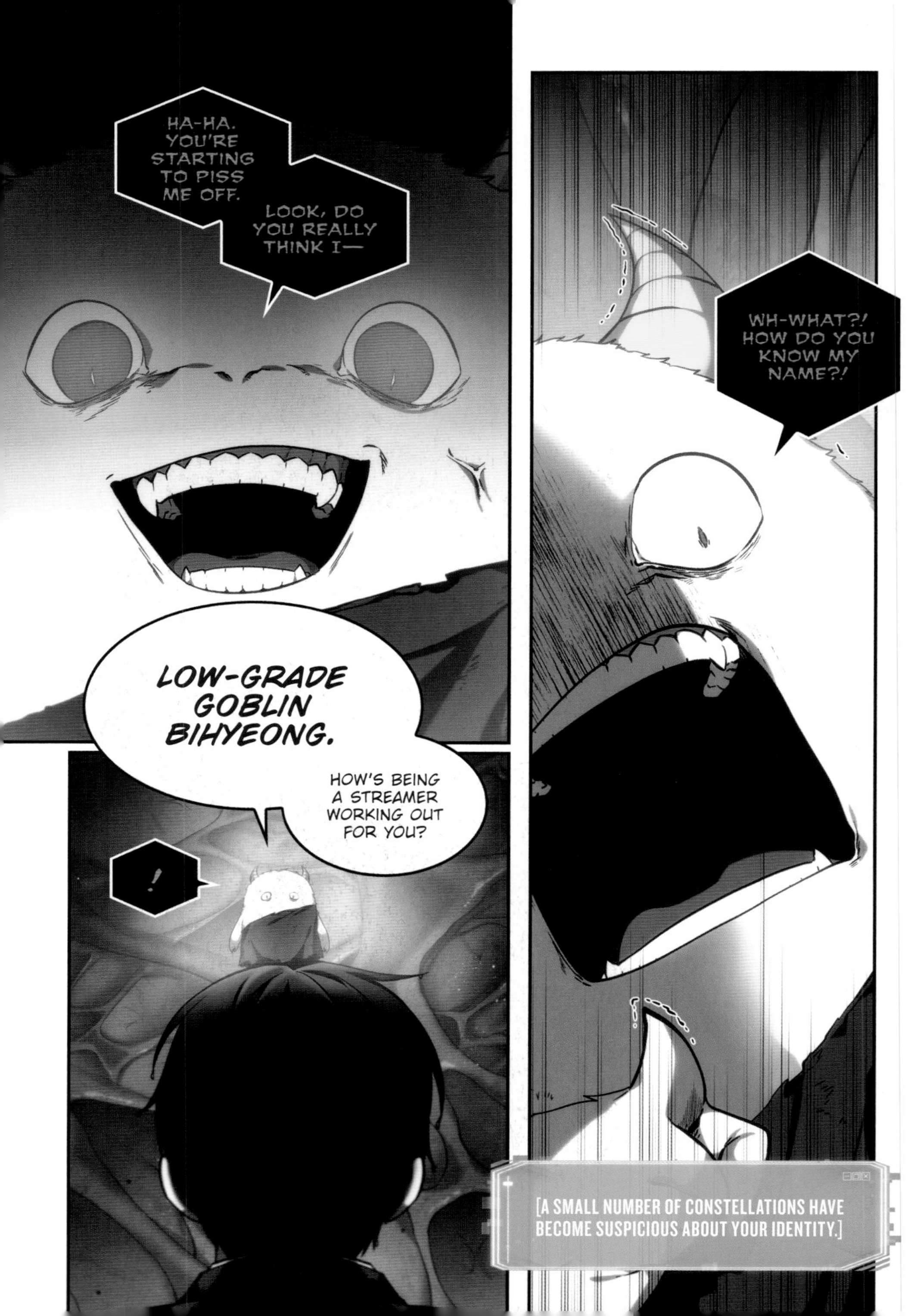
HA-HA. YOU'RE STARTING TO PISS ME OFF.
LOOK, DO YOU REALLY THINK I—
LOW-GRADE GOBLIN BIHYEONG.
HOW'S BEING A STREAMER WORKING OUT FOR YOU?
!
WH-WHAT?! HOW DO YOU KNOW MY NAME?!
[A SMALL NUMBER OF CONSTELLATIONS HAVE BECOME SUSPICIOUS ABOUT YOUR IDENTITY.]

STREAMING ISN'T SO HOT THESE DAYS, HUH?

MUST BE HARD WHEN THE CONSTELLATIONS ARE SO STINGY WITH COINS.

Why don't you shut off your channel for a bit so we can continue this talk?

!

WH-WHO THE HELL ARE YOU? HOW CAN A MERE HUMAN KNOW ABOUT—!

BZZT ZZZZT

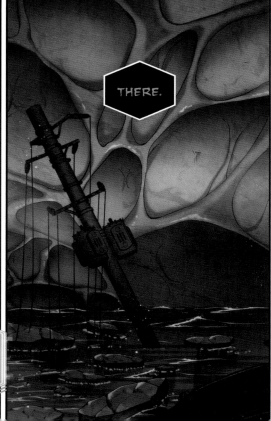

THERE.

[CONSTELLATION *SECRETIVE PLOTTER*'S EYES GLINT IN ANTICIPATION OF YOUR PLAN.]

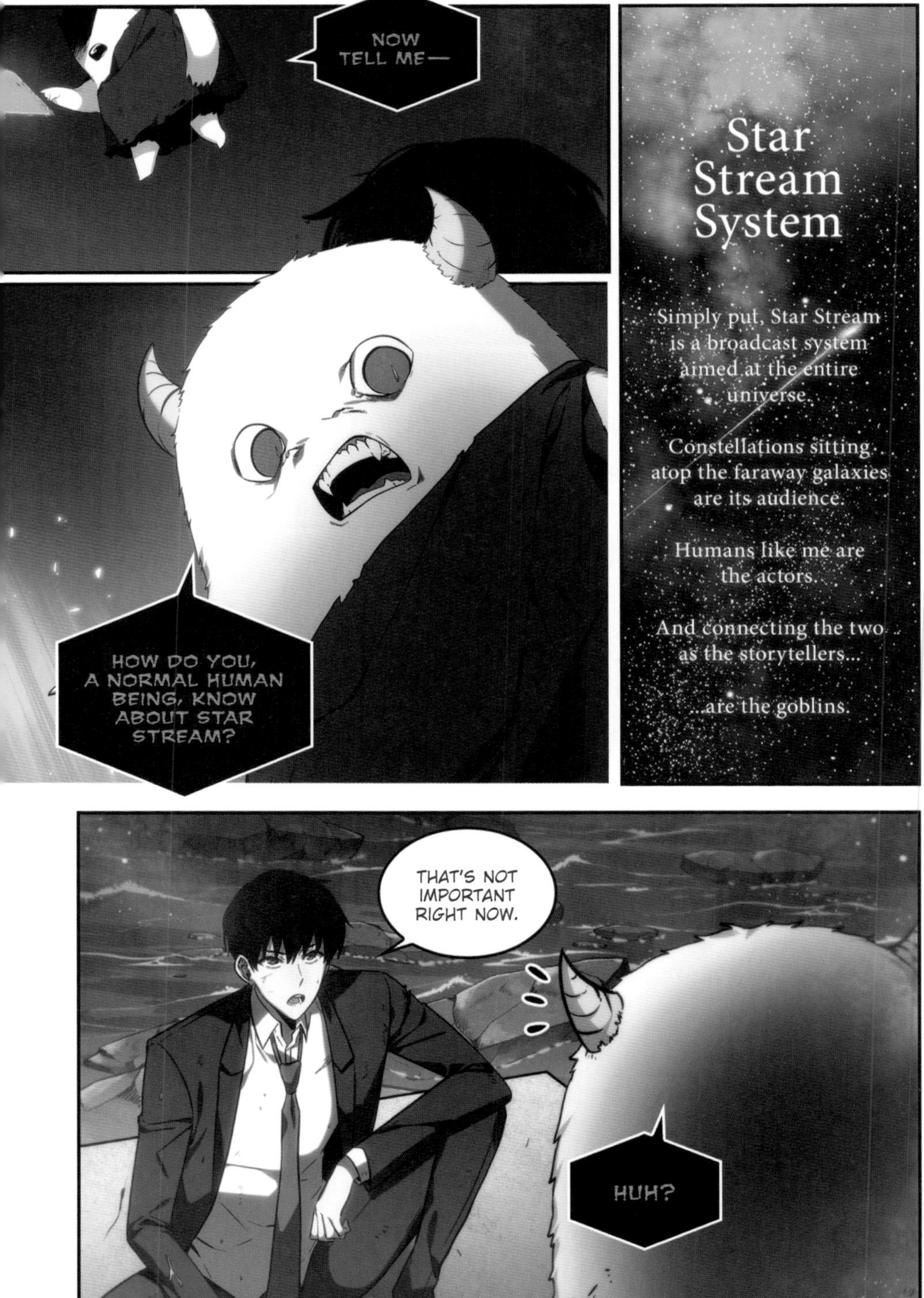
NOW TELL ME—
HOW DO YOU, A NORMAL HUMAN BEING, KNOW ABOUT STAR STREAM?
Star Stream System
Simply put, Star Stream is a broadcast system aimed at the entire universe.
Constellations sitting atop the faraway galaxies are its audience.
Humans like me are the actors.
And connecting the two as the storytellers...
...are the goblins.
THAT'S NOT IMPORTANT RIGHT NOW.
HUH?

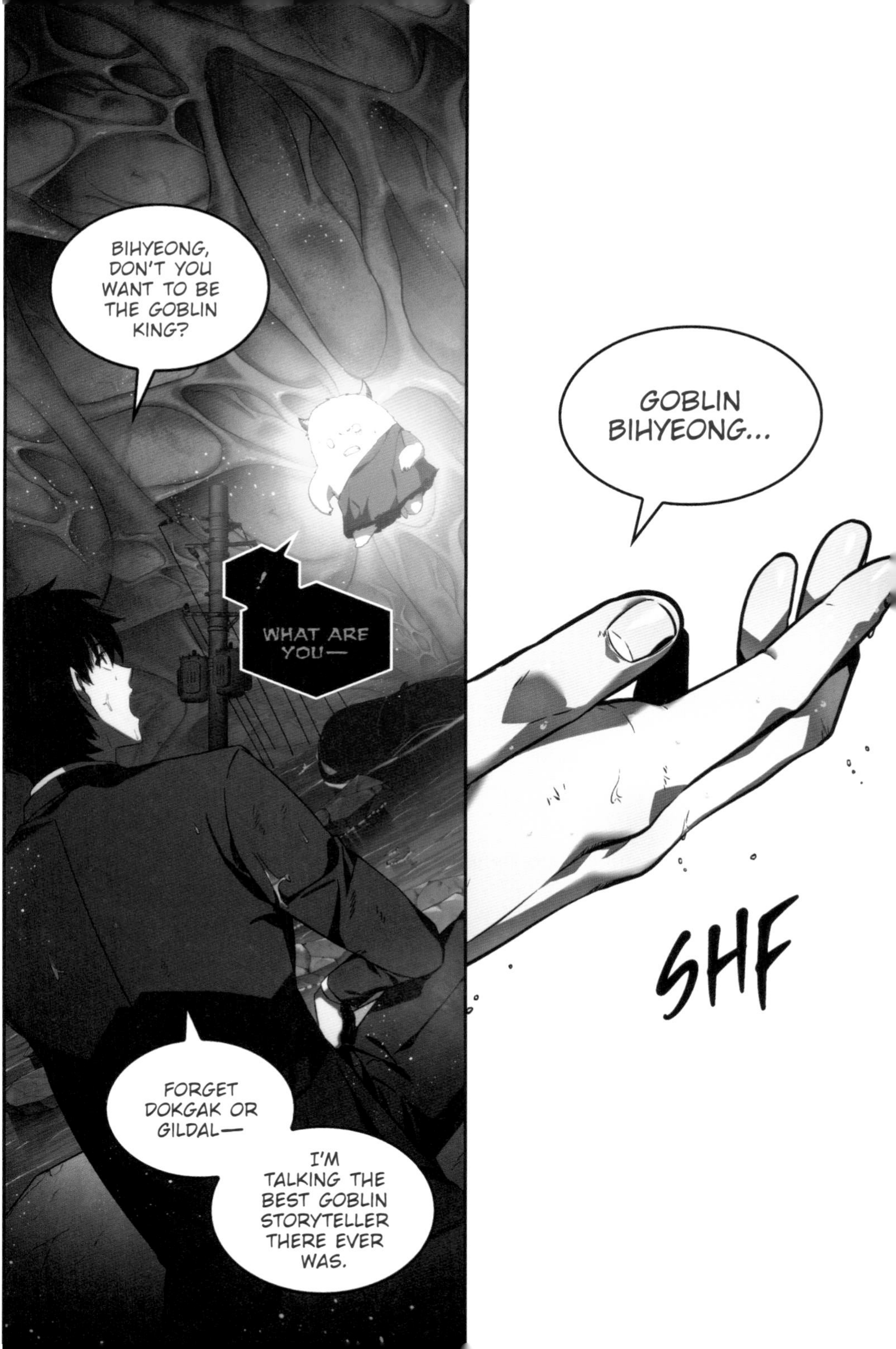

BIHYEONG, DON'T YOU WANT TO BE THE GOBLIN KING?
GOBLIN BIHYEONG...
!
WHAT ARE YOU—
SHF
FORGET DOKGAK OR GILDAL—
I'M TALKING THE BEST GOBLIN STORYTELLER THERE EVER WAS.

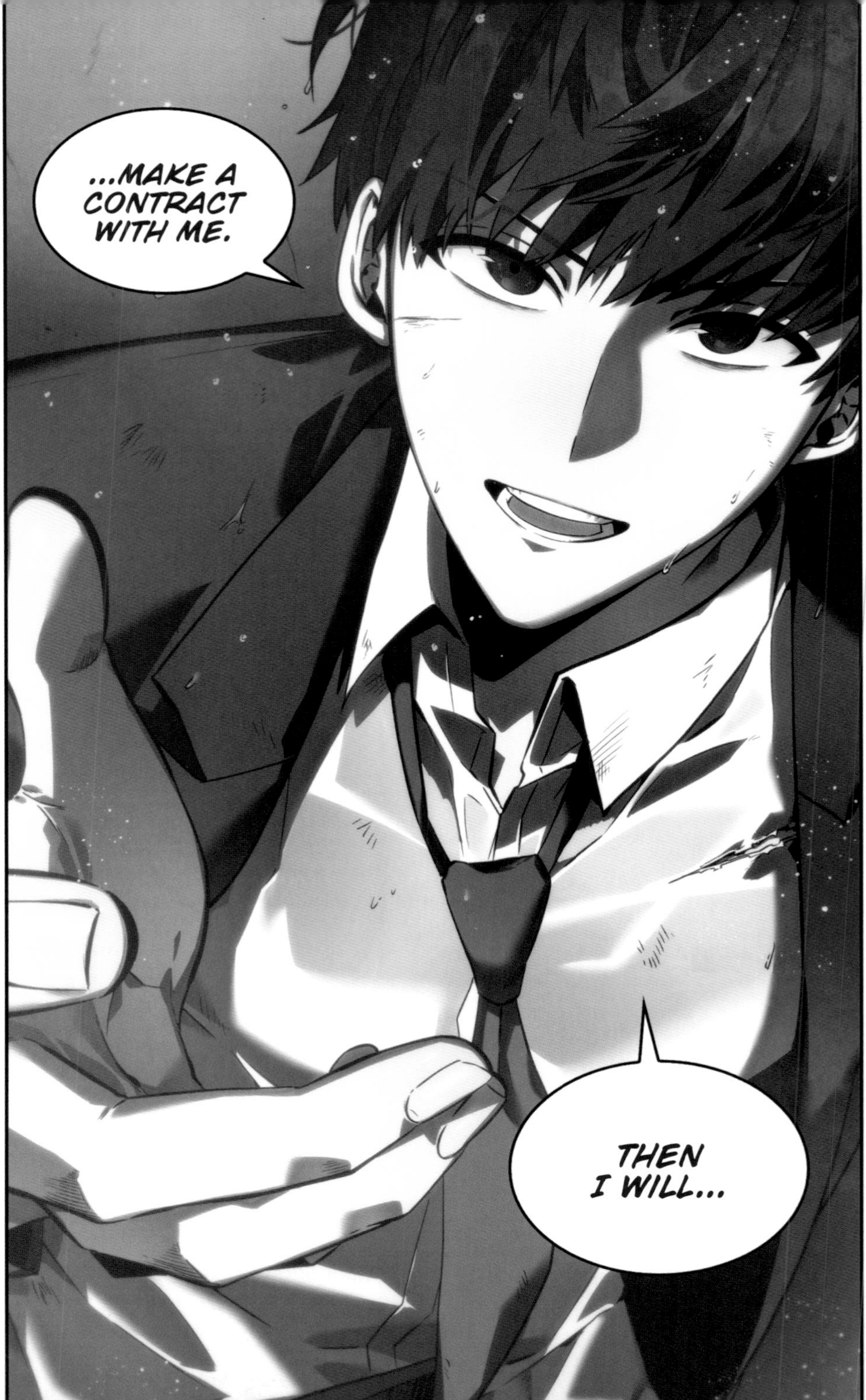
...MAKE A CONTRACT WITH ME.
THEN I WILL...

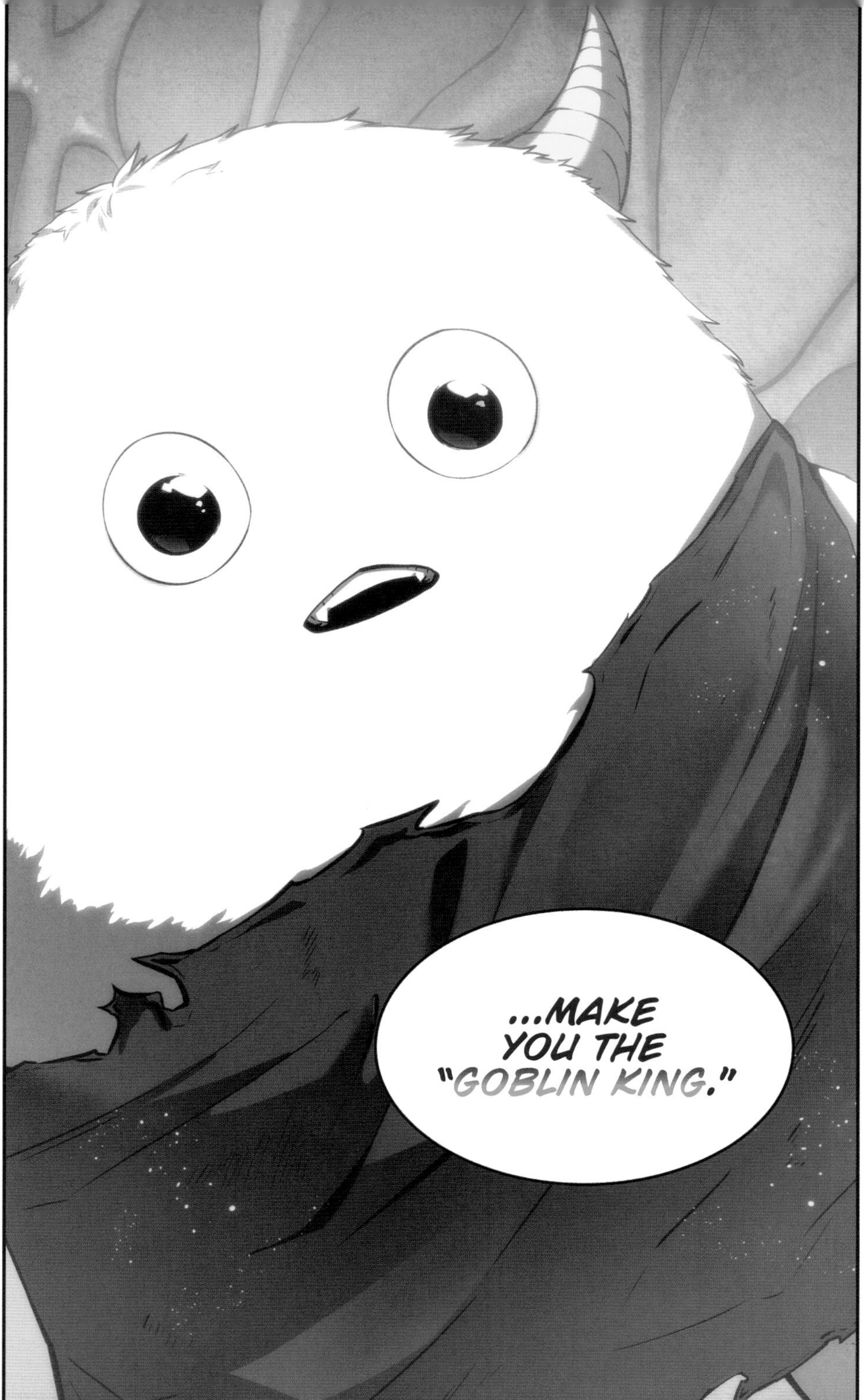
...MAKE YOU THE "GOBLIN KING."

EP. 03

Omniscient
Reader's
Viewpoint

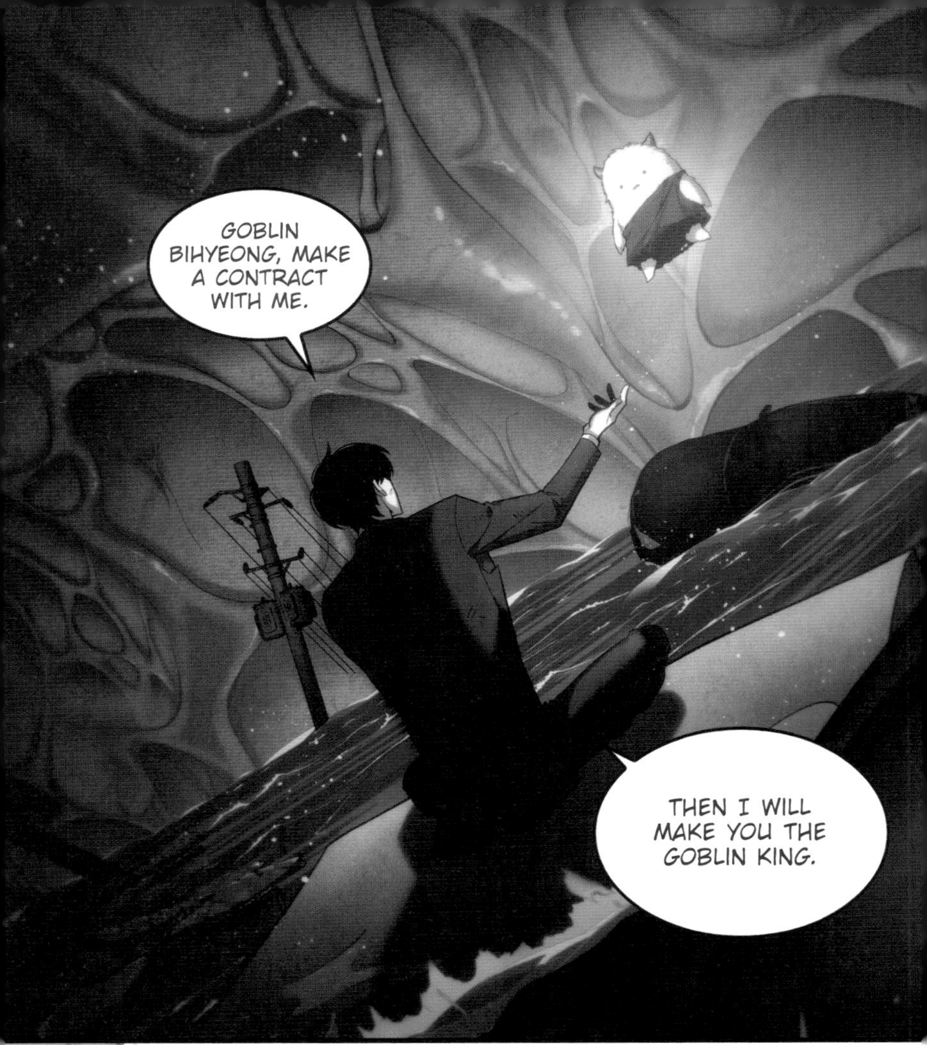
GOBLIN BIHYEONG, MAKE A CONTRACT WITH ME.
THEN I WILL MAKE YOU THE GOBLIN KING.
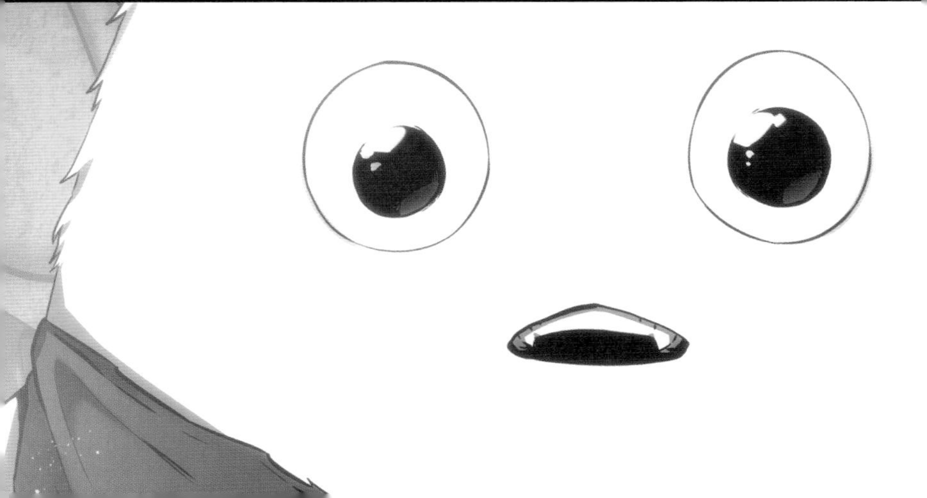

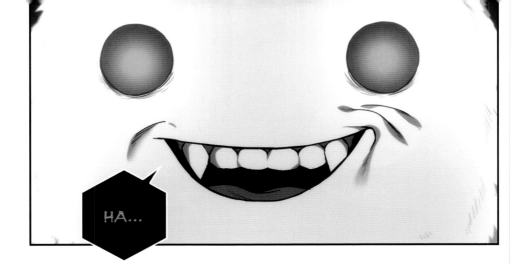

HA...

HA-HA-HA-HA-HA!

I SHOULD'VE REALIZED WHEN YOU TURNED DOWN ALL THE OFFERS DURING THE SPONSOR SELECTION!

Abyssal Black
Demonic Judg
Secretive Plott
risoner of Gol

THAT'S RIGHT.

DURING THE SPONSOR SELECTION THAT TOOK PLACE BEFORE CROSSING THE BRIDGE...

YOU'RE CRAZY! COMPLETELY INSANE!

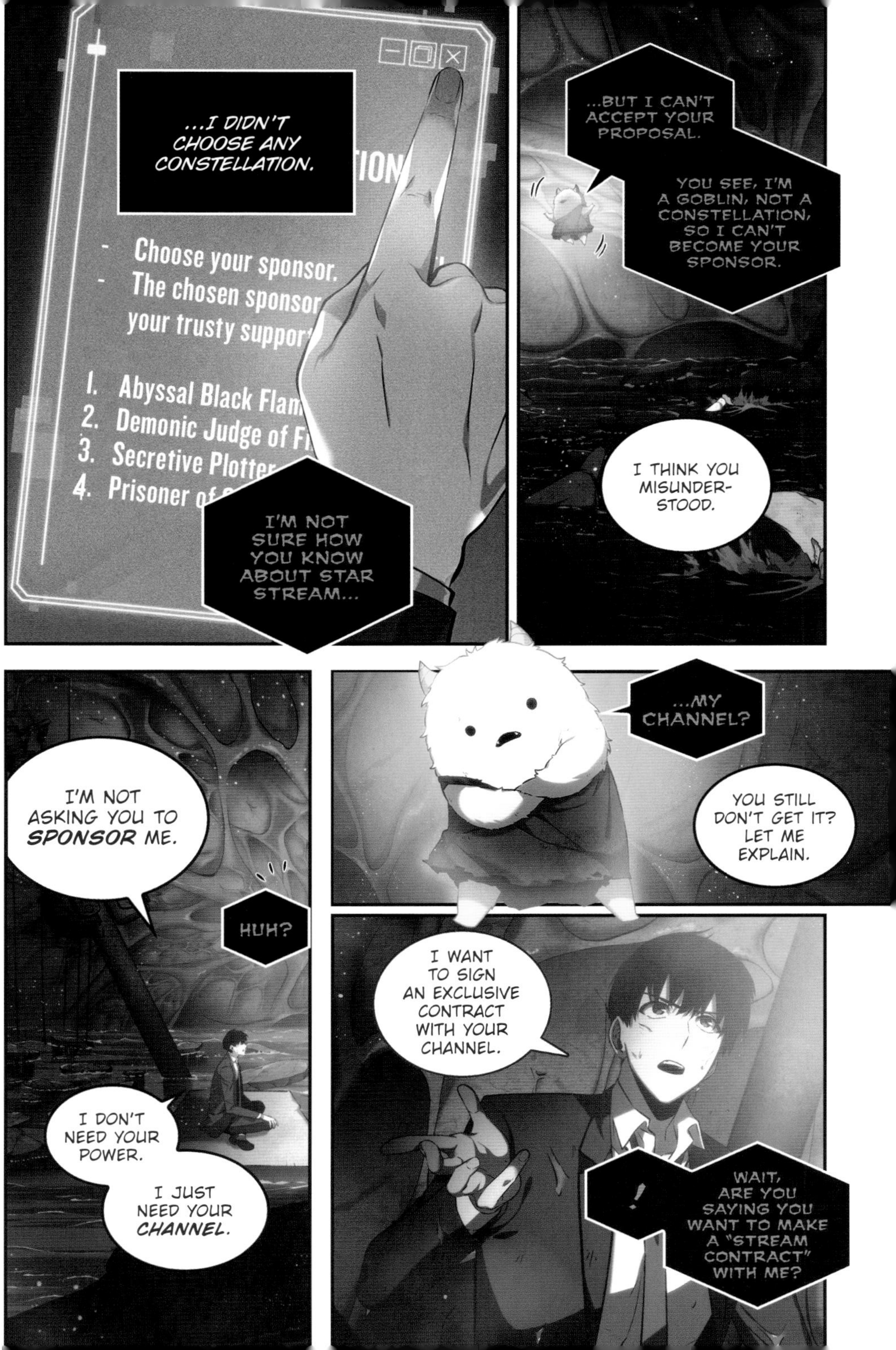

...I DIDN'T CHOOSE ANY CONSTELLATION.
- Choose your sponsor.
- The chosen sponsor
your trusty support
1. Abyssal Black Flam
2. Demonic Judge of Fi
3. Secretive Plotter
4. Prisoner of
I'M NOT SURE HOW YOU KNOW ABOUT STAR STREAM...
...BUT I CAN'T ACCEPT YOUR PROPOSAL.
YOU SEE, I'M A GOBLIN, NOT A CONSTELLATION, SO I CAN'T BECOME YOUR SPONSOR.
I THINK YOU MISUNDER-STOOD.
I'M NOT ASKING YOU TO SPONSOR ME.
HUH?
I DON'T NEED YOUR POWER.
I JUST NEED YOUR CHANNEL.
...MY CHANNEL?
YOU STILL DON'T GET IT? LET ME EXPLAIN.
I WANT TO SIGN AN EXCLUSIVE CONTRACT WITH YOUR CHANNEL.
!
WAIT, ARE YOU SAYING YOU WANT TO MAKE A "STREAM CONTRACT" WITH ME?

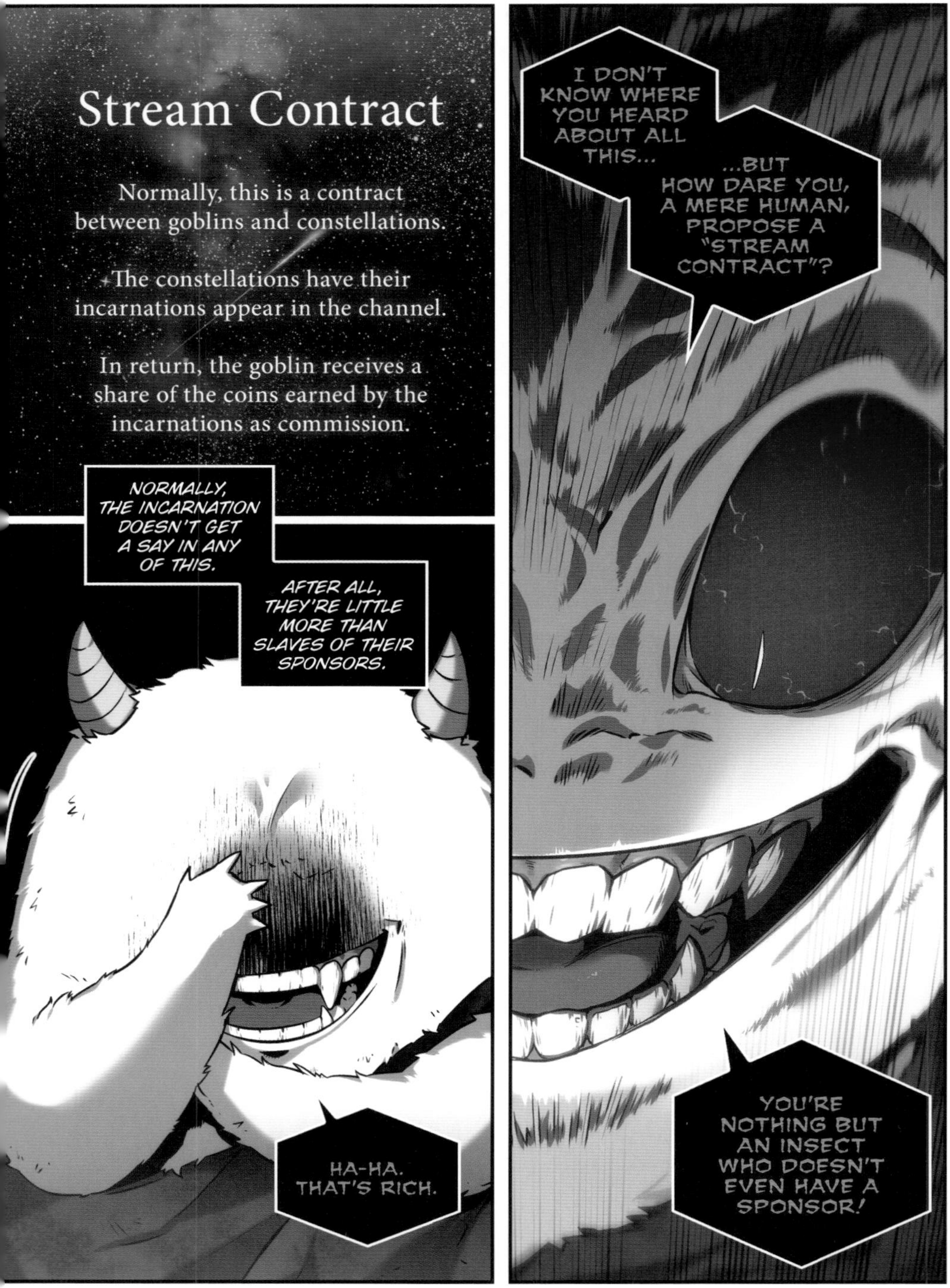

Stream Contract
Normally, this is a contract between goblins and constellations.
The constellations have their incarnations appear in the channel.
In return, the goblin receives a share of the coins earned by the incarnations as commission.
NORMALLY, THE INCARNATION DOESN'T GET A SAY IN ANY OF THIS.
AFTER ALL, THEY'RE LITTLE MORE THAN SLAVES OF THEIR SPONSORS.
HA-HA. THAT'S RICH.
I DON'T KNOW WHERE YOU HEARD ABOUT ALL THIS...
...BUT HOW DARE YOU, A MERE HUMAN, PROPOSE A "STREAM CONTRACT"?
YOU'RE NOTHING BUT AN INSECT WHO DOESN'T EVEN HAVE A SPONSOR!

IT'S PRECISELY BECAUSE I DON'T HAVE A SPONSOR THAT THIS IS A GOOD DEAL FOR YOU.

HUH?

WHY DO YOU THINK CONSTELLATIONS WATCH THESE CHANNELS IN THE FIRST PLACE?

THE SUBSCRIBERS OF STAR STREAM CAN BE DIVIDED INTO TWO BROAD CATEGORIES.

FIRST, THE "THRILL SEEKERS" WHO FLIP THROUGH THE CHANNELS TO PASS TIME.

AND SECOND, THE "INCARNATION SEEKERS" WHO ARE SEARCHING FOR PEOPLE TO SPONSOR.

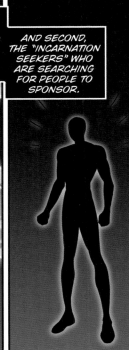

FOR YOUR CHANNEL TO SUCCEED, YOU HAVE TO SATISFY AT LEAST ONE OF THOSE GROUPS.

YOU PROVIDE EITHER GOOD ENTERTAINMENT, OR SUITABLE CANDIDATES TO SPONSOR.

YOU KNOW YOUR STUFF, I ADMIT, BUT WHAT DOES ANY OF THIS HAVE TO DO WITH YOU?

YOU STILL DON'T GET IT? NO WONDER YOUR SUBSCRIBER COUNT IS STUCK AT THREE DIGITS.

...SHUT UP AND GET TO THE POINT.

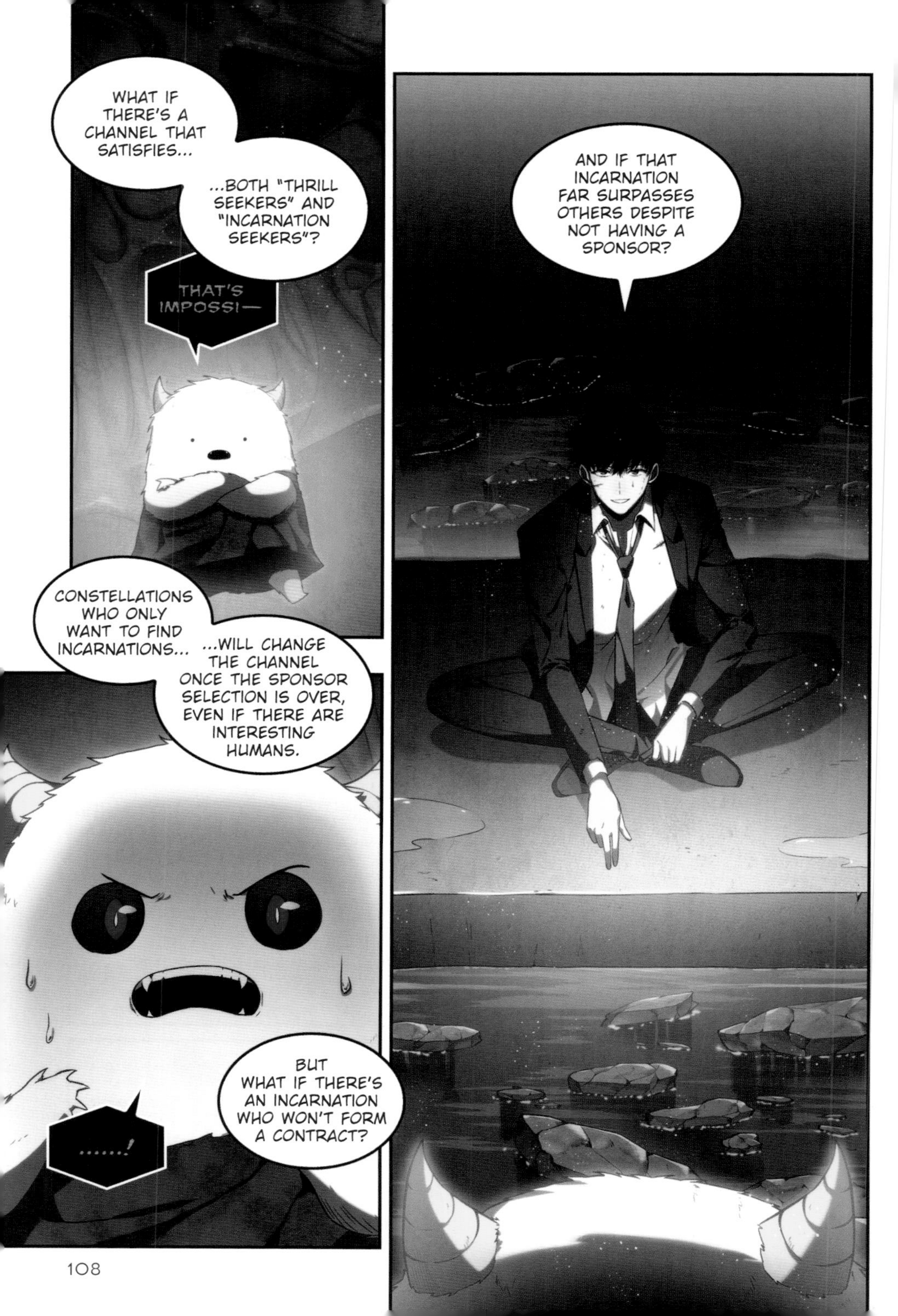
WHAT IF THERE'S A CHANNEL THAT SATISFIES...
...BOTH "THRILL SEEKERS" AND "INCARNATION SEEKERS"?
THAT'S IMPOSSI—
CONSTELLATIONS WHO ONLY WANT TO FIND INCARNATIONS...
...WILL CHANGE THE CHANNEL ONCE THE SPONSOR SELECTION IS OVER, EVEN IF THERE ARE INTERESTING HUMANS.
BUT WHAT IF THERE'S AN INCARNATION WHO WON'T FORM A CONTRACT?
.......!
AND IF THAT INCARNATION FAR SURPASSES OTHERS DESPITE NOT HAVING A SPONSOR?

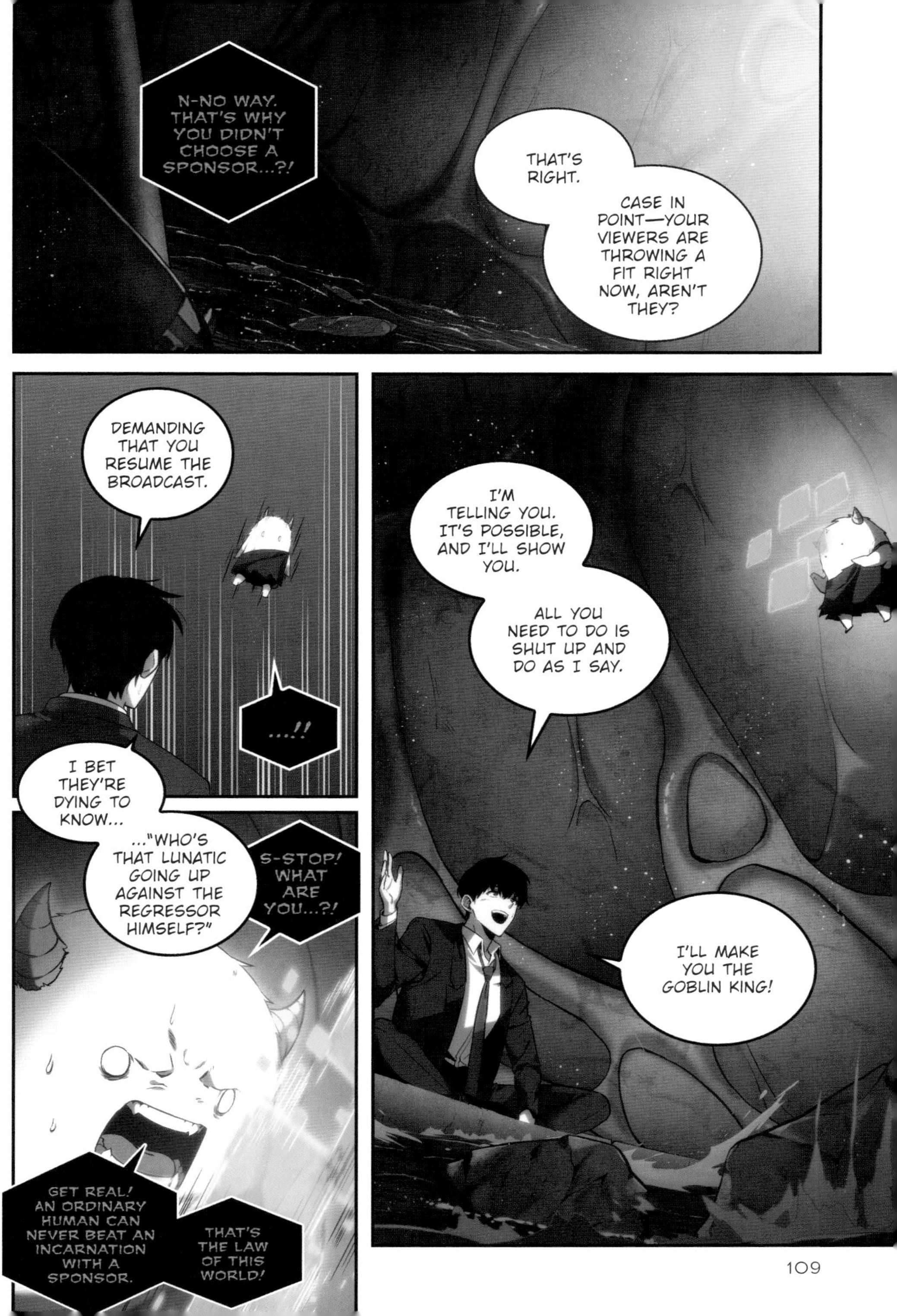

N-NO WAY. THAT'S WHY YOU DIDN'T CHOOSE A SPONSOR...?!
THAT'S RIGHT.
CASE IN POINT—YOUR VIEWERS ARE THROWING A FIT RIGHT NOW, AREN'T THEY?
DEMANDING THAT YOU RESUME THE BROADCAST.
...!!
I BET THEY'RE DYING TO KNOW...
..."WHO'S THAT LUNATIC GOING UP AGAINST THE REGRESSOR HIMSELF?"
S-STOP! WHAT ARE YOU...?!
GET REAL! AN ORDINARY HUMAN CAN NEVER BEAT AN INCARNATION WITH A SPONSOR.
THAT'S THE LAW OF THIS WORLD!
I'M TELLING YOU. IT'S POSSIBLE, AND I'LL SHOW YOU.
ALL YOU NEED TO DO IS SHUT UP AND DO AS I SAY.
I'LL MAKE YOU THE GOBLIN KING!

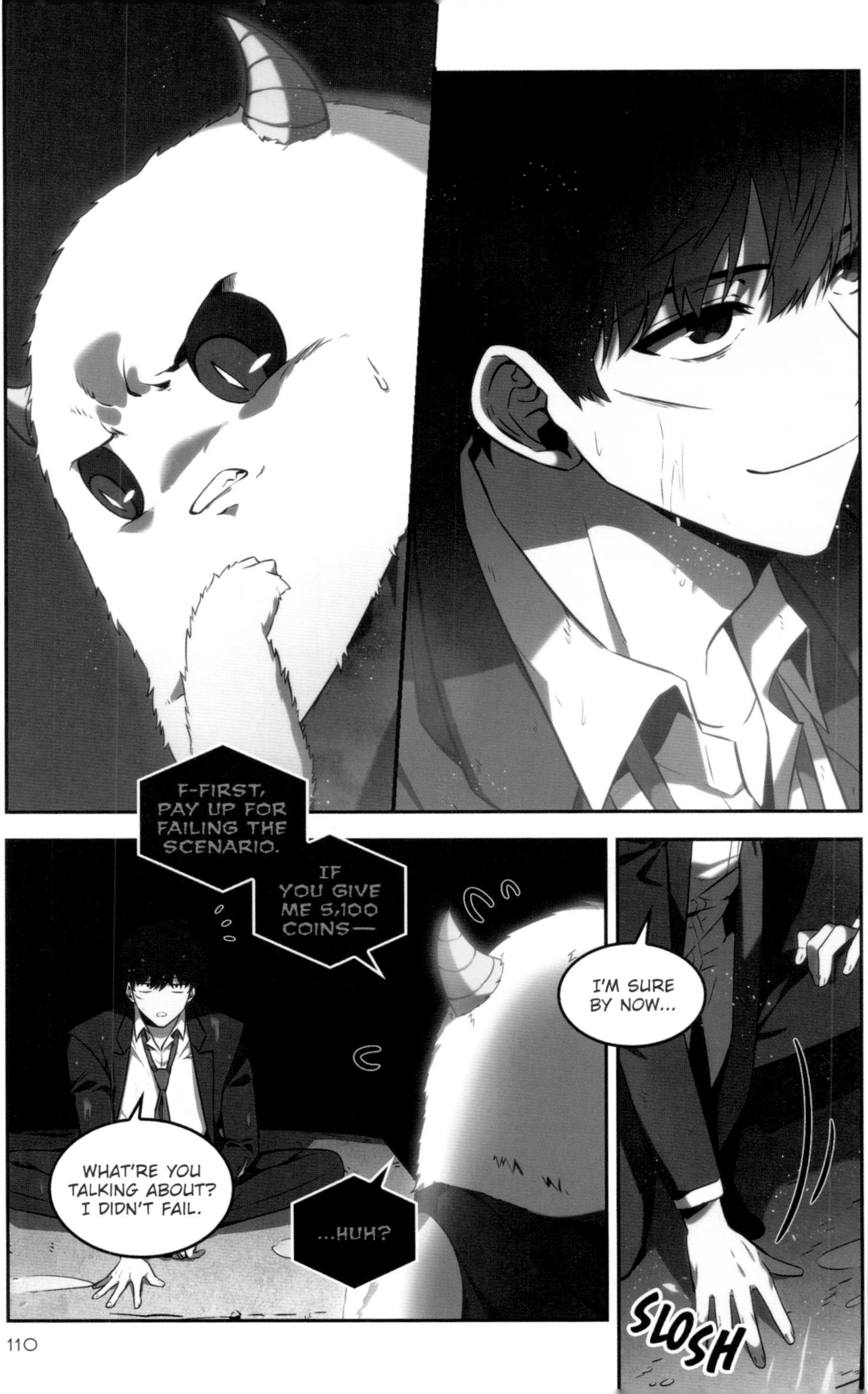
F-FIRST, PAY UP FOR FAILING THE SCENARIO.
IF YOU GIVE ME 5,100 COINS—
WHAT'RE YOU TALKING ABOUT? I DIDN'T FAIL.
...HUH?
I'M SURE BY NOW...
SLOSH

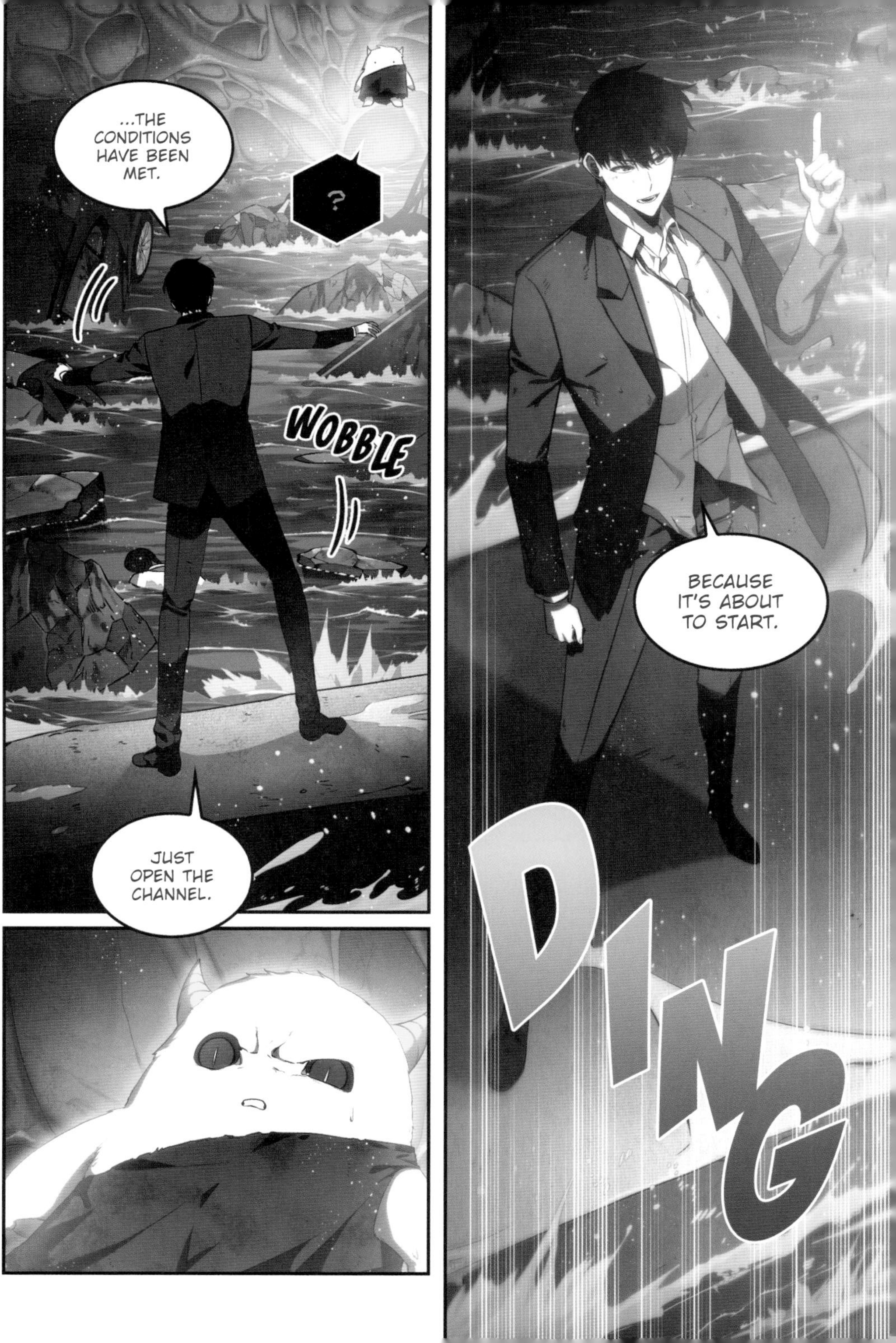
...THE CONDITIONS HAVE BEEN MET.
?
WOBBLE
JUST OPEN THE CHANNEL.
BECAUSE IT'S ABOUT TO START.
DING

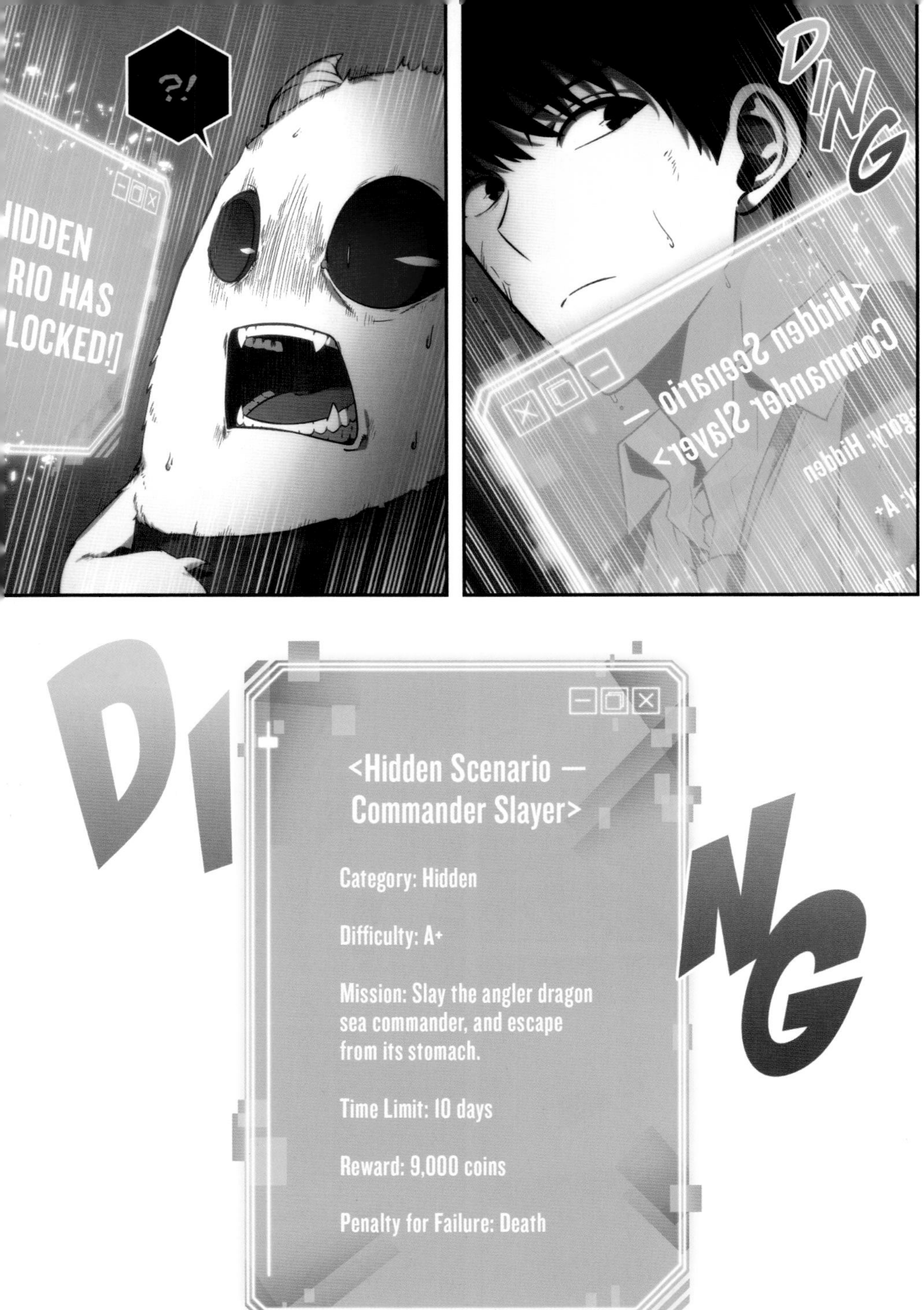
?!
IDDEN
RIO HAS
LOCKED!]
DING
DING
<Hidden Scenario —
Commander Slayer>
Category: Hidden
Difficulty: A+
Mission: Slay the angler dragon sea commander, and escape from its stomach.
Time Limit: 10 days
Reward: 9,000 coins
Penalty for Failure: Death

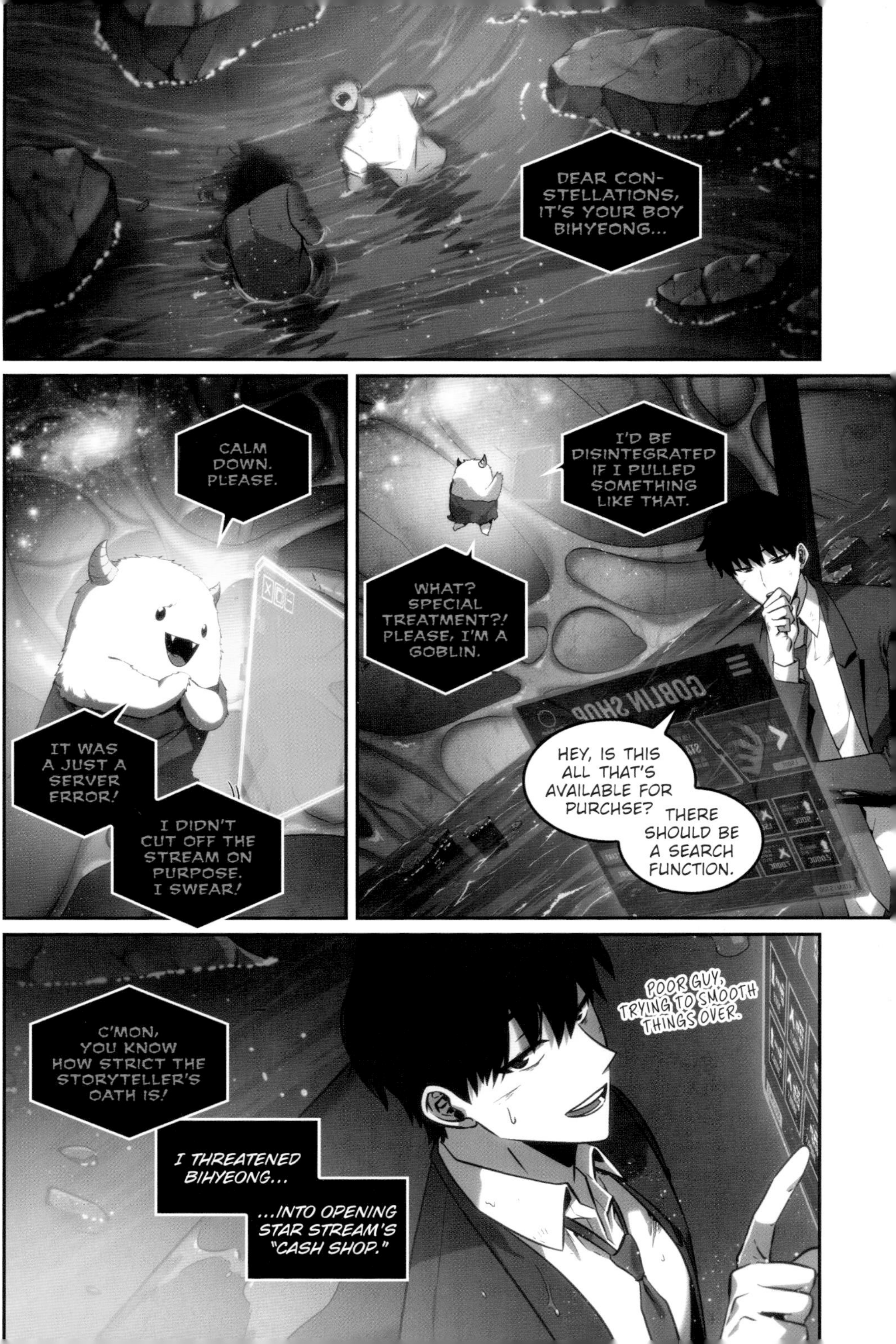
DEAR CON-STELLATIONS, IT'S YOUR BOY BIHYEONG...
CALM DOWN. PLEASE.
IT WAS A JUST A SERVER ERROR!
I DIDN'T CUT OFF THE STREAM ON PURPOSE. I SWEAR!
I'D BE DISINTEGRATED IF I PULLED SOMETHING LIKE THAT.
WHAT? SPECIAL TREATMENT?! PLEASE, I'M A GOBLIN.
GOBLIN SHOP
HEY, IS THIS ALL THAT'S AVAILABLE FOR PURCHSE?
THERE SHOULD BE A SEARCH FUNCTION.
C'MON, YOU KNOW HOW STRICT THE STORYTELLER'S OATH IS!
POOR GUY, TRYING TO SMOOTH THINGS OVER.
I THREATENED BIHYEONG...
...INTO OPENING STAR STREAM'S "CASH SHOP."

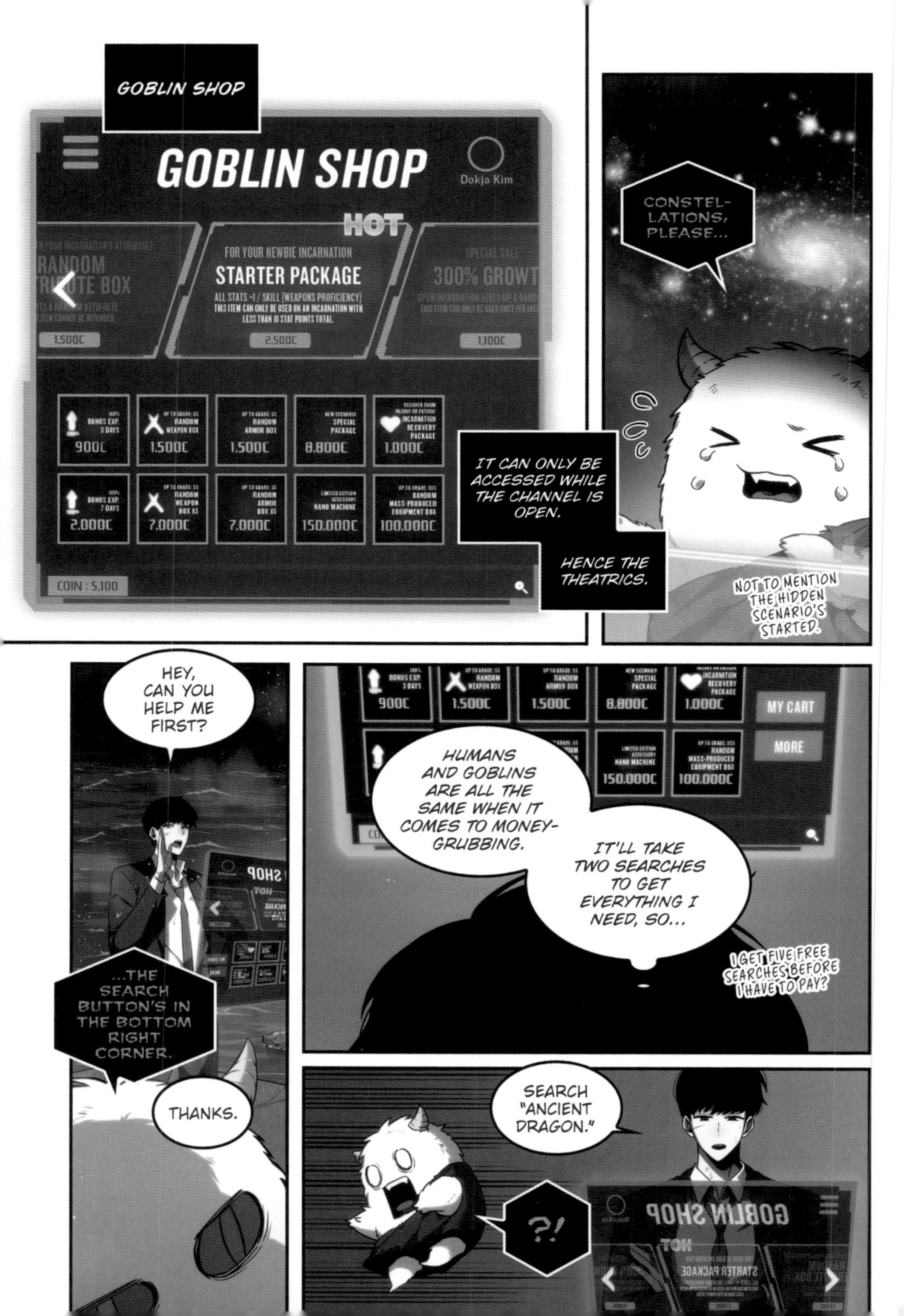
GOBLIN SHOP
GOBLIN SHOP
Dokja Kim
HOT
FOR YOUR NEWBIE INCARNATION
STARTER PACKAGE
ALL STATS +1 / SKILL [WEAPONS PROFICIENCY]
THIS ITEM CAN ONLY BE USED ON AN INCARNATION WITH LESS THAN 10 STAT POINTS TOTAL.
1,500C
2,500C
SPECIAL SALE
1,100C
100% BONUS EXP. 3 DAYS 900C
UP TO GRADE: SS RANDOM WEAPON BOX 1,500C
UP TO GRADE: SS RANDOM ARMOR BOX 1,500C
NEW SCENARIO SPECIAL PACKAGE 8,800C
RECOVER FROM INJURY OR FATIGUE INCARNATION RECOVERY PACKAGE 1,000C
100% BONUS EXP. 7 DAYS 2,000C
UP TO GRADE: SS RANDOM WEAPON BOX X5 7,000C
UP TO GRADE: SS RANDOM ARMOR BOX X5 7,000C
LIMITED EDITION ACCESSORY NANO MACHINE 150,000C
UP TO GRADE: SSS RANDOM MASS-PRODUCED EQUIPMENT BOX 100,000C
COIN : 5,100
IT CAN ONLY BE ACCESSED WHILE THE CHANNEL IS OPEN.
HENCE THE THEATRICS.
CONSTEL-LATIONS, PLEASE...
NOT TO MENTION THE HIDDEN SCENARIO'S STARTED.
HEY, CAN YOU HELP ME FIRST?
...THE SEARCH BUTTON'S IN THE BOTTOM RIGHT CORNER.
THANKS.
MY CART
MORE
HUMANS AND GOBLINS ARE ALL THE SAME WHEN IT COMES TO MONEY-GRUBBING.
I GET FIVE FREE SEARCHES BEFORE I HAVE TO PAY?
IT'LL TAKE TWO SEARCHES TO GET EVERYTHING I NEED, SO...
SEARCH "ANCIENT DRAGON."
?!

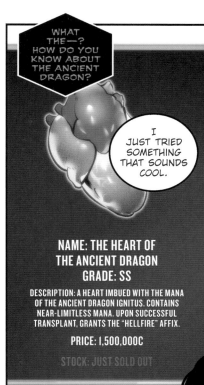

WHAT THE—? HOW DO YOU KNOW ABOUT THE ANCIENT DRAGON?

I JUST TRIED SOMETHING THAT SOUNDS COOL.

NAME: THE HEART OF THE ANCIENT DRAGON

GRADE: SS

DESCRIPTION: A HEART IMBUED WITH THE MANA OF THE ANCIENT DRAGON IGNITUS. CONTAINS NEAR-LIMITLESS MANA. UPON SUCCESSFUL TRANSPLANT, GRANTS THE "HELLFIRE" AFFIX.

PRICE: 1,500,000C

STOCK: JUST SOLD OUT

SOUNDS LIKE A LIE...

AS I THOUGHT, IT'S SOLD OUT...

ACCORDING TO TWSA, THE OWNER OF THIS HEART IS IN ITALY RIGHT NOW.

LUCKY BASTARD. HE HAS A FILTHY-RICH SPONSOR WHO BUYS HIM HIGH-LEVEL ITEMS LIKE THIS.

HOW THE HELL DID YOU KNOW ABOUT THOSE?

SEARCH "ARCH-DEMON'S EYEBALL."

SEARCH "WHITE STAR WEAPON AURA."

ALL THAT FUSS, AND YOU ENDED UP BUYING...

YOU DON'T NEED TO KNOW.

...FOUR BAGS OF MUCUS AND FOUR THORNS?

WHAT'RE YOU GONNA DO WITH THAT JUNK?

[ITEM]

STONE HOG'S SHARP THORN

STOCK: 17
PRICE: 100C

[ITEM]

HAMMER SEAHORSE'S MUCUS

STOCK: 124
PRICE: 100C

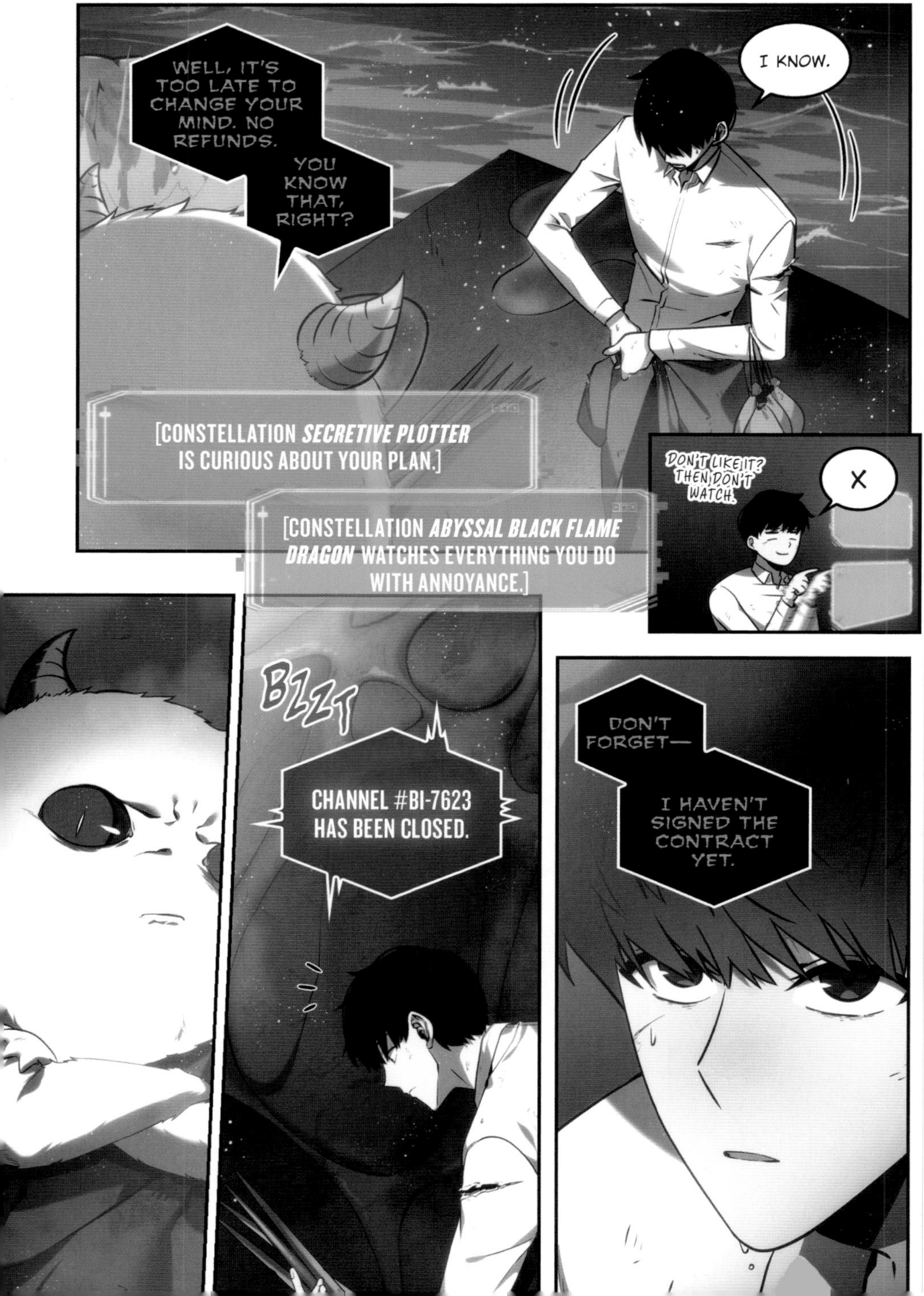
WELL, IT'S TOO LATE TO CHANGE YOUR MIND. NO REFUNDS.
YOU KNOW THAT, RIGHT?
I KNOW.
[CONSTELLATION SECRETIVE PLOTTER IS CURIOUS ABOUT YOUR PLAN.]
DON'T LIKE IT? THEN DON'T WATCH.
X
[CONSTELLATION ABYSSAL BLACK FLAME DRAGON WATCHES EVERYTHING YOU DO WITH ANNOYANCE.]
BZZT
CHANNEL #BI-7623 HAS BEEN CLOSED.
DON'T FORGET—
I HAVEN'T SIGNED THE CONTRACT YET.

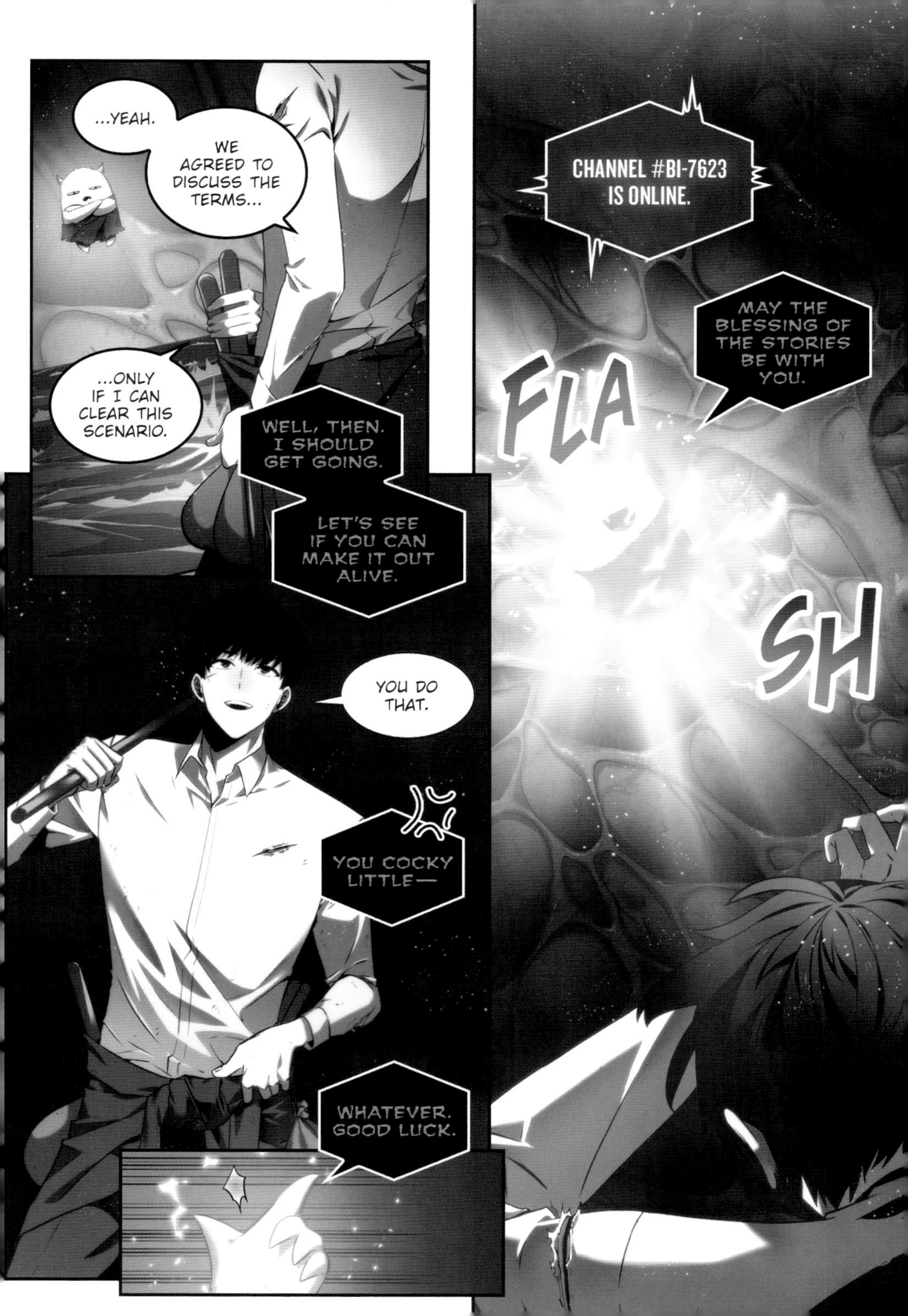
...YEAH.
WE AGREED TO DISCUSS THE TERMS...
...ONLY IF I CAN CLEAR THIS SCENARIO.
WELL, THEN. I SHOULD GET GOING.
LET'S SEE IF YOU CAN MAKE IT OUT ALIVE.
YOU DO THAT.
YOU COCKY LITTLE—
WHATEVER. GOOD LUCK.
CHANNEL #BI-7623 IS ONLINE.
MAY THE BLESSING OF THE STORIES BE WITH YOU.
FLASH

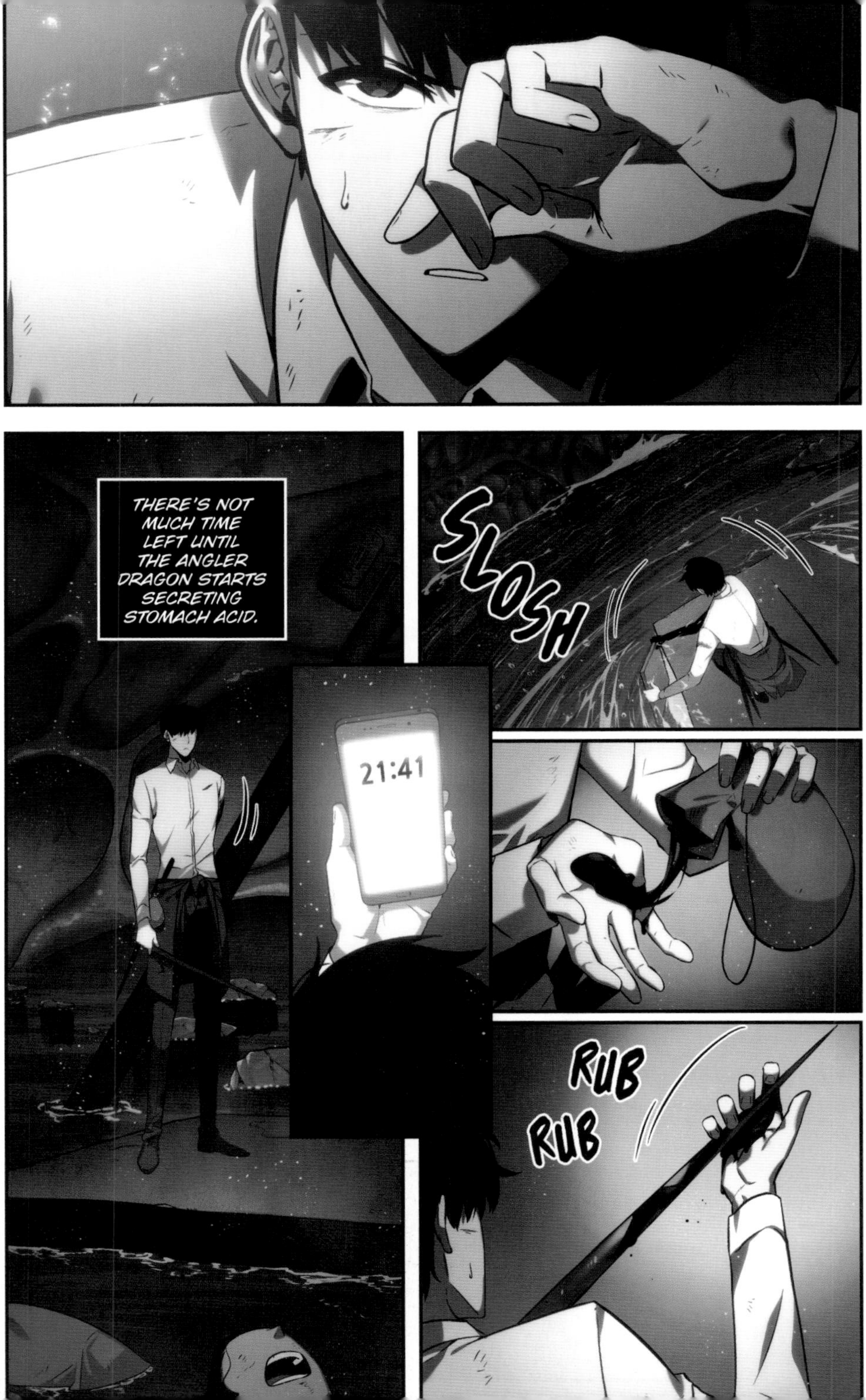
THERE'S NOT MUCH TIME LEFT UNTIL THE ANGLER DRAGON STARTS SECRETING STOMACH ACID.
SLOSH
21:41
RUB RUB

SHF

FSSS

PSHK

PSHK

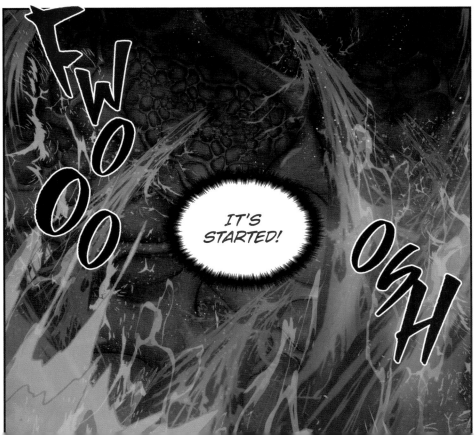

FWOOOO

IT'S STARTED!

OSSH

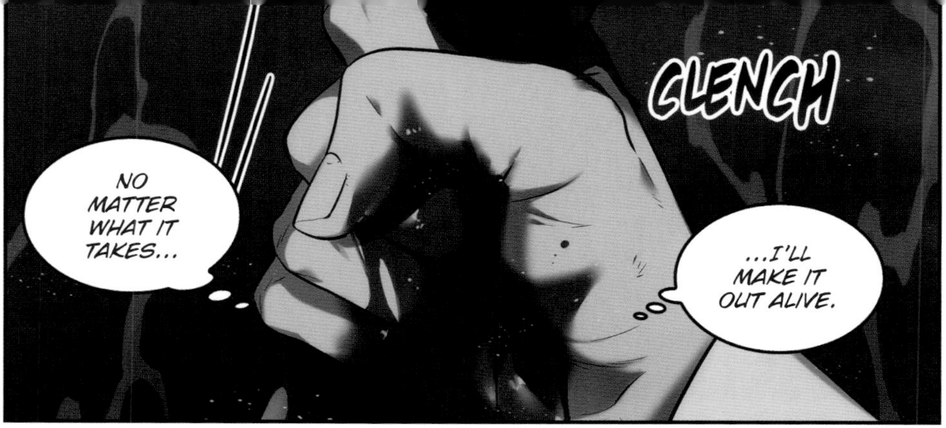
CLENCH
NO MATTER WHAT IT TAKES...
...I'LL MAKE IT OUT ALIVE.
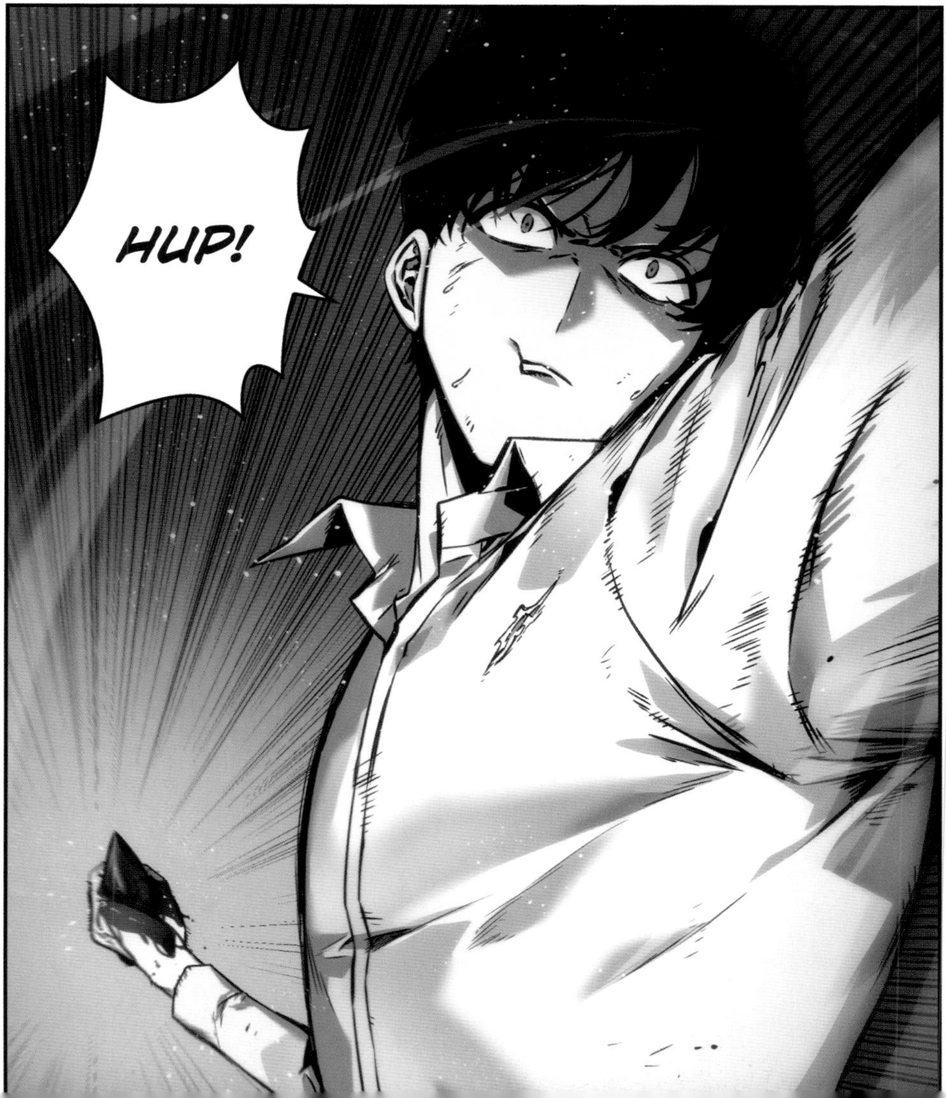
HUP!

EP. 03

Omniscient
Reader's
Viewpoint

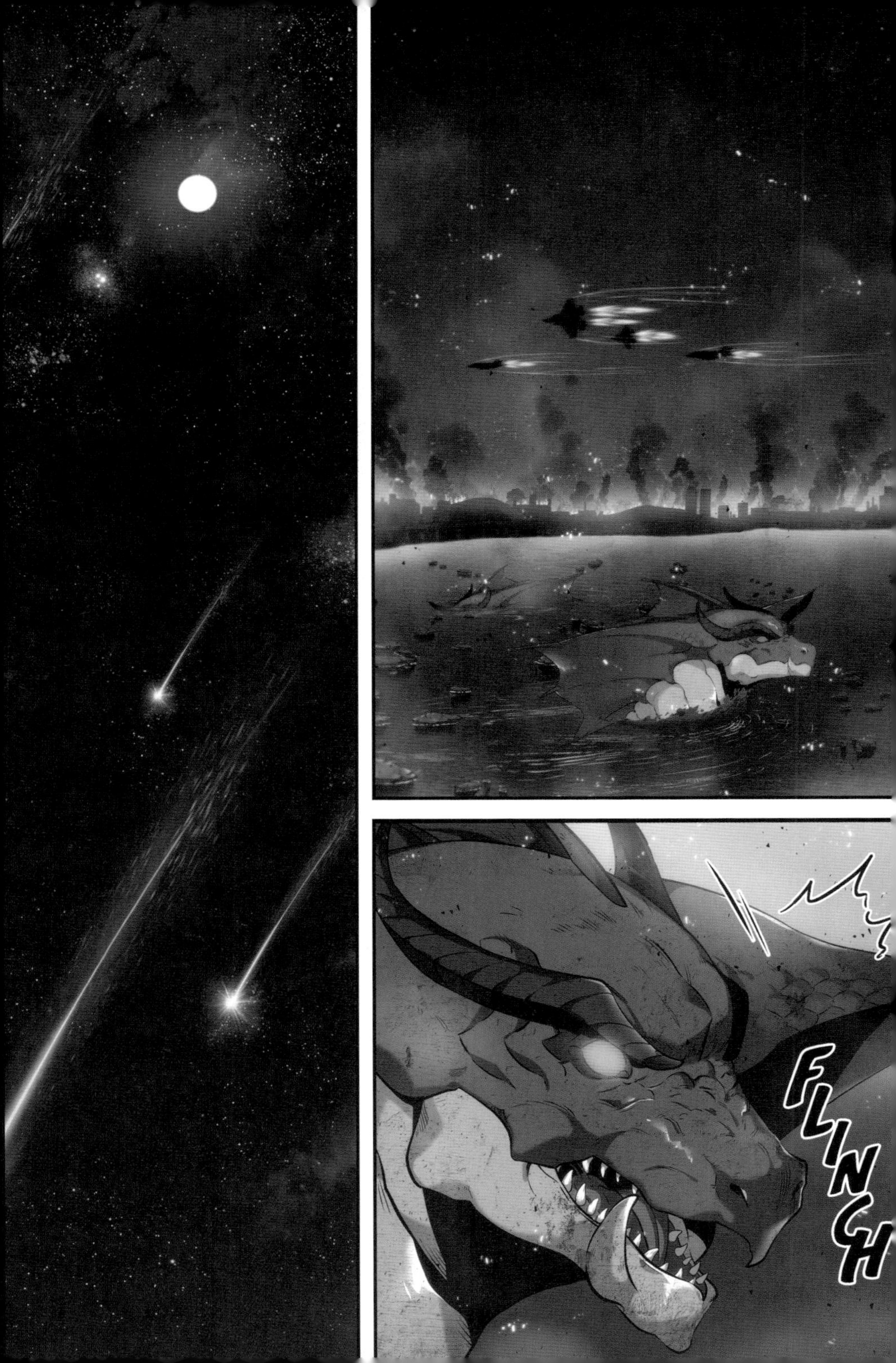
FLINCH

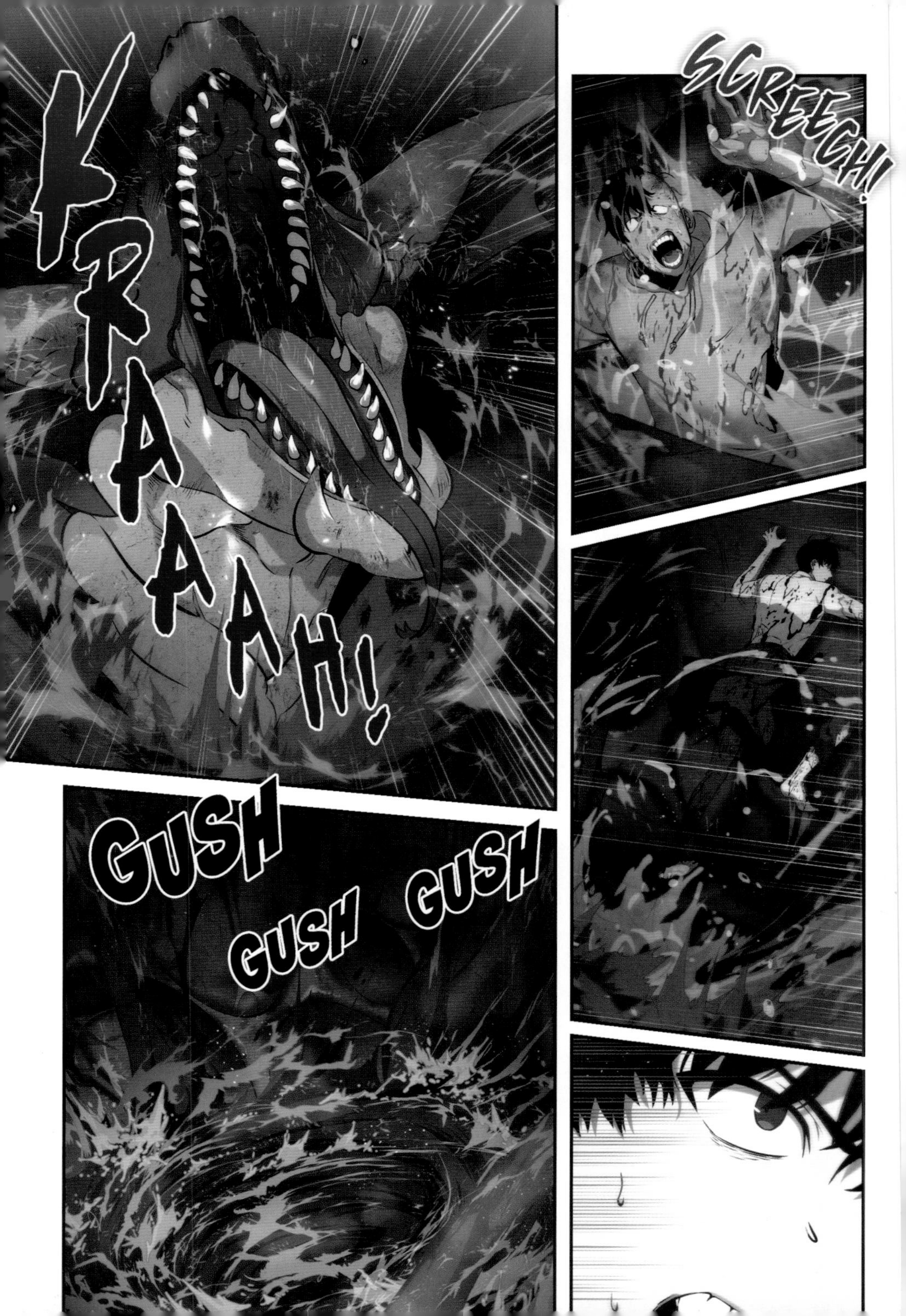
SCREECH!
KRAAAAH!
GUSH
GUSH
GUSH

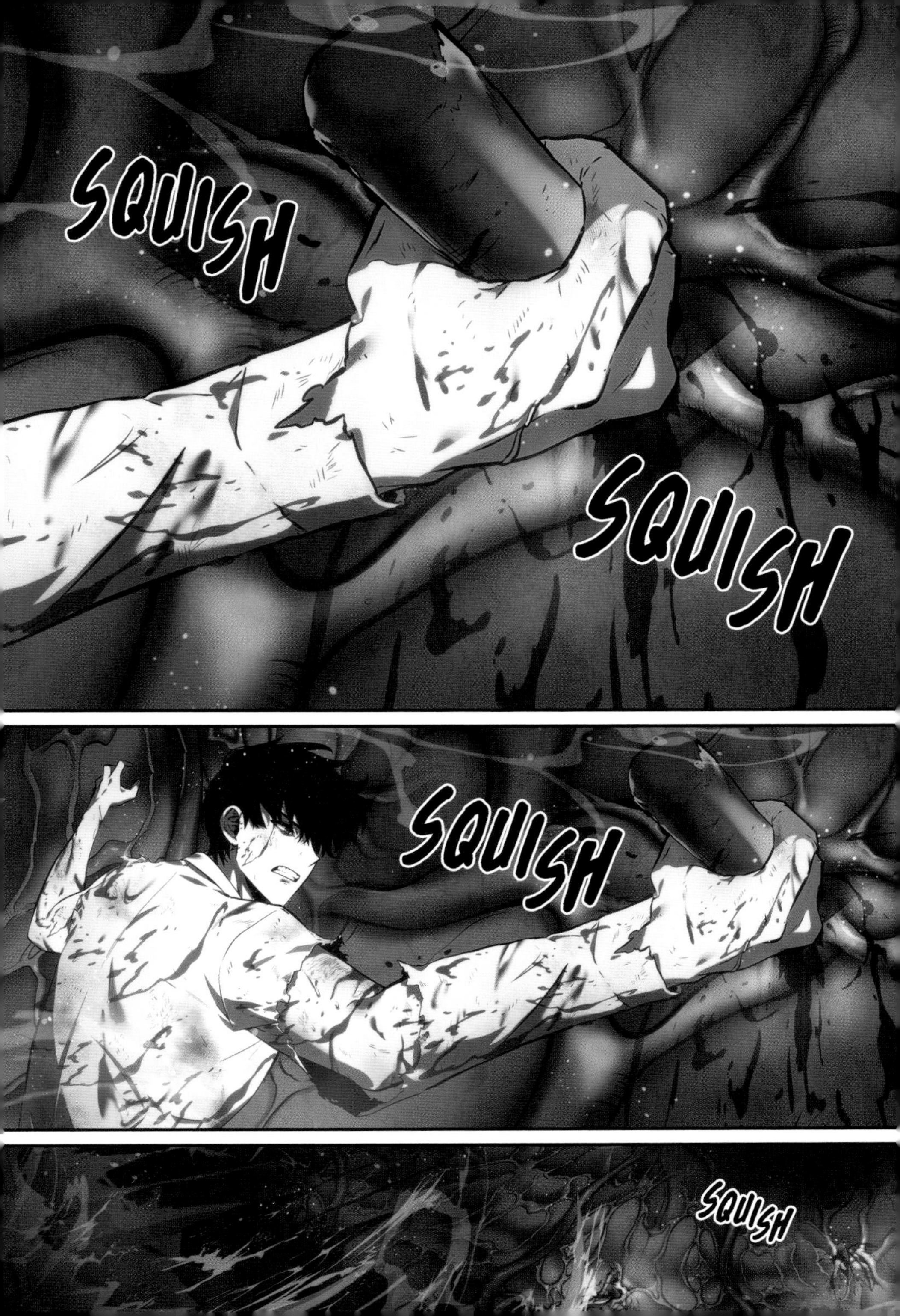
SQUISH
SQUISH
SQUISH
SQUISH

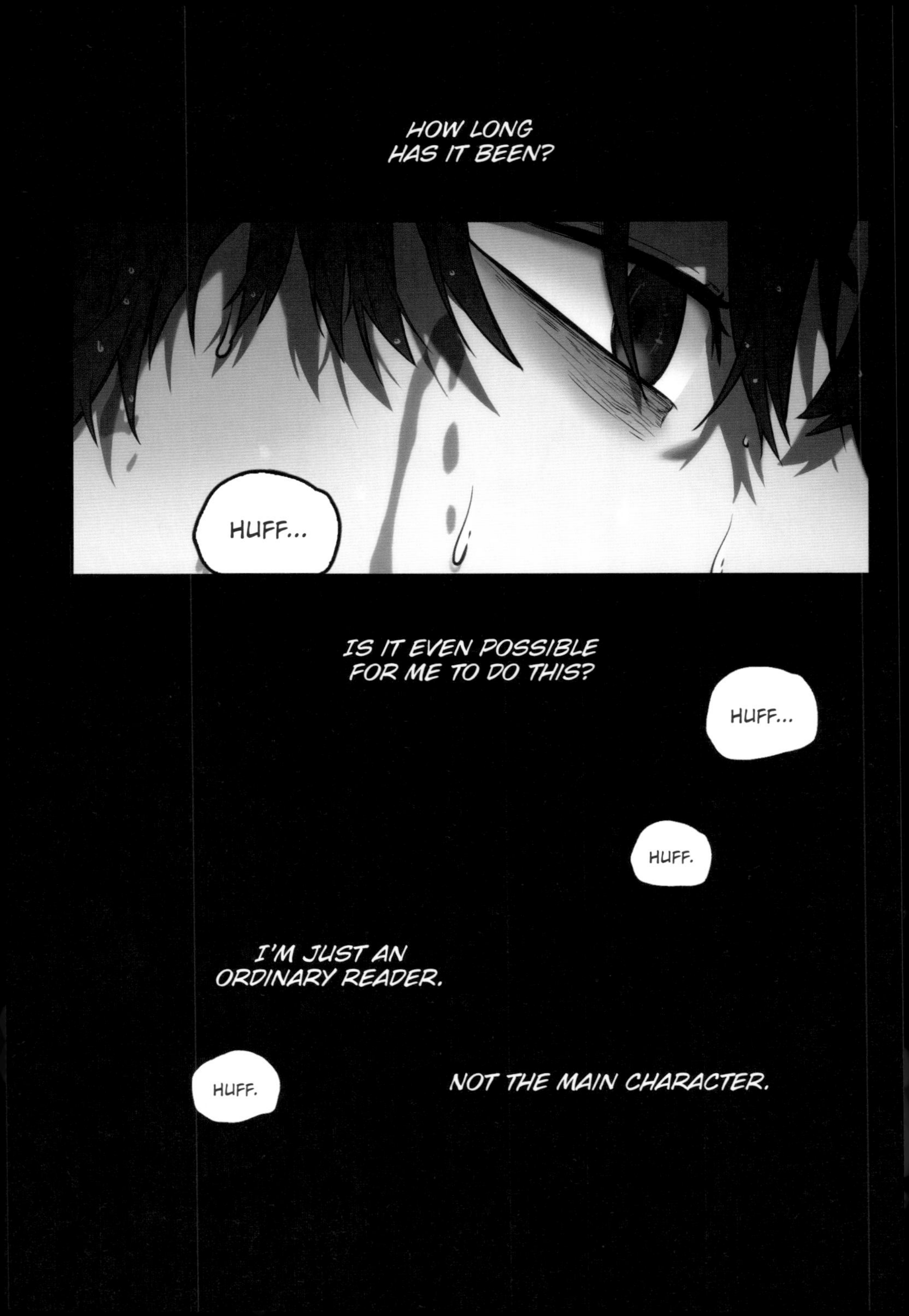
HOW LONG HAS IT BEEN?
HUFF...
IS IT EVEN POSSIBLE FOR ME TO DO THIS?
HUFF...
HUFF.
I'M JUST AN ORDINARY READER.
HUFF.
NOT THE MAIN CHARACTER.

...I WONDER IF MOTHER IS OKAY.

I'M SURE SHE IS. IT'S **MOTHER** WE'RE TALKING ABOUT.

BLINK

...THIS ISN'T A DREAM, IS IT?

STILL, I WISH IT WERE.

HUFF.

THE OLD WORLD WASN'T EXACTLY A PARADISE...

...BUT AT LEAST I DIDN'T HAVE TO WORRY ABOUT DYING...IN A FISH GUT...

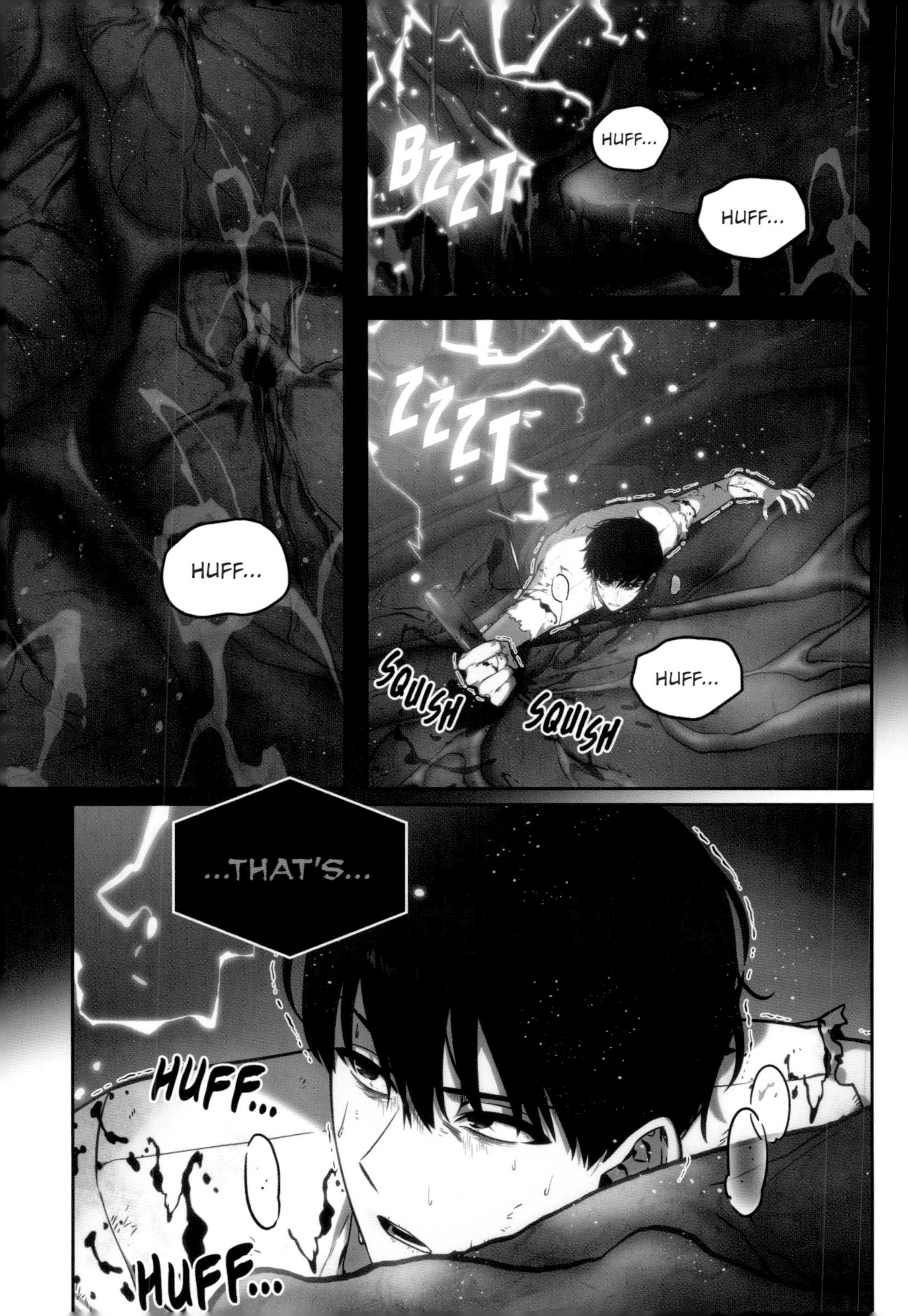
BZZT
HUFF...
HUFF...
HUFF...
ZZZT
SQUISH
SQUISH
HUFF...
...THAT'S...
HUFF...
HUFF...

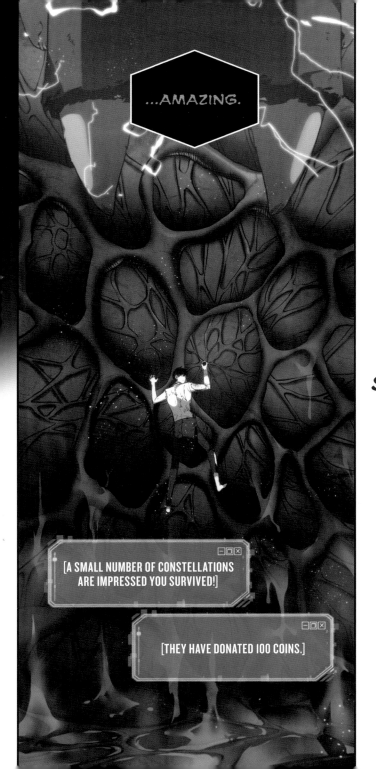

...AMAZING.

SINCE
THE
SCENARIO
STARTED
...

[A SMALL NUMBER OF CONSTELLATIONS
ARE IMPRESSED YOU SURVIVED!]

[THEY HAVE DONATED 100 COINS.]

...FOUR DAYS HAVE PASSED.

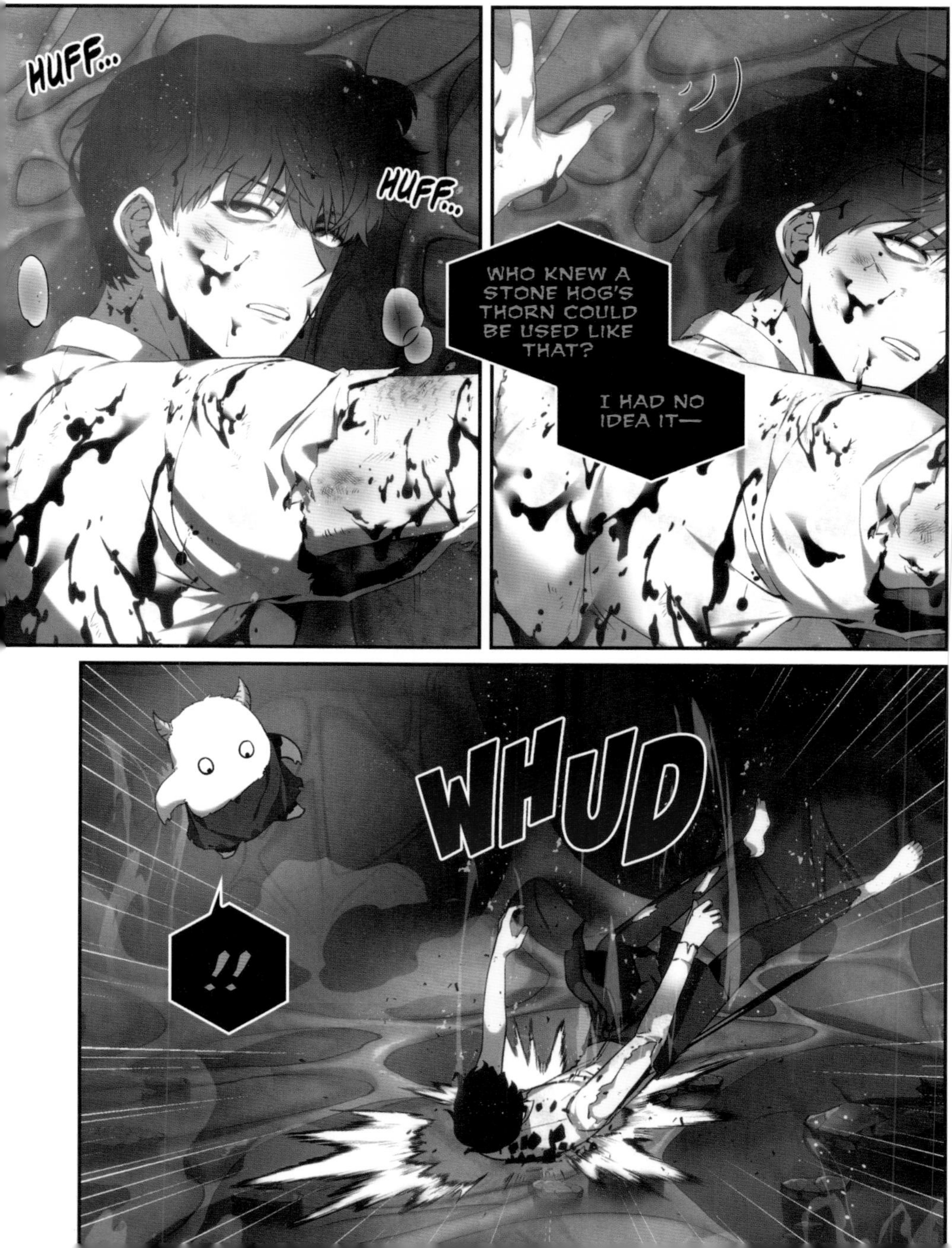
HUFF...
HUFF...
WHO KNEW A STONE HOG'S THORN COULD BE USED LIKE THAT?
I HAD NO IDEA IT—
WHUD
!!

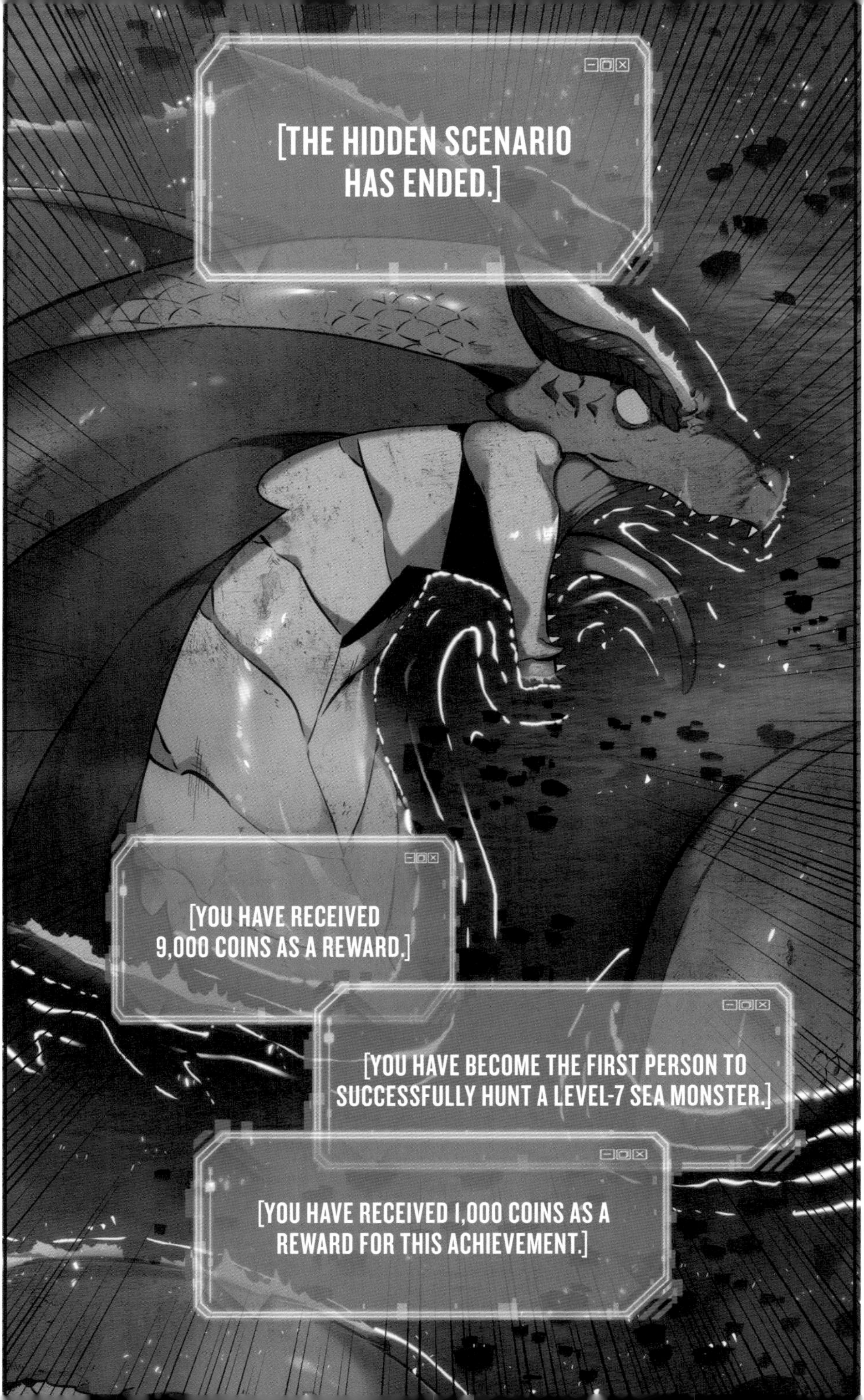
[THE HIDDEN SCENARIO HAS ENDED.]
[YOU HAVE RECEIVED 9,000 COINS AS A REWARD.]
[YOU HAVE BECOME THE FIRST PERSON TO SUCCESSFULLY HUNT A LEVEL-7 SEA MONSTER.]
[YOU HAVE RECEIVED 1,000 COINS AS A REWARD FOR THIS ACHIEVEMENT.]

HUFF...

HUFF...

PHEW.

I MADE IT...

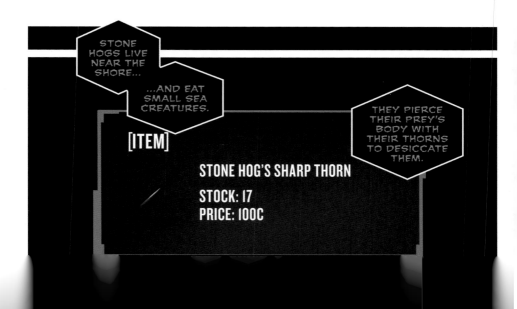

STONE HOGS LIVE NEAR THE SHORE...

...AND EAT SMALL SEA CREATURES.

THEY PIERCE THEIR PREY'S BODY WITH THEIR THORNS TO DESICCATE THEM.

[ITEM]

STONE HOG'S SHARP THORN

STOCK: 17
PRICE: 100C

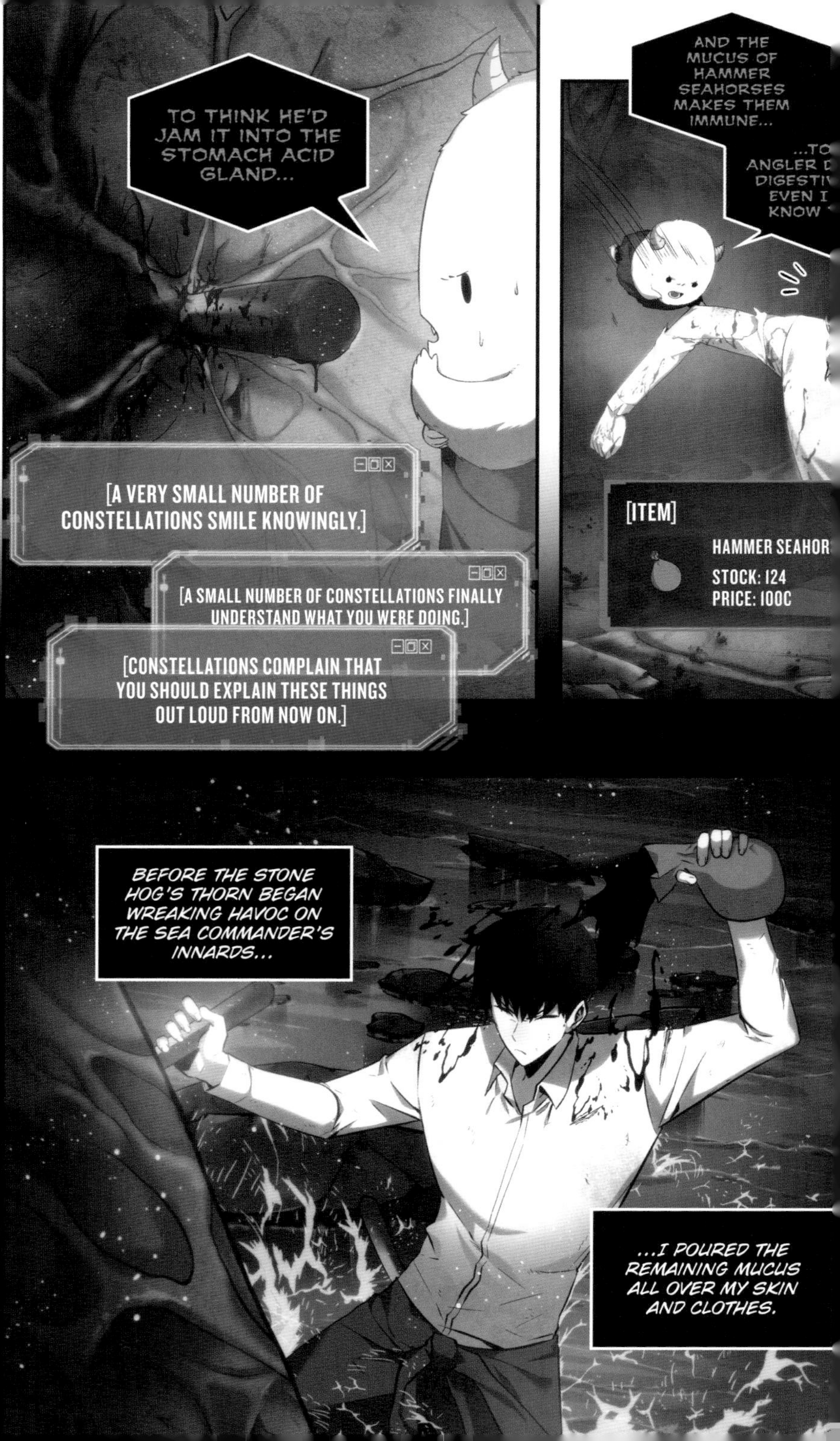
TO THINK HE'D JAM IT INTO THE STOMACH ACID GLAND...
[A VERY SMALL NUMBER OF CONSTELLATIONS SMILE KNOWINGLY.]
[A SMALL NUMBER OF CONSTELLATIONS FINALLY UNDERSTAND WHAT YOU WERE DOING.]
[CONSTELLATIONS COMPLAIN THAT YOU SHOULD EXPLAIN THESE THINGS OUT LOUD FROM NOW ON.]
AND THE MUCUS OF HAMMER SEAHORSES MAKES THEM IMMUNE...
[ITEM]
STOCK: 124
PRICE: 100C
BEFORE THE STONE HOG'S THORN BEGAN WREAKING HAVOC ON THE SEA COMMANDER'S INNARDS...
...I POURED THE REMAINING MUCUS ALL OVER MY SKIN AND CLOTHES.

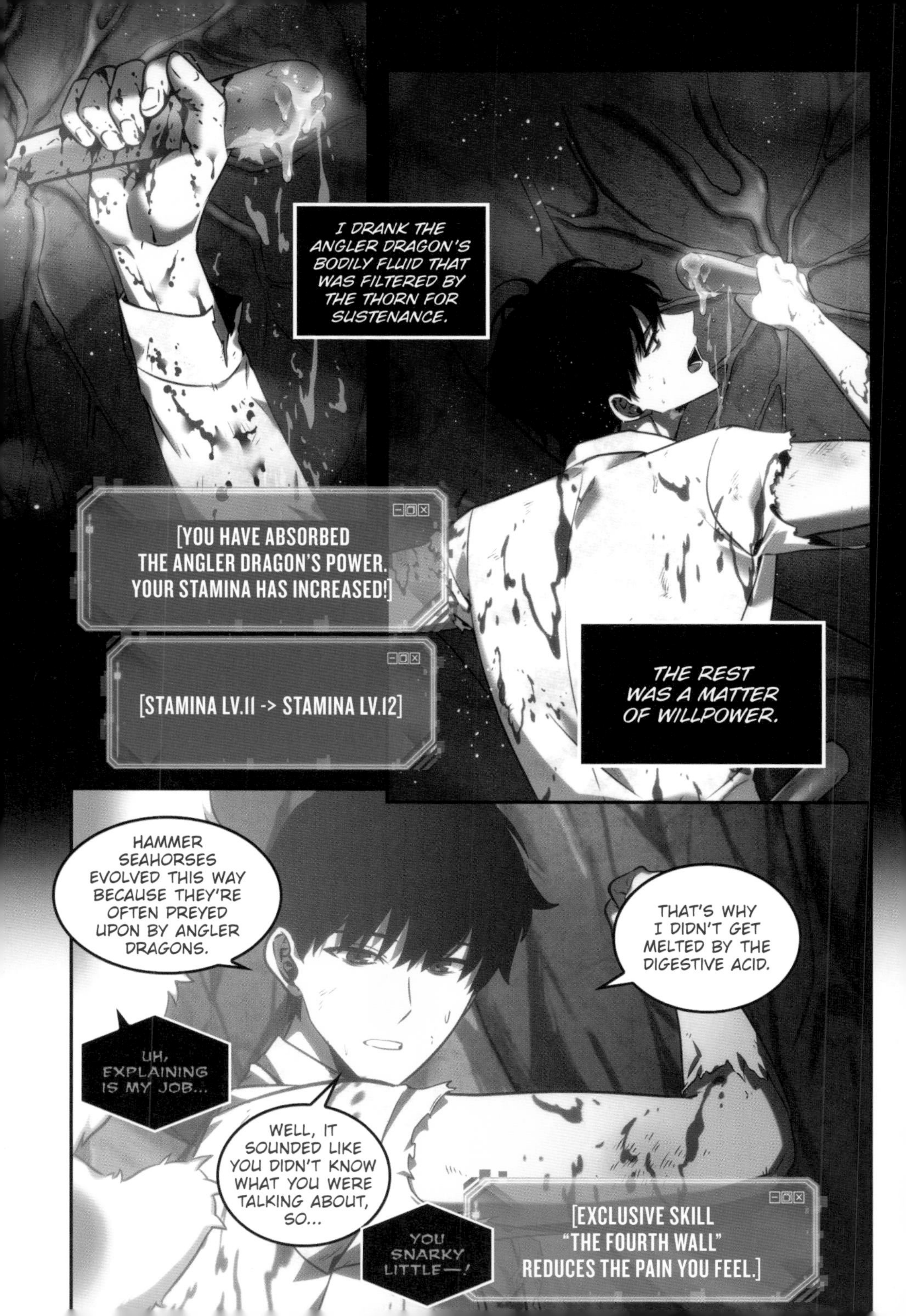
I DRANK THE ANGLER DRAGON'S BODILY FLUID THAT WAS FILTERED BY THE THORN FOR SUSTENANCE.
[YOU HAVE ABSORBED THE ANGLER DRAGON'S POWER. YOUR STAMINA HAS INCREASED!]
[STAMINA LV.11 -> STAMINA LV.12]
THE REST WAS A MATTER OF WILLPOWER.
HAMMER SEAHORSES EVOLVED THIS WAY BECAUSE THEY'RE OFTEN PREYED UPON BY ANGLER DRAGONS.
THAT'S WHY I DIDN'T GET MELTED BY THE DIGESTIVE ACID.
UH, EXPLAINING IS MY JOB...
WELL, IT SOUNDED LIKE YOU DIDN'T KNOW WHAT YOU WERE TALKING ABOUT, SO...
YOU SNARKY LITTLE—!
[EXCLUSIVE SKILL "THE FOURTH WALL" REDUCES THE PAIN YOU FEEL.]

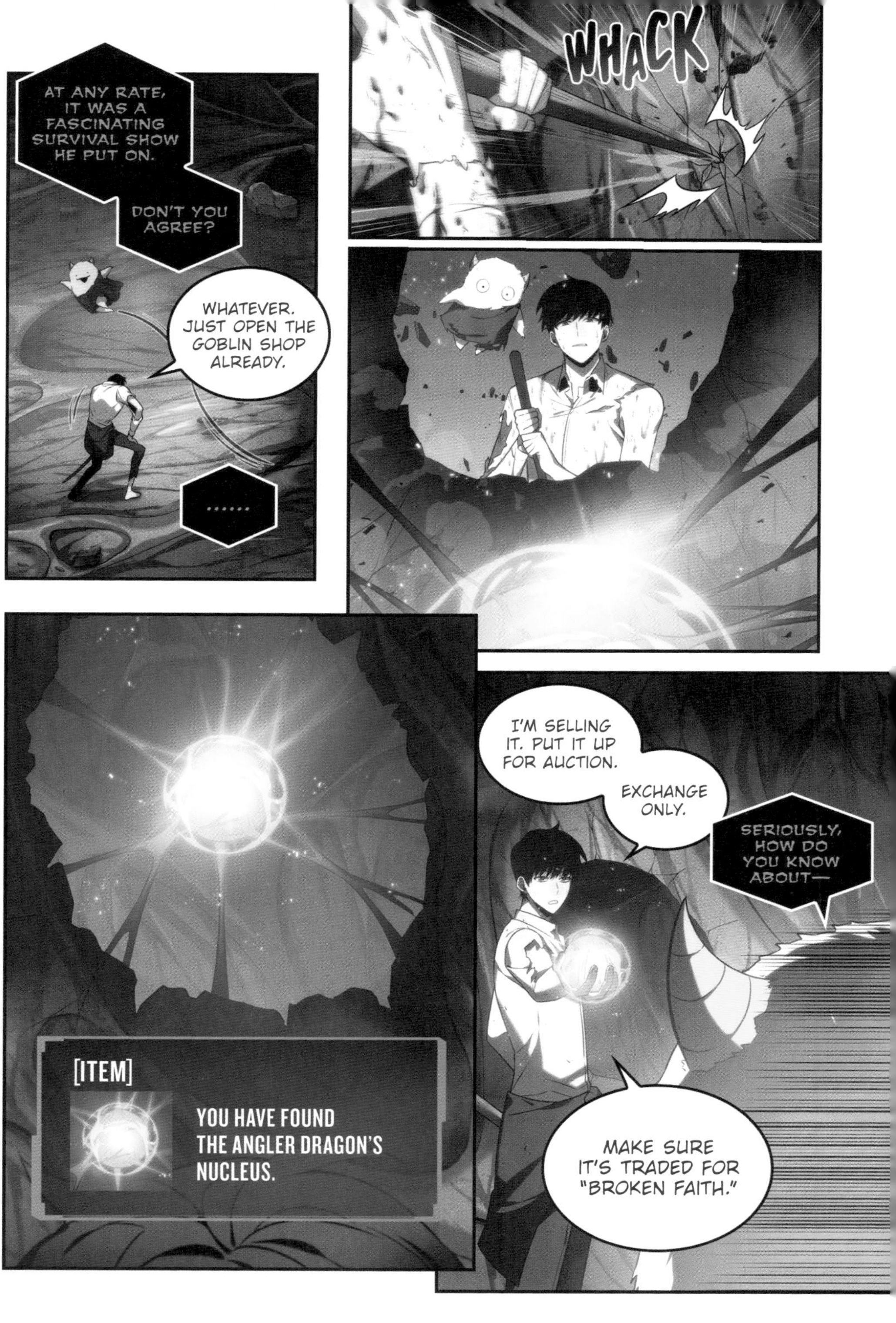
AT ANY RATE, IT WAS A FASCINATING SURVIVAL SHOW HE PUT ON.
DON'T YOU AGREE?
WHATEVER. JUST OPEN THE GOBLIN SHOP ALREADY.
......
WHACK
[ITEM]
YOU HAVE FOUND THE ANGLER DRAGON'S NUCLEUS.
I'M SELLING IT. PUT IT UP FOR AUCTION.
EXCHANGE ONLY.
SERIOUSLY, HOW DO YOU KNOW ABOUT—
MAKE SURE IT'S TRADED FOR "BROKEN FAITH."

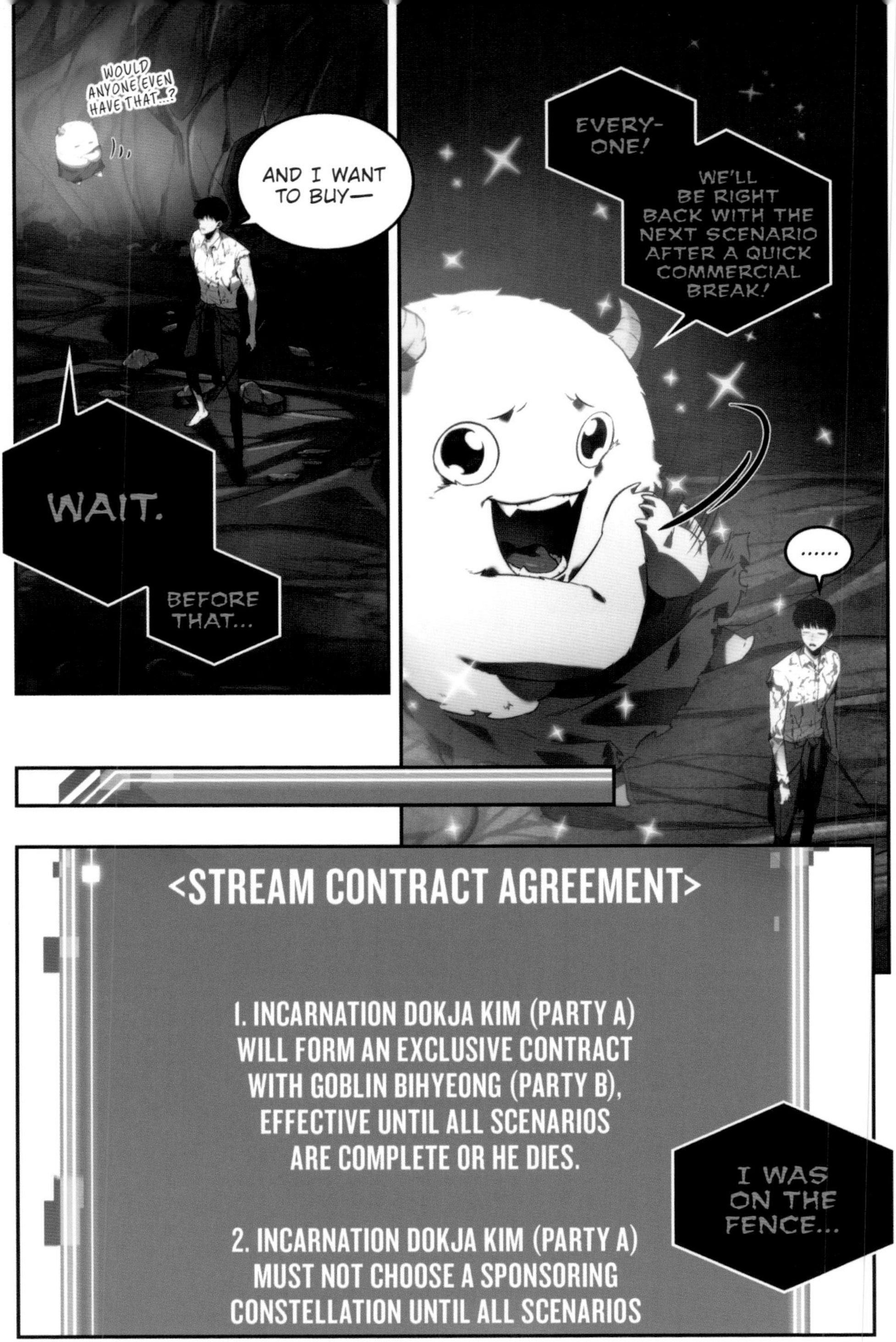

WOULD ANYONE EVEN HAVE THAT...?
AND I WANT TO BUY—
WAIT.
BEFORE THAT...
EVERY-ONE!
WE'LL BE RIGHT BACK WITH THE NEXT SCENARIO AFTER A QUICK COMMERCIAL BREAK!
......
<STREAM CONTRACT AGREEMENT>
1. INCARNATION DOKJA KIM (PARTY A) WILL FORM AN EXCLUSIVE CONTRACT WITH GOBLIN BIHYEONG (PARTY B), EFFECTIVE UNTIL ALL SCENARIOS ARE COMPLETE OR HE DIES.
2. INCARNATION DOKJA KIM (PARTY A) MUST NOT CHOOSE A SPONSORING CONSTELLATION UNTIL ALL SCENARIOS
I WAS ON THE FENCE...

...BUT WATCHING YOU CLEAR THIS SCENARIO CONVINCED ME.

...I'M PARTY A?

HUMANS LIKE COMING FIRST, RIGHT?

EVEN THOUGH IT'S MEANINGLESS HERE.

LET'S GIVE IT A SHOT.

THIS IS SURPRISINGLY WELL WRITTEN. NO HIDDEN TRICKS.

‹STREAM CONTRACT AGREEMENT›

EXCEPT FOR ONE THING.

1. INCARNATION DOKJA KIM (PARTY A) ...IVE CONTRACT ... (PARTY B), ...ENARIOS ...E DIES.

2. INCARNATION DOKJA KIM (PARTY A) MUST NOT CHOOSE A SPONSORING CONSTELLATION UNTIL ALL SCENARIOS ARE COMPLETE OR HE DIES.

3. INCARNATION DOKJA KIM (PARTY A) MUST ONLY APPEAR IN THE CHANNEL RUN BY BIHYEONG (PARTY B).

4. INCARNATION DOKJA KIM (PARTY A) AND BIHYEONG (PARTY B) WILL SHARE ALL PROFIT COMING FROM THE STREAM CONTRACT, DIVIDED BY A RATIO TO BE AGREED UPON.

THERE'S AN IMPORTANT PART THAT'S MISSING.

YOU MEAN SIGNATURES? YOU CAN JUST SAY YOU AGREE.

A STREAM CONTRACT IS A SOUL OATH, SO—

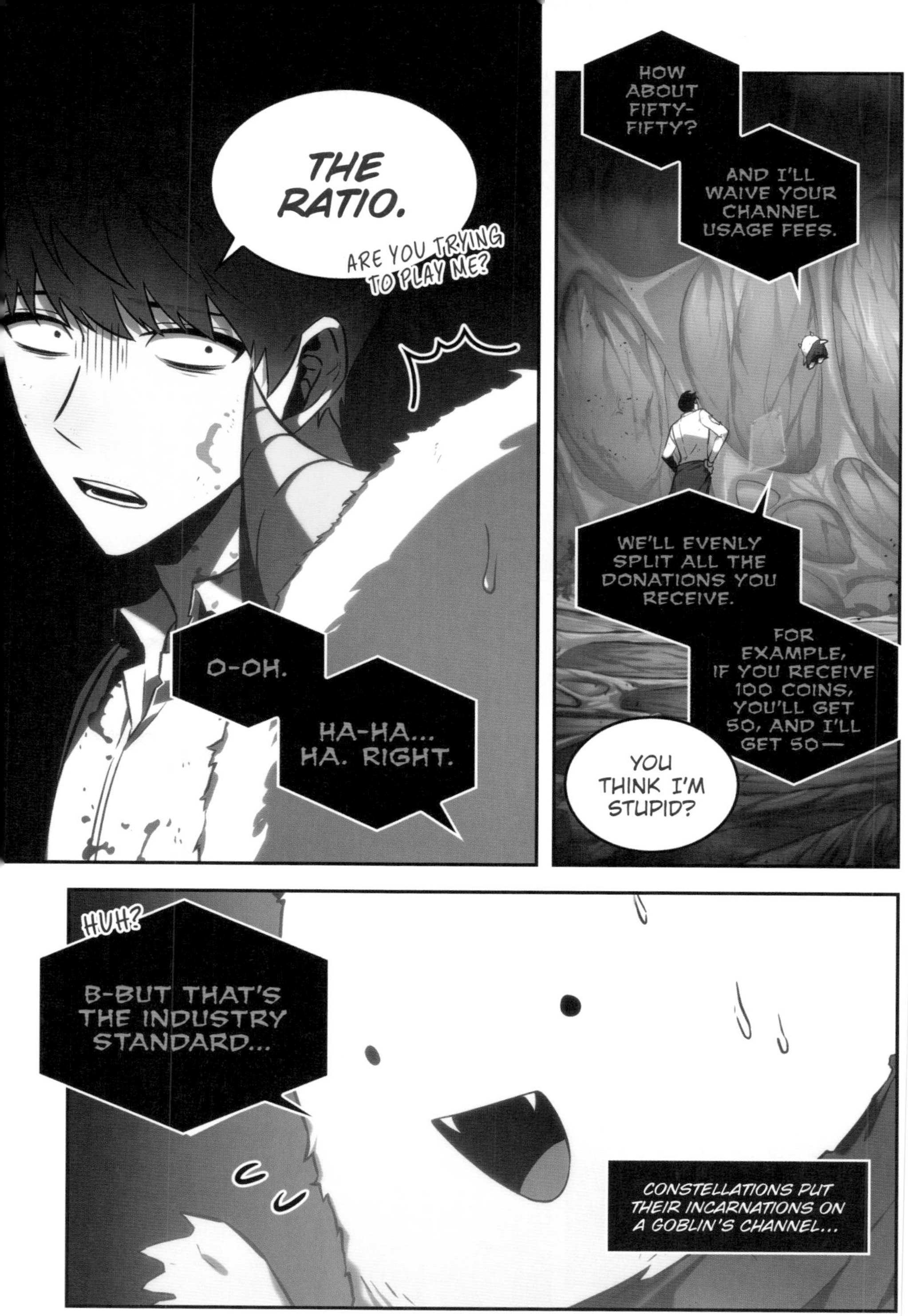
THE RATIO.
ARE YOU TRYING TO PLAY ME?
O-OH.
HA-HA... HA. RIGHT.
HOW ABOUT FIFTY-FIFTY?
AND I'LL WAIVE YOUR CHANNEL USAGE FEES.
WE'LL EVENLY SPLIT ALL THE DONATIONS YOU RECEIVE.
FOR EXAMPLE, IF YOU RECEIVE 100 COINS, YOU'LL GET 50, AND I'LL GET 50—
YOU THINK I'M STUPID?
HUH?
B-BUT THAT'S THE INDUSTRY STANDARD...
CONSTELLATIONS PUT THEIR INCARNATIONS ON A GOBLIN'S CHANNEL...

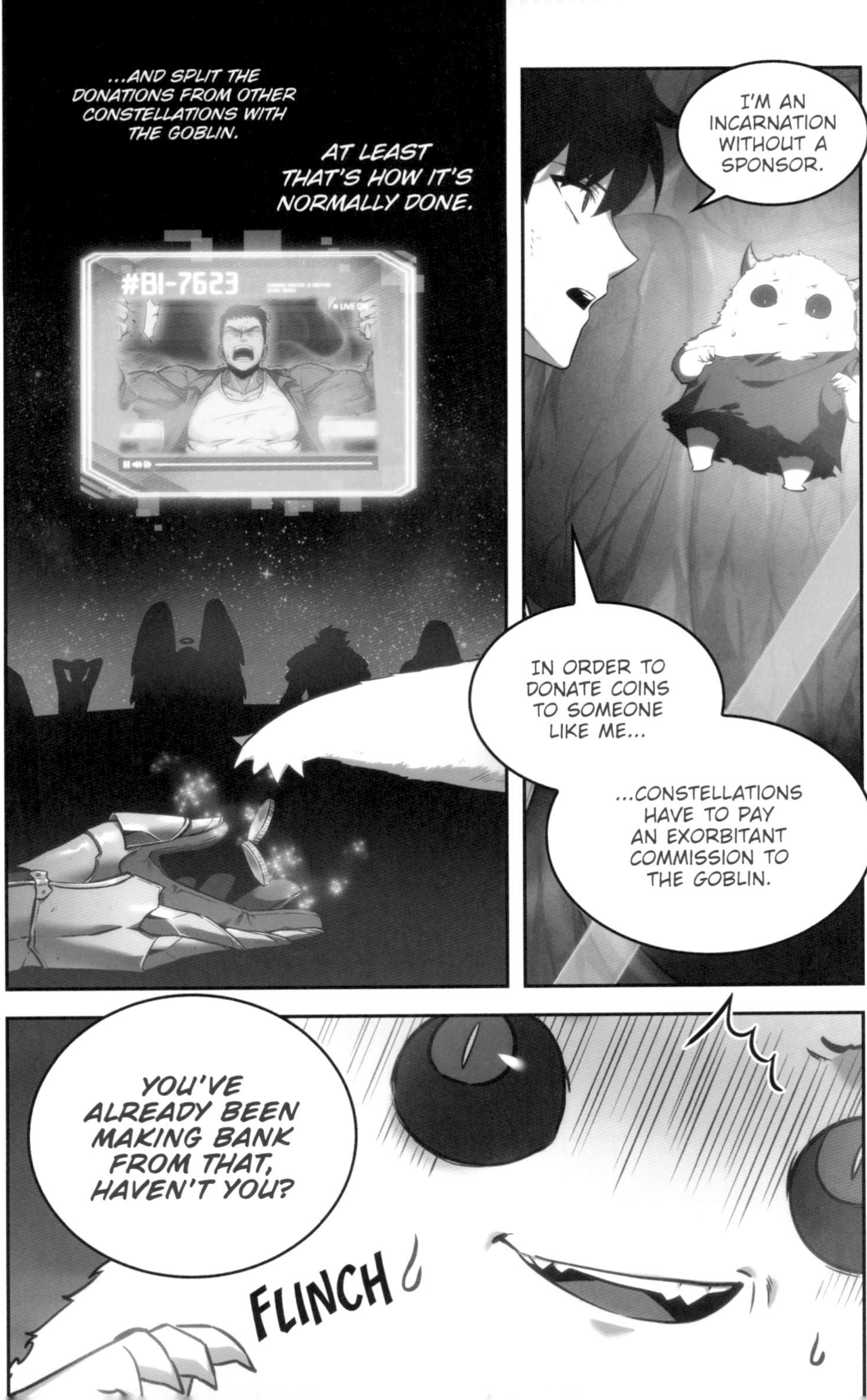
...AND SPLIT THE DONATIONS FROM OTHER CONSTELLATIONS WITH THE GOBLIN.
AT LEAST THAT'S HOW IT'S NORMALLY DONE.
#BI-7623
I'M AN INCARNATION WITHOUT A SPONSOR.
IN ORDER TO DONATE COINS TO SOMEONE LIKE ME...
...CONSTELLATIONS HAVE TO PAY AN EXORBITANT COMMISSION TO THE GOBLIN.
YOU'VE ALREADY BEEN MAKING BANK FROM THAT, HAVEN'T YOU?
FLINCH

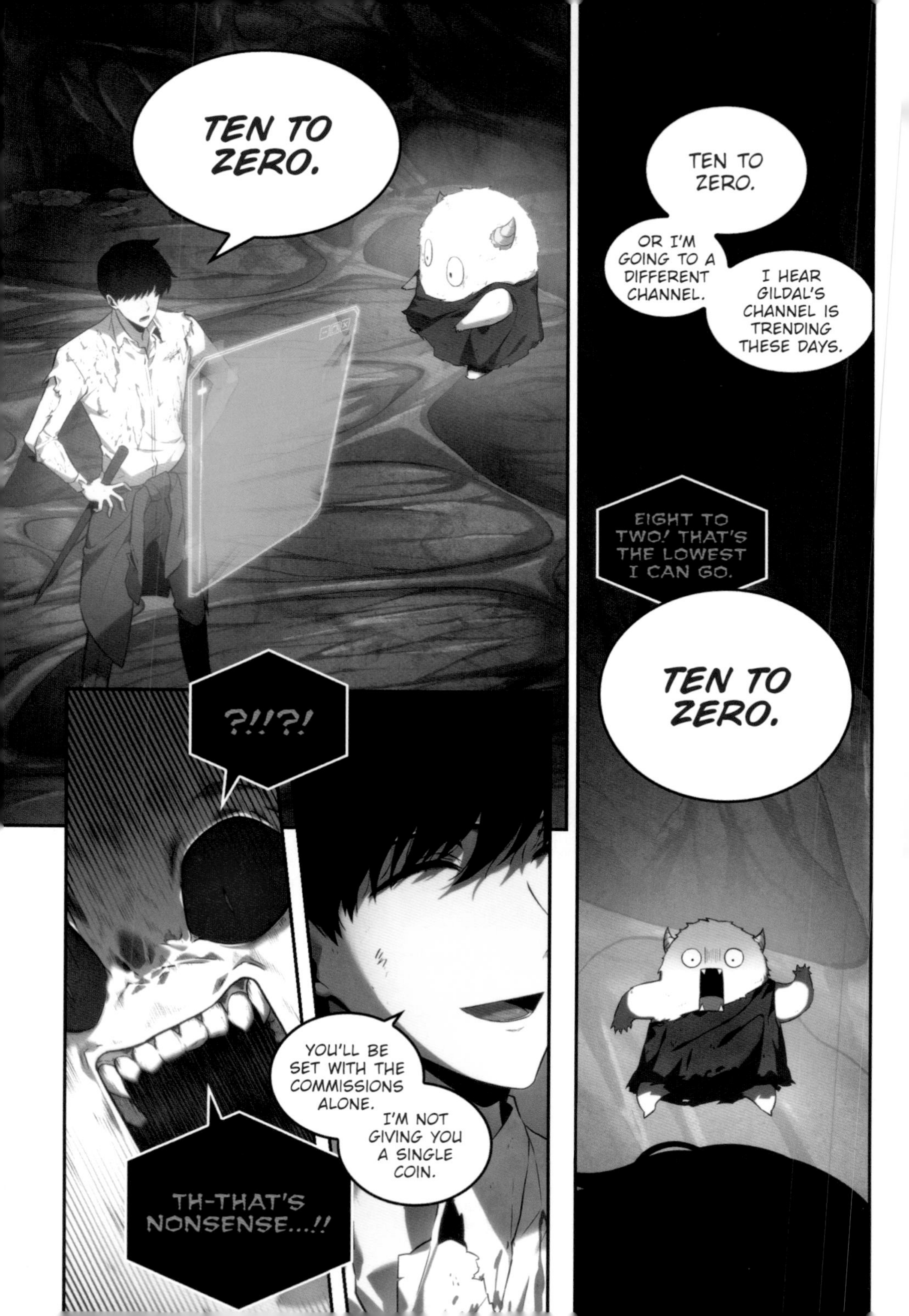
TEN TO ZERO.
TEN TO ZERO.
OR I'M GOING TO A DIFFERENT CHANNEL.
I HEAR GILDAL'S CHANNEL IS TRENDING THESE DAYS.
EIGHT TO TWO! THAT'S THE LOWEST I CAN GO.
TEN TO ZERO.
?!!?!
YOU'LL BE SET WITH THE COMMISSIONS ALONE.
I'M NOT GIVING YOU A SINGLE COIN.
TH-THAT'S NONSENSE...!!

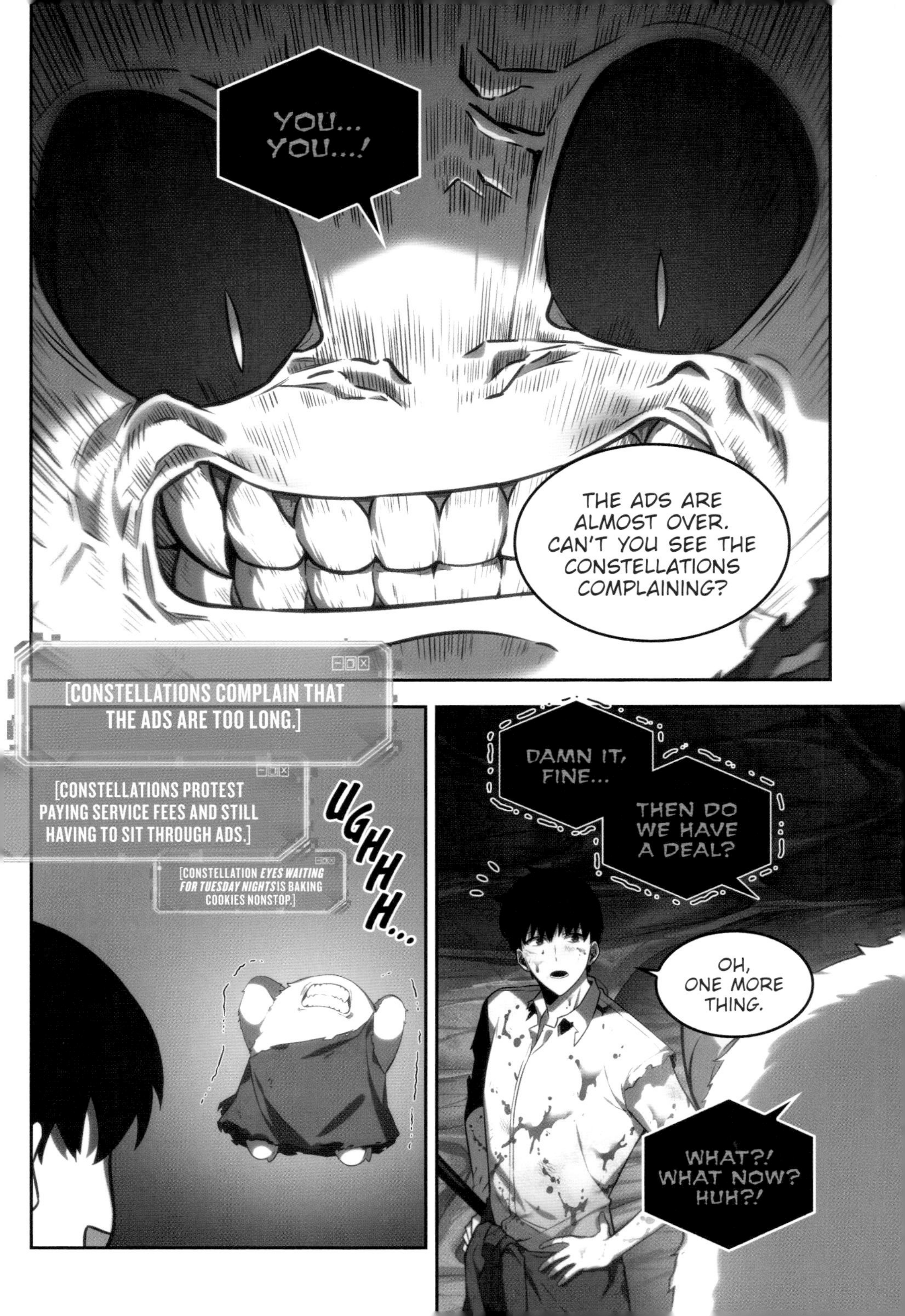
YOU...
YOU...!
THE ADS ARE ALMOST OVER. CAN'T YOU SEE THE CONSTELLATIONS COMPLAINING?
[CONSTELLATIONS COMPLAIN THAT THE ADS ARE TOO LONG.]
[CONSTELLATIONS PROTEST PAYING SERVICE FEES AND STILL HAVING TO SIT THROUGH ADS.]
[CONSTELLATION EYES WAITING FOR TUESDAY NIGHTS IS BAKING COOKIES NONSTOP.]
UGHHH...
DAMN IT, FINE...
THEN DO WE HAVE A DEAL?
OH, ONE MORE THING.
WHAT?! WHAT NOW? HUH?!

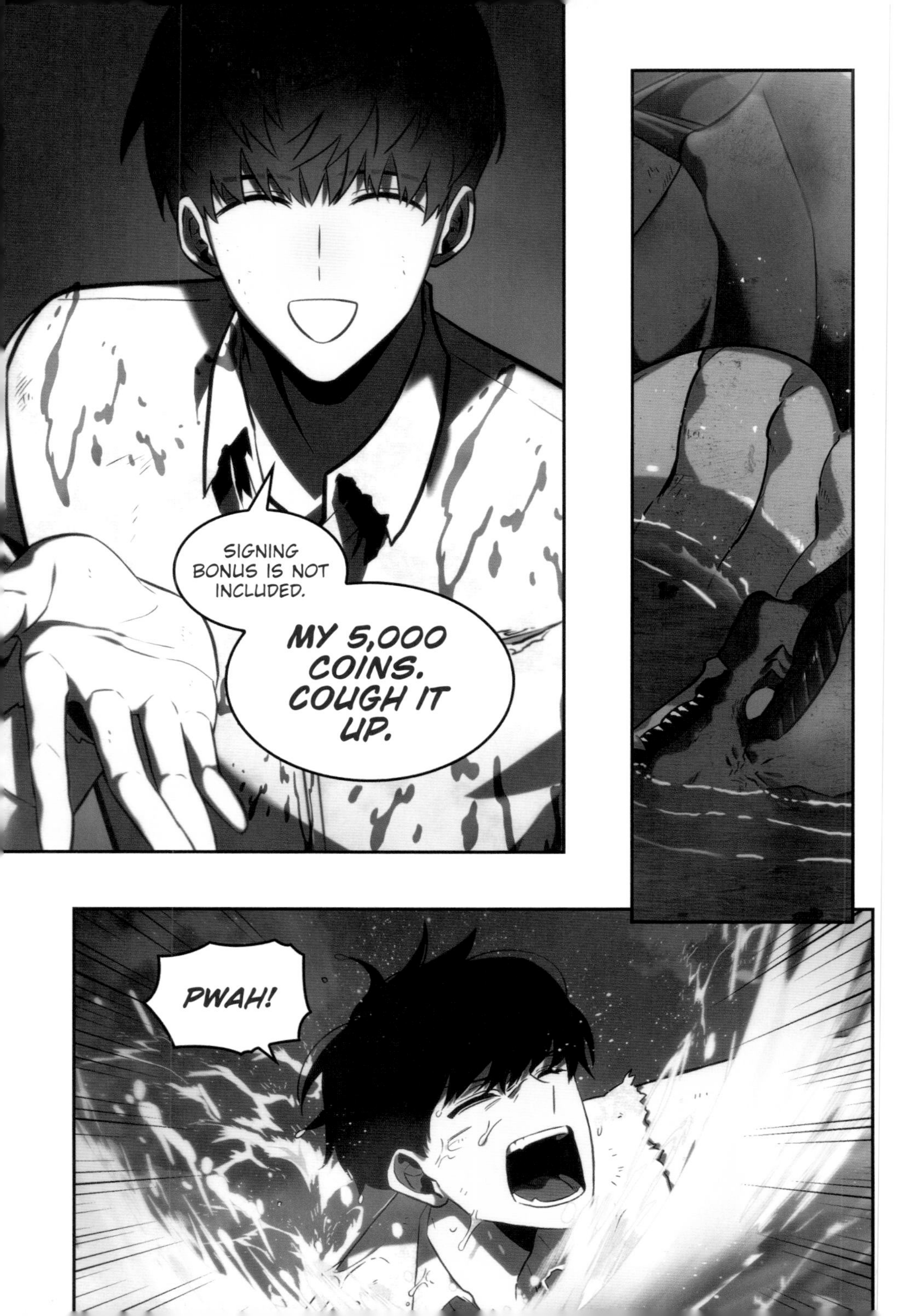
SIGNING BONUS IS NOT INCLUDED.
MY 5,000 COINS. COUGH IT UP.
PWAH!

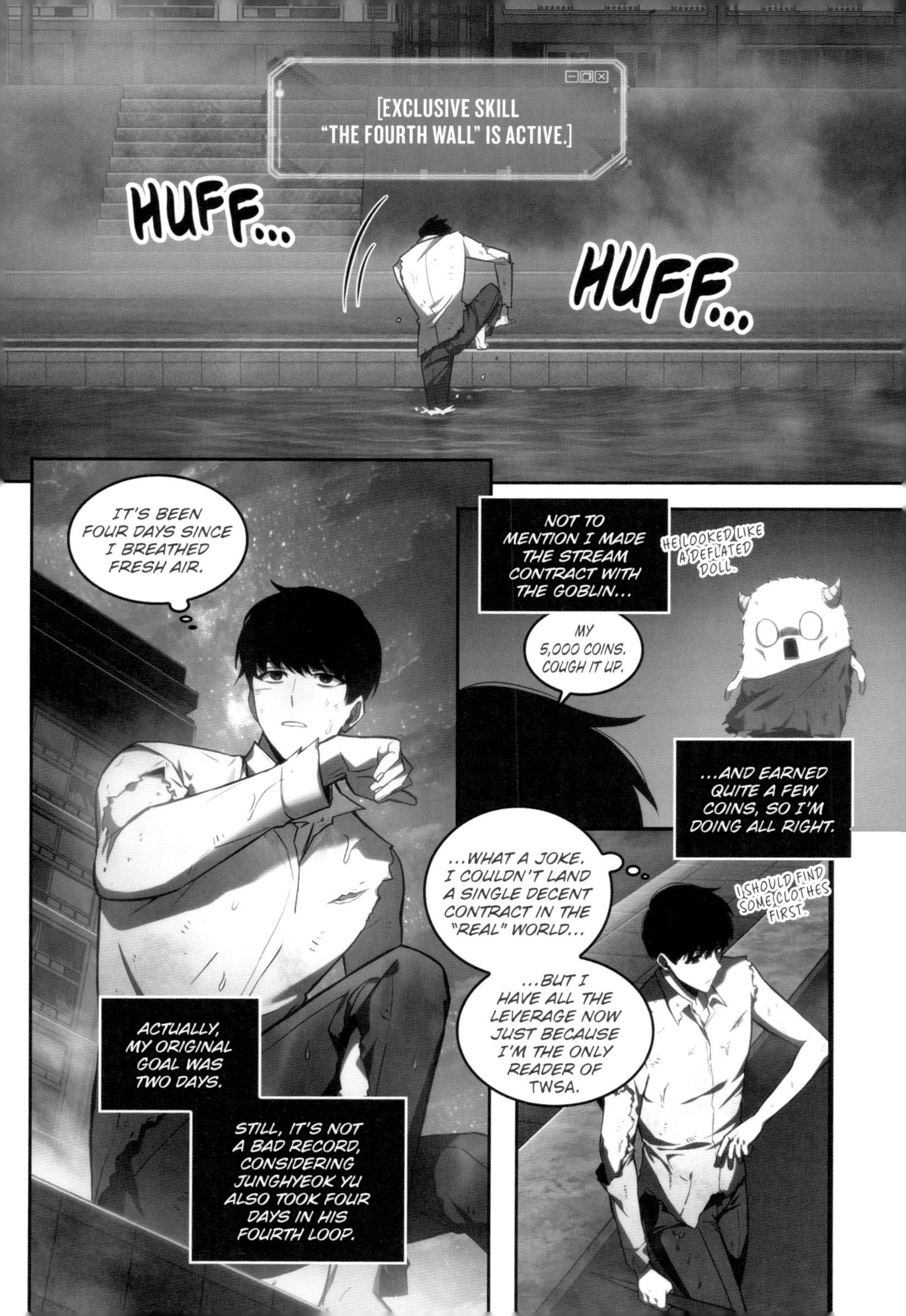
[EXCLUSIVE SKILL
"THE FOURTH WALL" IS ACTIVE.]
HUFF...
HUFF...
IT'S BEEN FOUR DAYS SINCE I BREATHED FRESH AIR.
ACTUALLY, MY ORIGINAL GOAL WAS TWO DAYS.
STILL, IT'S NOT A BAD RECORD, CONSIDERING JUNGHYEOK YU ALSO TOOK FOUR DAYS IN HIS FOURTH LOOP.
NOT TO MENTION I MADE THE STREAM CONTRACT WITH THE GOBLIN...
HE LOOKED LIKE A DEFLATED DOLL.
MY 5,000 COINS. COUGH IT UP.
...AND EARNED QUITE A FEW COINS, SO I'M DOING ALL RIGHT.
...WHAT A JOKE. I COULDN'T LAND A SINGLE DECENT CONTRACT IN THE "REAL" WORLD...
...BUT I HAVE ALL THE LEVERAGE NOW JUST BECAUSE I'M THE ONLY READER OF TWSA.
I SHOULD FIND SOME CLOTHES FIRST.

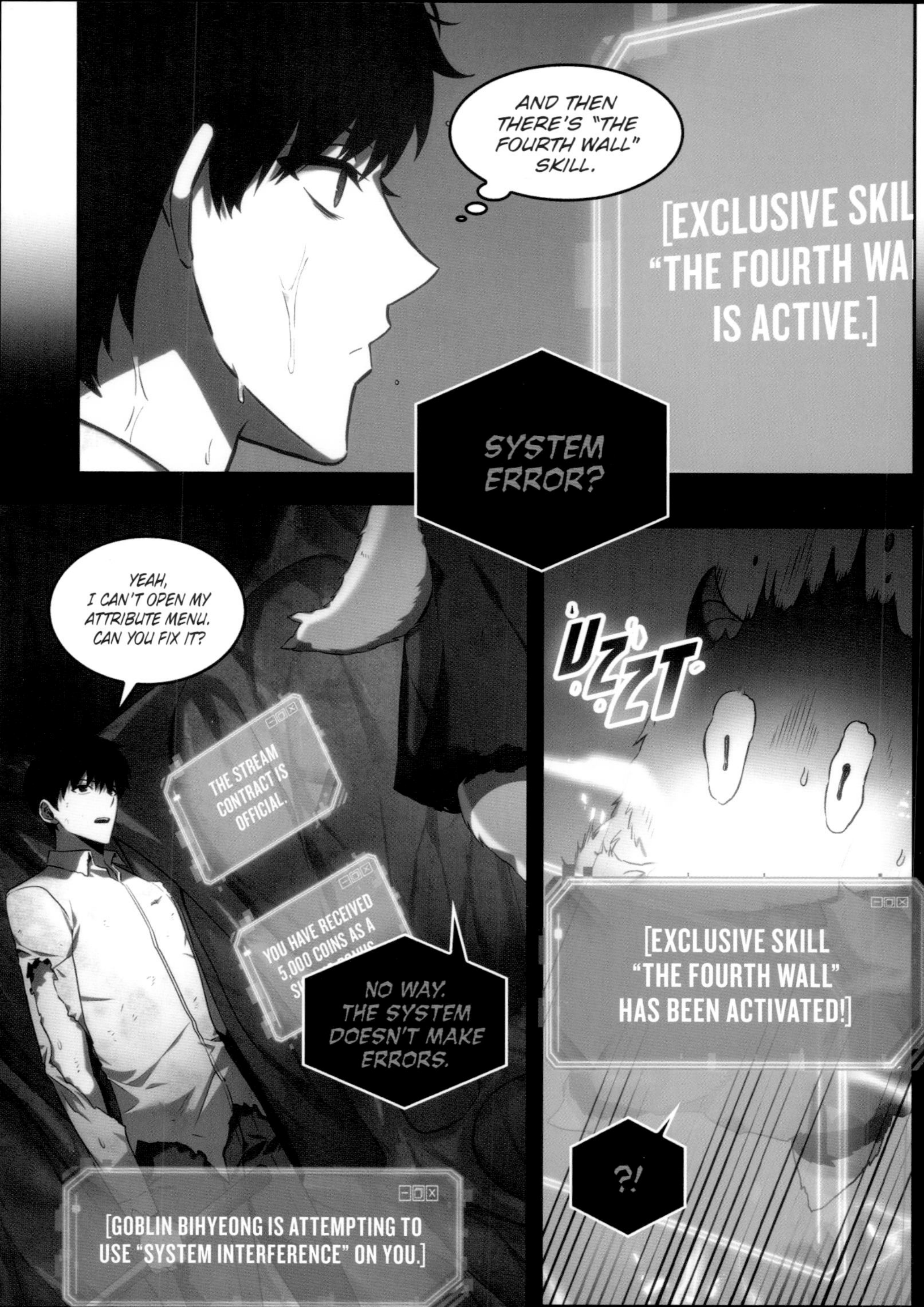
AND THEN THERE'S "THE FOURTH WALL" SKILL.
[EXCLUSIVE SKIL "THE FOURTH WA IS ACTIVE.]
SYSTEM ERROR?
YEAH, I CAN'T OPEN MY ATTRIBUTE MENU. CAN YOU FIX IT?
THE STREAM CONTRACT IS OFFICIAL.
YOU HAVE RECEIVED 5,000 COINS AS A
NO WAY. THE SYSTEM DOESN'T MAKE ERRORS.
[GOBLIN BIHYEONG IS ATTEMPTING TO USE "SYSTEM INTERFERENCE" ON YOU.]
VZZT
[EXCLUSIVE SKILL "THE FOURTH WALL" HAS BEEN ACTIVATED!]
?!

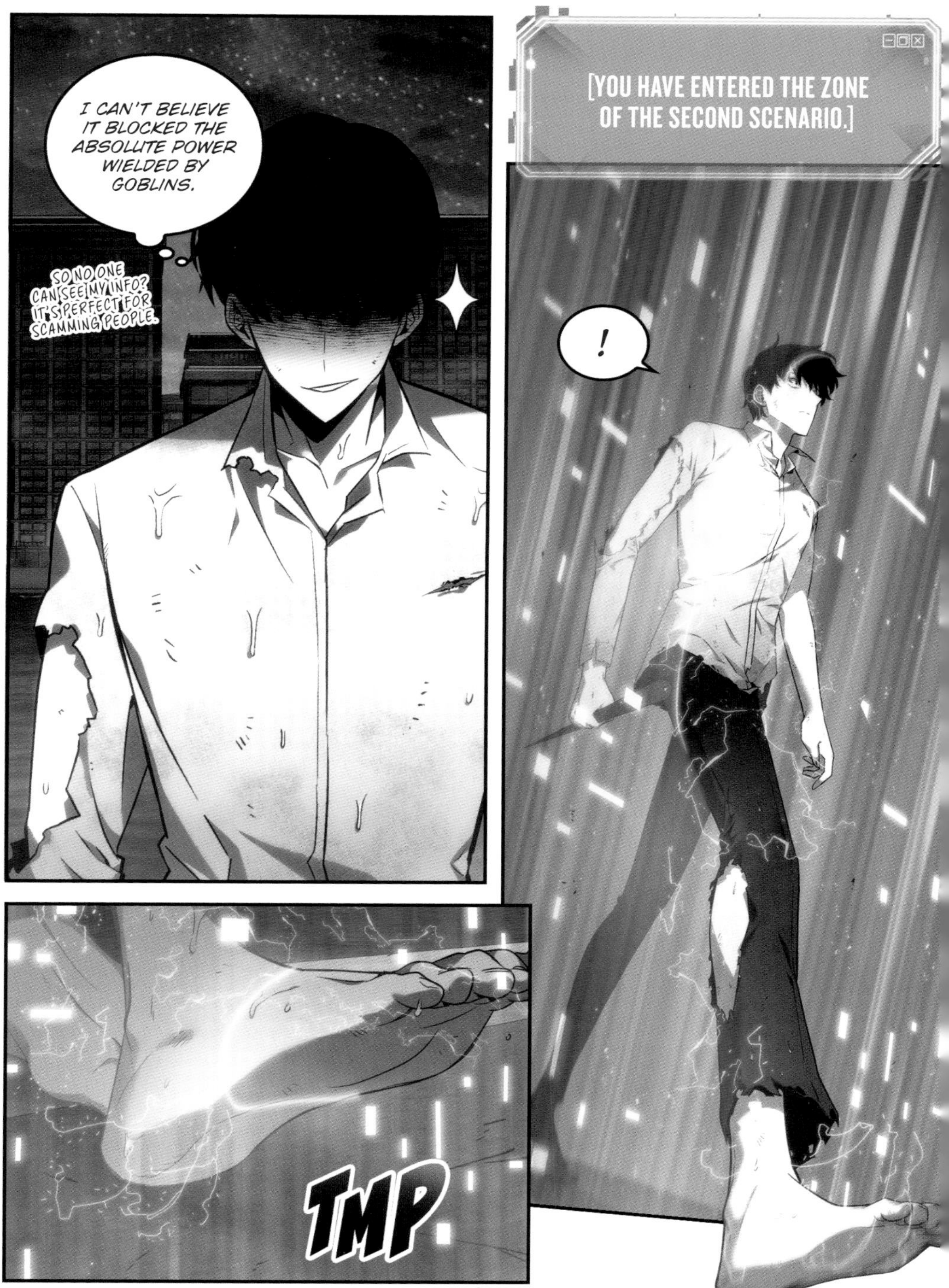
I CAN'T BELIEVE IT BLOCKED THE ABSOLUTE POWER WIELDED BY GOBLINS.
SO NO ONE CAN SEE MY INFO? IT'S PERFECT FOR SCAMMING PEOPLE.
TMP
[YOU HAVE ENTERED THE ZONE OF THE SECOND SCENARIO.]
!

UGH...!
I'M HERE...!
[THIS SCENARIO ZONE IS HEAVILY POLLUTED.]
[HOLD YOUR BREATH AND QUICKLY SEEK SHELTER IN AN UNDERGROUND AREA!]
[YOU ARE EXPOSED TO A POISONOUS FOG.]
[CONSTELLATION *ABYSSAL BLACK FLAME DRAGON* SMILES OMINOUSLY.]

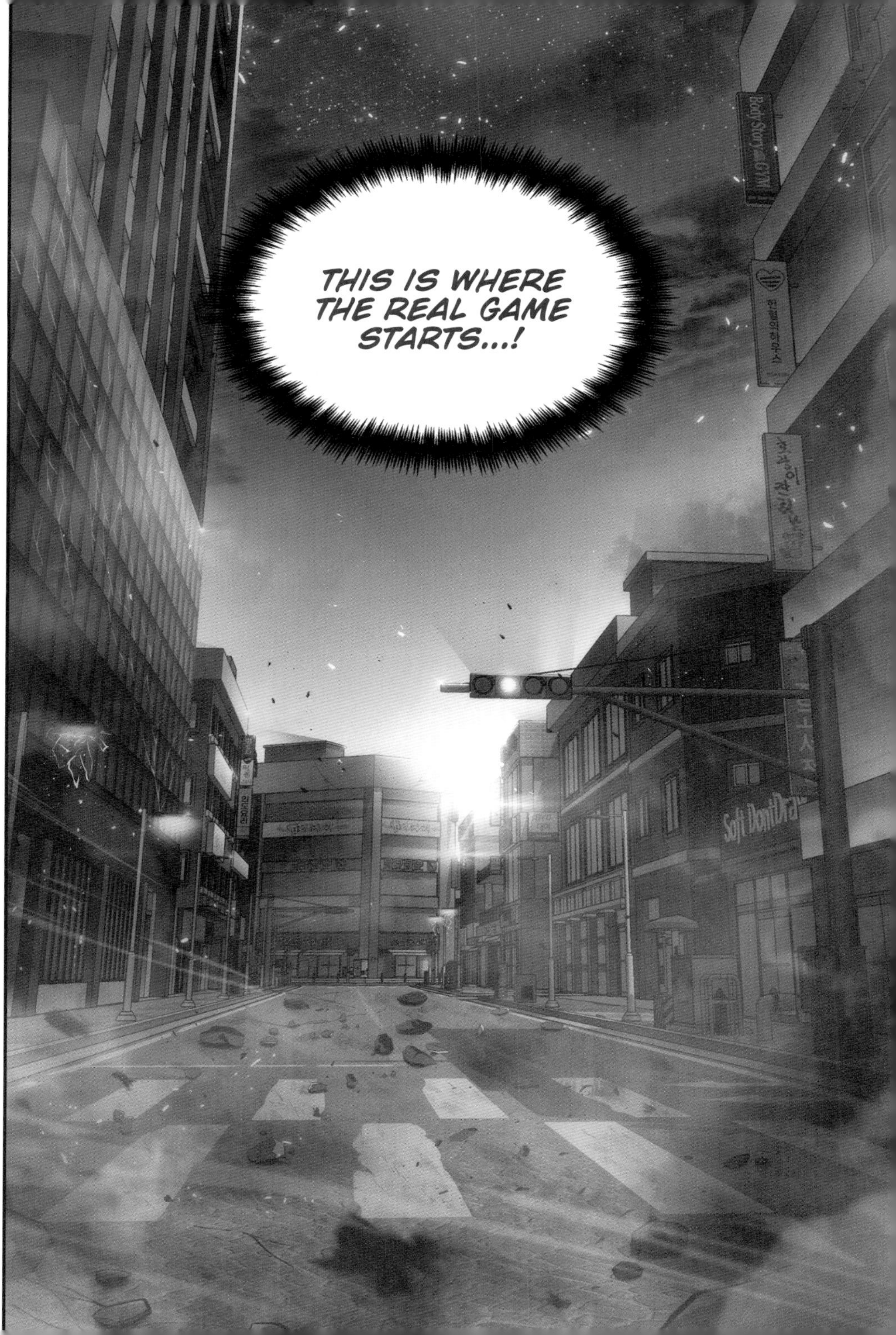
THIS IS WHERE THE REAL GAME STARTS...!

EP. 04

HYPOCRISY CAN BE A VIRTUE

EP. 04

Omniscient
Reader's
Viewpoint

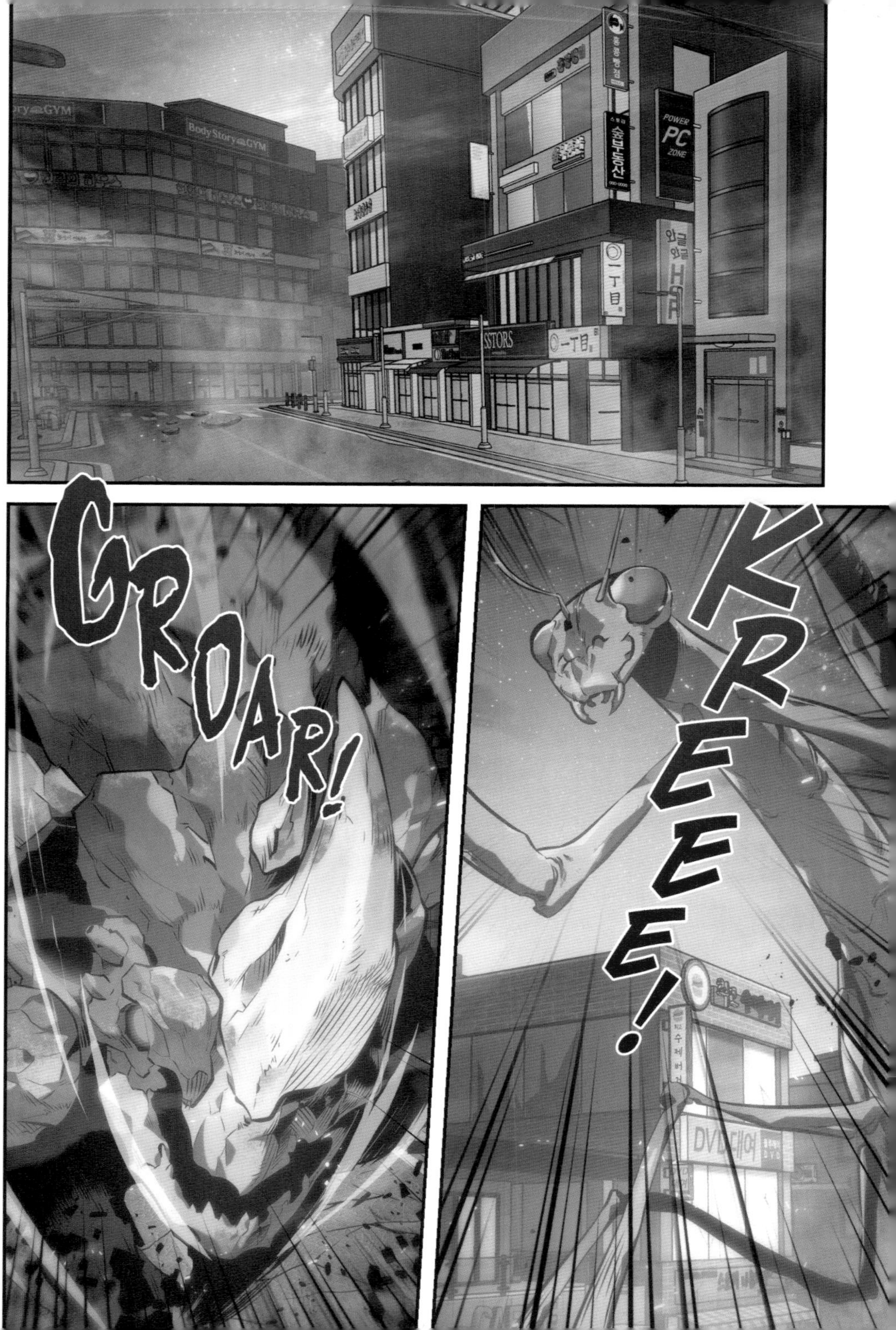

Body Story GYM
POWER PC ZONE
GROAR!
KREEEE!

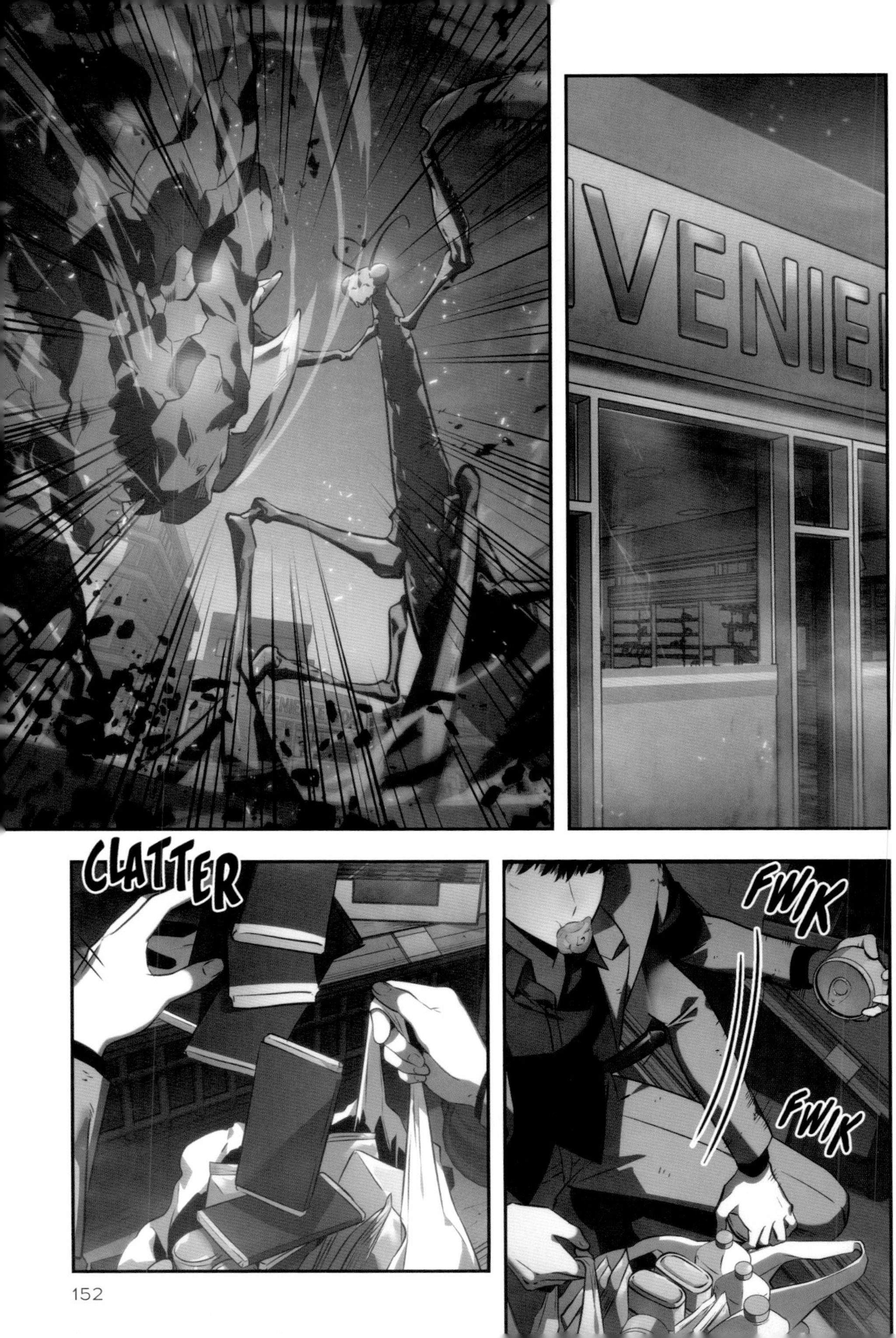
VENIE
FWIK
FWIK
CLATTER

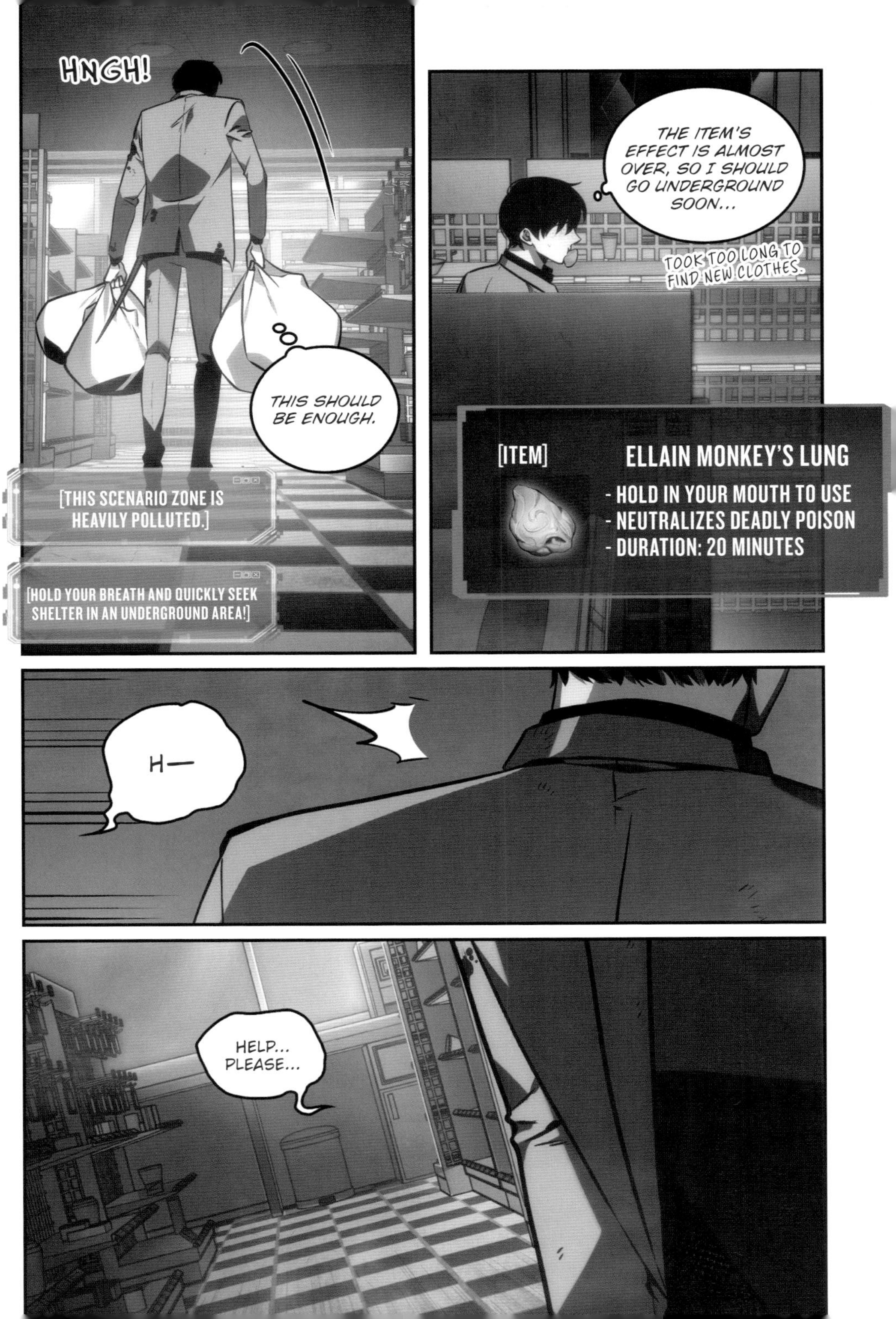
HNGH!
THIS SHOULD BE ENOUGH.
[THIS SCENARIO ZONE IS HEAVILY POLLUTED.]
[HOLD YOUR BREATH AND QUICKLY SEEK SHELTER IN AN UNDERGROUND AREA!]
THE ITEM'S EFFECT IS ALMOST OVER, SO I SHOULD GO UNDERGROUND SOON...
TOOK TOO LONG TO FIND NEW CLOTHES.
[ITEM]
ELLAIN MONKEY'S LUNG
- HOLD IN YOUR MOUTH TO USE
- NEUTRALIZES DEADLY POISON
- DURATION: 20 MINUTES
H—
HELP... PLEASE...

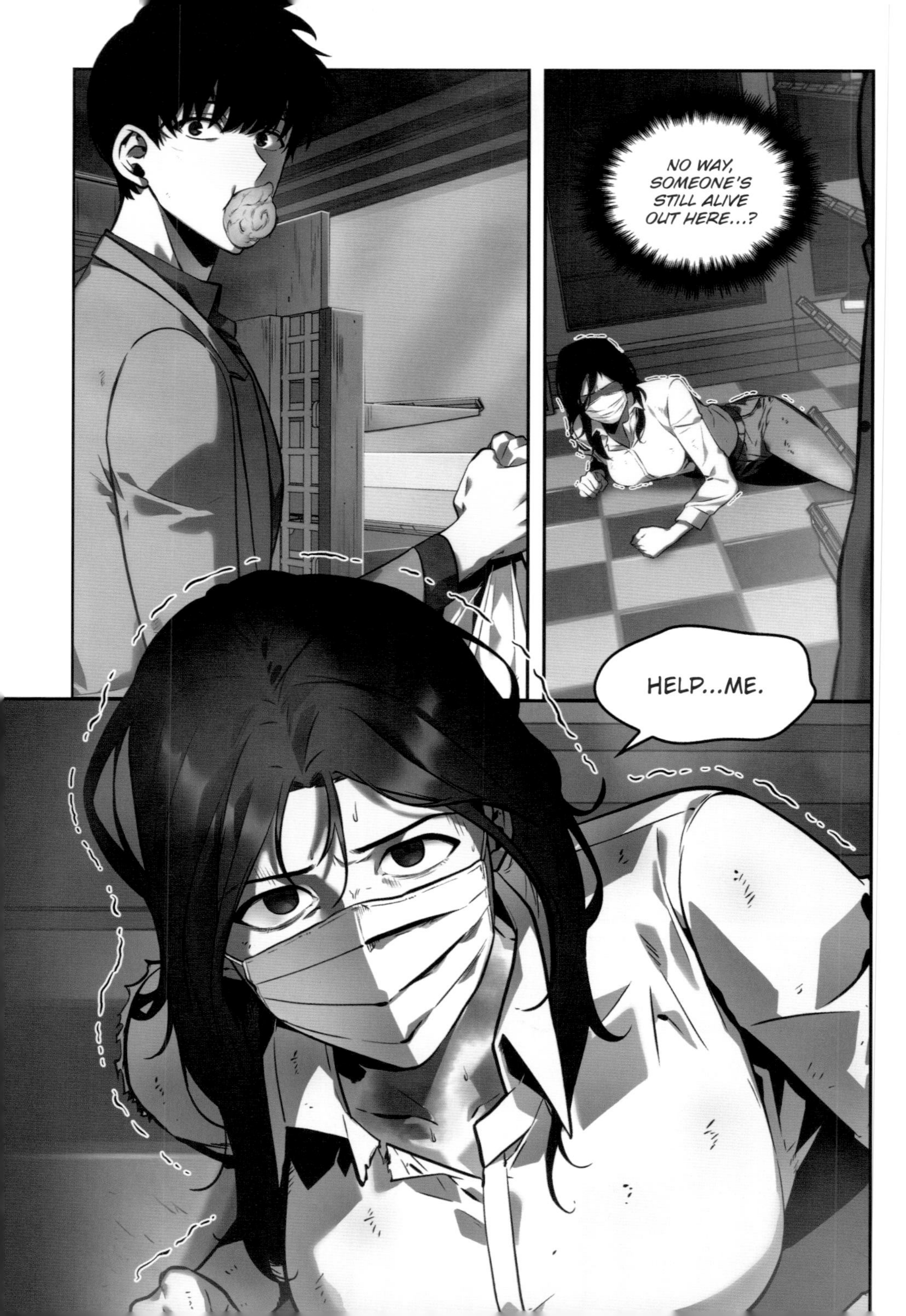
NO WAY, SOMEONE'S STILL ALIVE OUT HERE...?
HELP...ME.

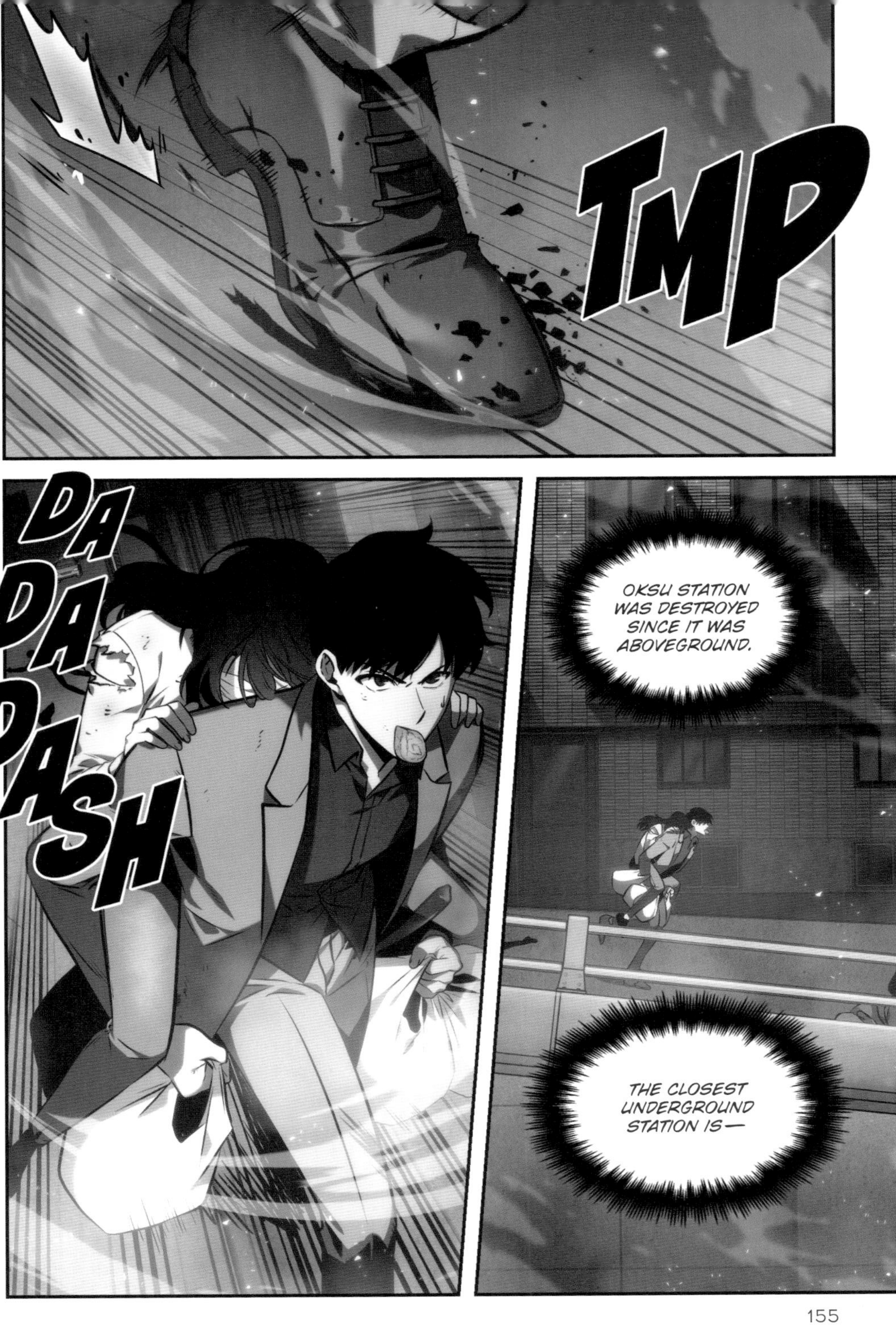
TMP
DA DA DA DASH
OKSU STATION WAS DESTROYED SINCE IT WAS ABOVEGROUND.
THE CLOSEST UNDERGROUND STATION IS—

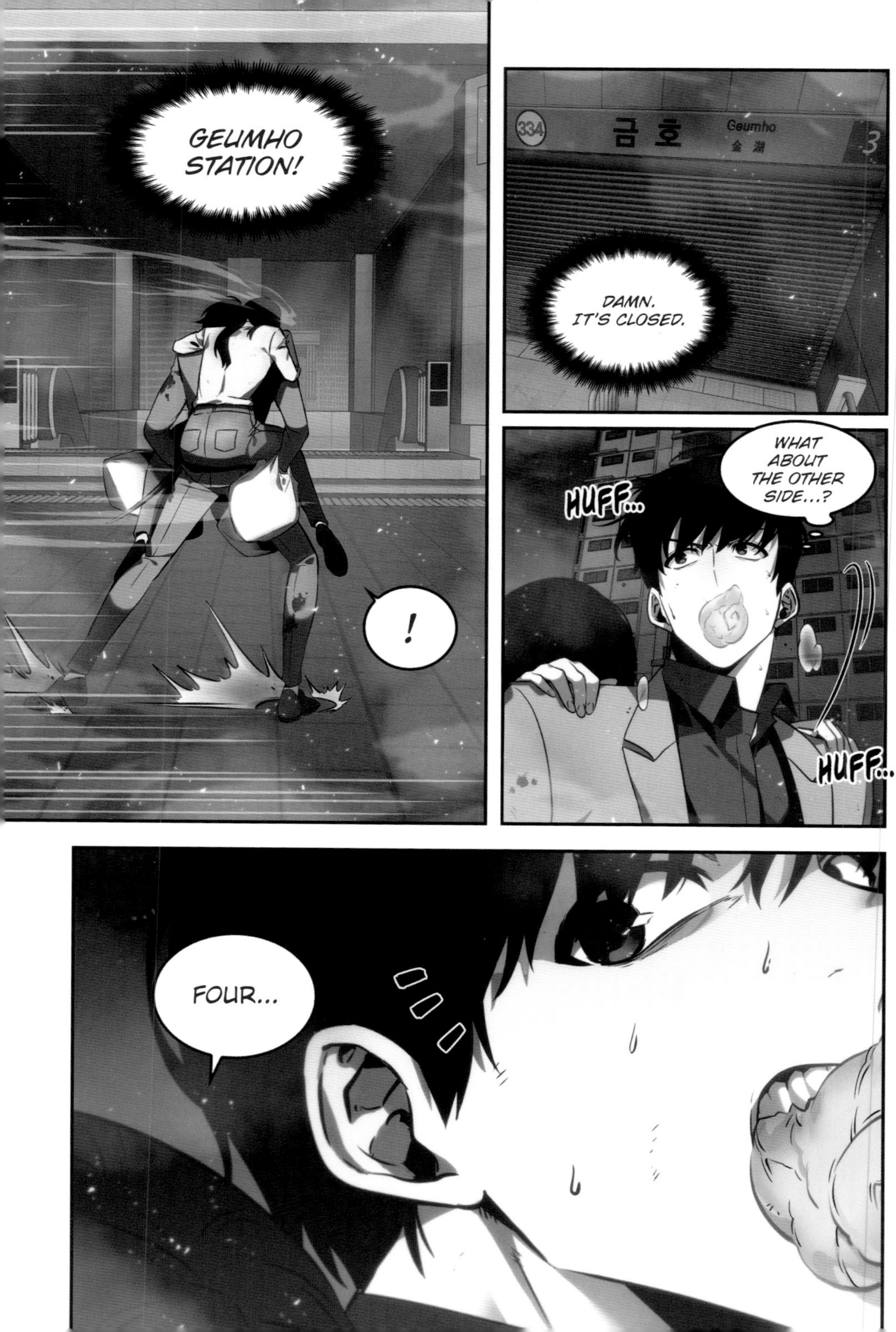
GEUMHO STATION!
!
334
금호
Geumho
金湖
3
DAMN. IT'S CLOSED.
HUFF...
WHAT ABOUT THE OTHER SIDE...?
HUFF...
FOUR...

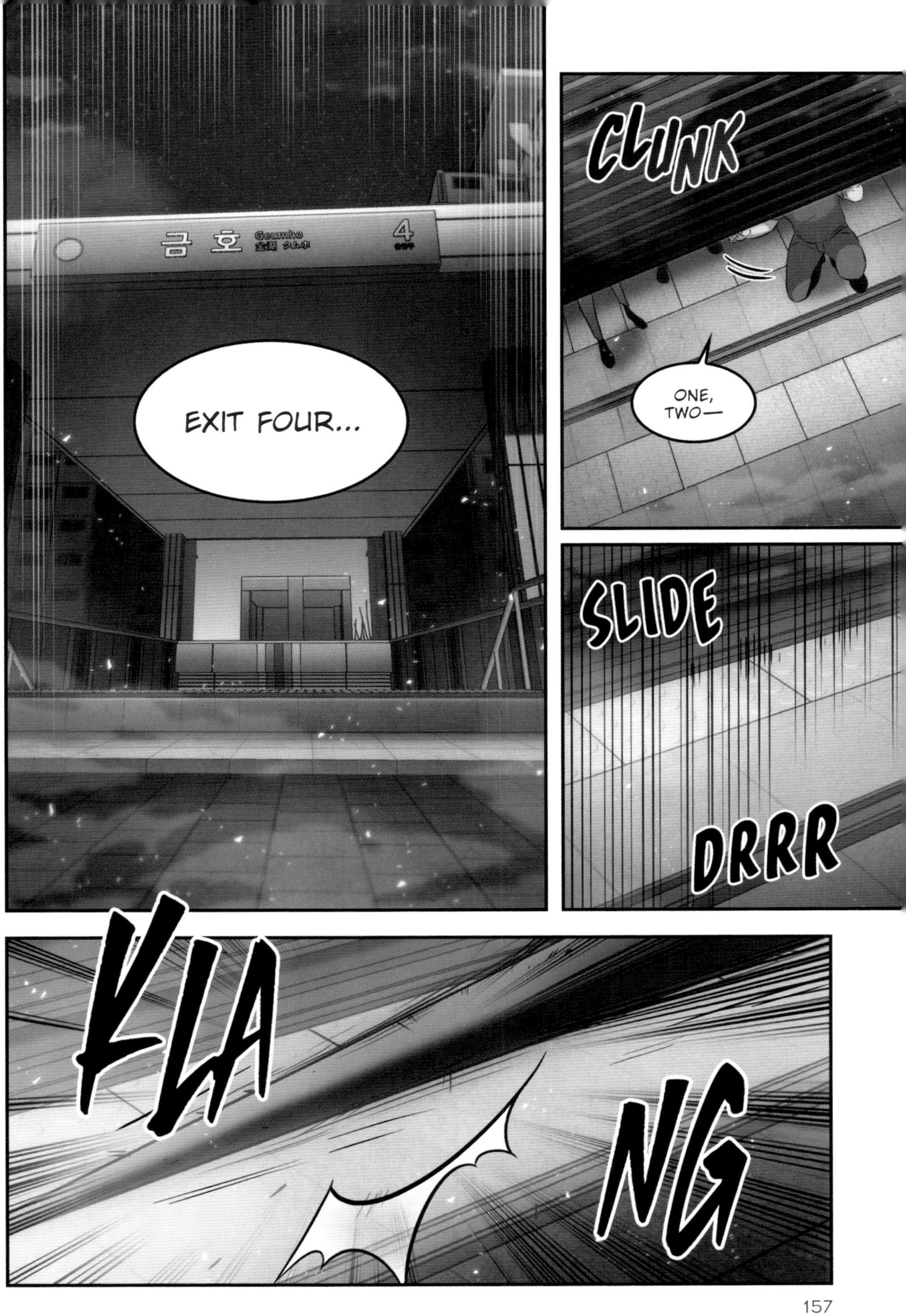

금호
Geumho
4
EXIT FOUR...
CLUNK
ONE, TWO—
SLIDE
DRRR
KLANG

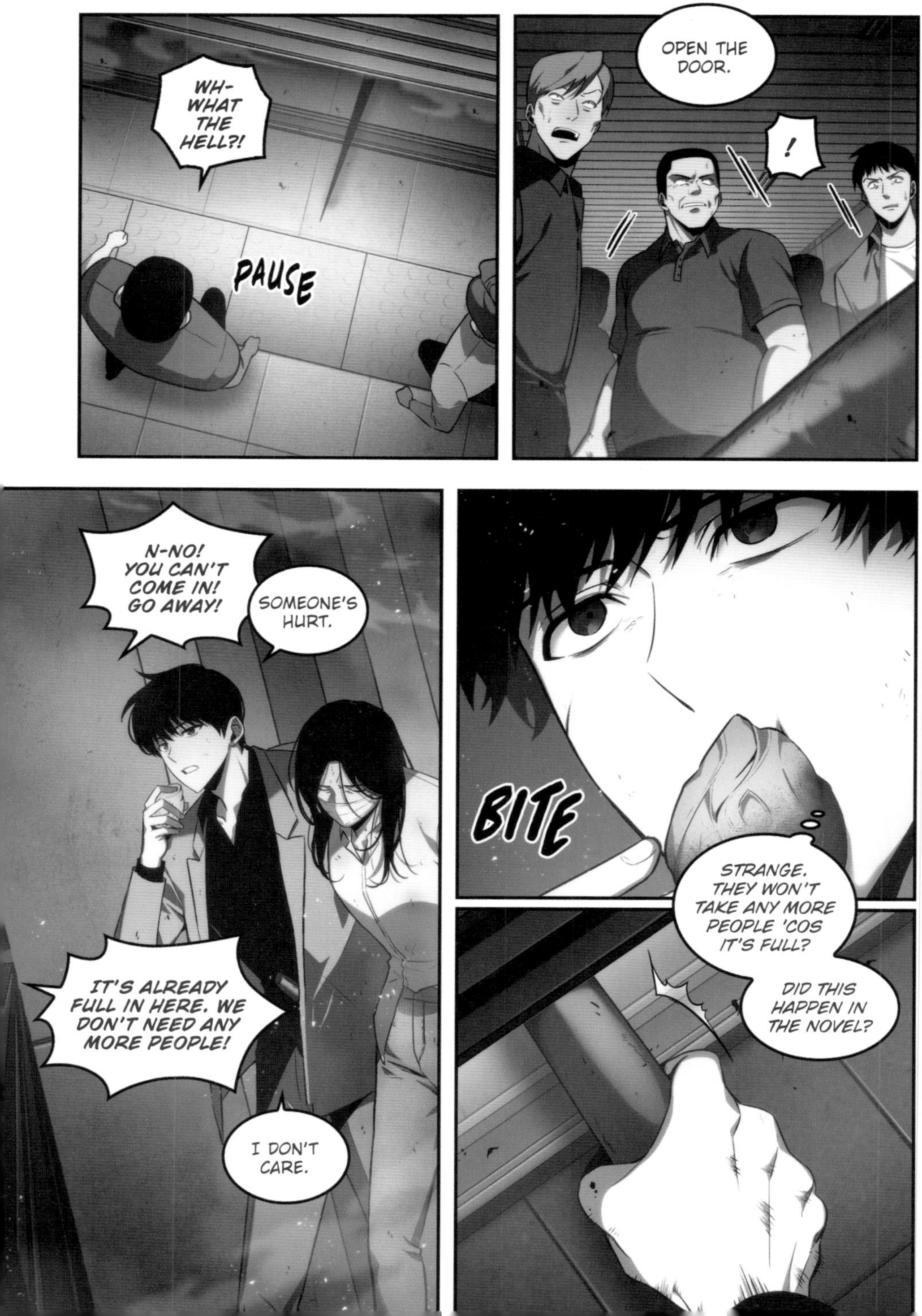
WH- WHAT THE HELL?!
PAUSE
OPEN THE DOOR.
!
N-NO! YOU CAN'T COME IN! GO AWAY!
SOMEONE'S HURT.
IT'S ALREADY FULL IN HERE. WE DON'T NEED ANY MORE PEOPLE!
I DON'T CARE.
BITE
STRANGE. THEY WON'T TAKE ANY MORE PEOPLE 'COS IT'S FULL?
DID THIS HAPPEN IN THE NOVEL?

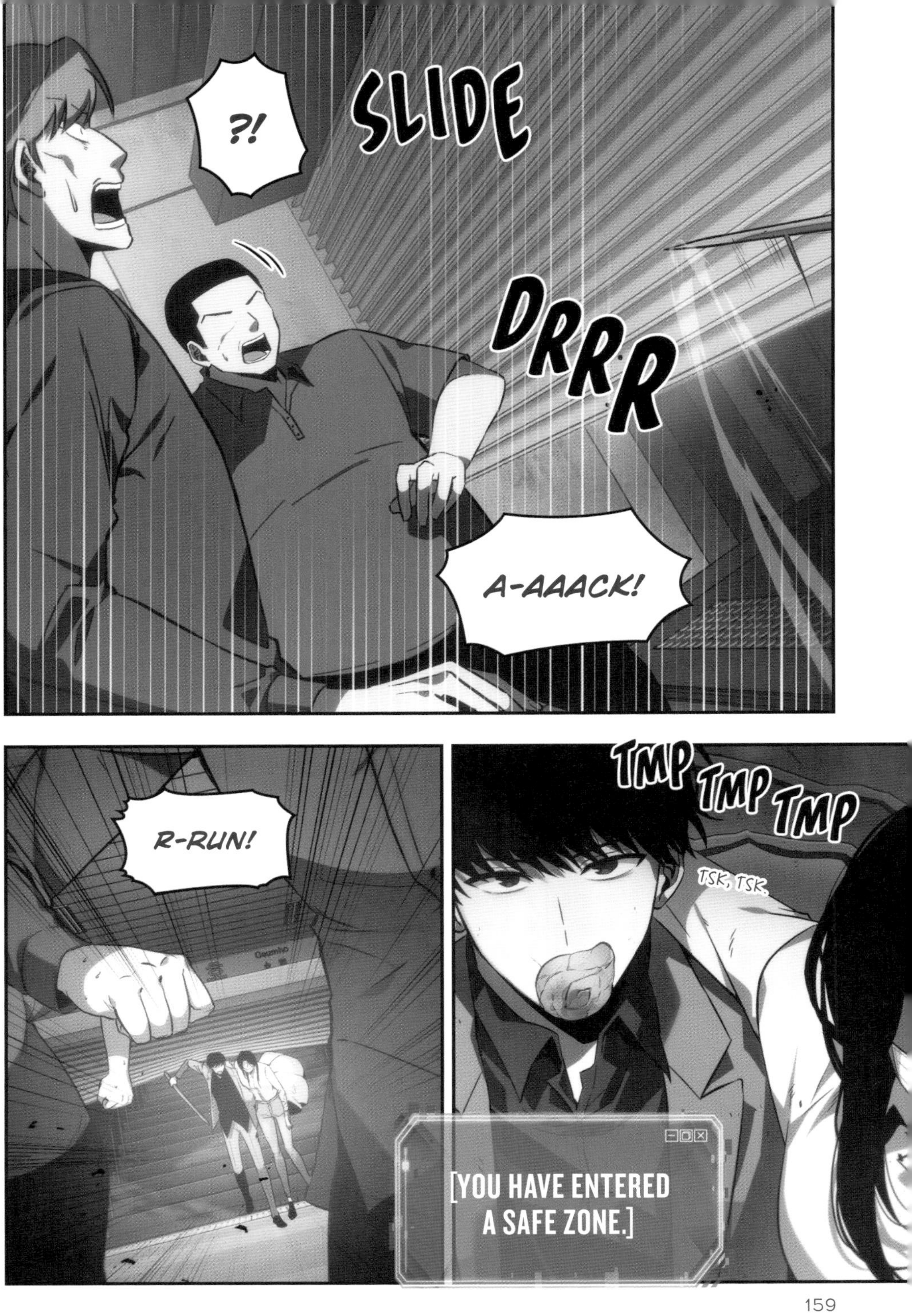
?!
SLIDE
DRRR
A-AAACK!
R-RUN!
TMP TMP TMP
TSK, TSK.
[YOU HAVE ENTERED A SAFE ZONE.]

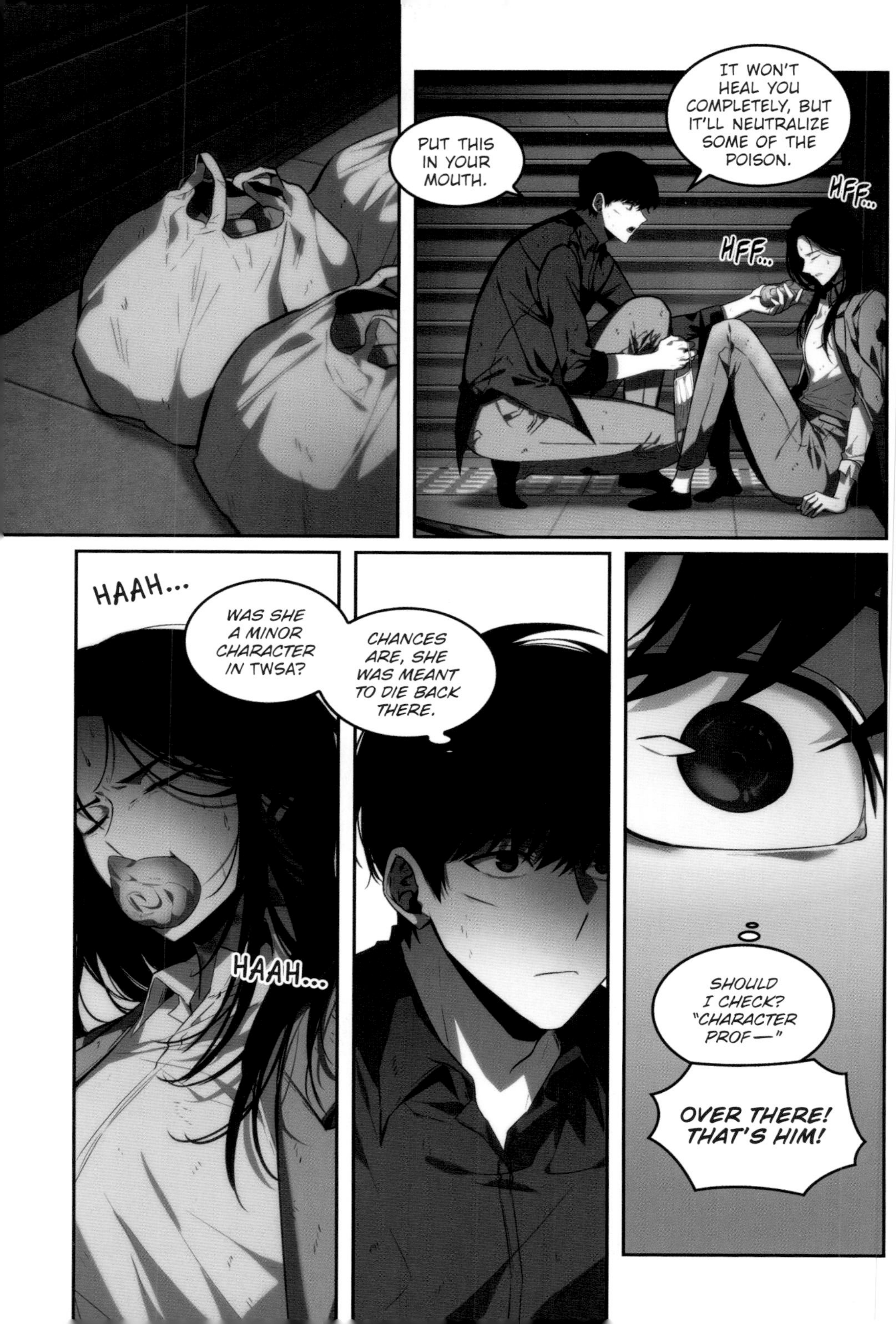
PUT THIS IN YOUR MOUTH.
IT WON'T HEAL YOU COMPLETELY, BUT IT'LL NEUTRALIZE SOME OF THE POISON.
HFF...
HFF...
HAAH...
HAAH...
WAS SHE A MINOR CHARACTER IN TWSA?
CHANCES ARE, SHE WAS MEANT TO DIE BACK THERE.
SHOULD I CHECK? "CHARACTER PROF—"
OVER THERE! THAT'S HIM!

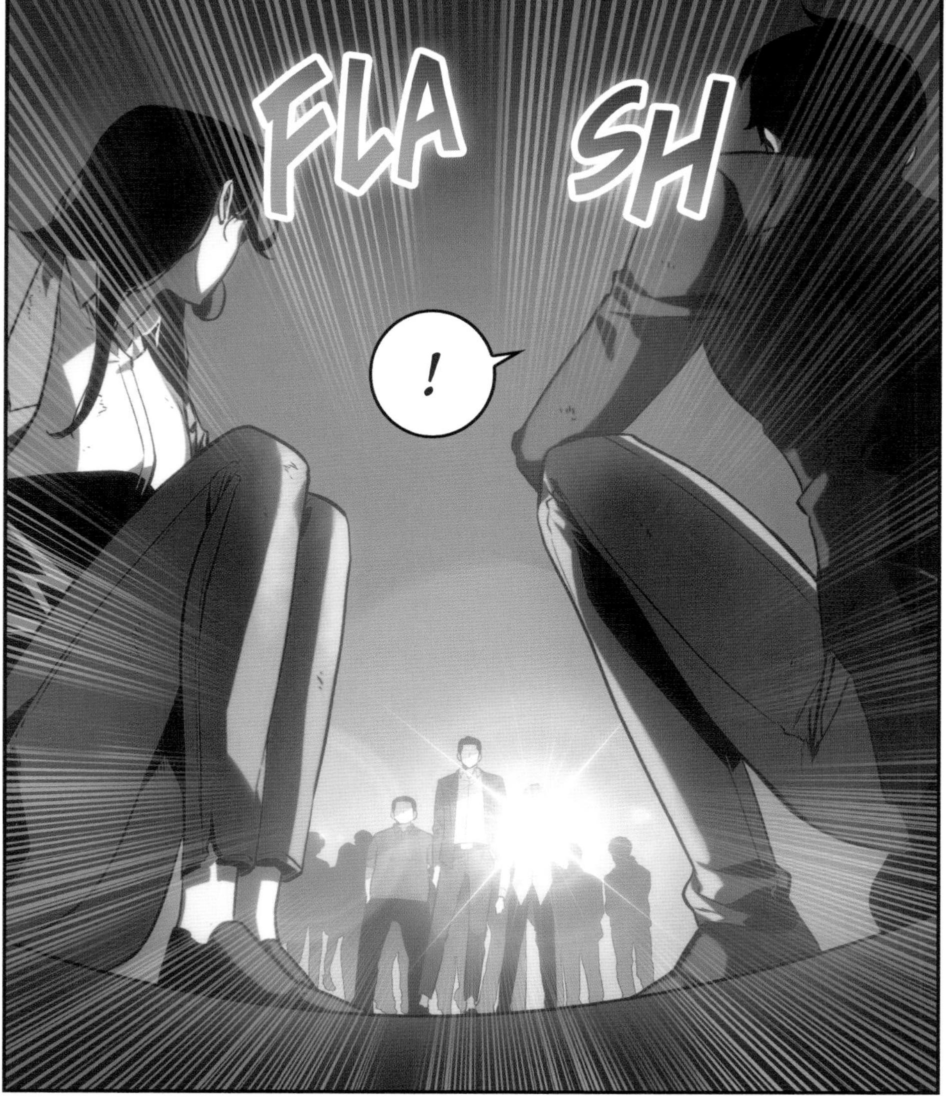
FLASH
!
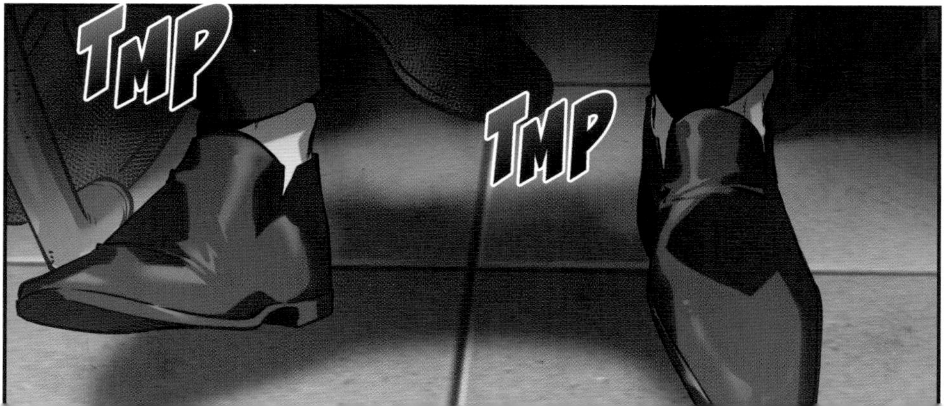
TMP
TMP

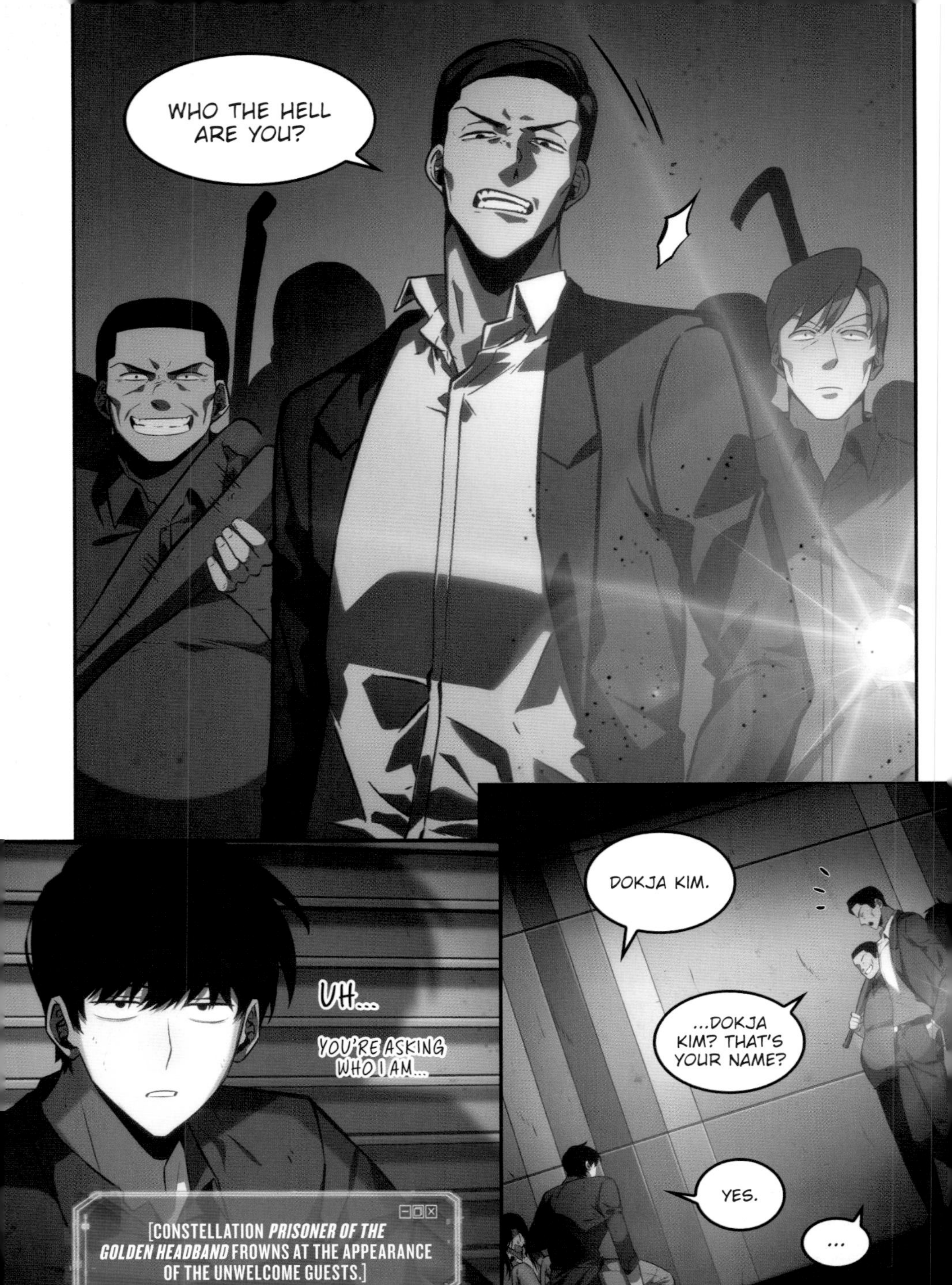
WHO THE HELL ARE YOU?
UH...
YOU'RE ASKING WHO I AM...
[CONSTELLATION *PRISONER OF THE GOLDEN HEADBAND* FROWNS AT THE APPEARANCE OF THE UNWELCOME GUESTS.]
DOKJA KIM.
...DOKJA KIM? THAT'S YOUR NAME?
YES.
...

TRYING TO TALK LIKE JUNGHYEOK YU.

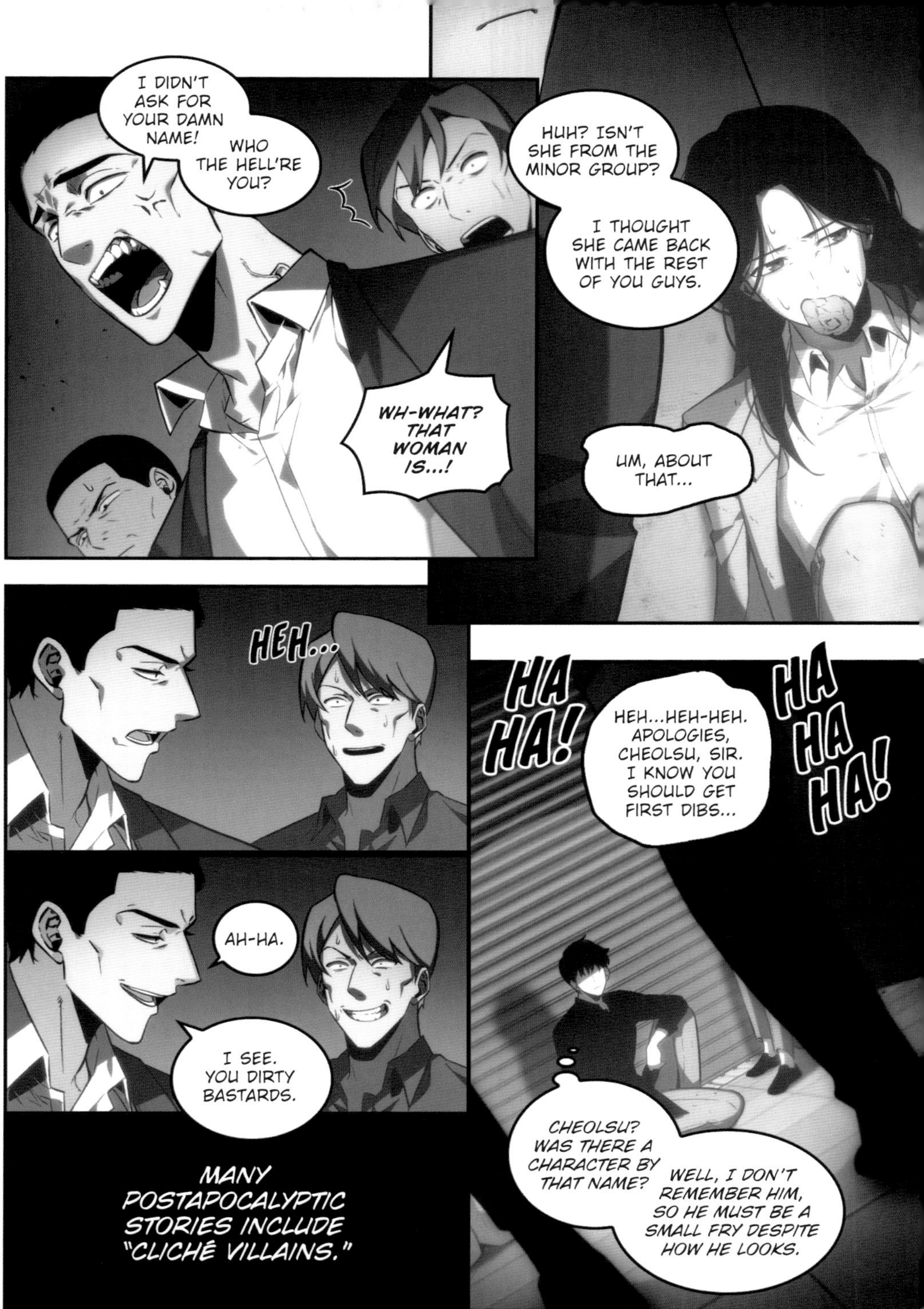
I DIDN'T ASK FOR YOUR DAMN NAME!
WHO THE HELL'RE YOU?
WH-WHAT? THAT WOMAN IS...!
HUH? ISN'T SHE FROM THE MINOR GROUP?
I THOUGHT SHE CAME BACK WITH THE REST OF YOU GUYS.
UM, ABOUT THAT...
HEH...
HA HA!
HA HA HA HA!
HEH...HEH-HEH. APOLOGIES, CHEOLSU, SIR. I KNOW YOU SHOULD GET FIRST DIBS...
AH-HA.
I SEE. YOU DIRTY BASTARDS.
MANY POSTAPOCALYPTIC STORIES INCLUDE "CLICHÉ VILLAINS."
CHEOLSU? WAS THERE A CHARACTER BY THAT NAME?
WELL, I DON'T REMEMBER HIM, SO HE MUST BE A SMALL FRY DESPITE HOW HE LOOKS.

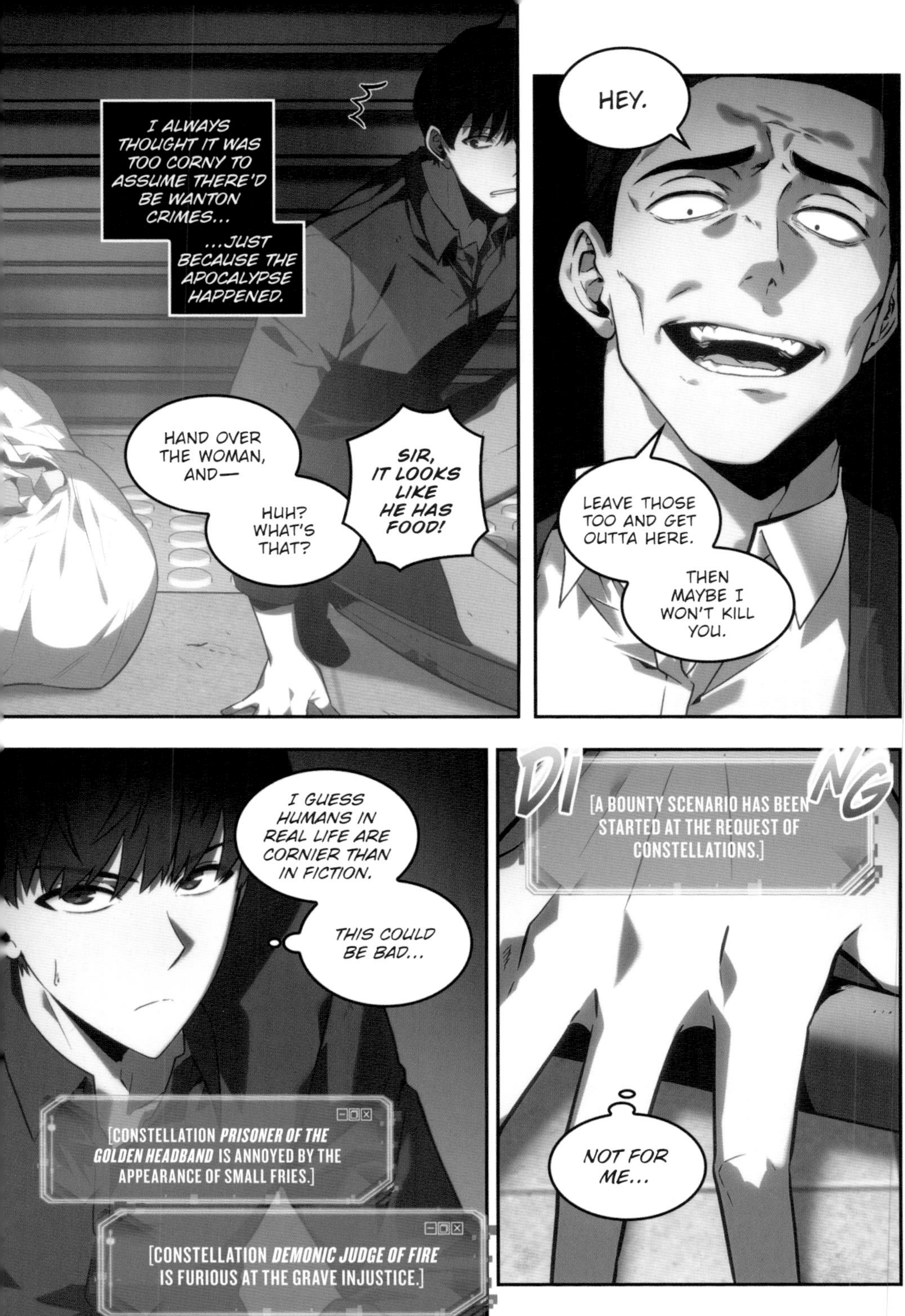
I ALWAYS THOUGHT IT WAS TOO CORNY TO ASSUME THERE'D BE WANTON CRIMES...
...JUST BECAUSE THE APOCALYPSE HAPPENED.
HAND OVER THE WOMAN, AND—
HUH? WHAT'S THAT?
SIR, IT LOOKS LIKE HE HAS FOOD!
HEY.
LEAVE THOSE TOO AND GET OUTTA HERE.
THEN MAYBE I WON'T KILL YOU.
I GUESS HUMANS IN REAL LIFE ARE CORNIER THAN IN FICTION.
THIS COULD BE BAD...
[CONSTELLATION PRISONER OF THE GOLDEN HEADBAND IS ANNOYED BY THE APPEARANCE OF SMALL FRIES.]
[CONSTELLATION DEMONIC JUDGE OF FIRE IS FURIOUS AT THE GRAVE INJUSTICE.]
DING
[A BOUNTY SCENARIO HAS BEEN STARTED AT THE REQUEST OF CONSTELLATIONS.]
NOT FOR ME...

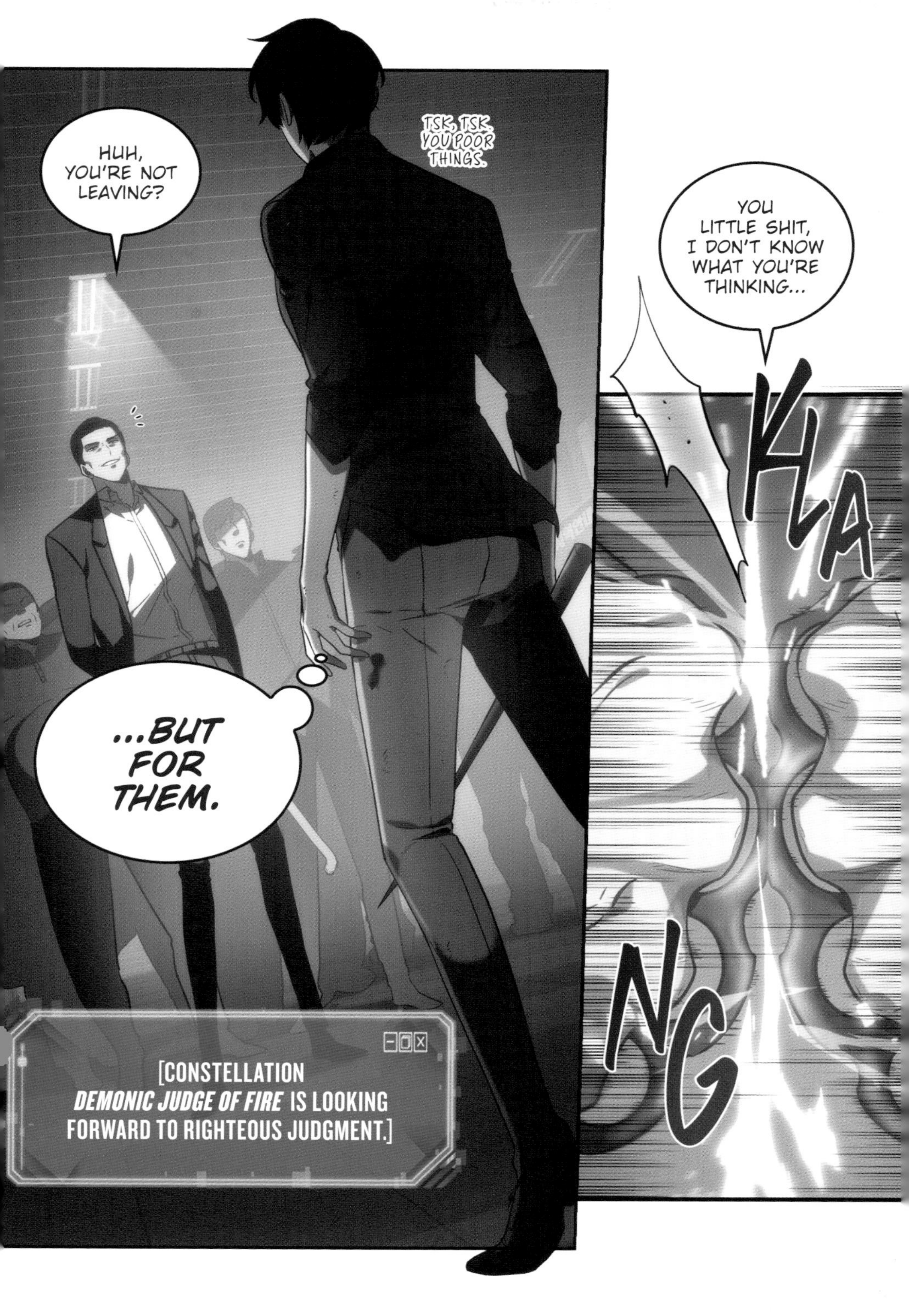
HUH, YOU'RE NOT LEAVING?
TSK, TSK. YOU POOR THINGS.
...BUT FOR THEM.
[CONSTELLATION *DEMONIC JUDGE OF FIRE* IS LOOKING FORWARD TO RIGHTEOUS JUDGMENT.]
YOU LITTLE SHIT, I DON'T KNOW WHAT YOU'RE THINKING...
KLANG

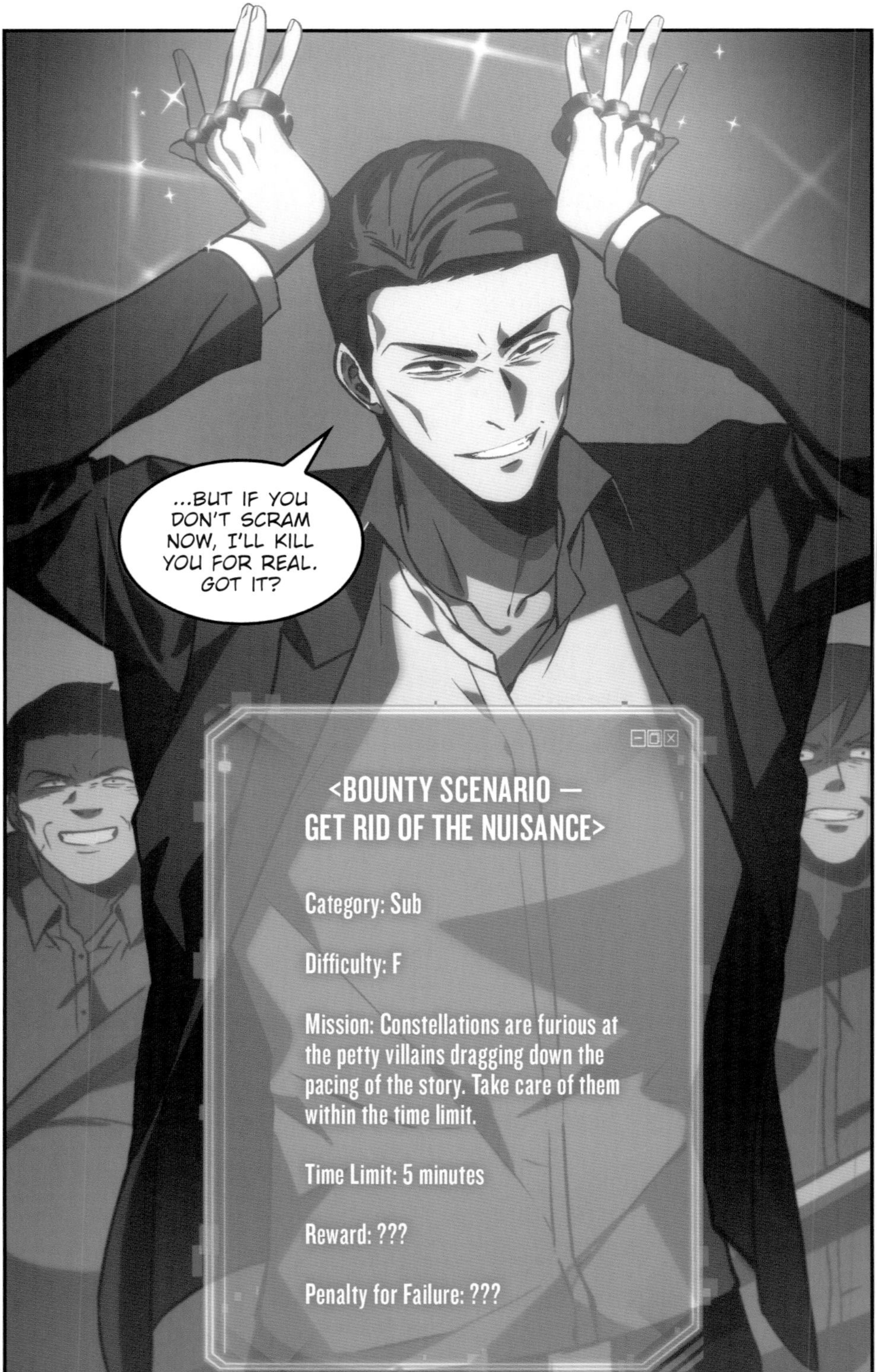
...BUT IF YOU DON'T SCRAM NOW, I'LL KILL YOU FOR REAL. GOT IT?
<BOUNTY SCENARIO — GET RID OF THE NUISANCE>
Category: Sub
Difficulty: F
Mission: Constellations are furious at the petty villains dragging down the pacing of the story. Take care of them within the time limit.
Time Limit: 5 minutes
Reward: ???
Penalty for Failure: ???

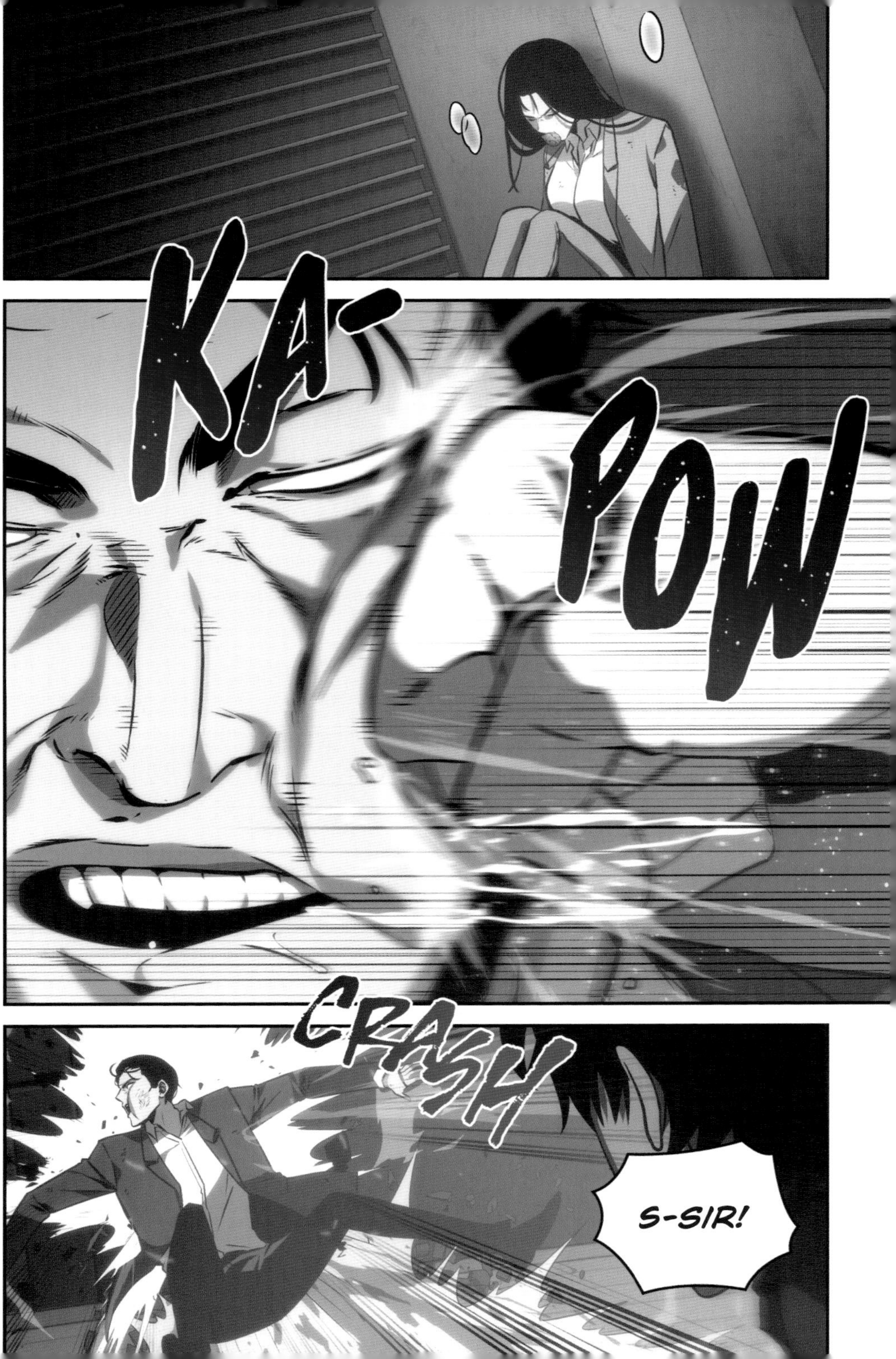
KA-
POW
CRASH
S-SIR!

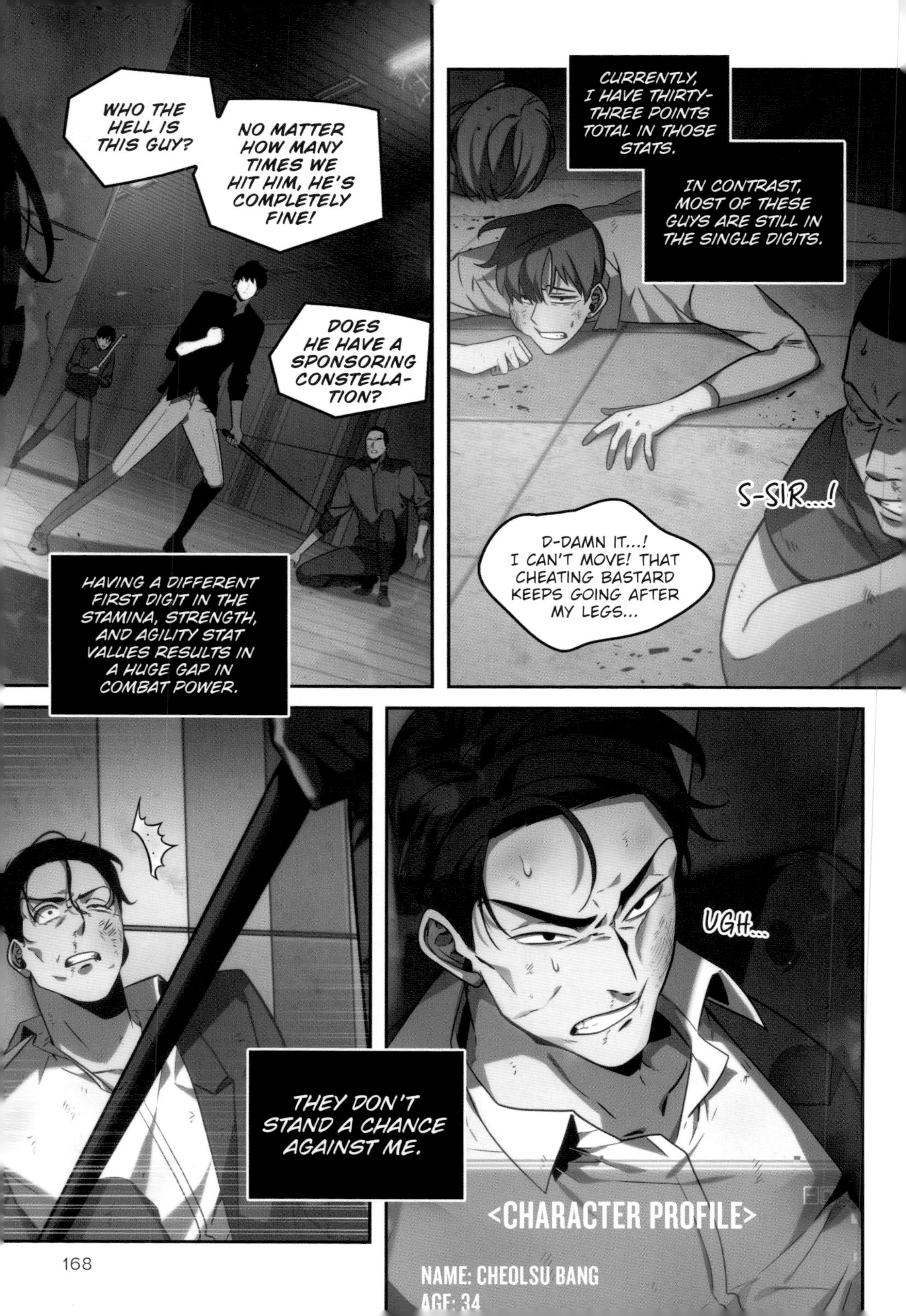
WHO THE HELL IS THIS GUY?
NO MATTER HOW MANY TIMES WE HIT HIM, HE'S COMPLETELY FINE!
DOES HE HAVE A SPONSORING CONSTELLA-TION?
HAVING A DIFFERENT FIRST DIGIT IN THE STAMINA, STRENGTH, AND AGILITY STAT VALUES RESULTS IN A HUGE GAP IN COMBAT POWER.
CURRENTLY, I HAVE THIRTY-THREE POINTS TOTAL IN THOSE STATS.
IN CONTRAST, MOST OF THESE GUYS ARE STILL IN THE SINGLE DIGITS.
S-SIR...!
D-DAMN IT...! I CAN'T MOVE! THAT CHEATING BASTARD KEEPS GOING AFTER MY LEGS...
THEY DON'T STAND A CHANCE AGAINST ME.
UGH...
<CHARACTER PROFILE>
NAME: CHEOLSU BANG
AGE: 34

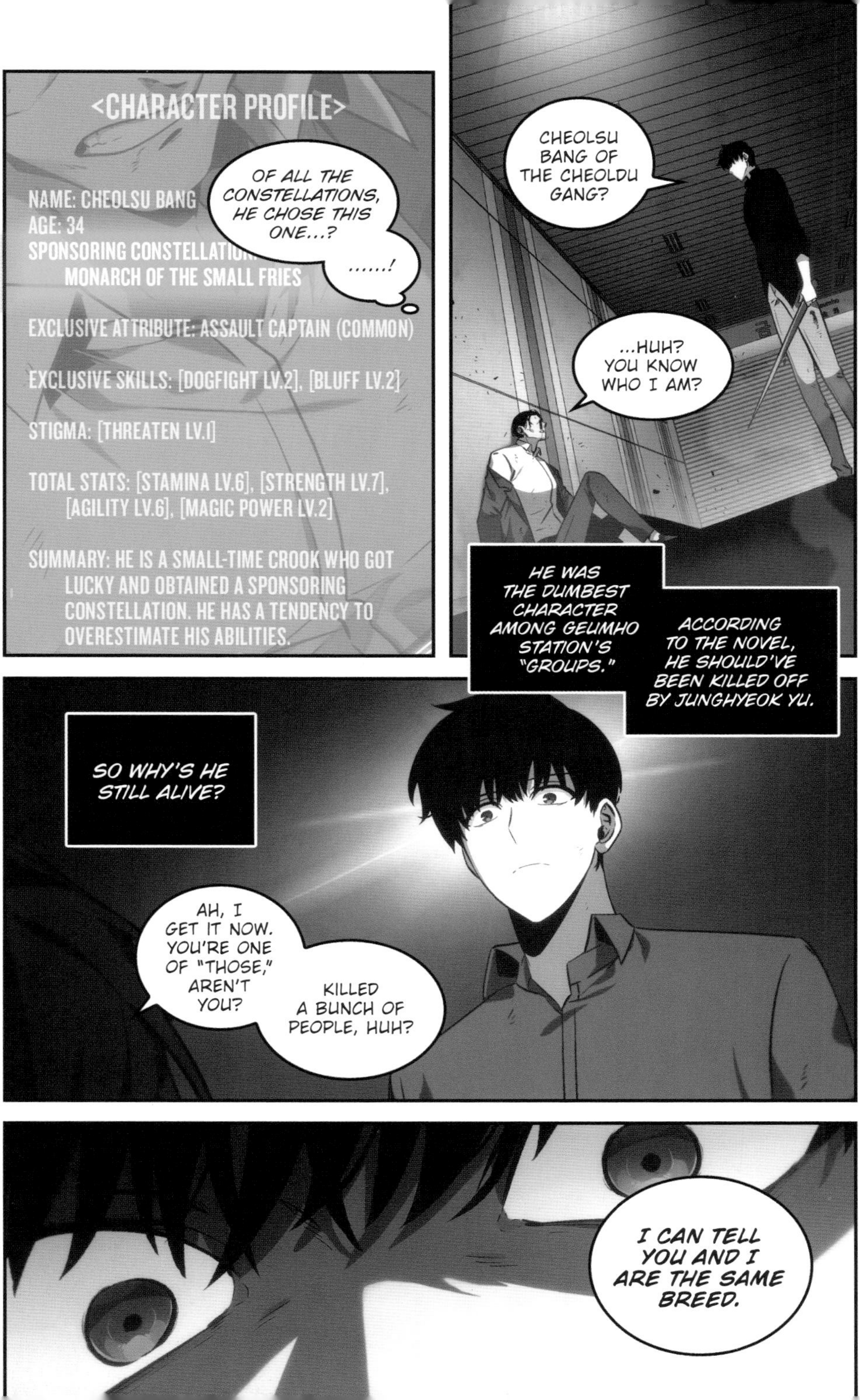
<CHARACTER PROFILE>
NAME: CHEOLSU BANG
AGE: 34
SPONSORING CONSTELLATI
MONARCH OF THE SMALL FRIES
EXCLUSIVE ATTRIBUTE: ASSAULT CAPTAIN (COMMON)
EXCLUSIVE SKILLS: [DOGFIGHT LV.2], [BLUFF LV.2]
STIGMA: [THREATEN LV.1]
TOTAL STATS: [STAMINA LV.6], [STRENGTH LV.7], [AGILITY LV.6], [MAGIC POWER LV.2]
SUMMARY: HE IS A SMALL-TIME CROOK WHO GOT LUCKY AND OBTAINED A SPONSORING CONSTELLATION. HE HAS A TENDENCY TO OVERESTIMATE HIS ABILITIES.
OF ALL THE CONSTELLATIONS, HE CHOSE THIS ONE...?
......!
CHEOLSU BANG OF THE CHEOLDU GANG?
...HUH? YOU KNOW WHO I AM?
HE WAS THE DUMBEST CHARACTER AMONG GEUMHO STATION'S "GROUPS."
ACCORDING TO THE NOVEL, HE SHOULD'VE BEEN KILLED OFF BY JUNGHYEOK YU.
SO WHY'S HE STILL ALIVE?
AH, I GET IT NOW. YOU'RE ONE OF "THOSE," AREN'T YOU?
KILLED A BUNCH OF PEOPLE, HUH?
I CAN TELL YOU AND I ARE THE SAME BREED.

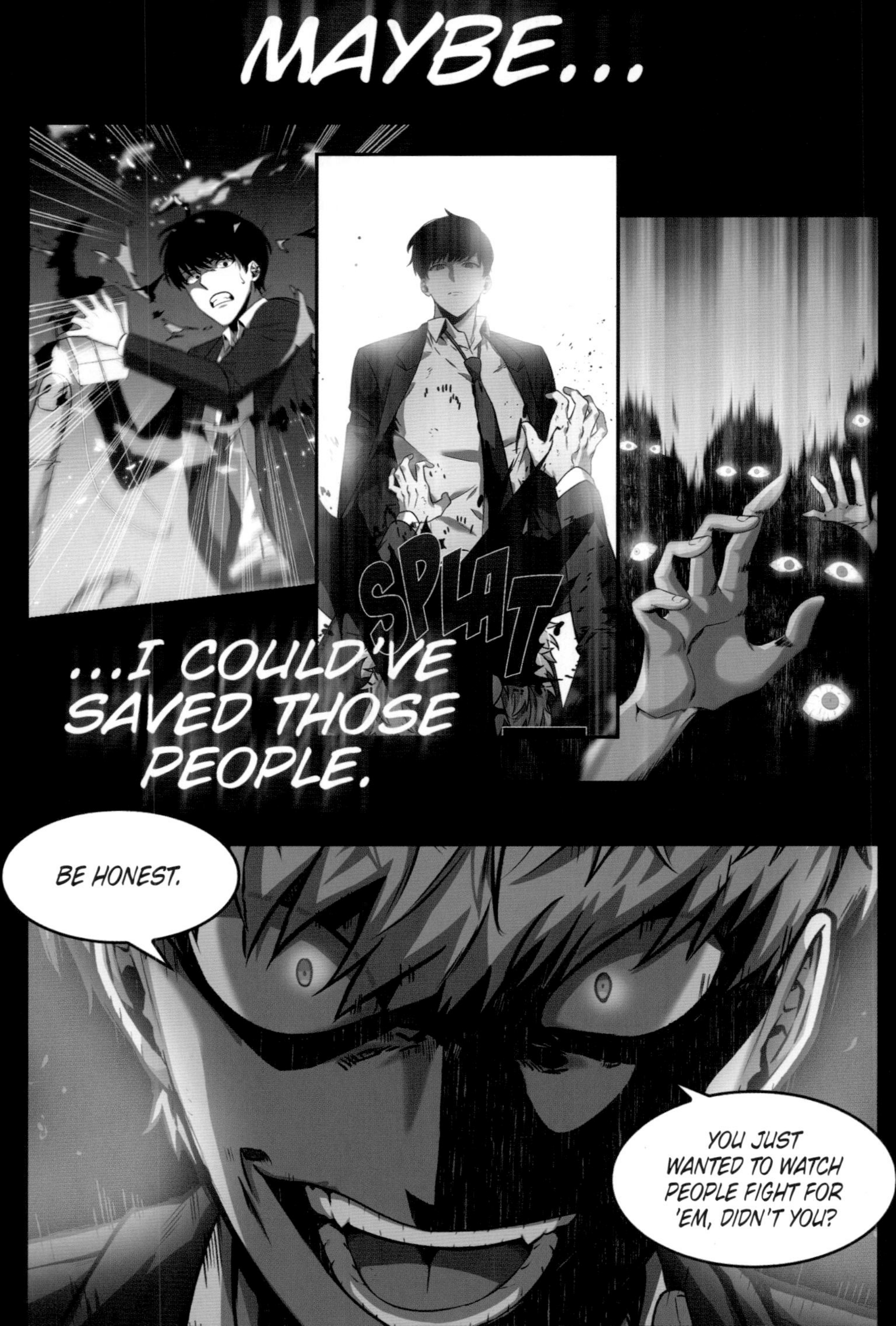
MAYBE...
SPLAT
...I COULD'VE SAVED THOSE PEOPLE.
BE HONEST.
YOU JUST WANTED TO WATCH PEOPLE FIGHT FOR 'EM, DIDN'T YOU?

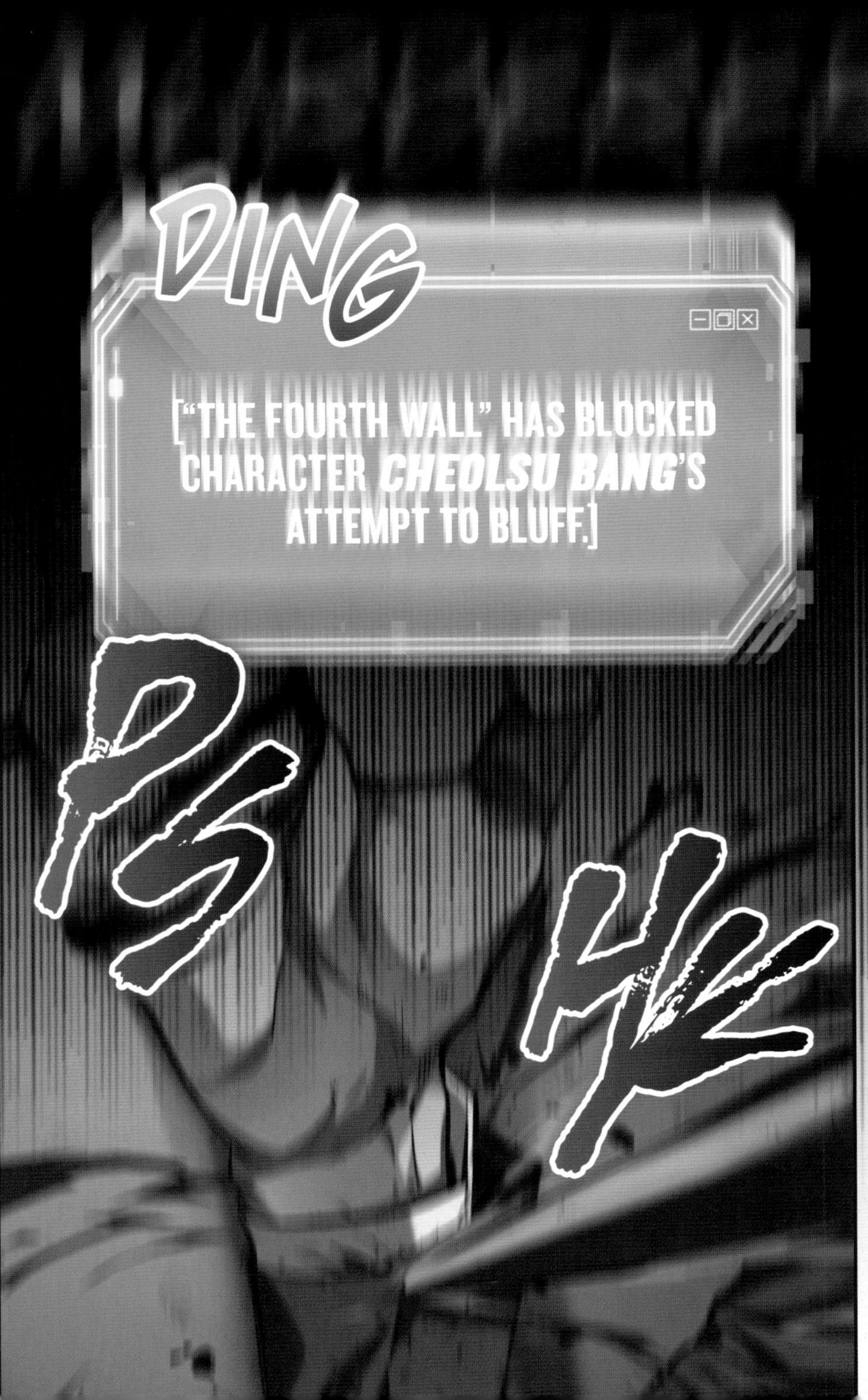
DING
["THE FOURTH WALL" HAS BLOCKED CHARACTER *CHEOLSU BANG*'S ATTEMPT TO BLUFF.]
PSHK

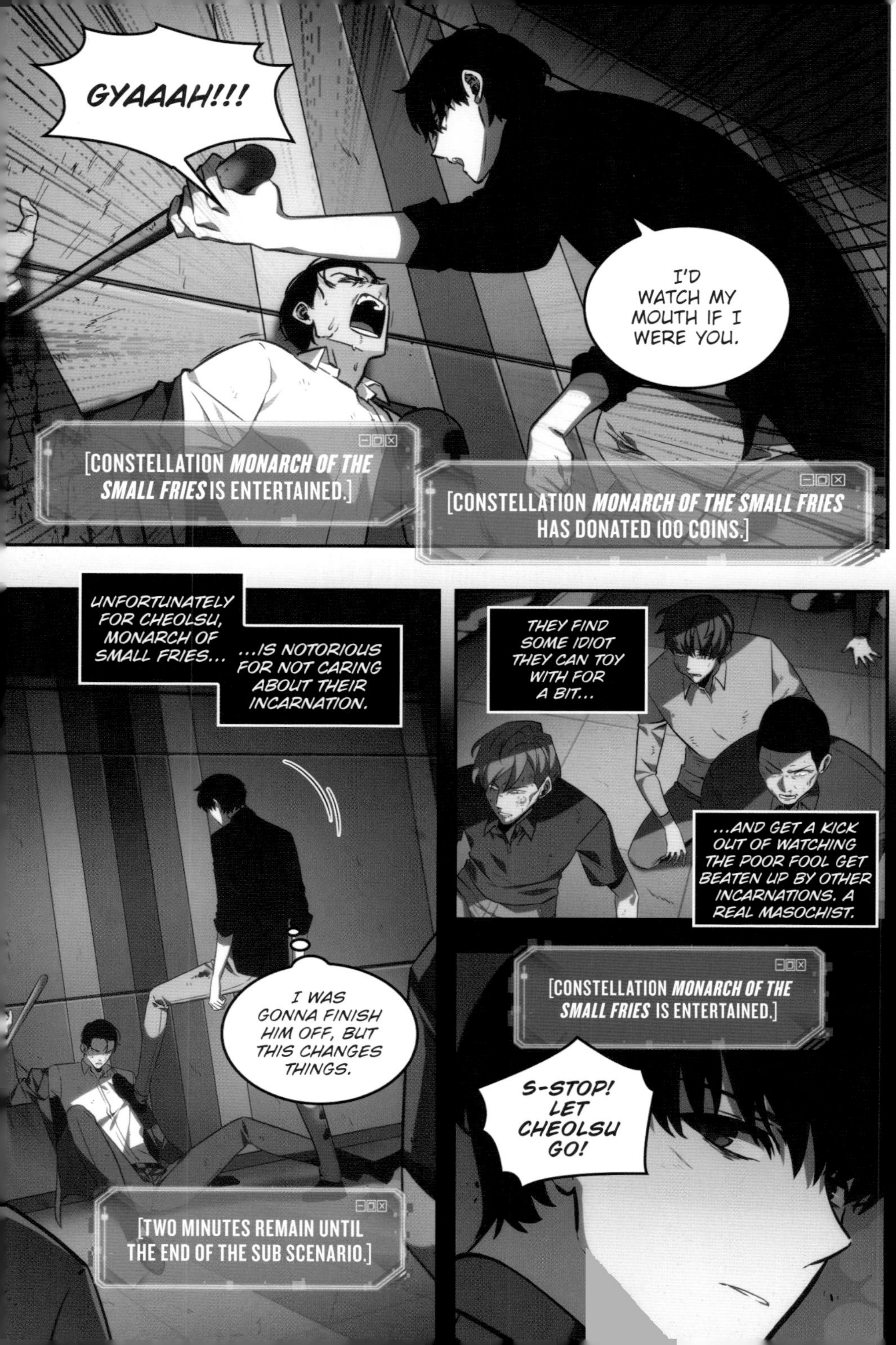
GYAAAH!!!
I'D WATCH MY MOUTH IF I WERE YOU.
[CONSTELLATION MONARCH OF THE SMALL FRIES IS ENTERTAINED.]
[CONSTELLATION MONARCH OF THE SMALL FRIES HAS DONATED 100 COINS.]
UNFORTUNATELY FOR CHEOLSU, MONARCH OF SMALL FRIES...
...IS NOTORIOUS FOR NOT CARING ABOUT THEIR INCARNATION.
THEY FIND SOME IDIOT THEY CAN TOY WITH FOR A BIT...
...AND GET A KICK OUT OF WATCHING THE POOR FOOL GET BEATEN UP BY OTHER INCARNATIONS. A REAL MASOCHIST.
I WAS GONNA FINISH HIM OFF, BUT THIS CHANGES THINGS.
[TWO MINUTES REMAIN UNTIL THE END OF THE SUB SCENARIO.]
[CONSTELLATION MONARCH OF THE SMALL FRIES IS ENTERTAINED.]
S-STOP! LET CHEOLSU GO!

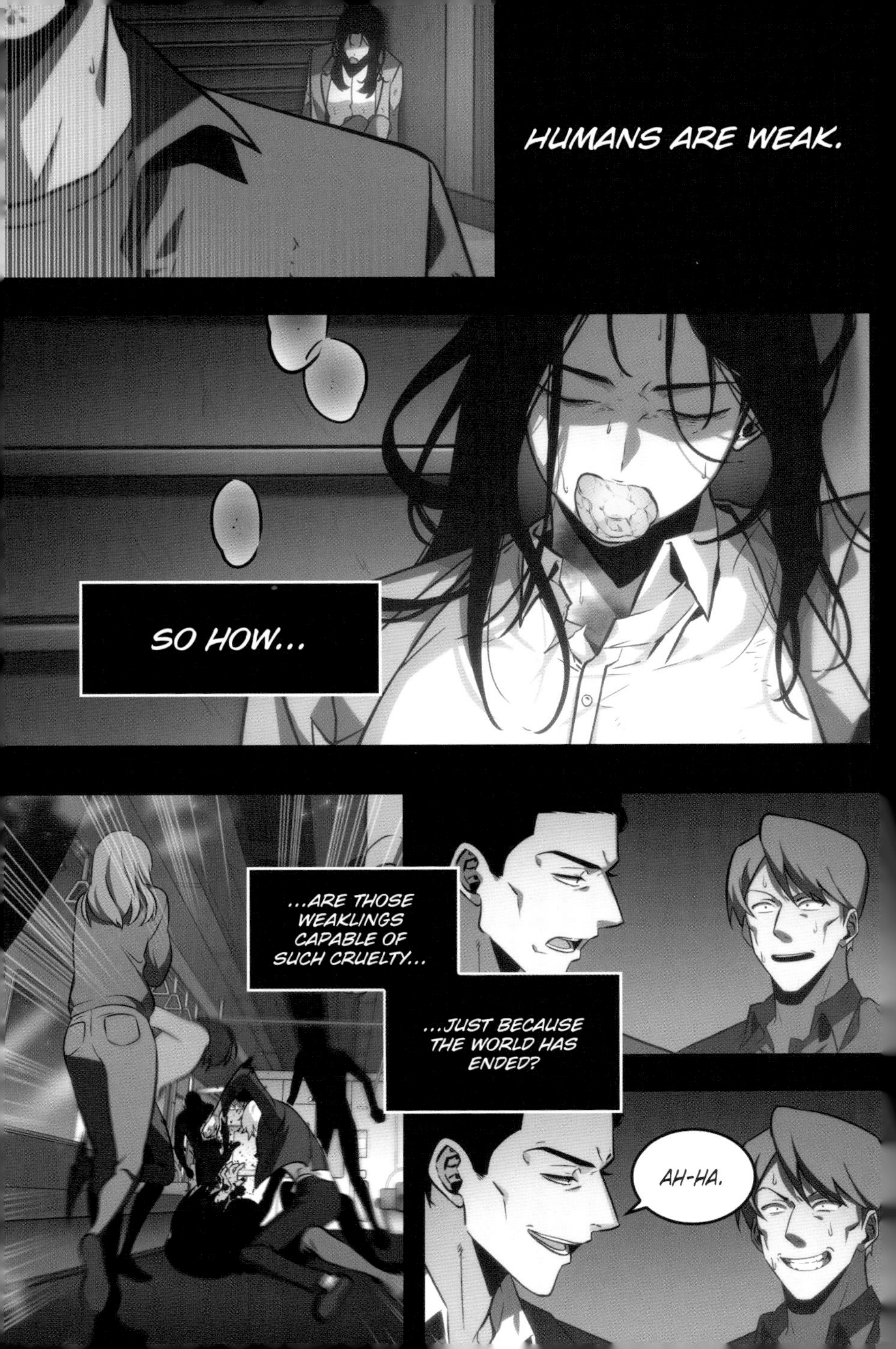
HUMANS ARE WEAK.
SO HOW...
...ARE THOSE WEAKLINGS CAPABLE OF SUCH CRUELTY...
...JUST BECAUSE THE WORLD HAS ENDED?
AH-HA.

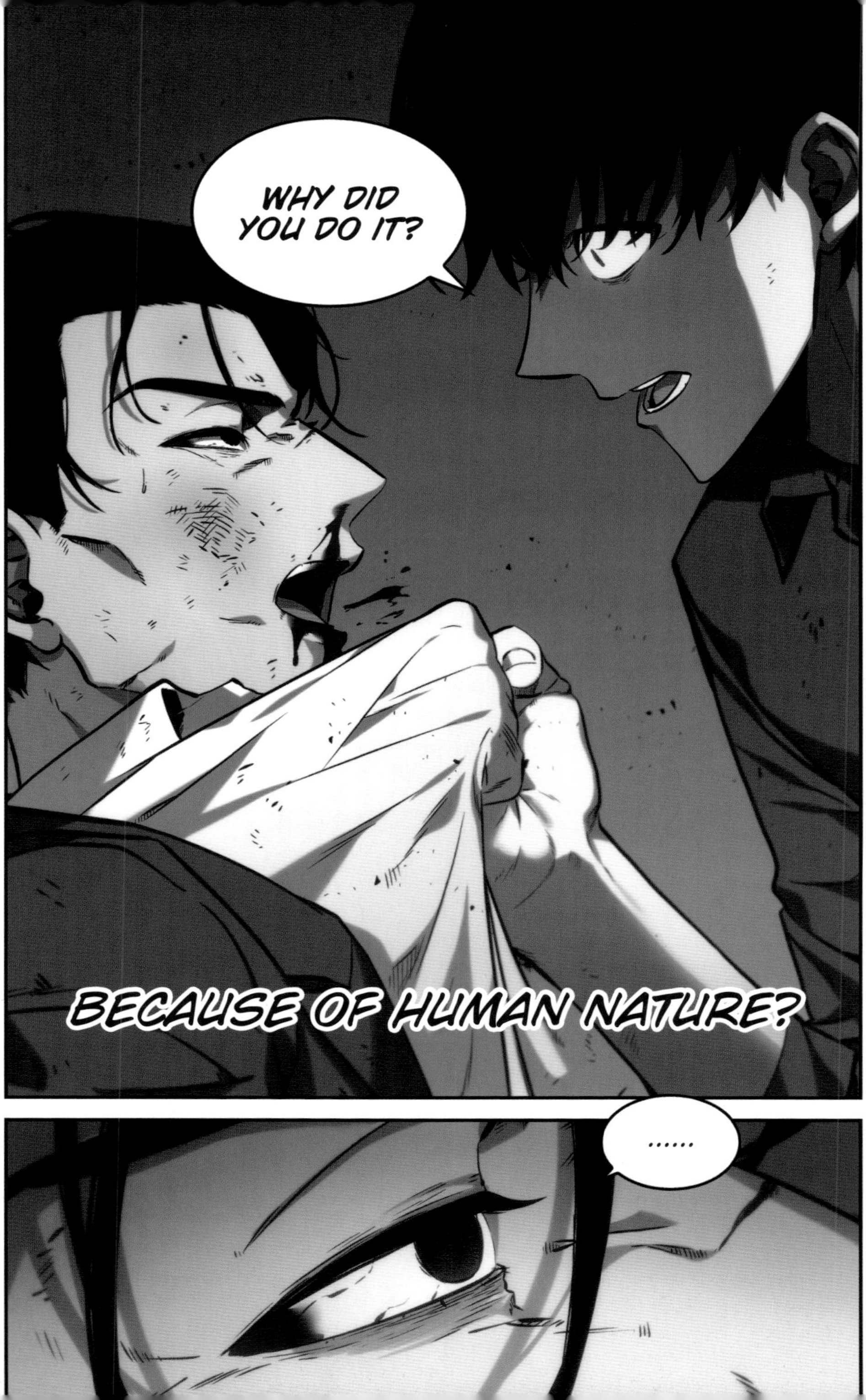
WHY DID YOU DO IT?
BECAUSE OF HUMAN NATURE?
......

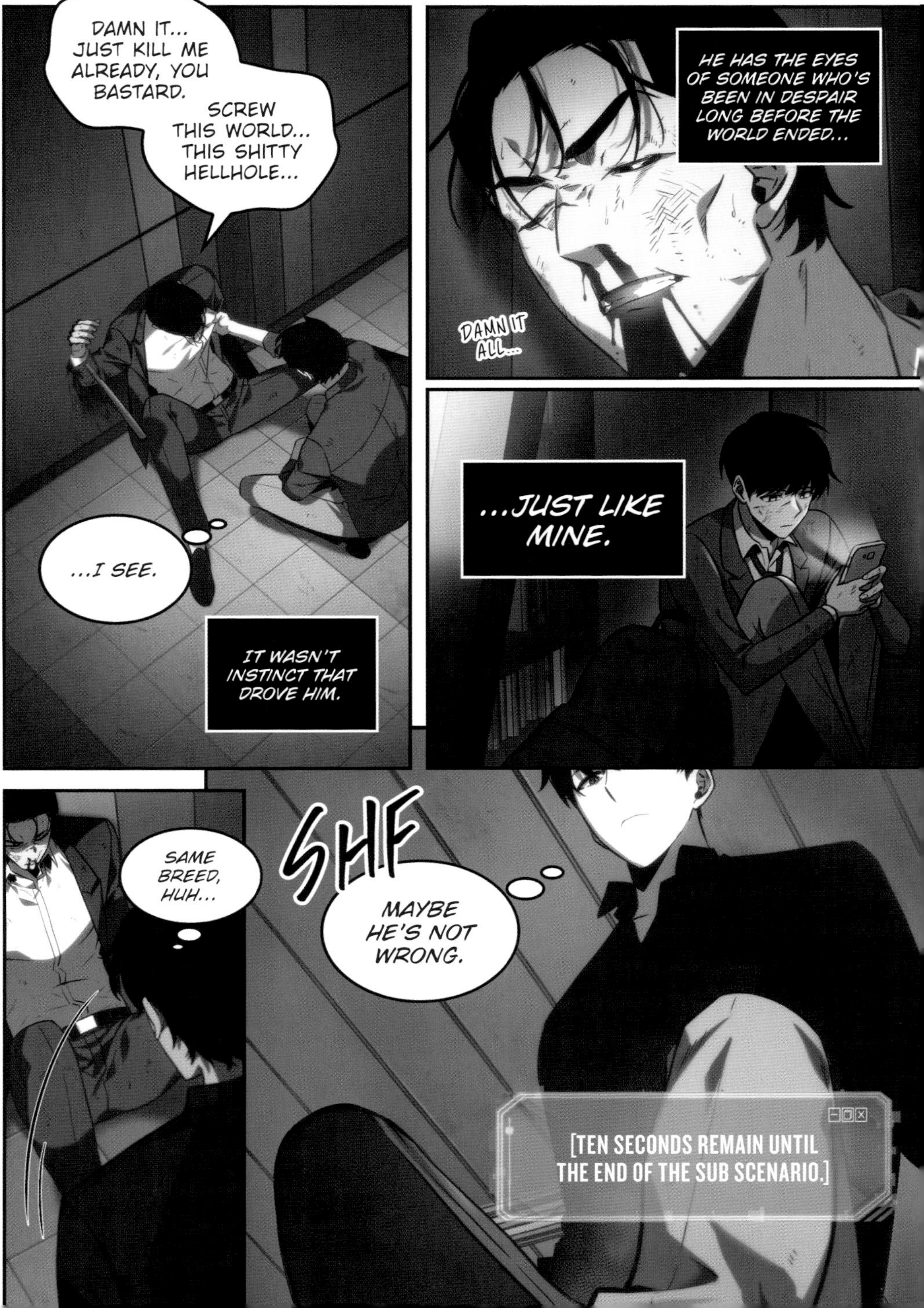
DAMN IT... JUST KILL ME ALREADY, YOU BASTARD.
SCREW THIS WORLD... THIS SHITTY HELLHOLE...
HE HAS THE EYES OF SOMEONE WHO'S BEEN IN DESPAIR LONG BEFORE THE WORLD ENDED...
DAMN IT ALL...
...I SEE.
IT WASN'T INSTINCT THAT DROVE HIM.
...JUST LIKE MINE.
SAME BREED, HUH...
SHF
MAYBE HE'S NOT WRONG.
[TEN SECONDS REMAIN UNTIL THE END OF THE SUB SCENARIO.]

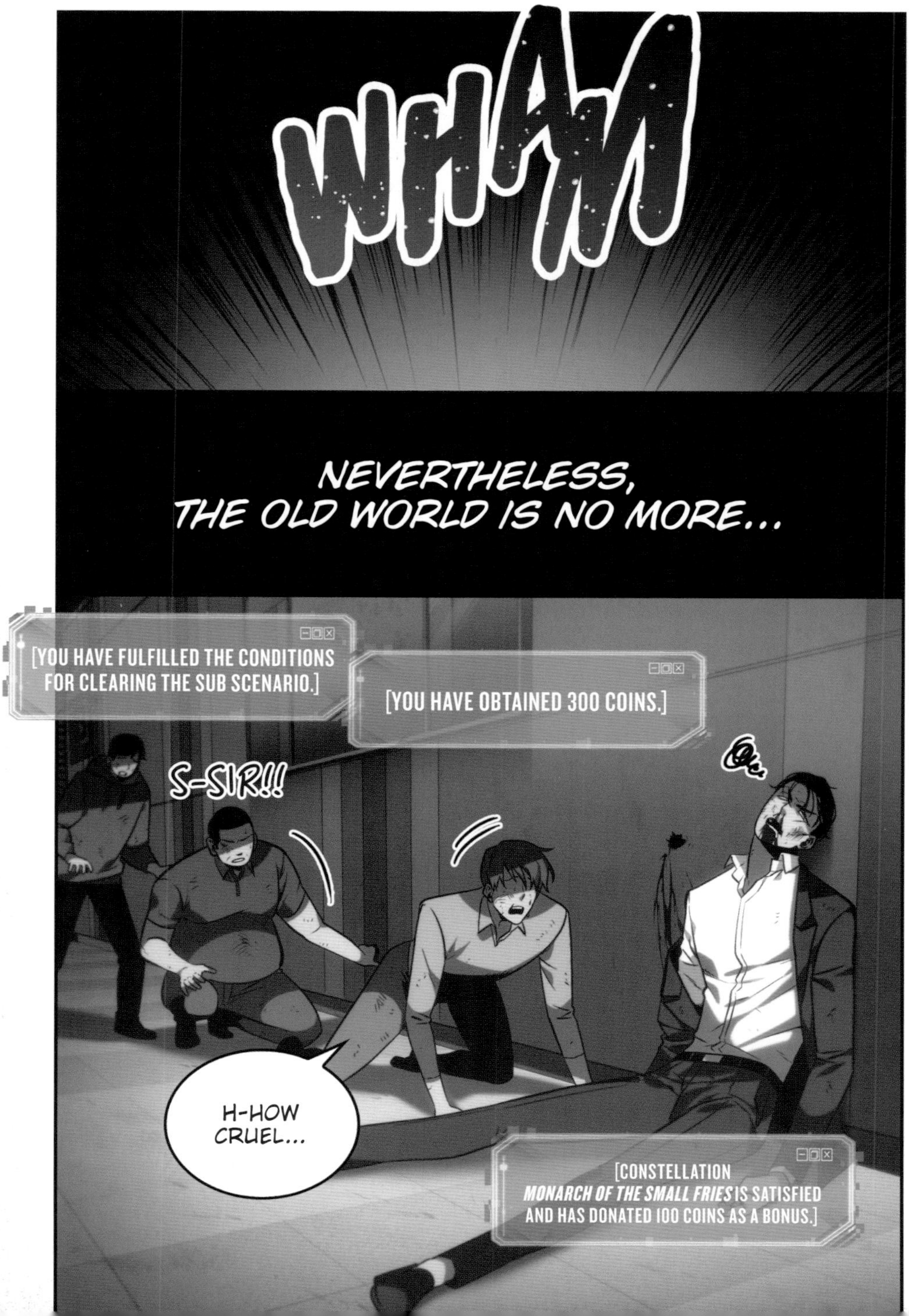
WHAM
NEVERTHELESS, THE OLD WORLD IS NO MORE...
[YOU HAVE FULFILLED THE CONDITIONS FOR CLEARING THE SUB SCENARIO.]
[YOU HAVE OBTAINED 300 COINS.]
S-SIR!!
H-HOW CRUEL...
[CONSTELLATION MONARCH OF THE SMALL FRIES IS SATISFIED AND HAS DONATED 100 COINS AS A BONUS.]

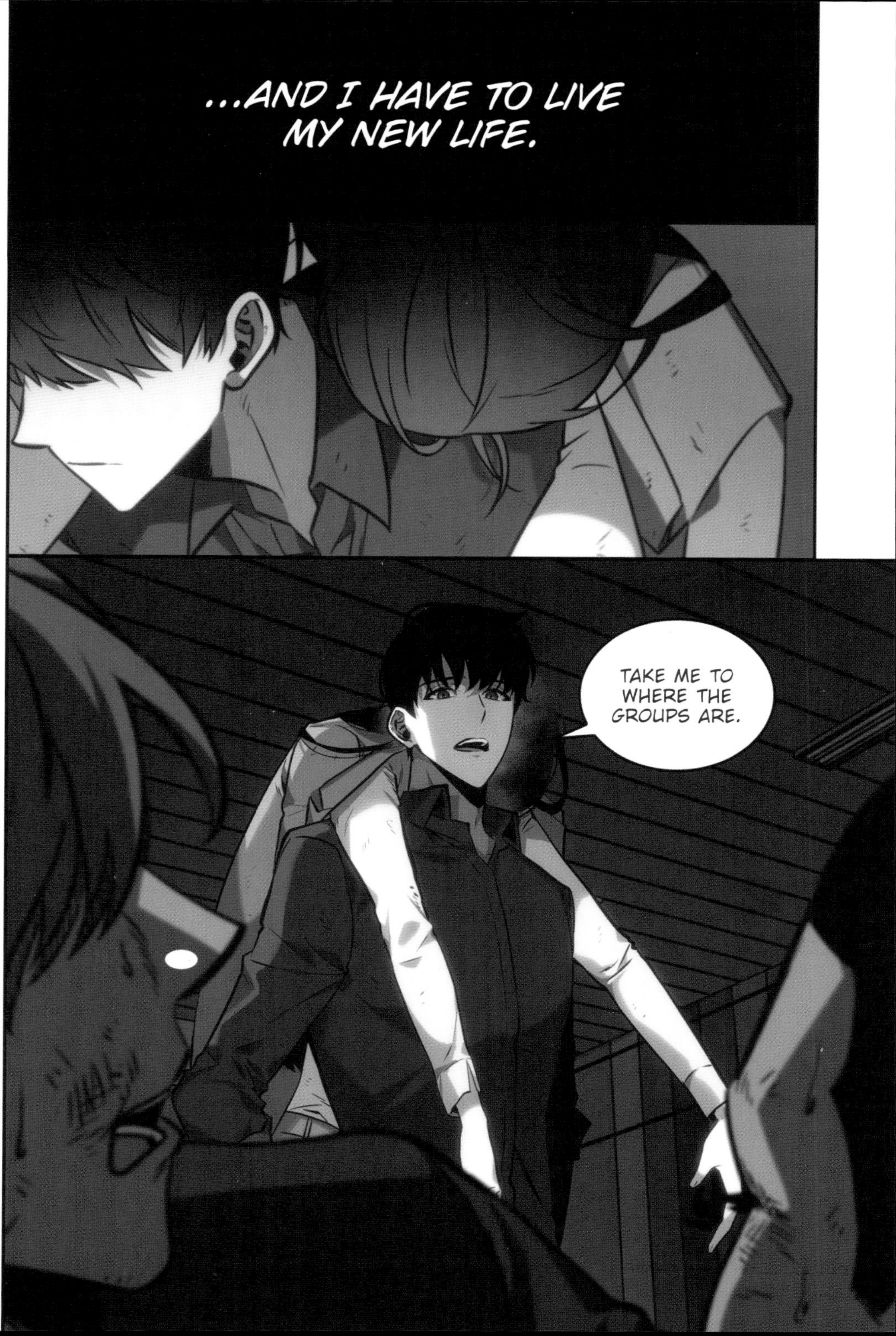
...AND I HAVE TO LIVE MY NEW LIFE.
TAKE ME TO WHERE THE GROUPS ARE.

EP. 04

Omniscient
Reader's
Viewpoint

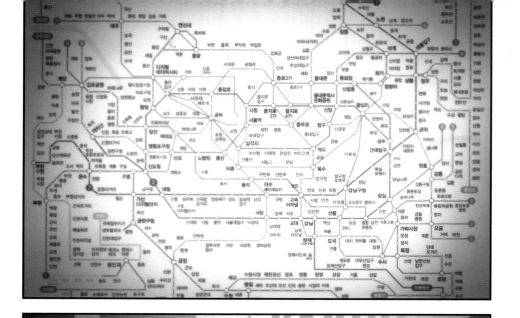

TIGOGAE | YAKSU

GEUMHO

334

금호

Geumho
金湖

HUH?

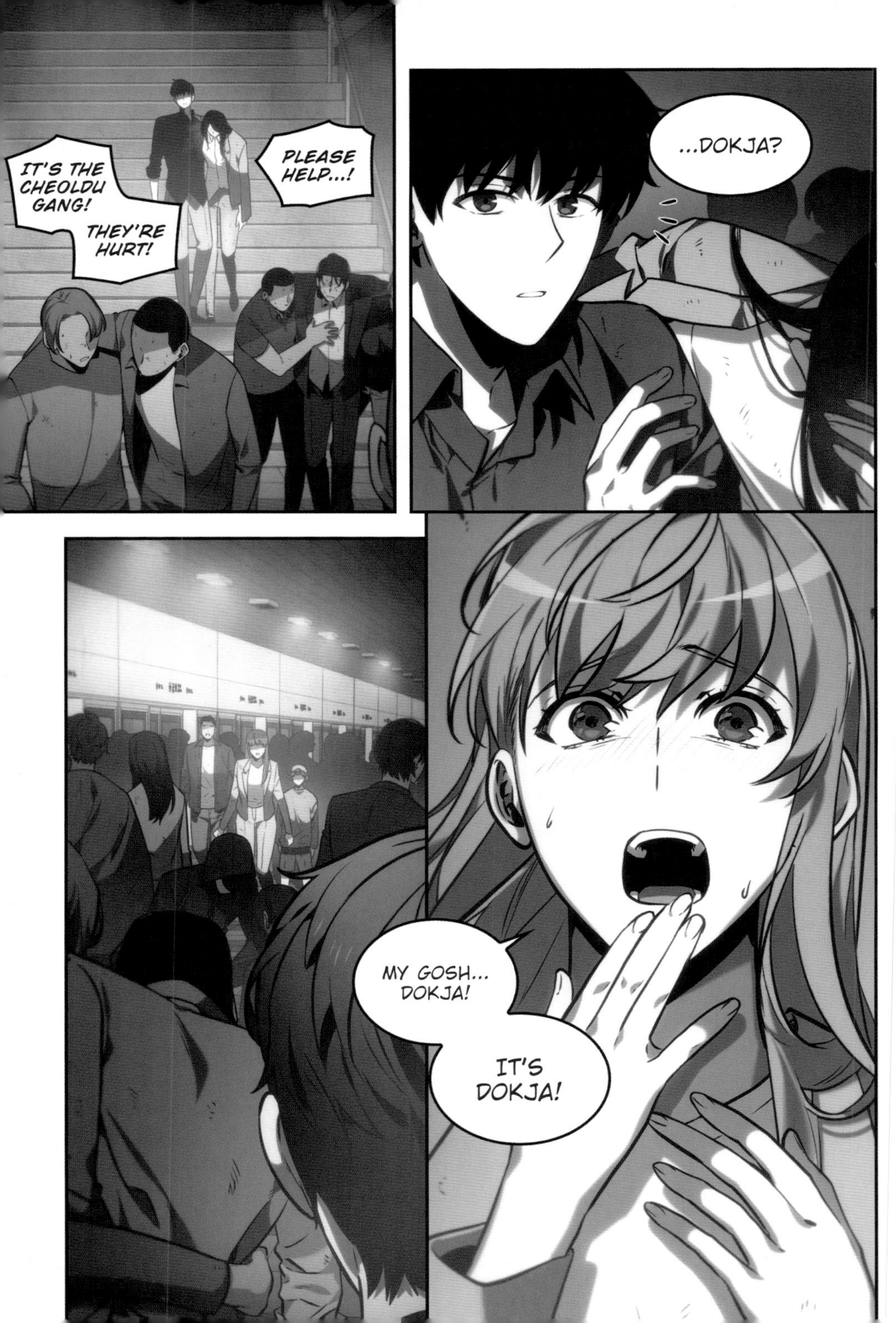
IT'S THE CHEOLDU GANG!
THEY'RE HURT!
PLEASE HELP...!
...DOKJA?
MY GOSH... DOKJA!
IT'S DOKJA!

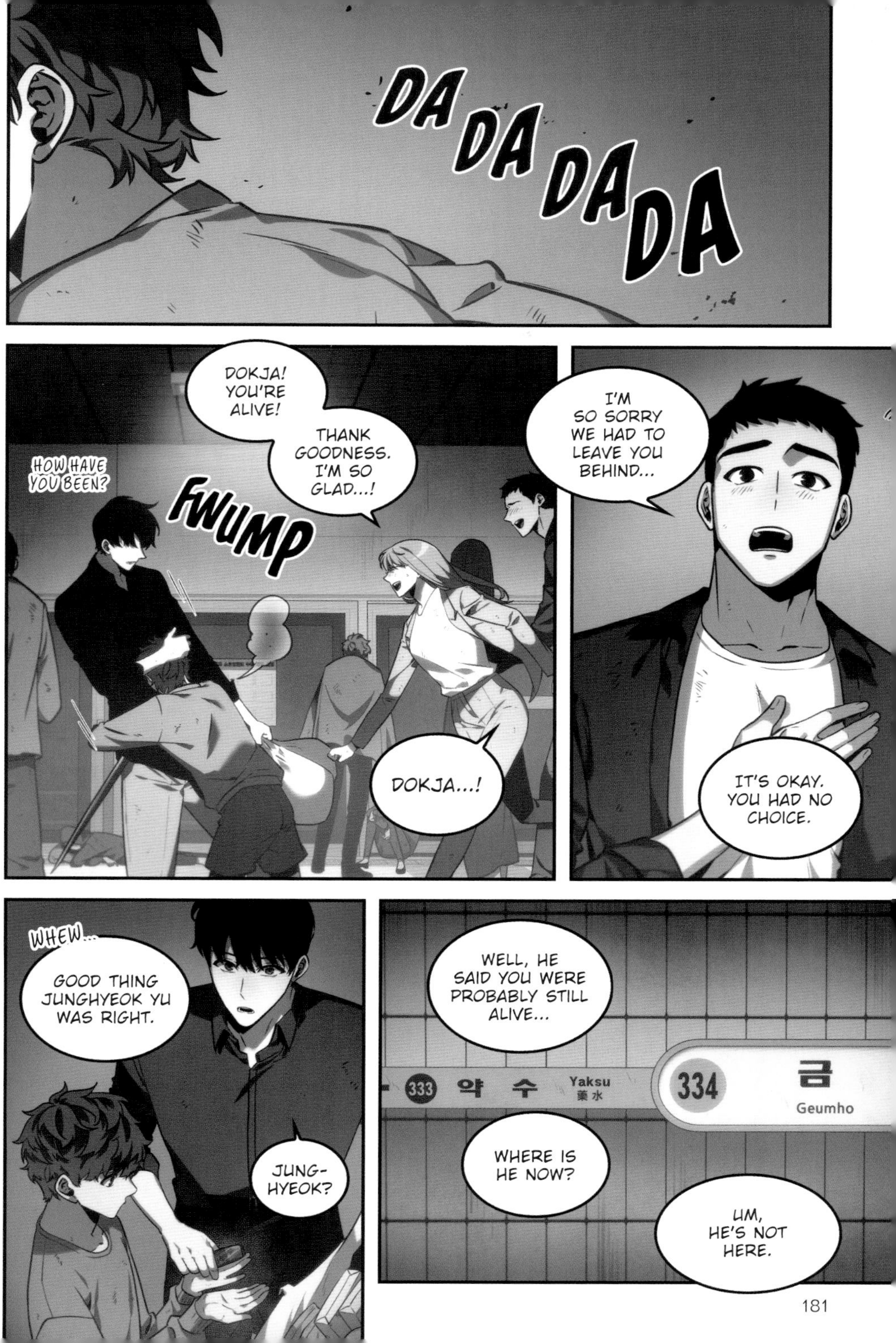

DA DA DA DA
DOKJA! YOU'RE ALIVE!
THANK GOODNESS. I'M SO GLAD...!
HOW HAVE YOU BEEN?
FWUMP
DOKJA...!
I'M SO SORRY WE HAD TO LEAVE YOU BEHIND...
IT'S OKAY. YOU HAD NO CHOICE.
WHEW...
GOOD THING JUNGHYEOK YU WAS RIGHT.
JUNG-HYEOK?
WELL, HE SAID YOU WERE PROBABLY STILL ALIVE...
333 약 수 Yaksu 藥水
334 금 Geumho
WHERE IS HE NOW?
UM, HE'S NOT HERE.

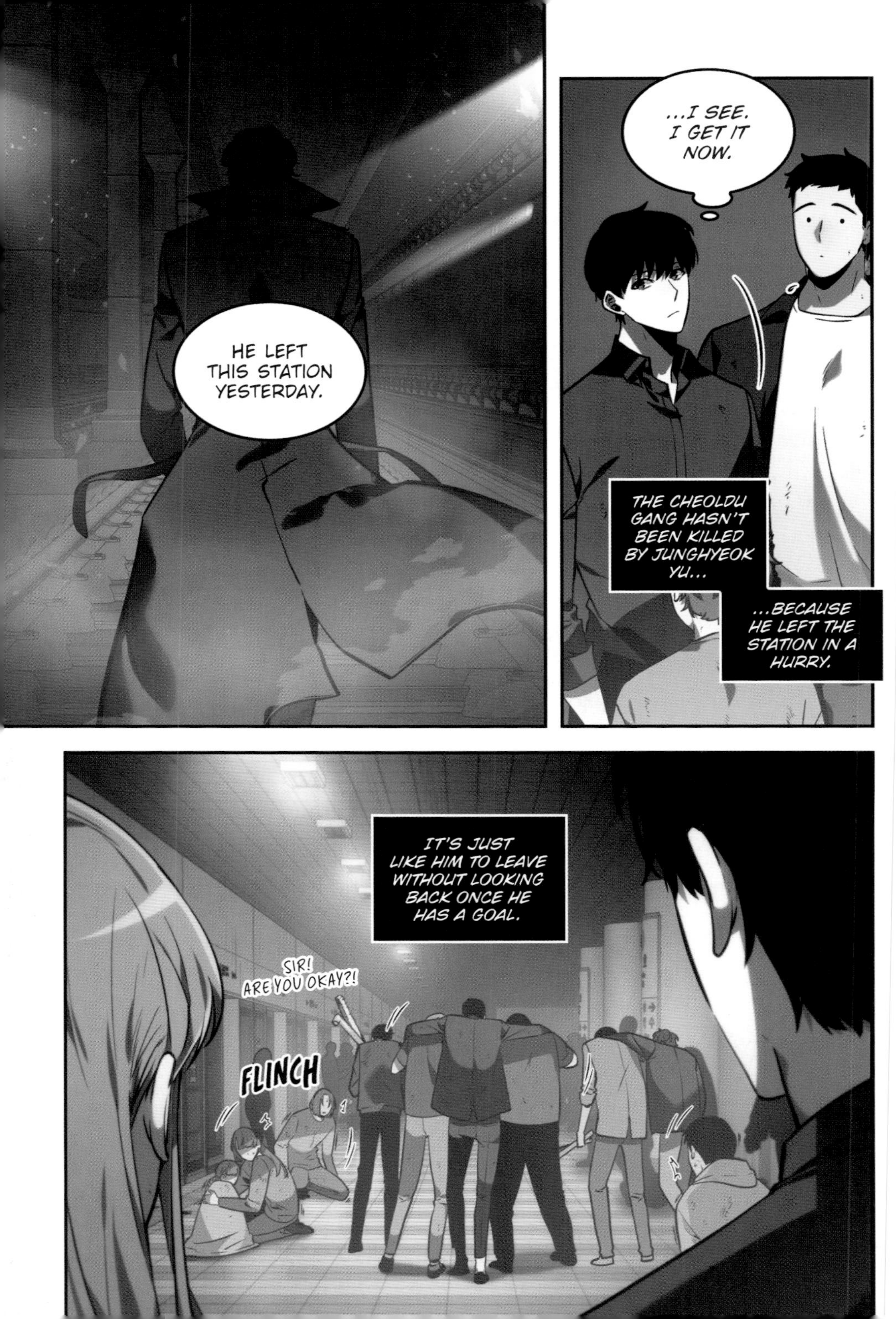
HE LEFT THIS STATION YESTERDAY.
...I SEE. I GET IT NOW.
THE CHEOLDU GANG HASN'T BEEN KILLED BY JUNGHYEOK YU...
...BECAUSE HE LEFT THE STATION IN A HURRY.
IT'S JUST LIKE HIM TO LEAVE WITHOUT LOOKING BACK ONCE HE HAS A GOAL.
SIR! ARE YOU OKAY?!
FLINCH

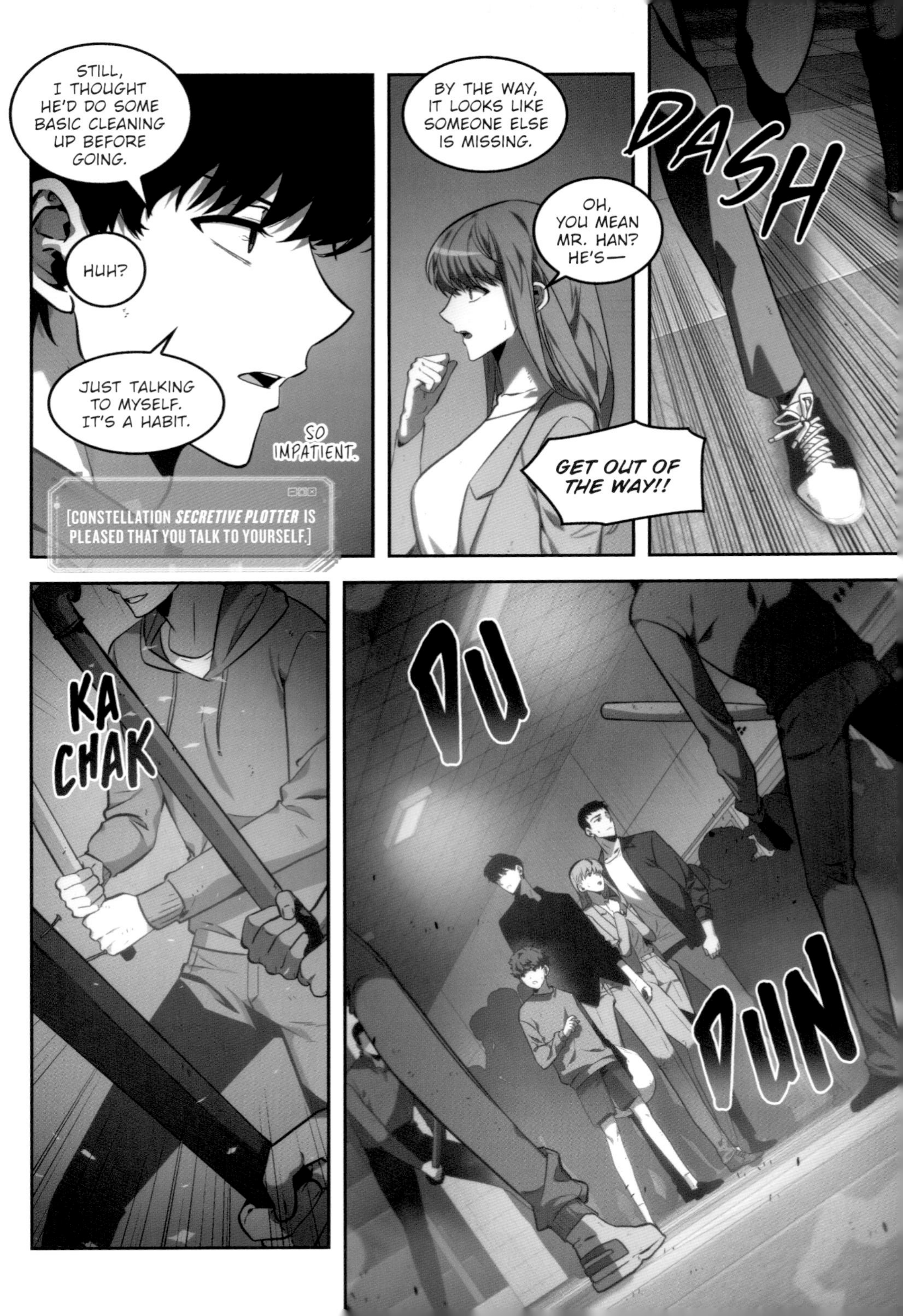
STILL, I THOUGHT HE'D DO SOME BASIC CLEANING UP BEFORE GOING.
HUH?
JUST TALKING TO MYSELF. IT'S A HABIT.
SO IMPATIENT.
[CONSTELLATION SECRETIVE PLOTTER IS PLEASED THAT YOU TALK TO YOURSELF.]
BY THE WAY, IT LOOKS LIKE SOMEONE ELSE IS MISSING.
OH, YOU MEAN MR. HAN? HE'S—
GET OUT OF THE WAY!!
DASH
KA CHAK
DU
DUN

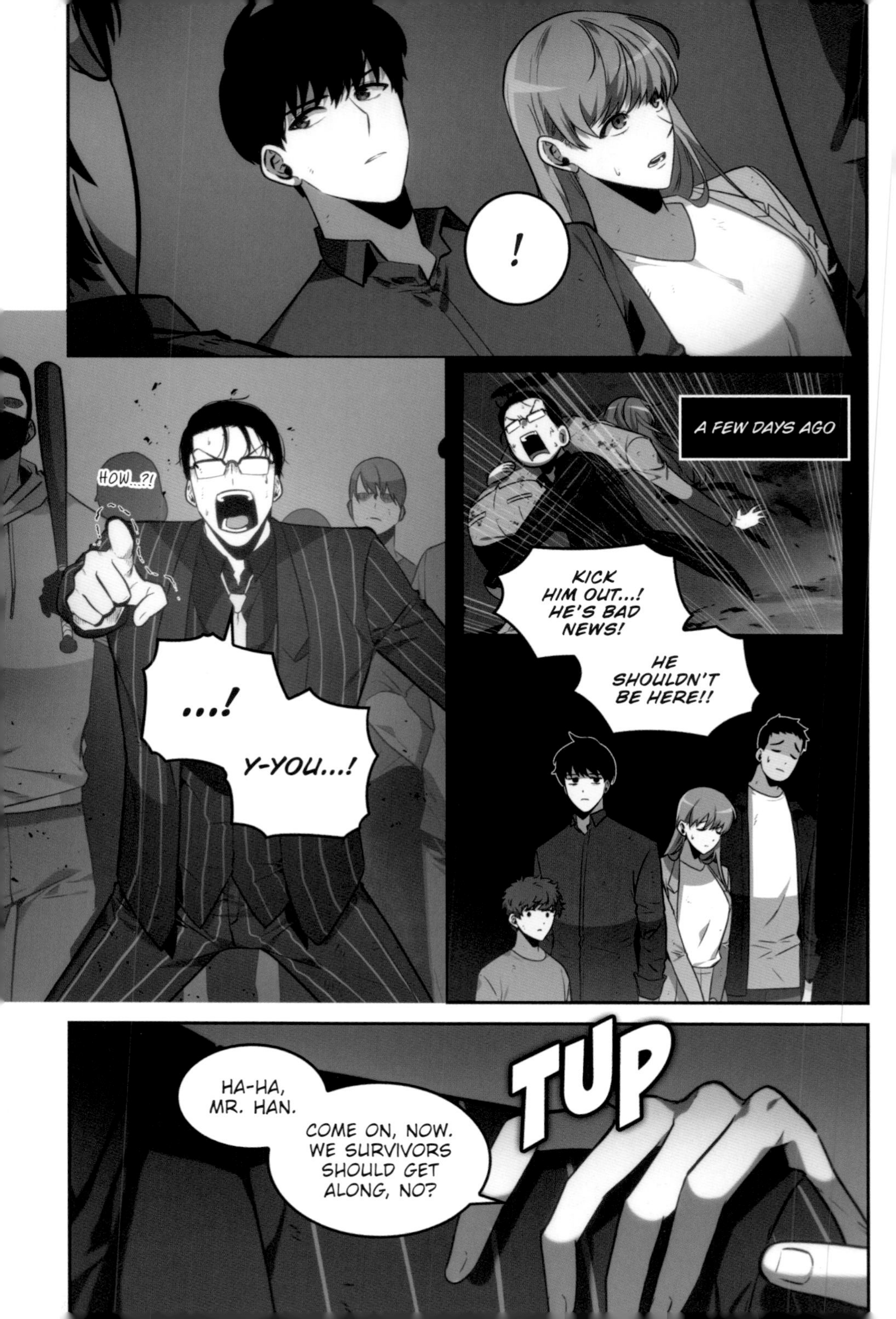
!
HOW...?!
...!
Y-YOU...!
A FEW DAYS AGO
KICK HIM OUT...! HE'S BAD NEWS!
HE SHOULDN'T BE HERE!!
TUP
HA-HA, MR. HAN.
COME ON, NOW. WE SURVIVORS SHOULD GET ALONG, NO?

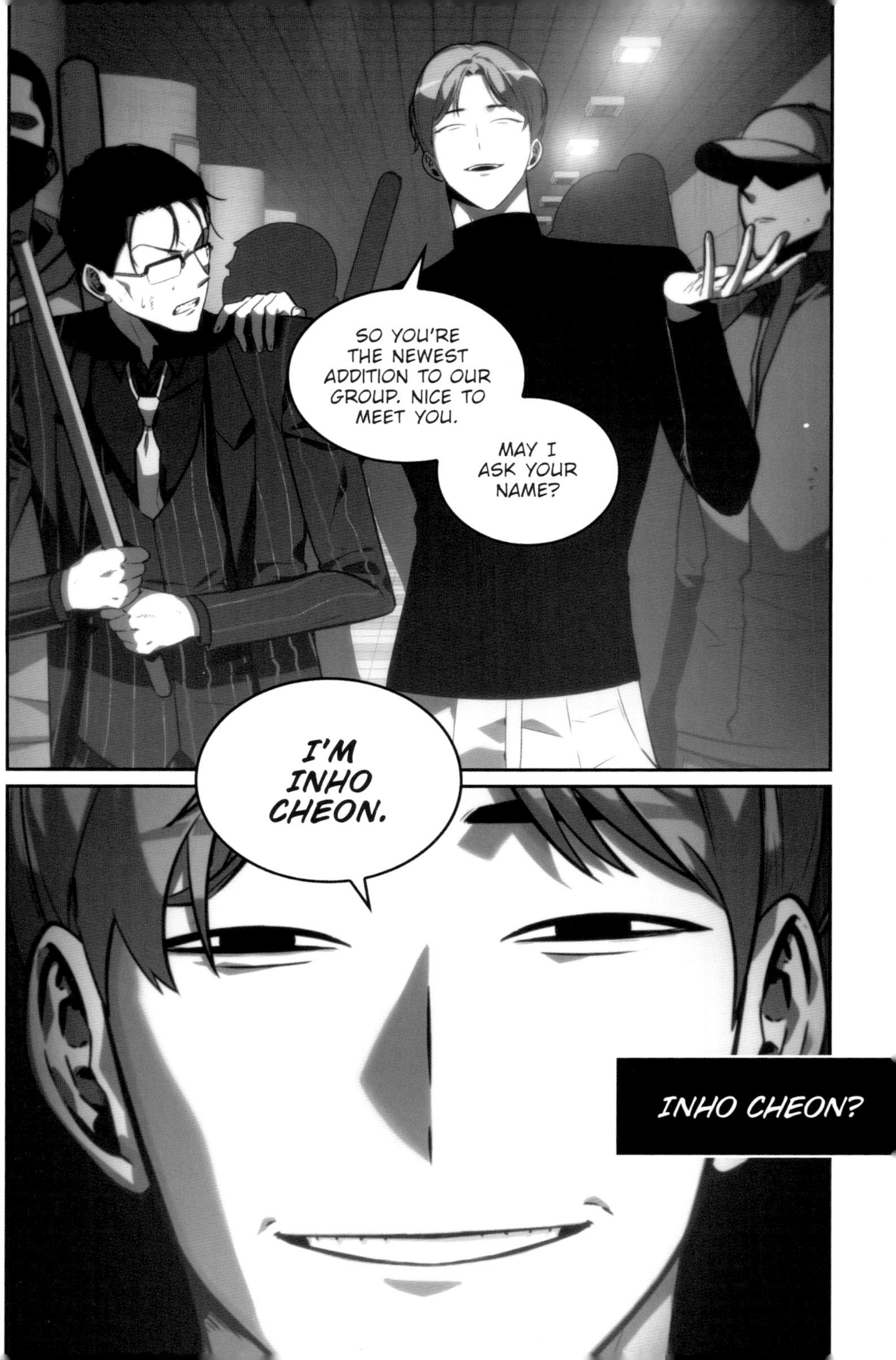
SO YOU'RE THE NEWEST ADDITION TO OUR GROUP. NICE TO MEET YOU.
MAY I ASK YOUR NAME?
I'M INHO CHEON.
INHO CHEON?

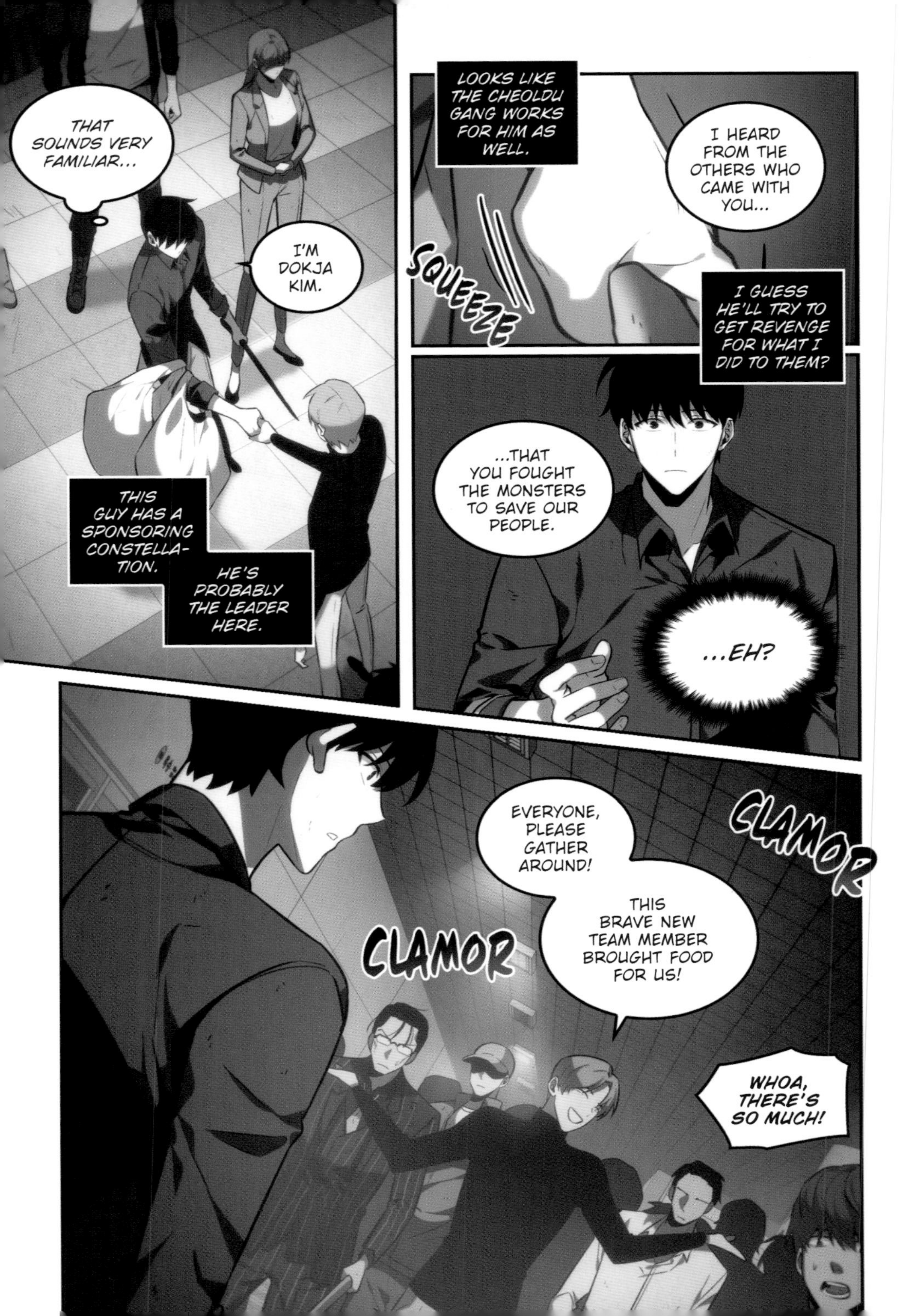
THAT SOUNDS VERY FAMILIAR...
I'M DOKJA KIM.
THIS GUY HAS A SPONSORING CONSTELLATION.
HE'S PROBABLY THE LEADER HERE.
LOOKS LIKE THE CHEOLDU GANG WORKS FOR HIM AS WELL.
I HEARD FROM THE OTHERS WHO CAME WITH YOU...
SQUEEEZE
I GUESS HE'LL TRY TO GET REVENGE FOR WHAT I DID TO THEM?
...THAT YOU FOUGHT THE MONSTERS TO SAVE OUR PEOPLE.
...EH?
EVERYONE, PLEASE GATHER AROUND!
CLAMOR
THIS BRAVE NEW TEAM MEMBER BROUGHT FOOD FOR US!
CLAMOR
WHOA, THERE'S SO MUCH!

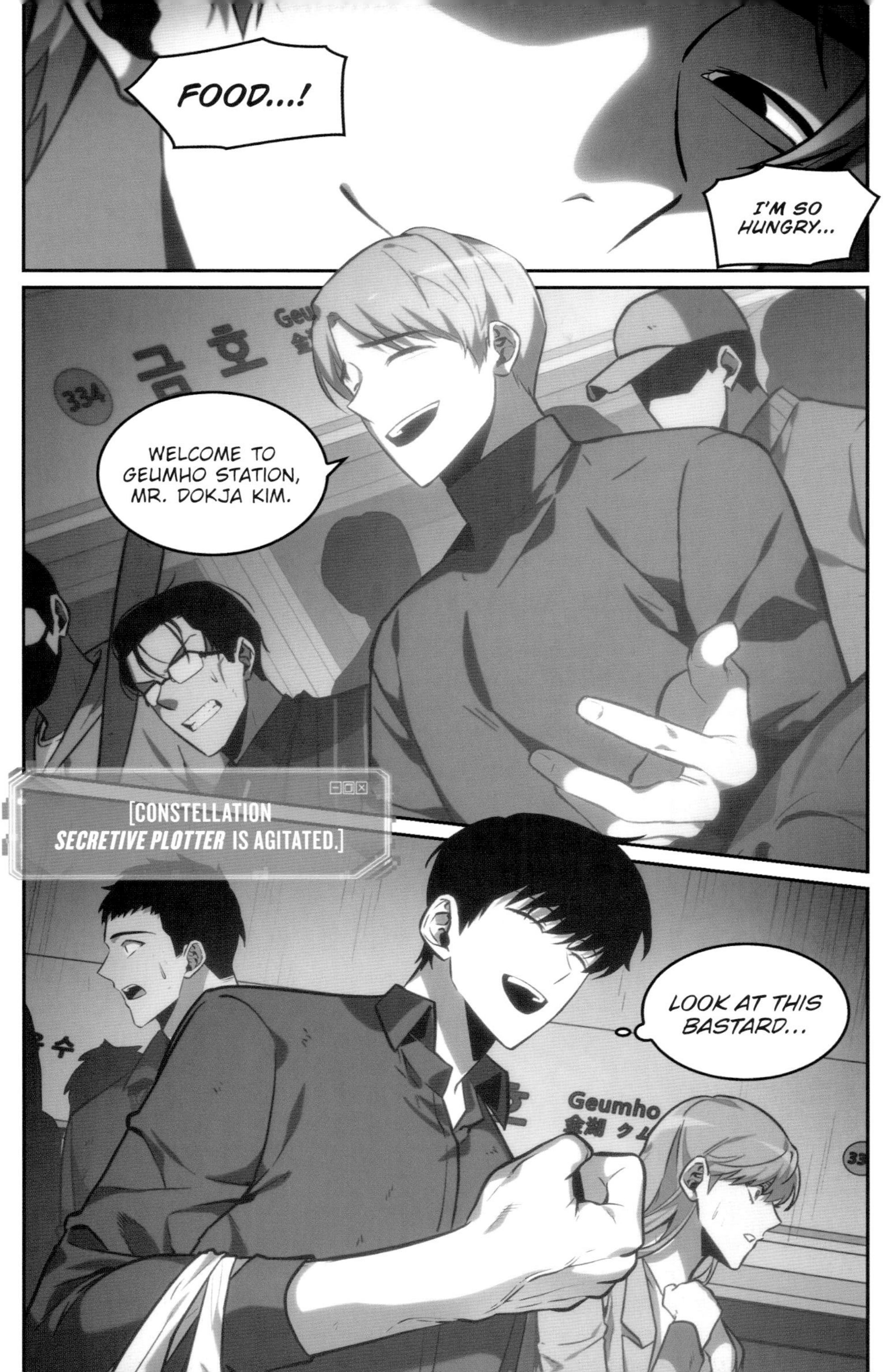
FOOD...!
I'M SO HUNGRY...
금호
Geum
334
WELCOME TO GEUMHO STATION, MR. DOKJA KIM.
[CONSTELLATION SECRETIVE PLOTTER IS AGITATED.]
LOOK AT THIS BASTARD...
Geumho

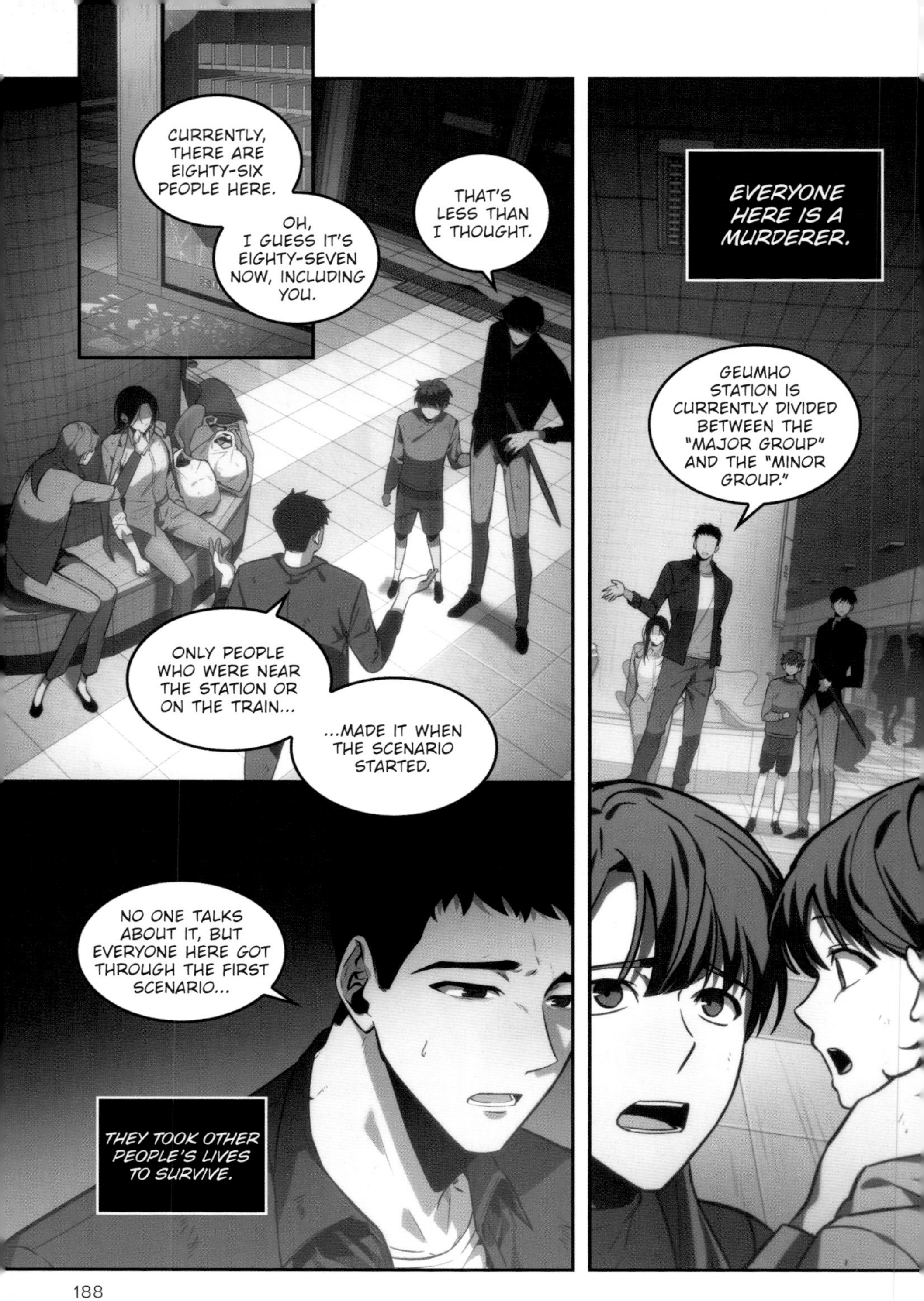

CURRENTLY, THERE ARE EIGHTY-SIX PEOPLE HERE.
OH, I GUESS IT'S EIGHTY-SEVEN NOW, INCLUDING YOU.
THAT'S LESS THAN I THOUGHT.
ONLY PEOPLE WHO WERE NEAR THE STATION OR ON THE TRAIN...
...MADE IT WHEN THE SCENARIO STARTED.
NO ONE TALKS ABOUT IT, BUT EVERYONE HERE GOT THROUGH THE FIRST SCENARIO...
THEY TOOK OTHER PEOPLE'S LIVES TO SURVIVE.
EVERYONE HERE IS A MURDERER.
GEUMHO STATION IS CURRENTLY DIVIDED BETWEEN THE "MAJOR GROUP" AND THE "MINOR GROUP."

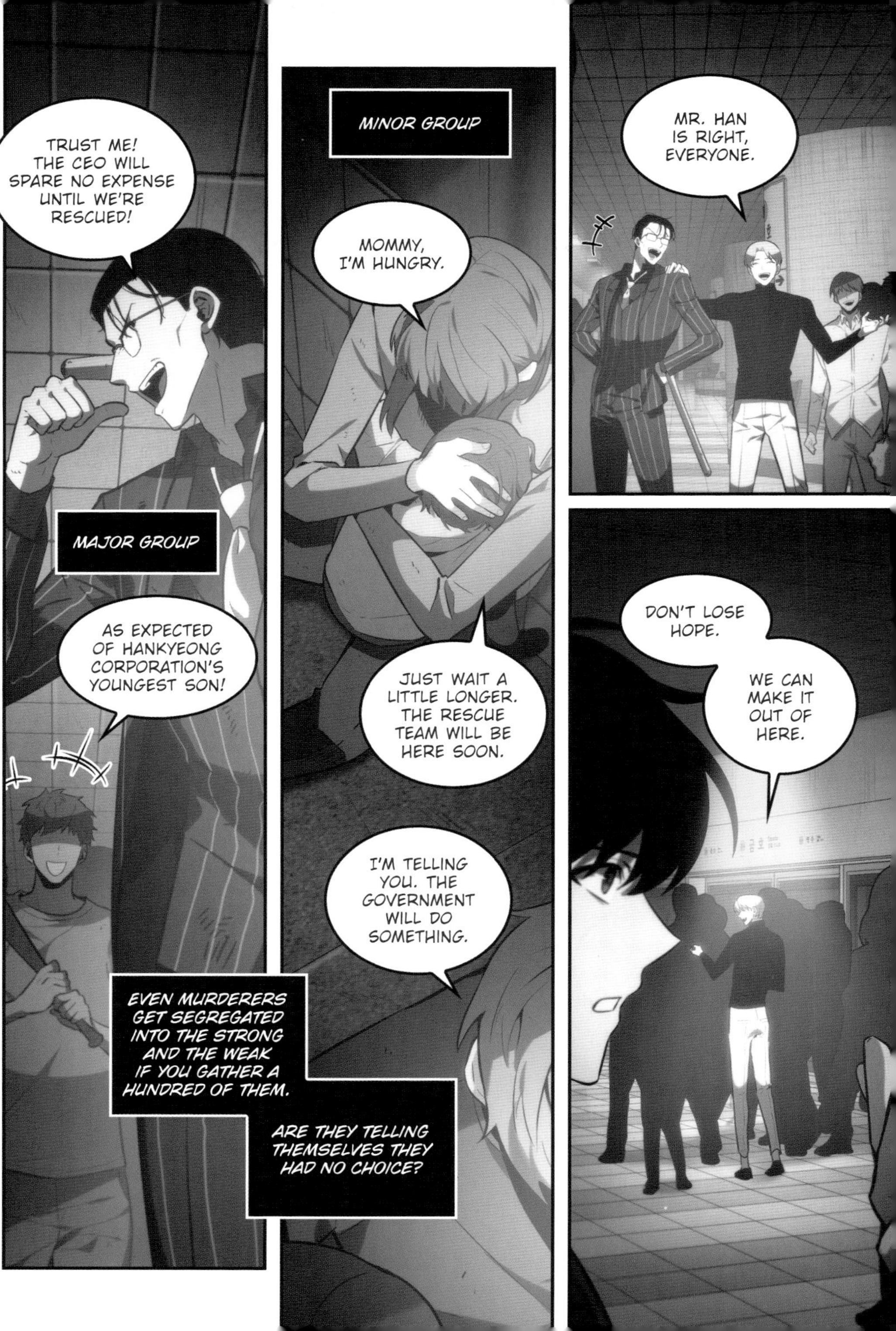
TRUST ME! THE CEO WILL SPARE NO EXPENSE UNTIL WE'RE RESCUED!
MAJOR GROUP
AS EXPECTED OF HANKYEONG CORPORATION'S YOUNGEST SON!
MINOR GROUP
MOMMY, I'M HUNGRY.
JUST WAIT A LITTLE LONGER. THE RESCUE TEAM WILL BE HERE SOON.
I'M TELLING YOU. THE GOVERNMENT WILL DO SOMETHING.
EVEN MURDERERS GET SEGREGATED INTO THE STRONG AND THE WEAK IF YOU GATHER A HUNDRED OF THEM.
ARE THEY TELLING THEMSELVES THEY HAD NO CHOICE?
MR. HAN IS RIGHT, EVERYONE.
DON'T LOSE HOPE.
WE CAN MAKE IT OUT OF HERE.

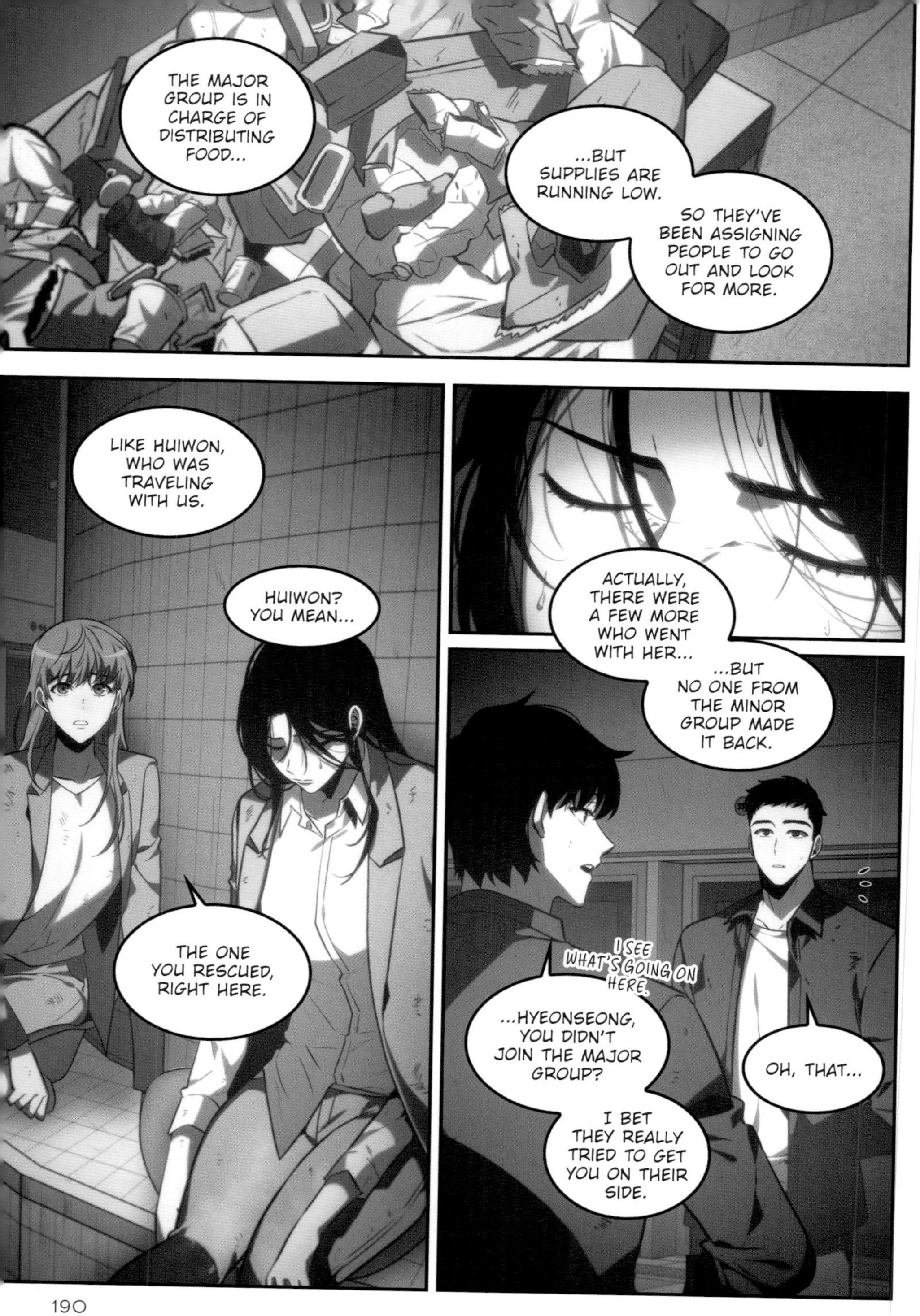
THE MAJOR GROUP IS IN CHARGE OF DISTRIBUTING FOOD...
...BUT SUPPLIES ARE RUNNING LOW.
SO THEY'VE BEEN ASSIGNING PEOPLE TO GO OUT AND LOOK FOR MORE.
LIKE HUIWON, WHO WAS TRAVELING WITH US.
HUIWON? YOU MEAN...
THE ONE YOU RESCUED, RIGHT HERE.
ACTUALLY, THERE WERE A FEW MORE WHO WENT WITH HER...
...BUT NO ONE FROM THE MINOR GROUP MADE IT BACK.
I SEE WHAT'S GOING ON HERE.
...HYEONSEONG, YOU DIDN'T JOIN THE MAJOR GROUP?
I BET THEY REALLY TRIED TO GET YOU ON THEIR SIDE.
OH, THAT...

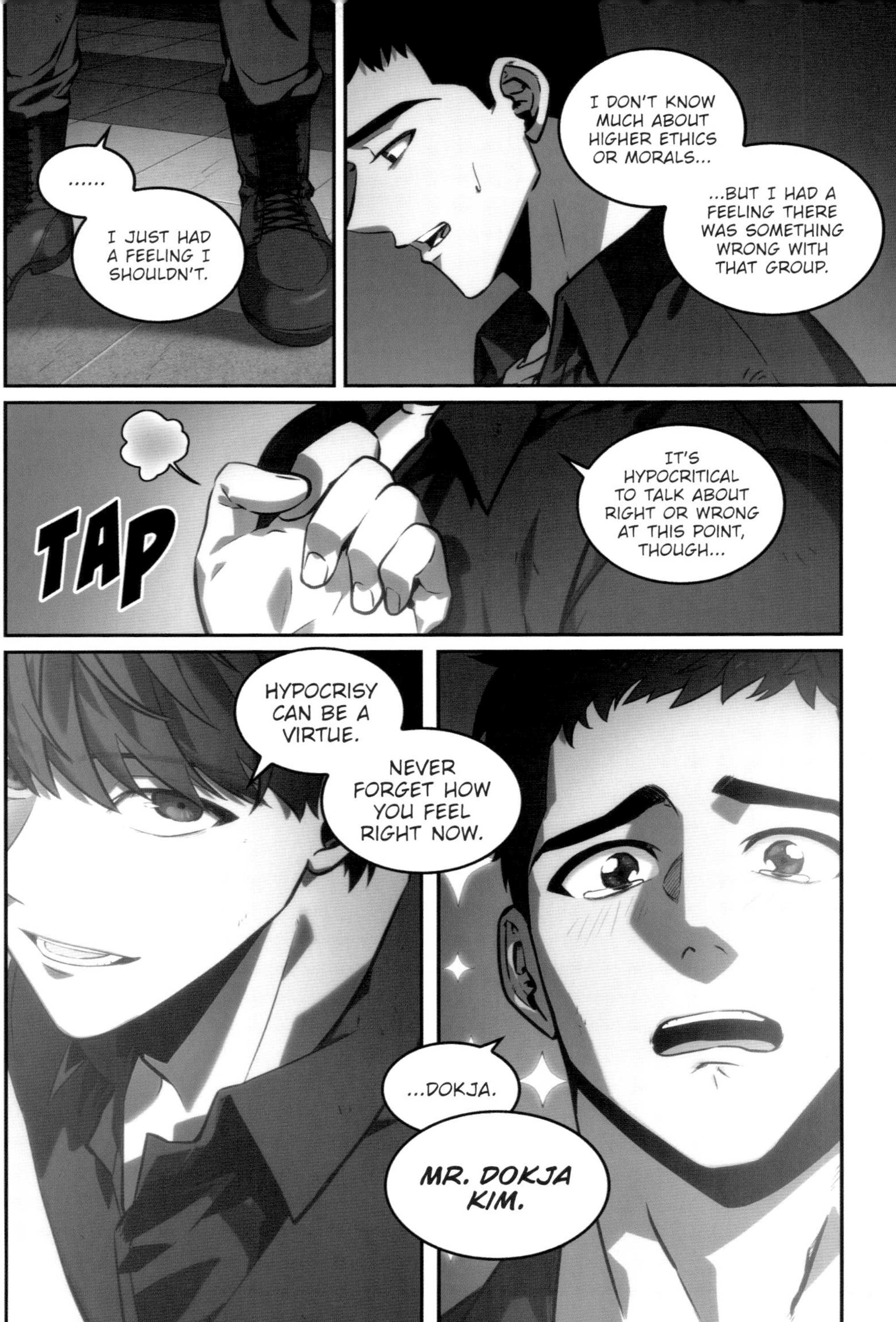
......
I JUST HAD A FEELING I SHOULDN'T.
I DON'T KNOW MUCH ABOUT HIGHER ETHICS OR MORALS...
...BUT I HAD A FEELING THERE WAS SOMETHING WRONG WITH THAT GROUP.
TAP
IT'S HYPOCRITICAL TO TALK ABOUT RIGHT OR WRONG AT THIS POINT, THOUGH...
HYPOCRISY CAN BE A VIRTUE.
NEVER FORGET HOW YOU FEEL RIGHT NOW.
...DOKJA.
MR. DOKJA KIM.

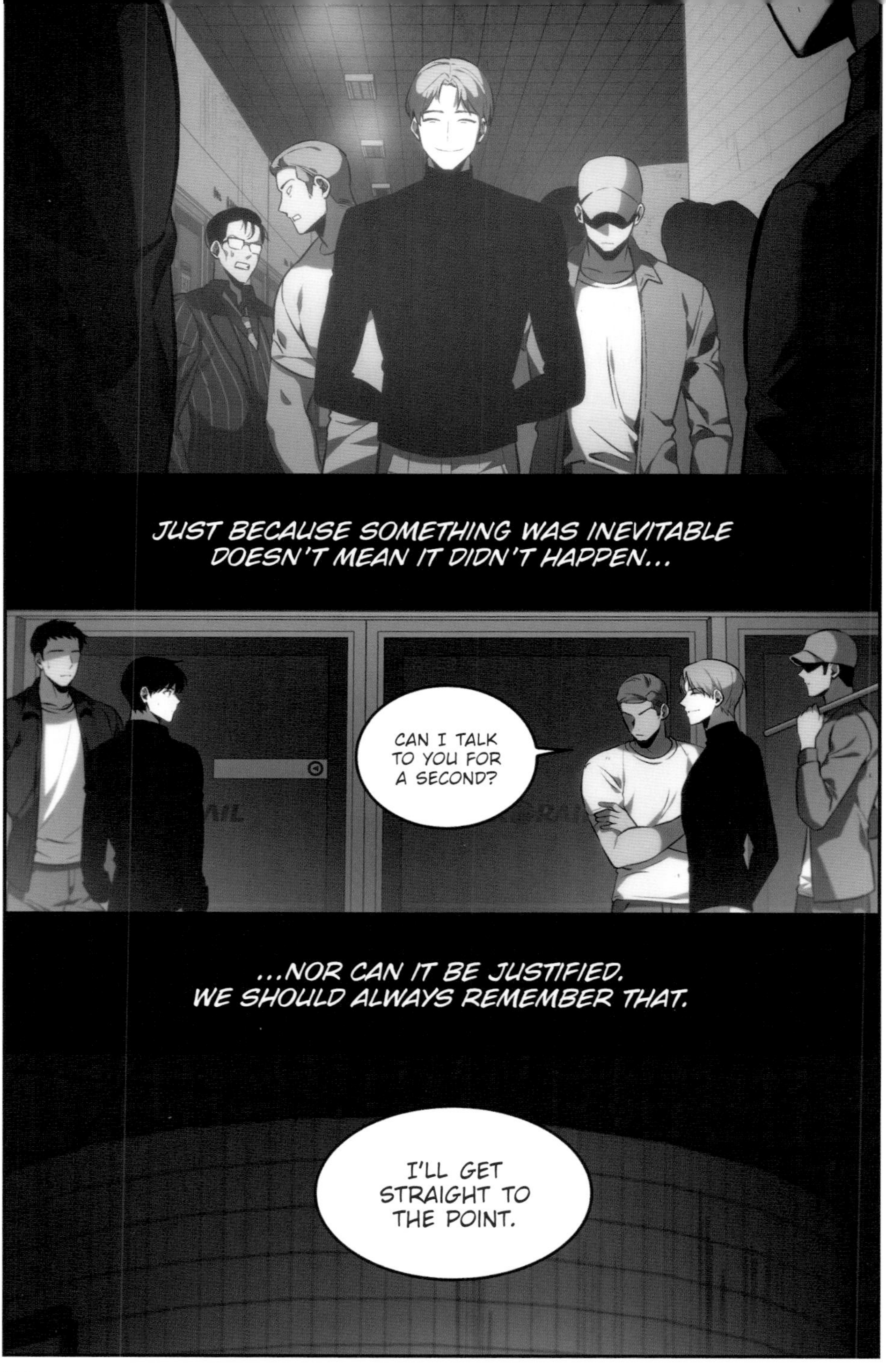
JUST BECAUSE SOMETHING WAS INEVITABLE DOESN'T MEAN IT DIDN'T HAPPEN...
CAN I TALK TO YOU FOR A SECOND?
...NOR CAN IT BE JUSTIFIED. WE SHOULD ALWAYS REMEMBER THAT.
I'LL GET STRAIGHT TO THE POINT.

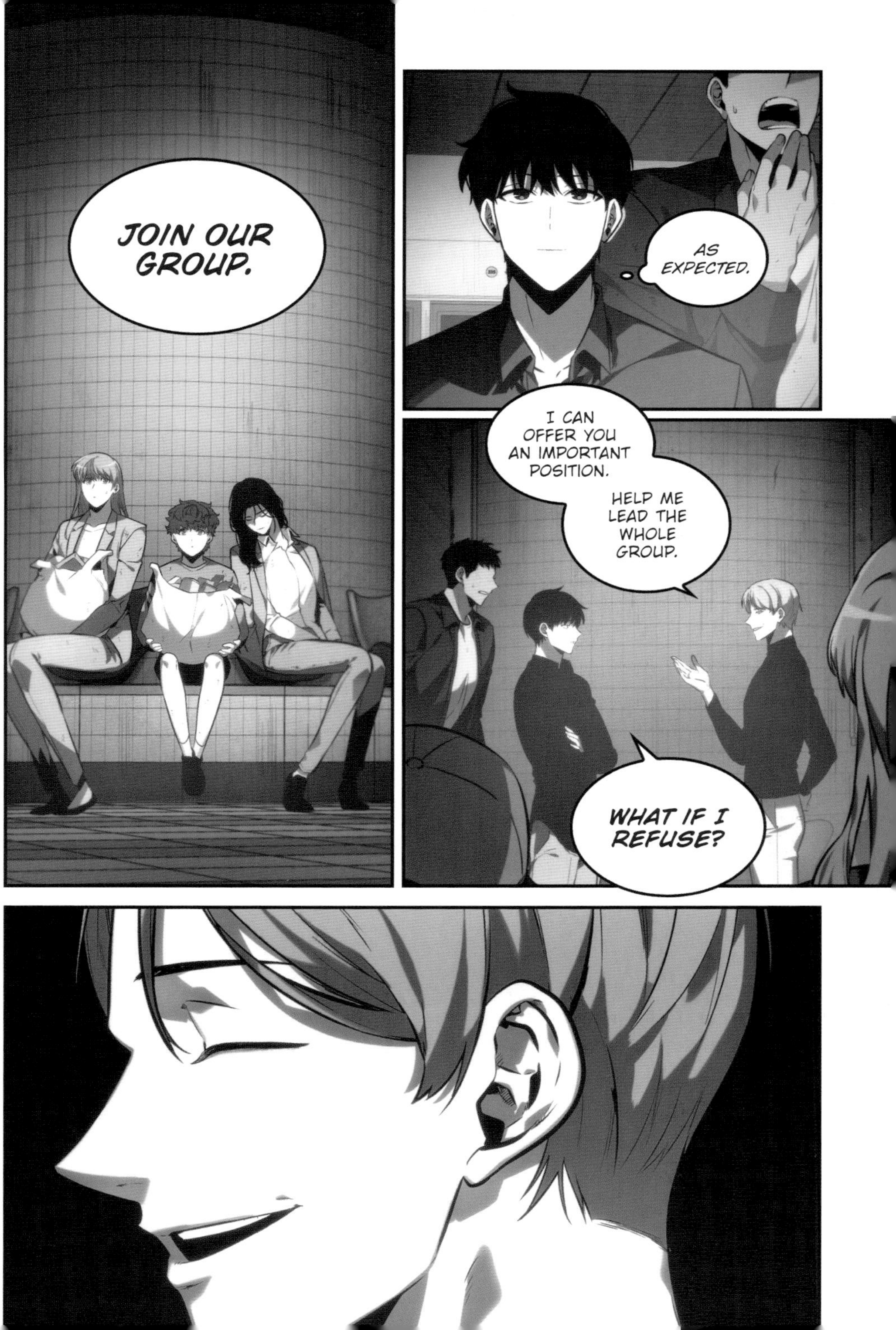
JOIN OUR GROUP.
AS EXPECTED.
I CAN OFFER YOU AN IMPORTANT POSITION.
HELP ME LEAD THE WHOLE GROUP.
WHAT IF I REFUSE?

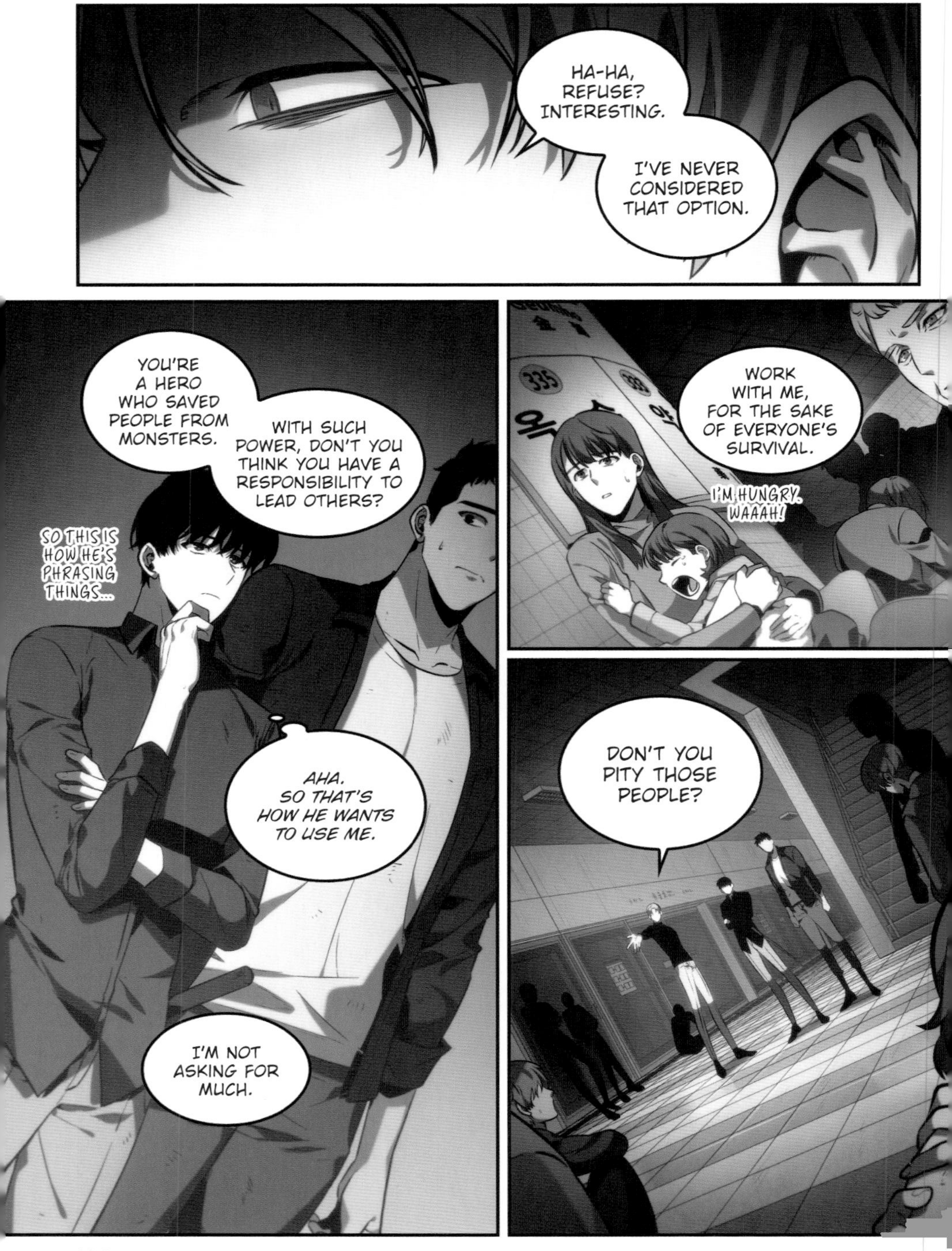

HA-HA, REFUSE? INTERESTING.
I'VE NEVER CONSIDERED THAT OPTION.
YOU'RE A HERO WHO SAVED PEOPLE FROM MONSTERS.
WITH SUCH POWER, DON'T YOU THINK YOU HAVE A RESPONSIBILITY TO LEAD OTHERS?
SO THIS IS HOW HE'S PHRASING THINGS...
AHA. SO THAT'S HOW HE WANTS TO USE ME.
I'M NOT ASKING FOR MUCH.
WORK WITH ME, FOR THE SAKE OF EVERYONE'S SURVIVAL.
I'M HUNGRY. WAAAH!
DON'T YOU PITY THOSE PEOPLE?

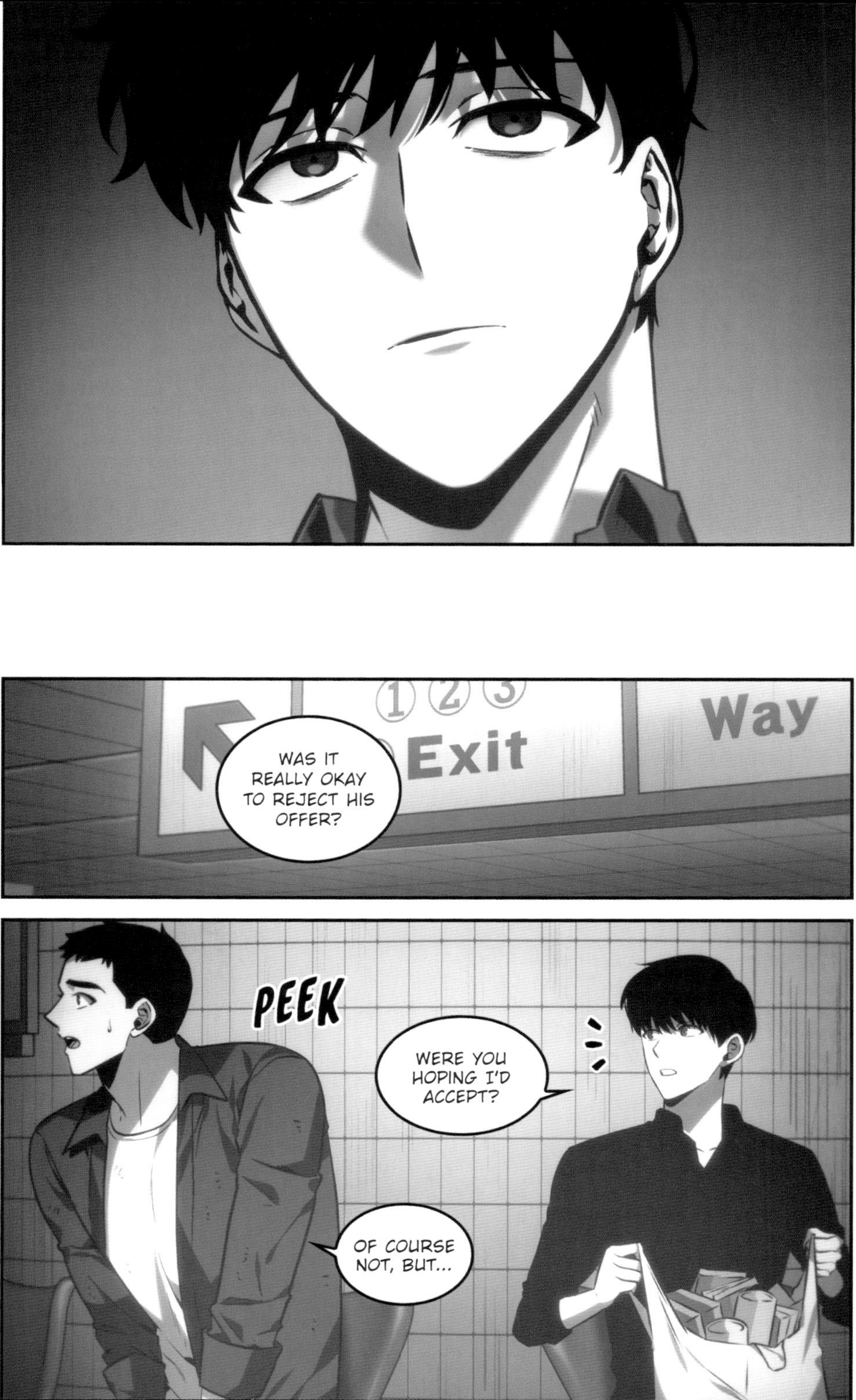
1 2 3
Exit
Way
WAS IT REALLY OKAY TO REJECT HIS OFFER?
PEEK
WERE YOU HOPING I'D ACCEPT?
OF COURSE NOT, BUT...

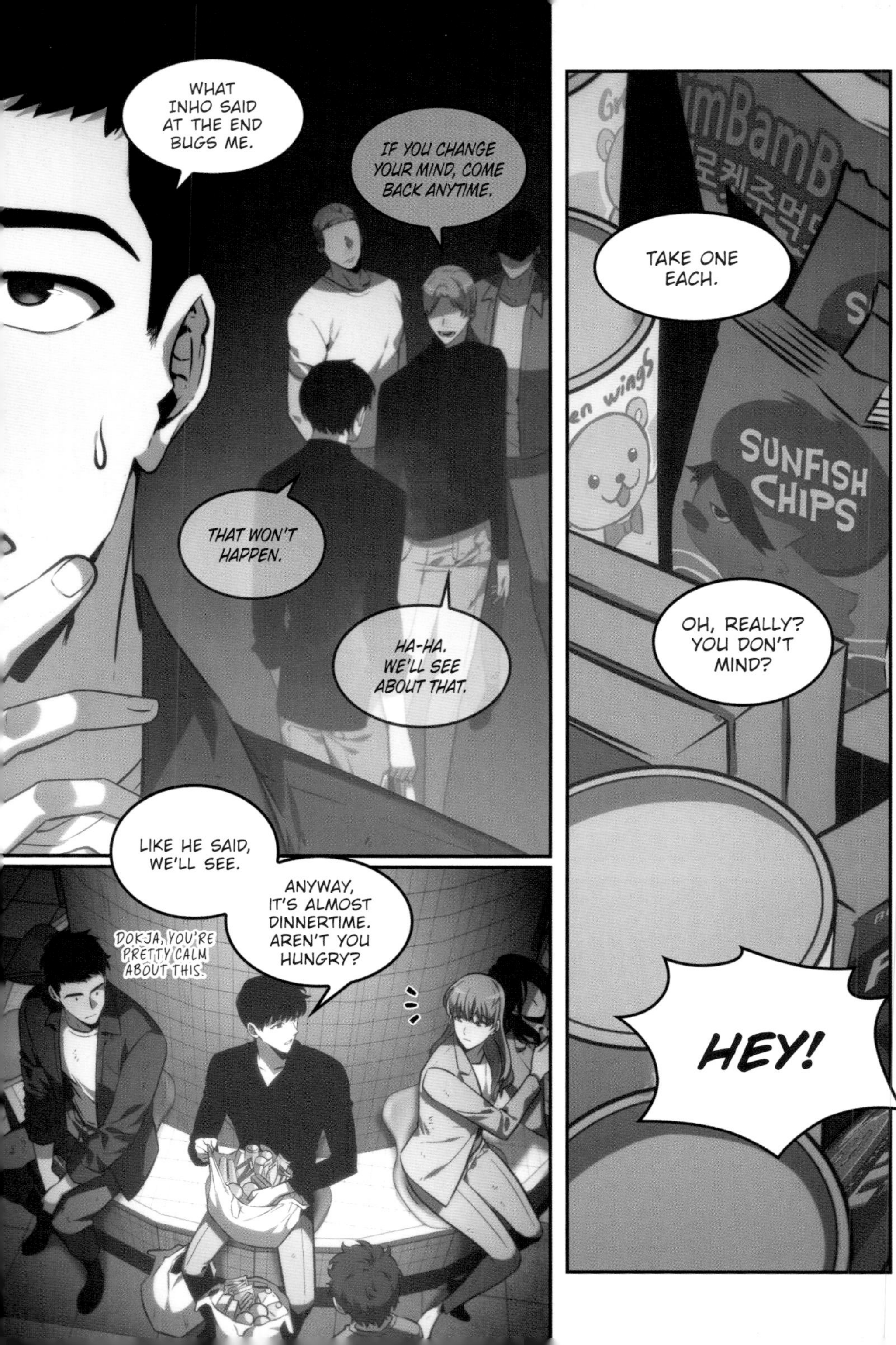

WHAT INHO SAID AT THE END BUGS ME.
IF YOU CHANGE YOUR MIND, COME BACK ANYTIME.
THAT WON'T HAPPEN.
HA-HA. WE'LL SEE ABOUT THAT.
LIKE HE SAID, WE'LL SEE.
ANYWAY, IT'S ALMOST DINNERTIME. AREN'T YOU HUNGRY?
DOKJA, YOU'RE PRETTY CALM ABOUT THIS.
TAKE ONE EACH.
SUNFISH CHIPS
OH, REALLY? YOU DON'T MIND?
HEY!

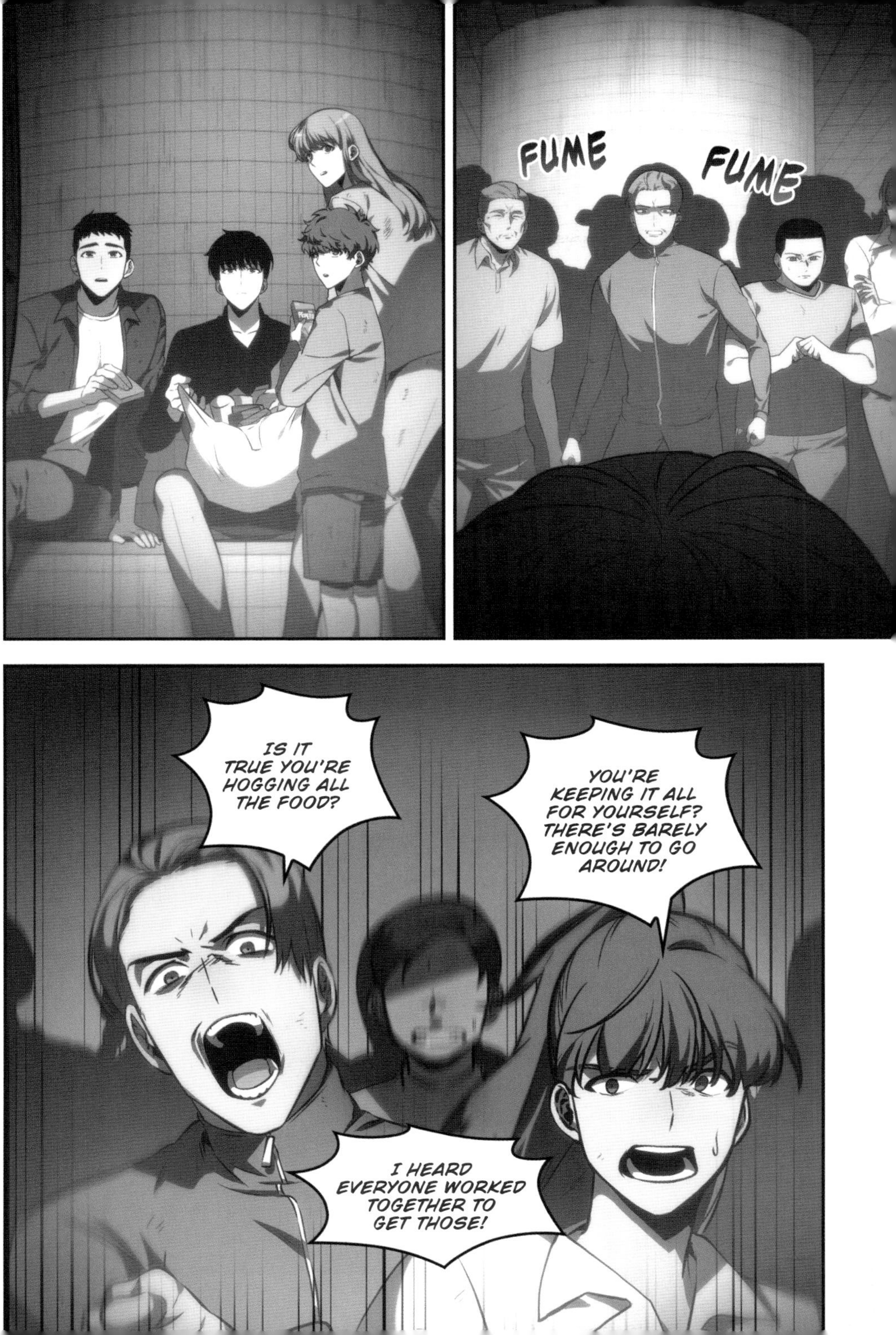
FUME
FUME
IS IT TRUE YOU'RE HOGGING ALL THE FOOD?
YOU'RE KEEPING IT ALL FOR YOURSELF? THERE'S BARELY ENOUGH TO GO AROUND!
I HEARD EVERYONE WORKED TOGETHER TO GET THOSE!

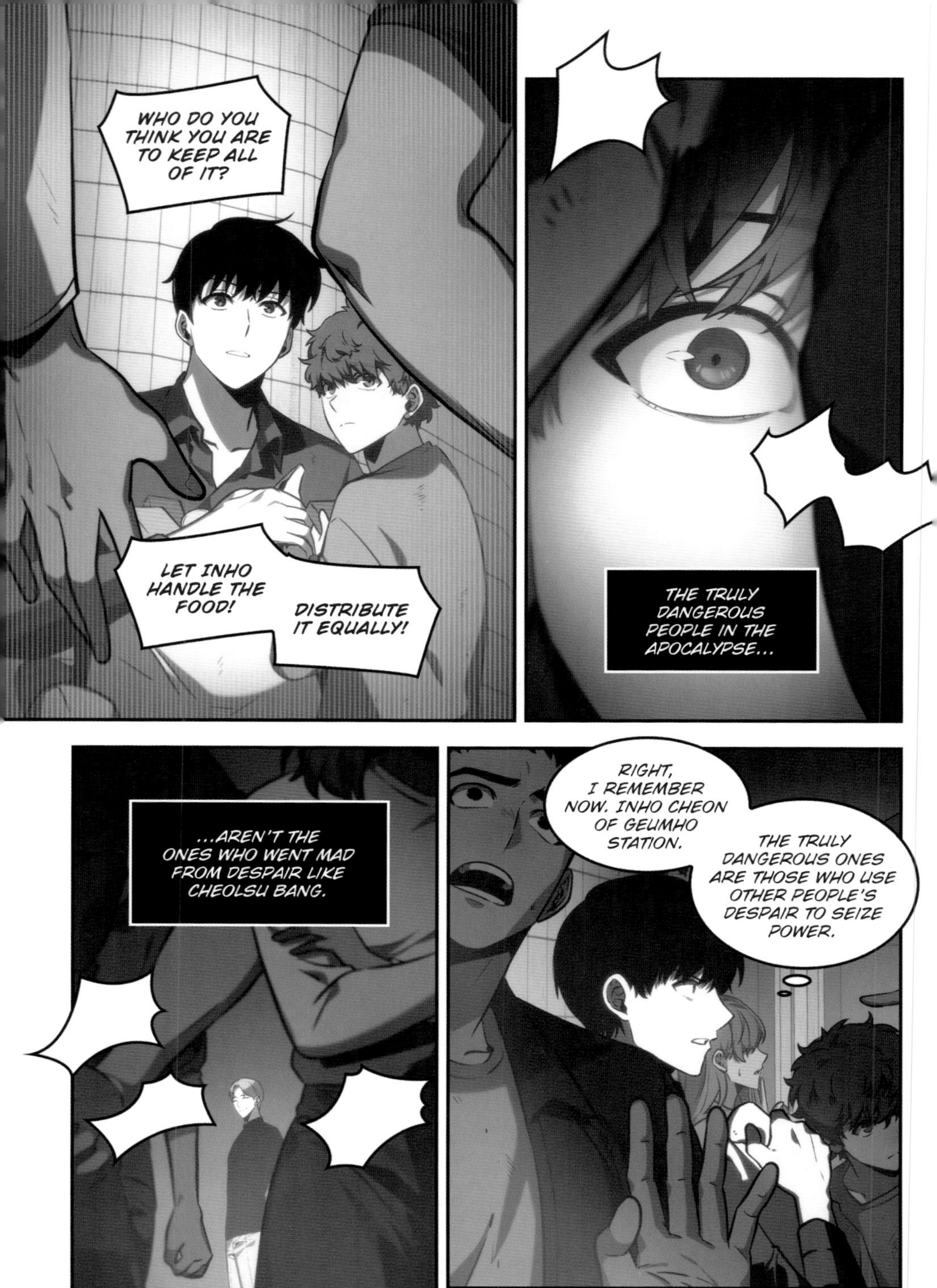
WHO DO YOU THINK YOU ARE TO KEEP ALL OF IT?
LET INHO HANDLE THE FOOD!
DISTRIBUTE IT EQUALLY!
THE TRULY DANGEROUS PEOPLE IN THE APOCALYPSE...
...AREN'T THE ONES WHO WENT MAD FROM DESPAIR LIKE CHEOLSU BANG.
RIGHT, I REMEMBER NOW. INHO CHEON OF GEUMHO STATION.
THE TRULY DANGEROUS ONES ARE THOSE WHO USE OTHER PEOPLE'S DESPAIR TO SEIZE POWER.

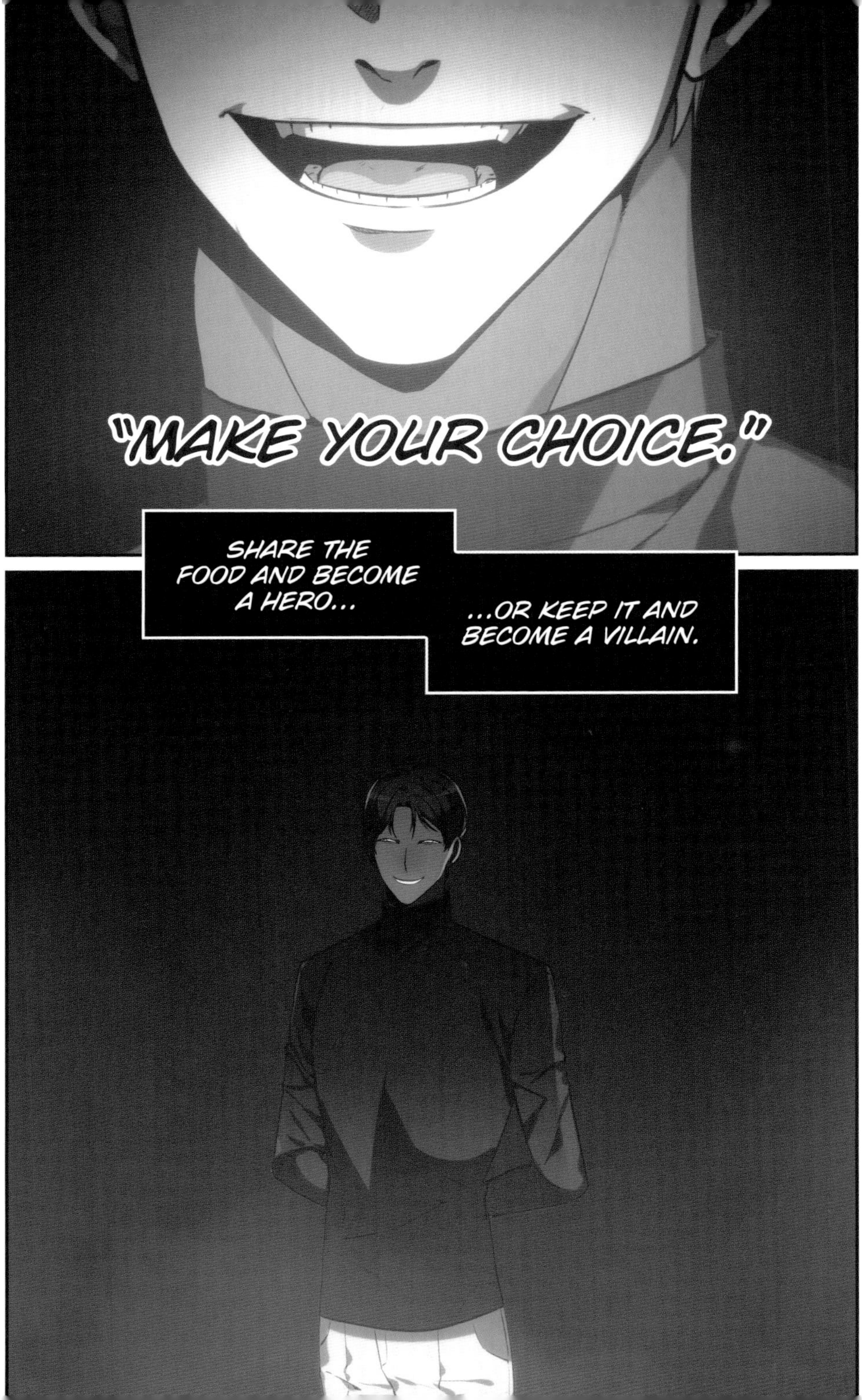
"MAKE YOUR CHOICE."
SHARE THE FOOD AND BECOME A HERO...
...OR KEEP IT AND BECOME A VILLAIN.

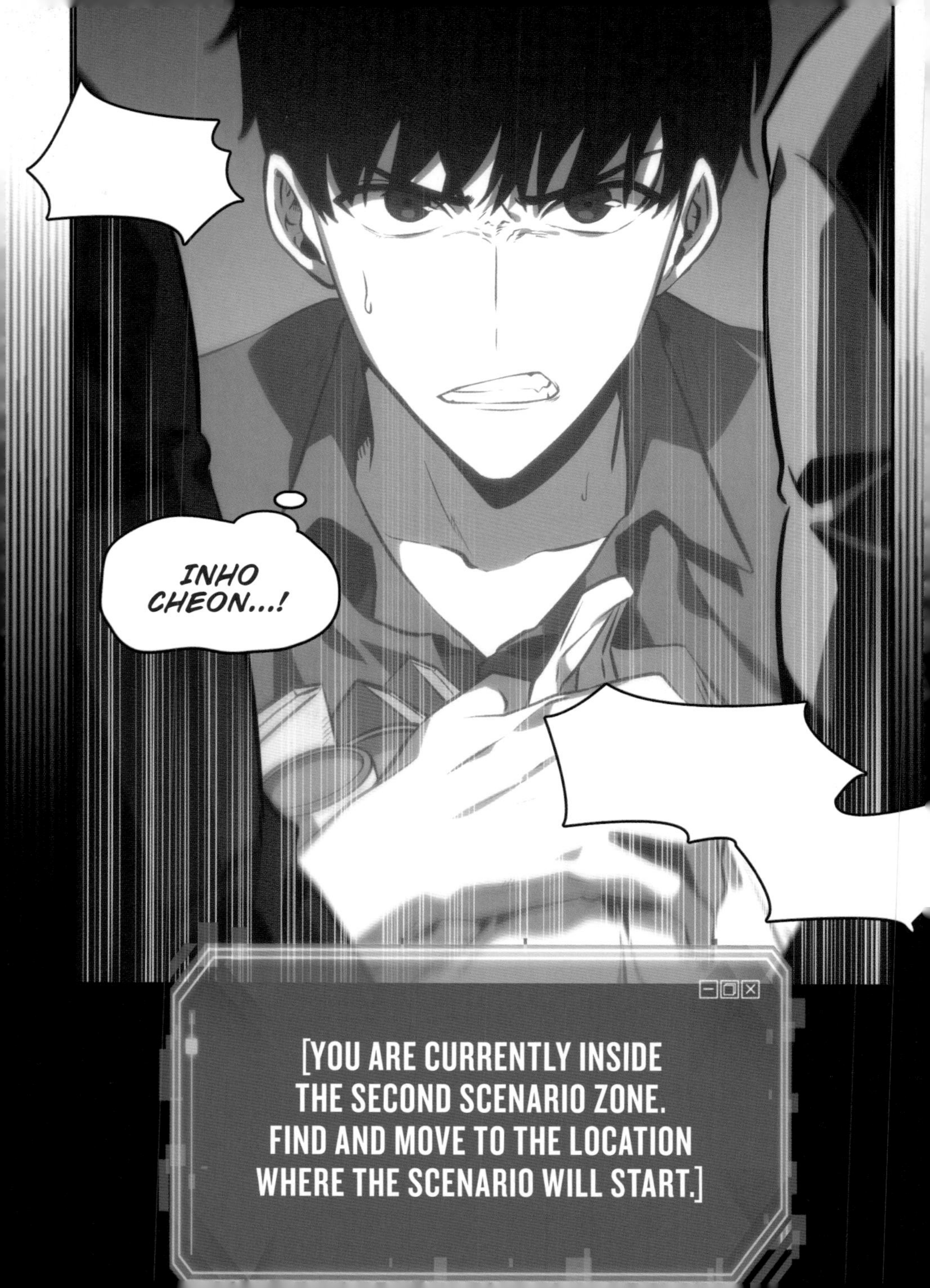
INHO CHEON...!
[YOU ARE CURRENTLY INSIDE THE SECOND SCENARIO ZONE. FIND AND MOVE TO THE LOCATION WHERE THE SCENARIO WILL START.]

EP. 04

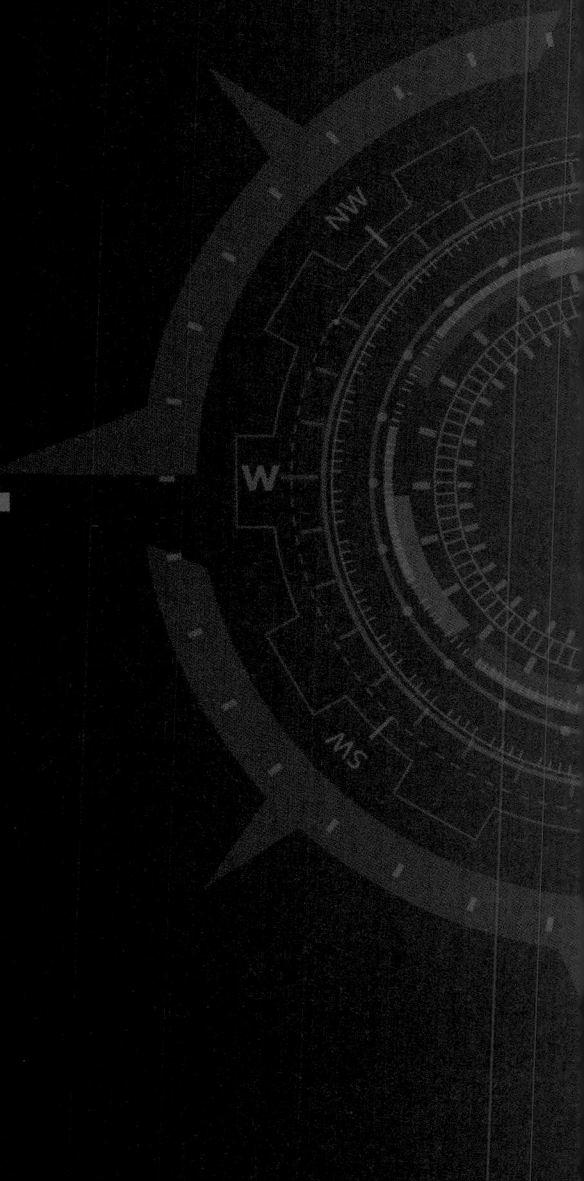
NW
W
SW

Omniscient Reader's Viewpoint

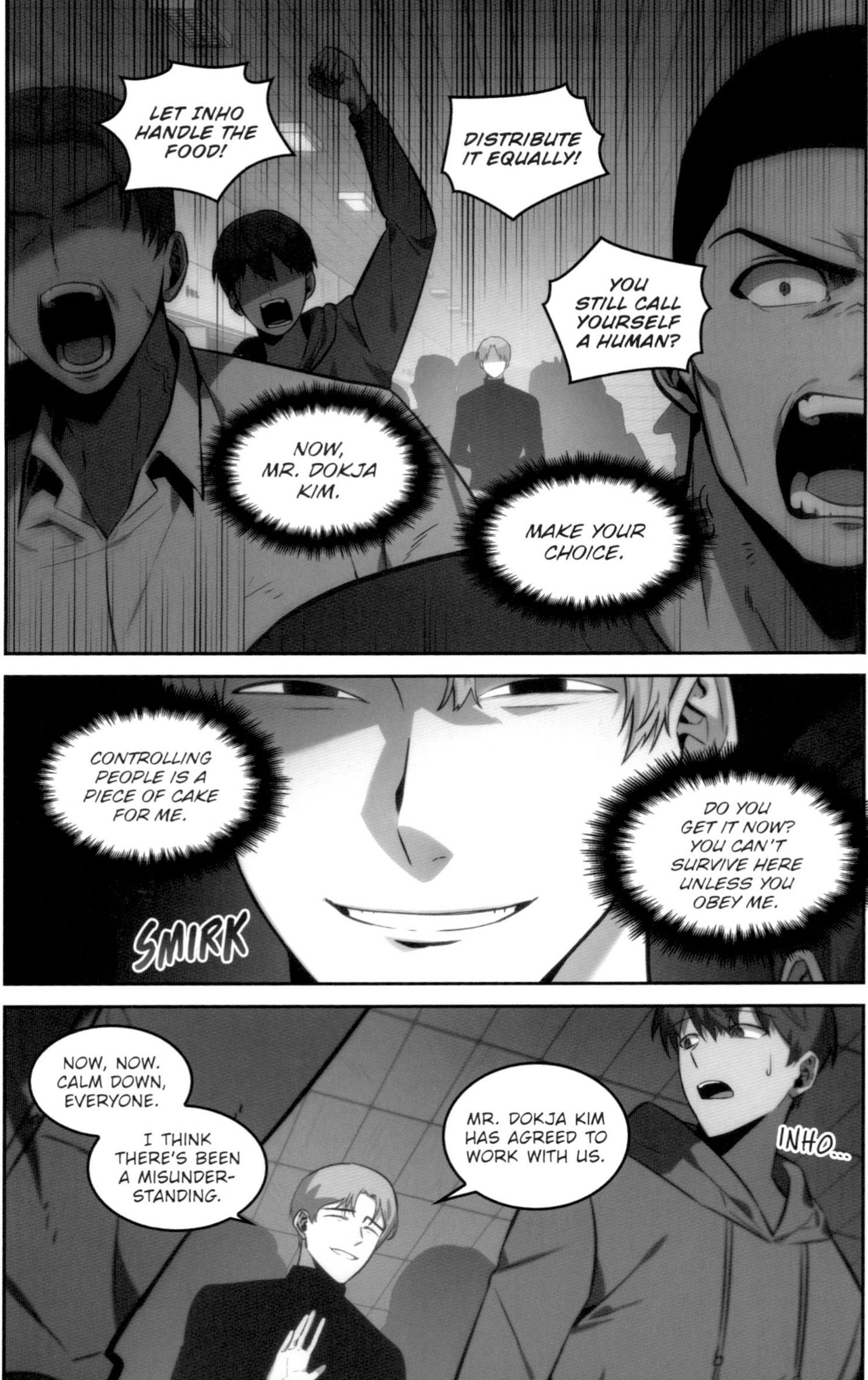

LET INHO HANDLE THE FOOD!
DISTRIBUTE IT EQUALLY!
YOU STILL CALL YOURSELF A HUMAN?
NOW, MR. DOKJA KIM.
MAKE YOUR CHOICE.
CONTROLLING PEOPLE IS A PIECE OF CAKE FOR ME.
DO YOU GET IT NOW? YOU CAN'T SURVIVE HERE UNLESS YOU OBEY ME.
SMIRK
NOW, NOW. CALM DOWN, EVERYONE.
I THINK THERE'S BEEN A MISUNDER-STANDING.
MR. DOKJA KIM HAS AGREED TO WORK WITH US.
INHO...

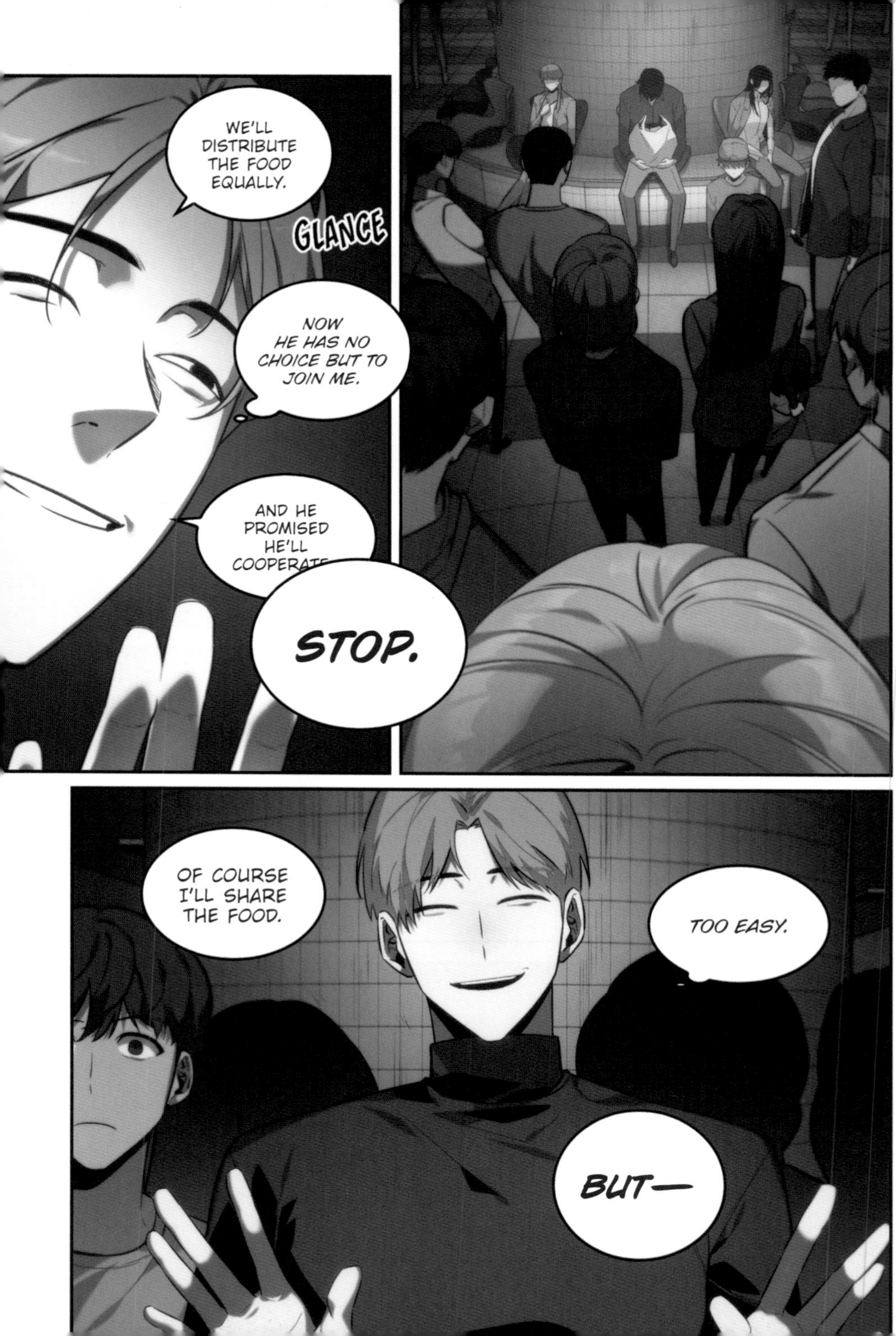
WE'LL DISTRIBUTE THE FOOD EQUALLY.
GLANCE
NOW HE HAS NO CHOICE BUT TO JOIN ME.
AND HE PROMISED HE'LL COOPERAT
STOP.
OF COURSE I'LL SHARE THE FOOD.
TOO EASY.
BUT—

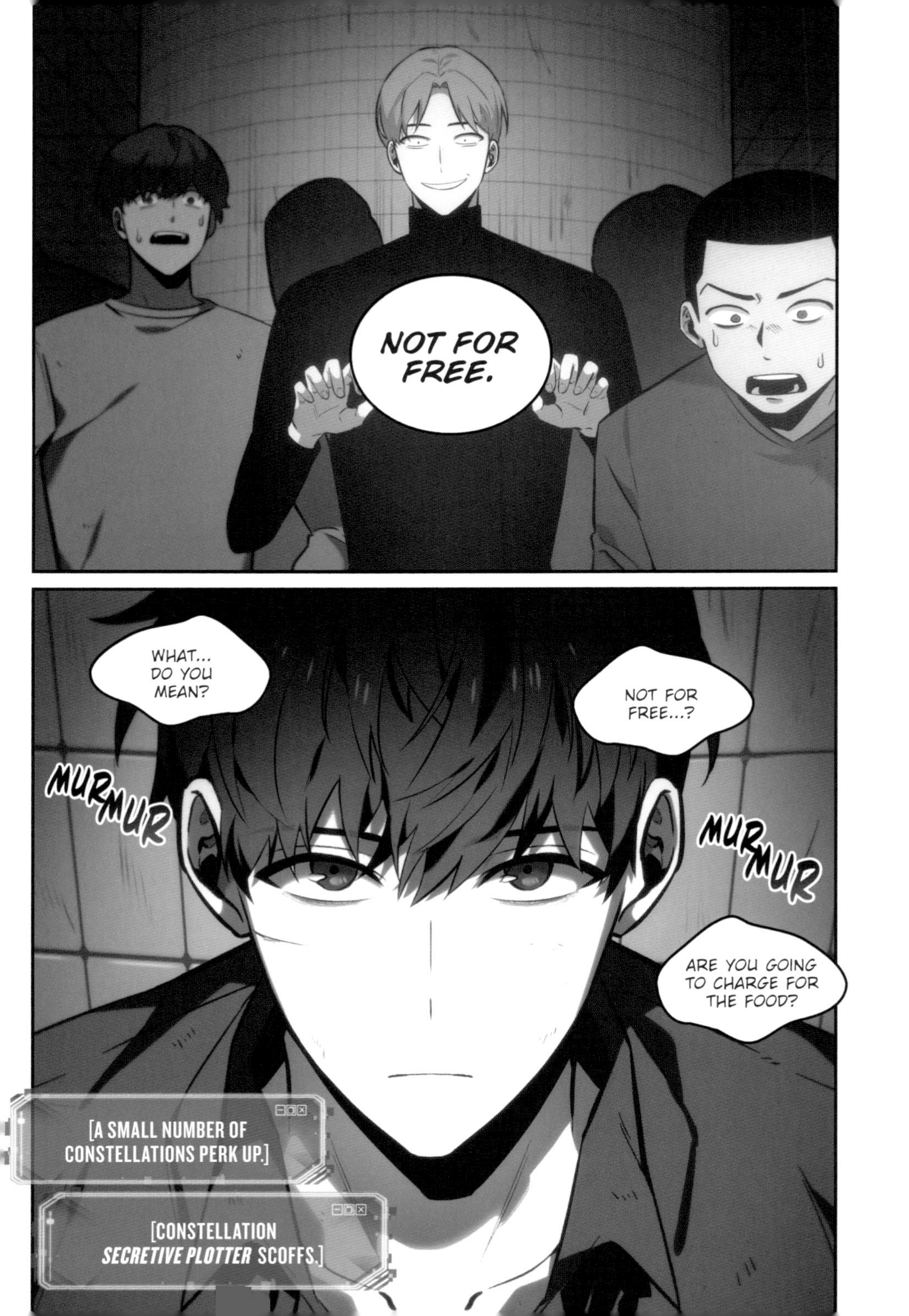
NOT FOR FREE.
WHAT... DO YOU MEAN?
NOT FOR FREE...?
MURMUR
MURMUR
ARE YOU GOING TO CHARGE FOR THE FOOD?
[A SMALL NUMBER OF CONSTELLATIONS PERK UP.]
[CONSTELLATION *SECRETIVE PLOTTER* SCOFFS.]

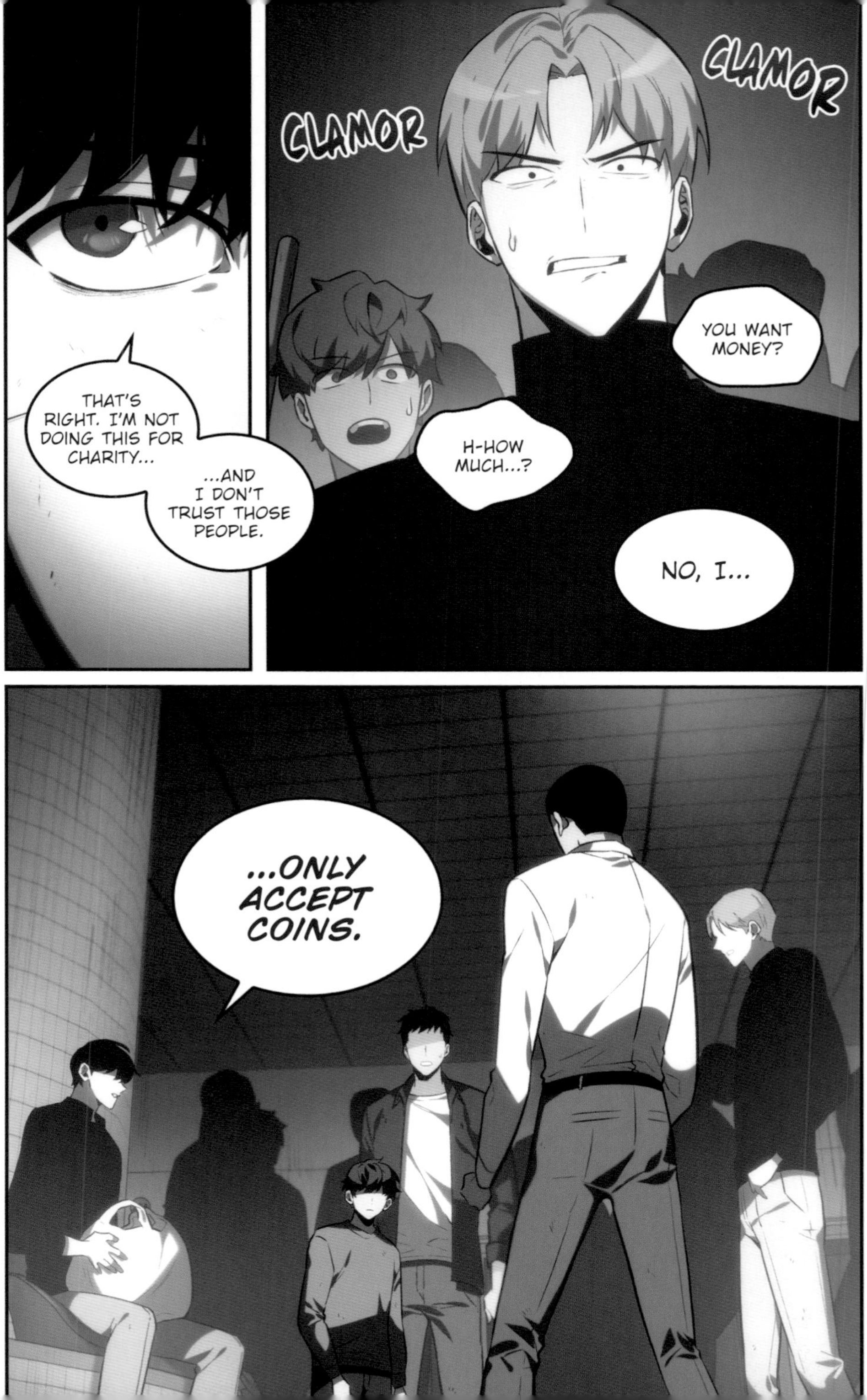
CLAMOR
CLAMOR
THAT'S RIGHT. I'M NOT DOING THIS FOR CHARITY...
...AND I DON'T TRUST THOSE PEOPLE.
YOU WANT MONEY?
H-HOW MUCH...?
NO, I...
...ONLY ACCEPT COINS.

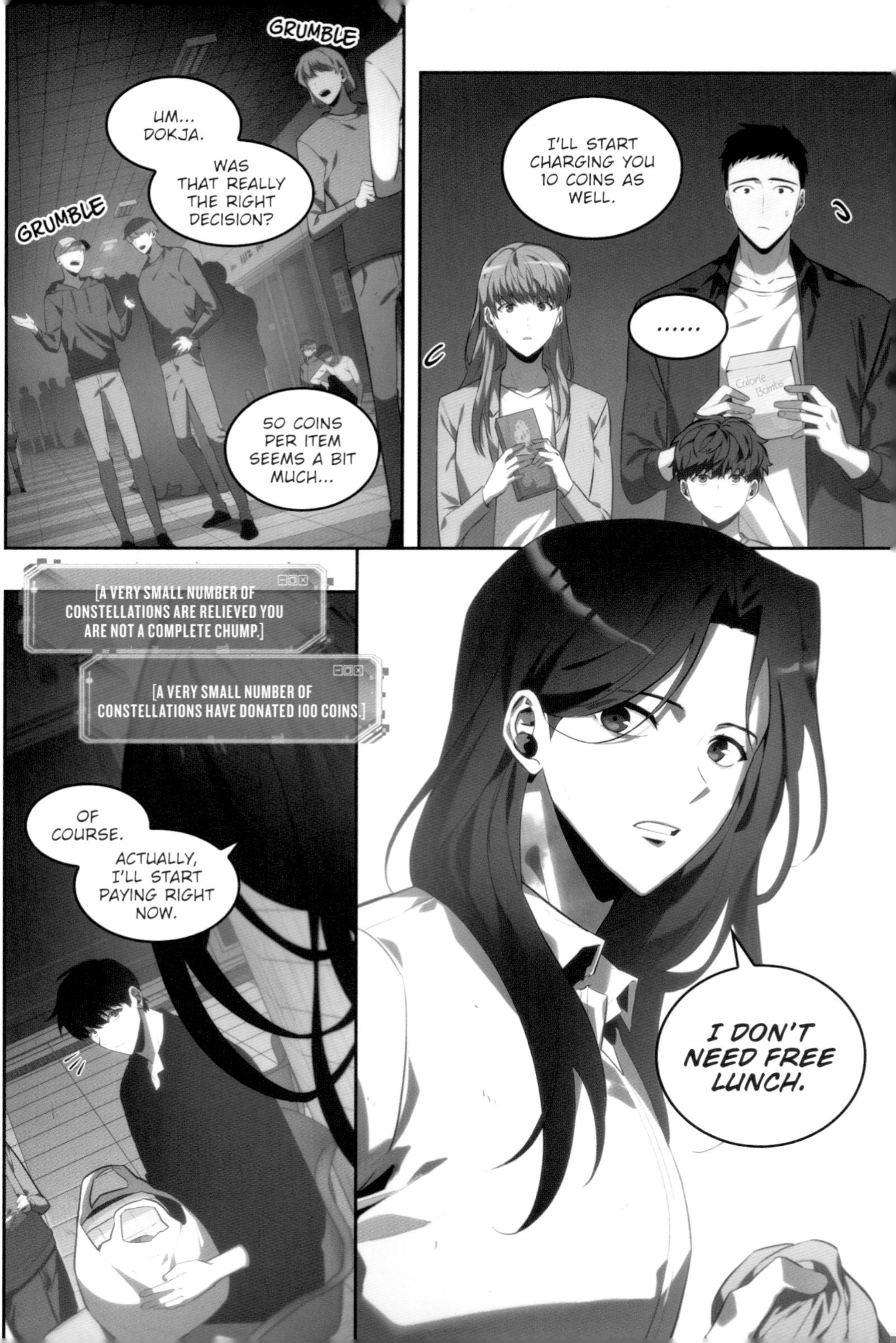
GRUMBLE
UM... DOKJA.
WAS THAT REALLY THE RIGHT DECISION?
GRUMBLE
50 COINS PER ITEM SEEMS A BIT MUCH...
I'LL START CHARGING YOU 10 COINS AS WELL.
......
Calorie Bombs
[A VERY SMALL NUMBER OF CONSTELLATIONS ARE RELIEVED YOU ARE NOT A COMPLETE CHUMP.]
[A VERY SMALL NUMBER OF CONSTELLATIONS HAVE DONATED 100 COINS.]
OF COURSE.
ACTUALLY, I'LL START PAYING RIGHT NOW.
I DON'T NEED FREE LUNCH.

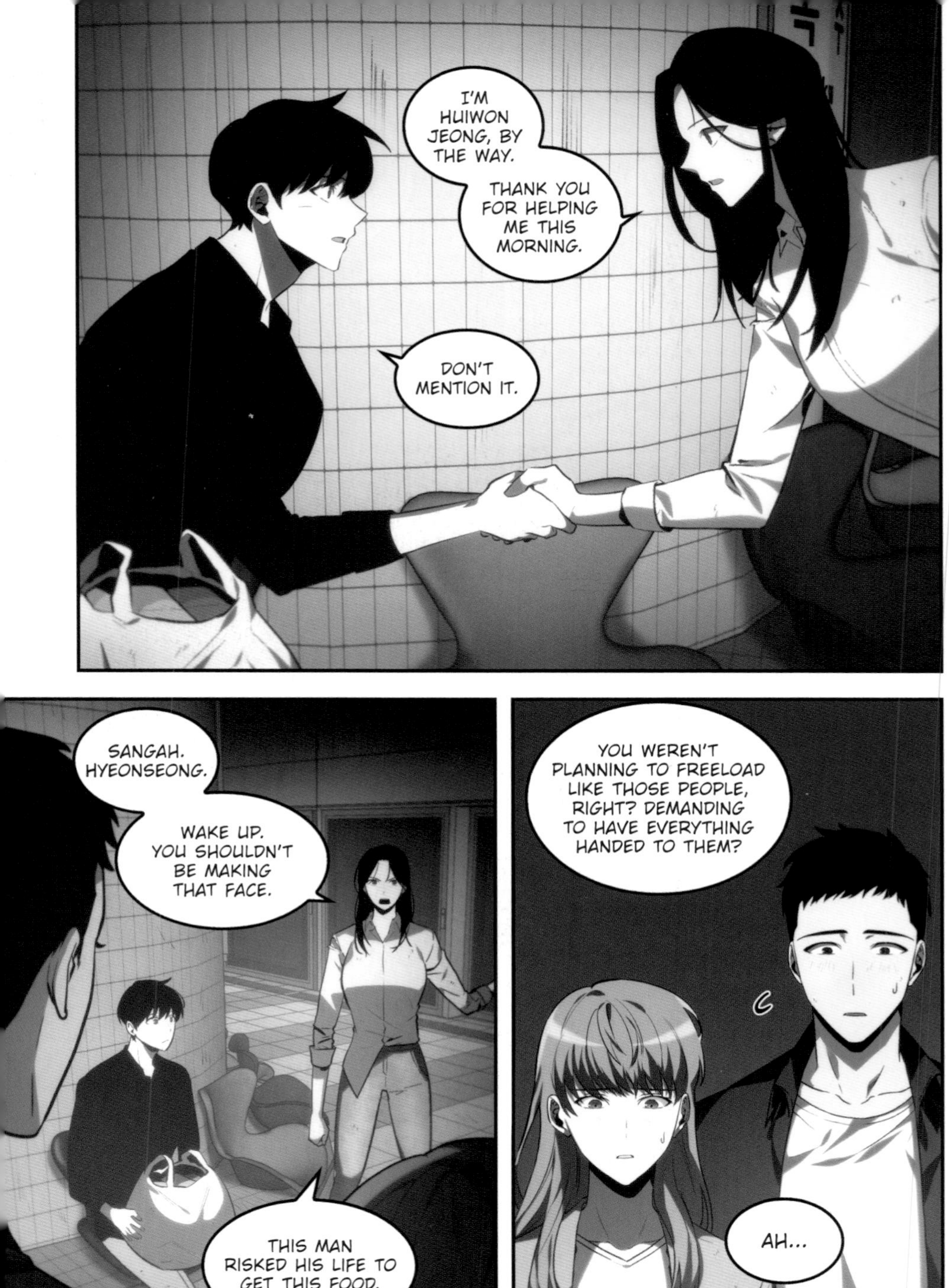
I'M HUIWON JEONG, BY THE WAY.
THANK YOU FOR HELPING ME THIS MORNING.
DON'T MENTION IT.
SANGAH. HYEONSEONG.
WAKE UP. YOU SHOULDN'T BE MAKING THAT FACE.
THIS MAN RISKED HIS LIFE TO GET THIS FOOD.
YOU WEREN'T PLANNING TO FREELOAD LIKE THOSE PEOPLE, RIGHT? DEMANDING TO HAVE EVERYTHING HANDED TO THEM?
AH...

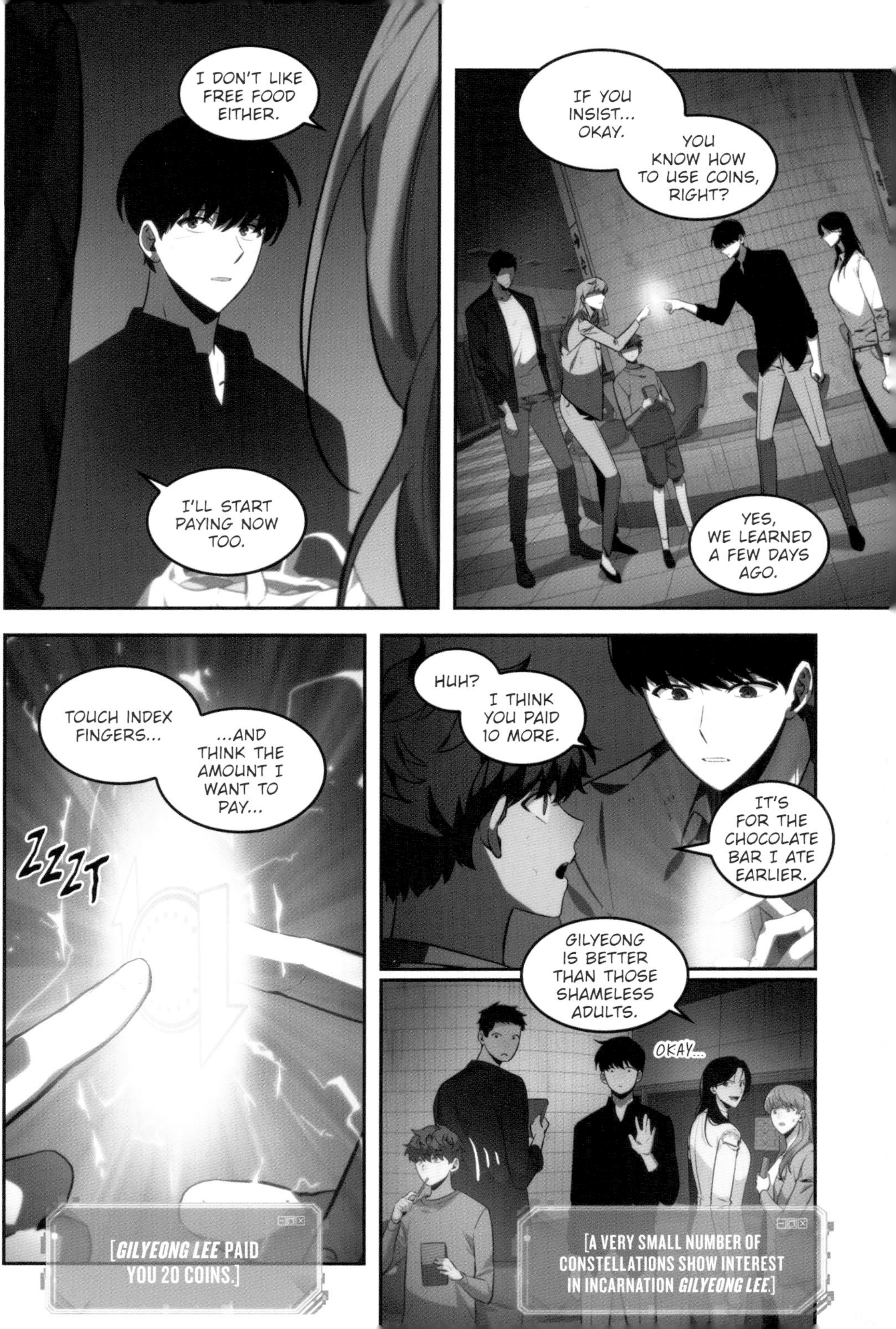

I DON'T LIKE FREE FOOD EITHER.
I'LL START PAYING NOW TOO.
IF YOU INSIST... OKAY.
YOU KNOW HOW TO USE COINS, RIGHT?
YES, WE LEARNED A FEW DAYS AGO.
TOUCH INDEX FINGERS...
...AND THINK THE AMOUNT I WANT TO PAY...
ZZZT
[GILYEONG LEE PAID YOU 20 COINS.]
HUH?
I THINK YOU PAID 10 MORE.
IT'S FOR THE CHOCOLATE BAR I ATE EARLIER.
GILYEONG IS BETTER THAN THOSE SHAMELESS ADULTS.
OKAY...
[A VERY SMALL NUMBER OF CONSTELLATIONS SHOW INTEREST IN INCARNATION GILYEONG LEE.]

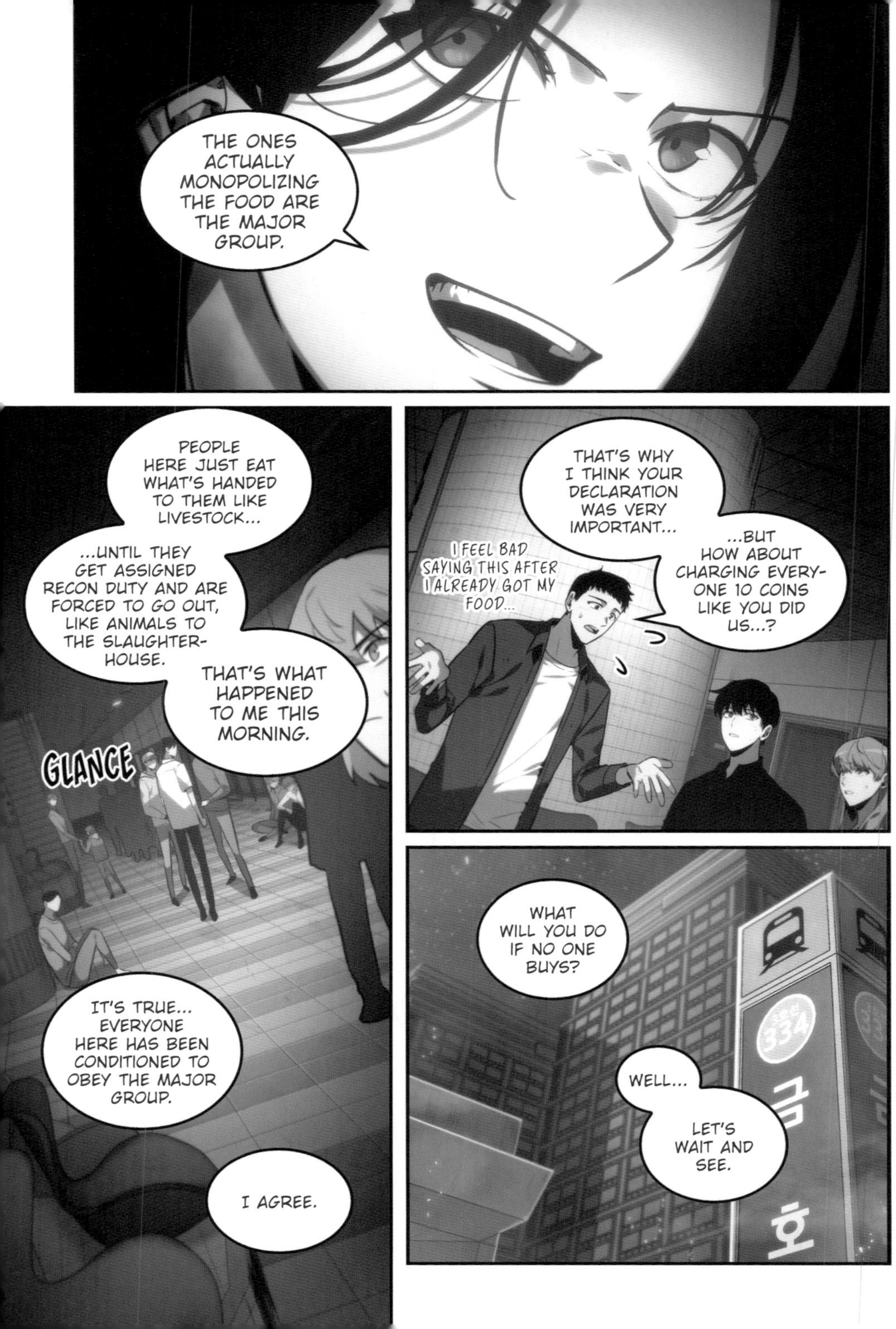
THE ONES ACTUALLY MONOPOLIZING THE FOOD ARE THE MAJOR GROUP.
PEOPLE HERE JUST EAT WHAT'S HANDED TO THEM LIKE LIVESTOCK...
...UNTIL THEY GET ASSIGNED RECON DUTY AND ARE FORCED TO GO OUT, LIKE ANIMALS TO THE SLAUGHTER-HOUSE.
THAT'S WHAT HAPPENED TO ME THIS MORNING.
GLANCE
IT'S TRUE... EVERYONE HERE HAS BEEN CONDITIONED TO OBEY THE MAJOR GROUP.
I AGREE.
THAT'S WHY I THINK YOUR DECLARATION WAS VERY IMPORTANT...
I FEEL BAD SAYING THIS AFTER I ALREADY GOT MY FOOD...
...BUT HOW ABOUT CHARGING EVERY-ONE 10 COINS LIKE YOU DID US...?
WHAT WILL YOU DO IF NO ONE BUYS?
334
금
호
WELL...
LET'S WAIT AND SEE.

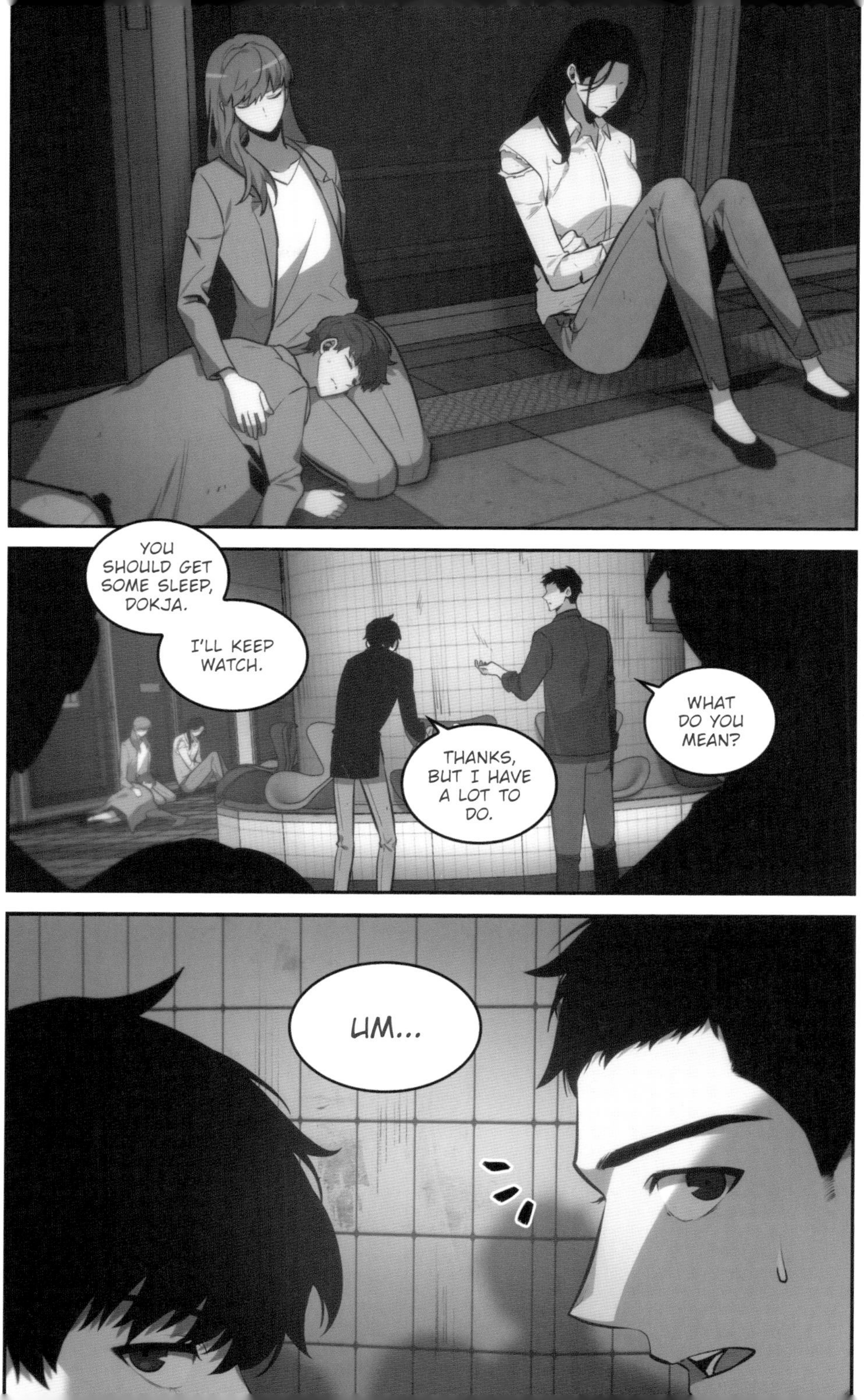
YOU SHOULD GET SOME SLEEP, DOKJA.
I'LL KEEP WATCH.
THANKS, BUT I HAVE A LOT TO DO.
WHAT DO YOU MEAN?
UM...

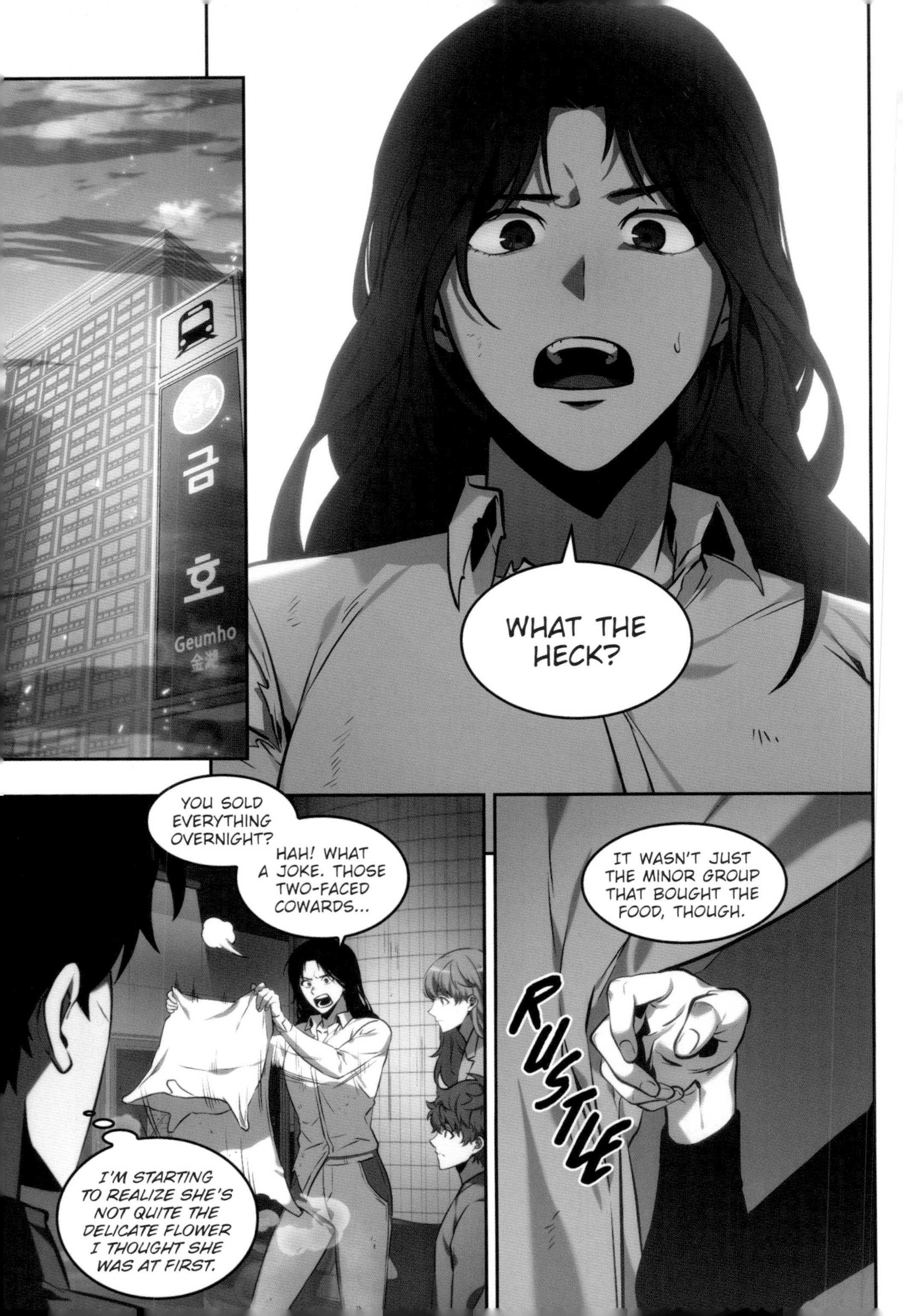

금
호
Geumho
WHAT THE HECK?
YOU SOLD EVERYTHING OVERNIGHT?
HAH! WHAT A JOKE. THOSE TWO-FACED COWARDS...
I'M STARTING TO REALIZE SHE'S NOT QUITE THE DELICATE FLOWER I THOUGHT SHE WAS AT FIRST.
IT WASN'T JUST THE MINOR GROUP THAT BOUGHT THE FOOD, THOUGH.
RUSTLE

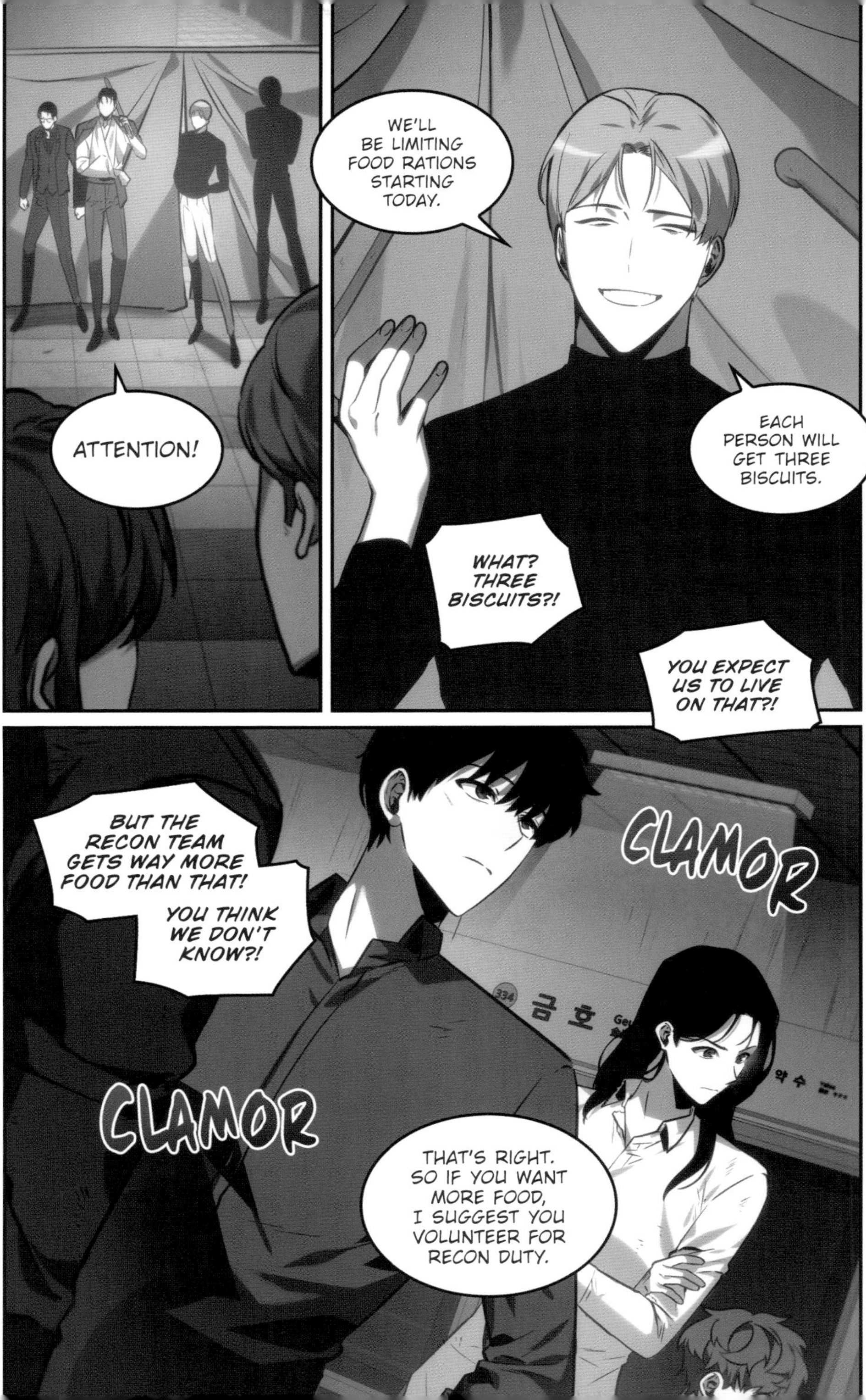
ATTENTION!
WE'LL BE LIMITING FOOD RATIONS STARTING TODAY.
EACH PERSON WILL GET THREE BISCUITS.
WHAT? THREE BISCUITS?!
YOU EXPECT US TO LIVE ON THAT?!
CLAMOR
BUT THE RECON TEAM GETS WAY MORE FOOD THAN THAT!
YOU THINK WE DON'T KNOW?!
334 금호
약수
CLAMOR
THAT'S RIGHT. SO IF YOU WANT MORE FOOD, I SUGGEST YOU VOLUNTEER FOR RECON DUTY.

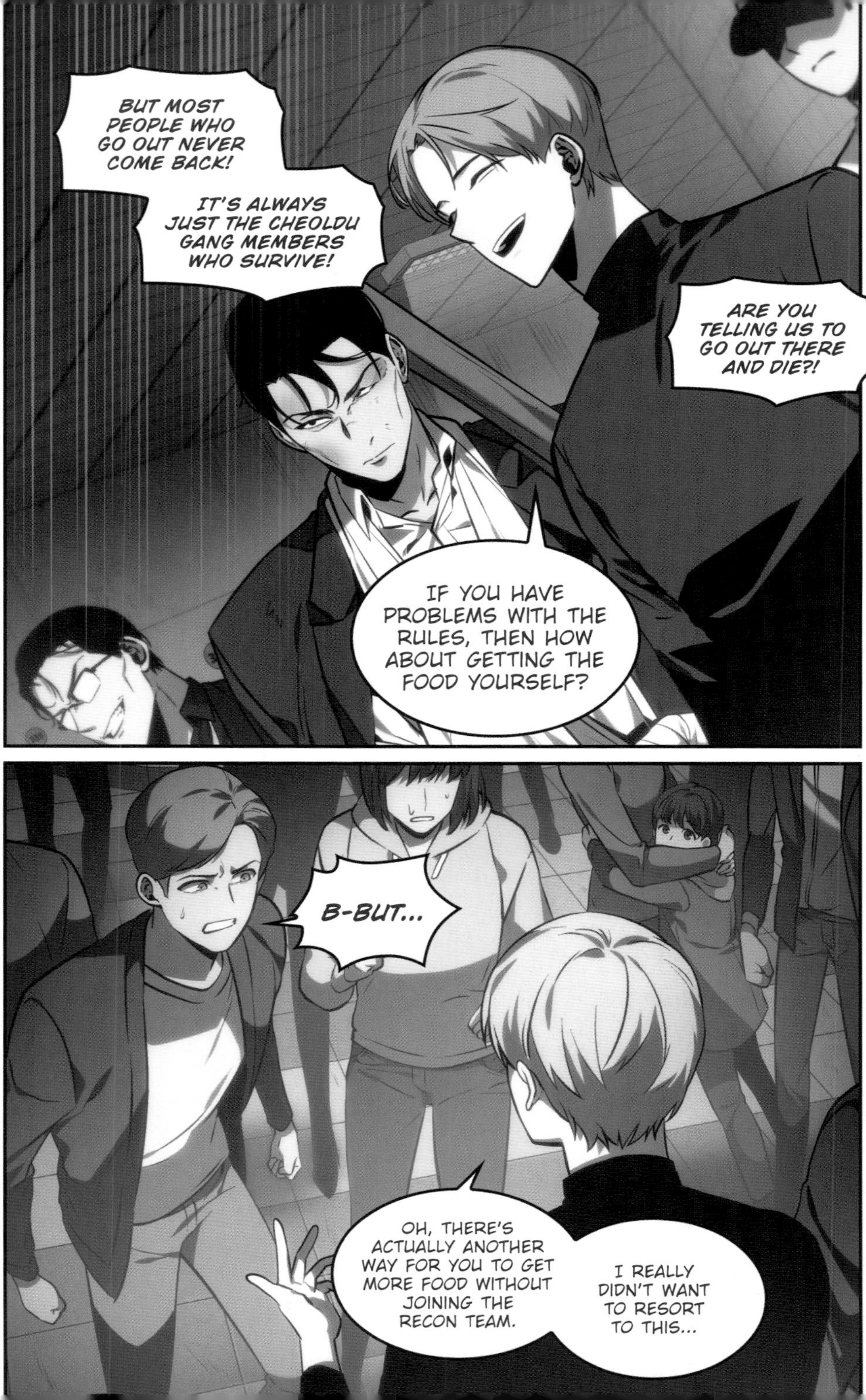
BUT MOST PEOPLE WHO GO OUT NEVER COME BACK!
IT'S ALWAYS JUST THE CHEOLDU GANG MEMBERS WHO SURVIVE!
ARE YOU TELLING US TO GO OUT THERE AND DIE?!
IF YOU HAVE PROBLEMS WITH THE RULES, THEN HOW ABOUT GETTING THE FOOD YOURSELF?
B-BUT...
OH, THERE'S ACTUALLY ANOTHER WAY FOR YOU TO GET MORE FOOD WITHOUT JOINING THE RECON TEAM.
I REALLY DIDN'T WANT TO RESORT TO THIS...

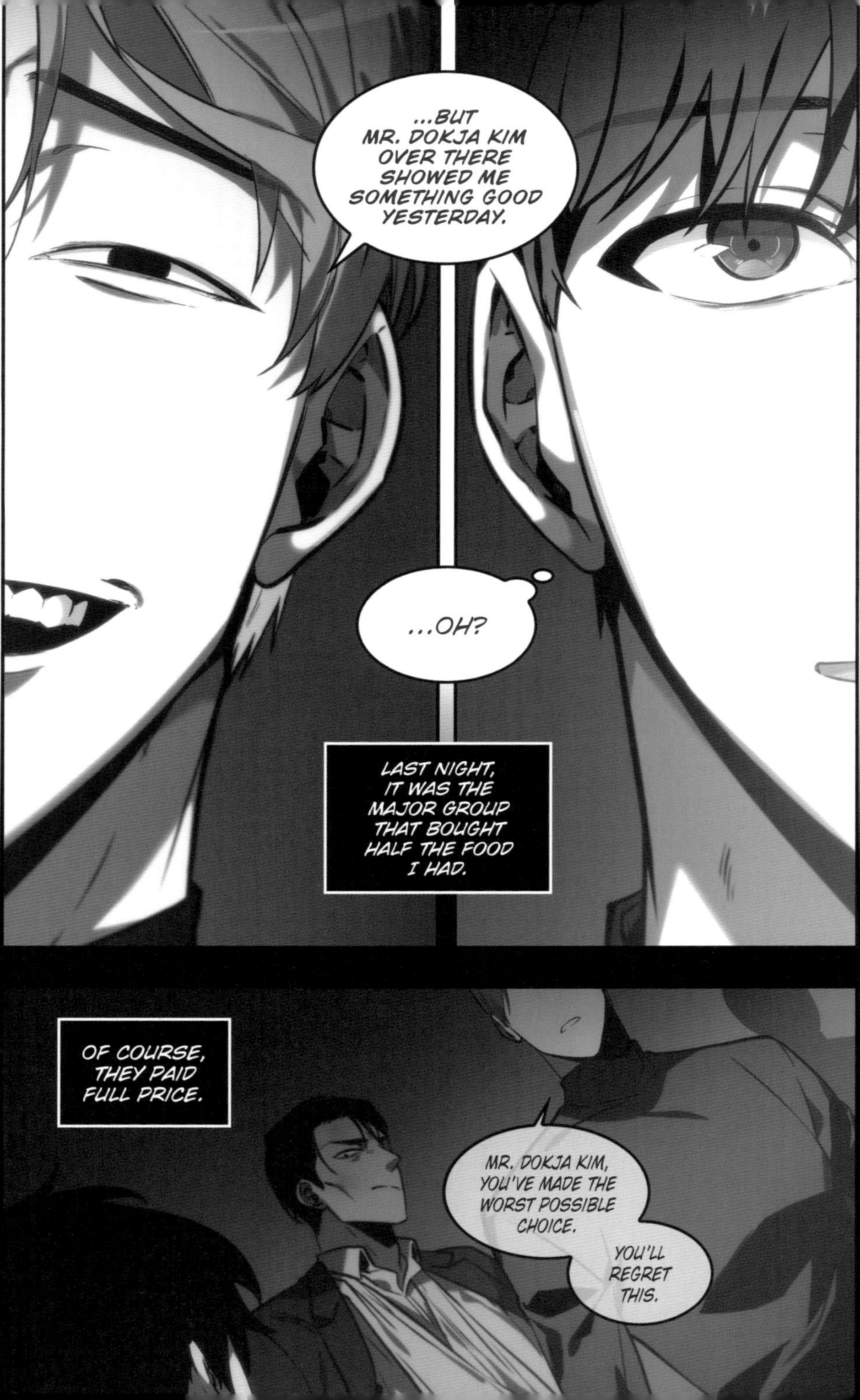
...BUT MR. DOKJA KIM OVER THERE SHOWED ME SOMETHING GOOD YESTERDAY.
...OH?
LAST NIGHT, IT WAS THE MAJOR GROUP THAT BOUGHT HALF THE FOOD I HAD.
OF COURSE, THEY PAID FULL PRICE.
MR. DOKJA KIM, YOU'VE MADE THE WORST POSSIBLE CHOICE.
YOU'LL REGRET THIS.

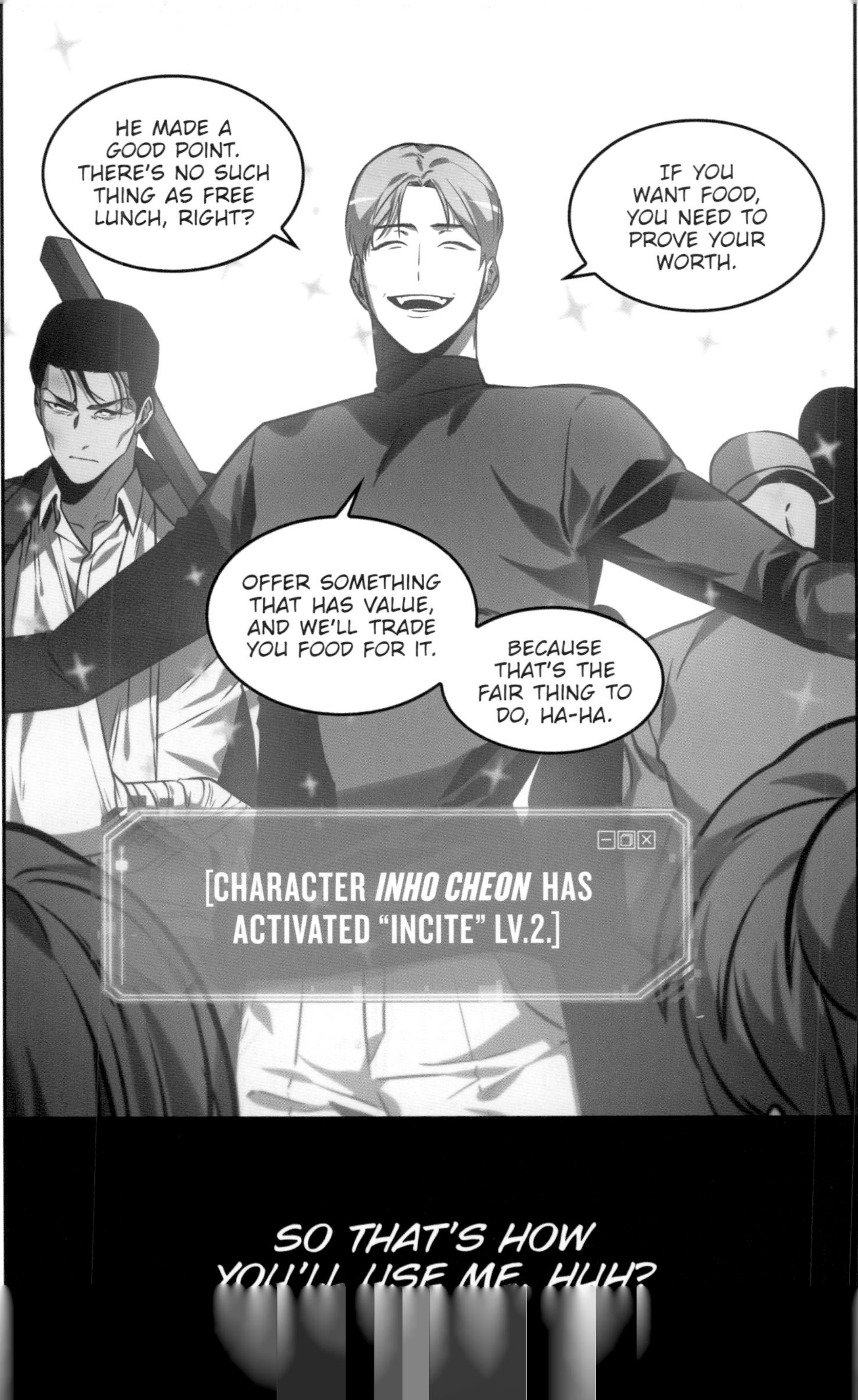
HE MADE A GOOD POINT. THERE'S NO SUCH THING AS FREE LUNCH, RIGHT?
IF YOU WANT FOOD, YOU NEED TO PROVE YOUR WORTH.
OFFER SOMETHING THAT HAS VALUE, AND WE'LL TRADE YOU FOOD FOR IT.
BECAUSE THAT'S THE FAIR THING TO DO, HA-HA.
[CHARACTER *INHO CHEON* HAS ACTIVATED "INCITE" LV.2.]
SO THAT'S HOW YOU'LL USE ME, HUH?

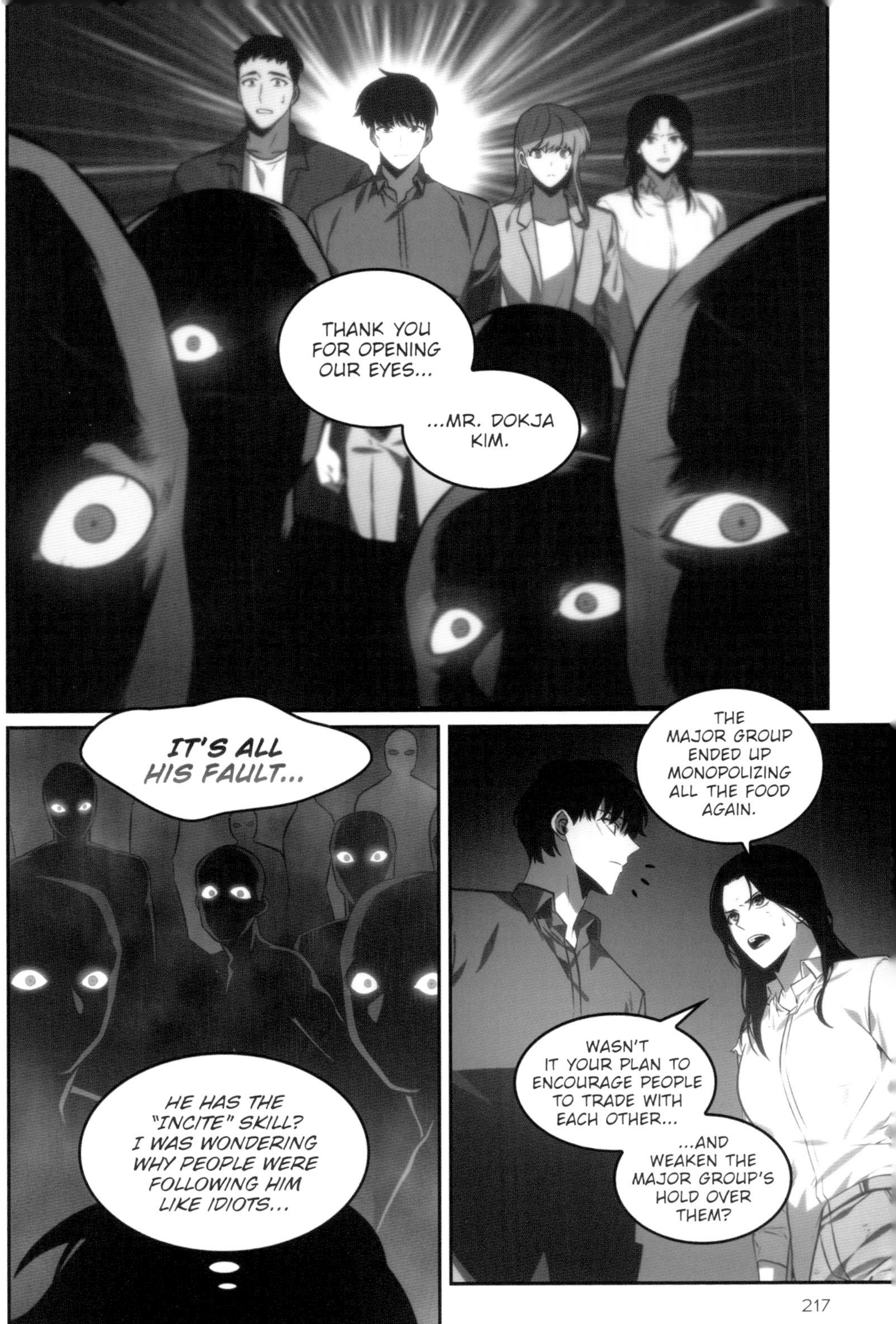
THANK YOU FOR OPENING OUR EYES...
...MR. DOKJA KIM.
IT'S ALL HIS FAULT...
HE HAS THE "INCITE" SKILL? I WAS WONDERING WHY PEOPLE WERE FOLLOWING HIM LIKE IDIOTS...
THE MAJOR GROUP ENDED UP MONOPOLIZING ALL THE FOOD AGAIN.
WASN'T IT YOUR PLAN TO ENCOURAGE PEOPLE TO TRADE WITH EACH OTHER...
...AND WEAKEN THE MAJOR GROUP'S HOLD OVER THEM?

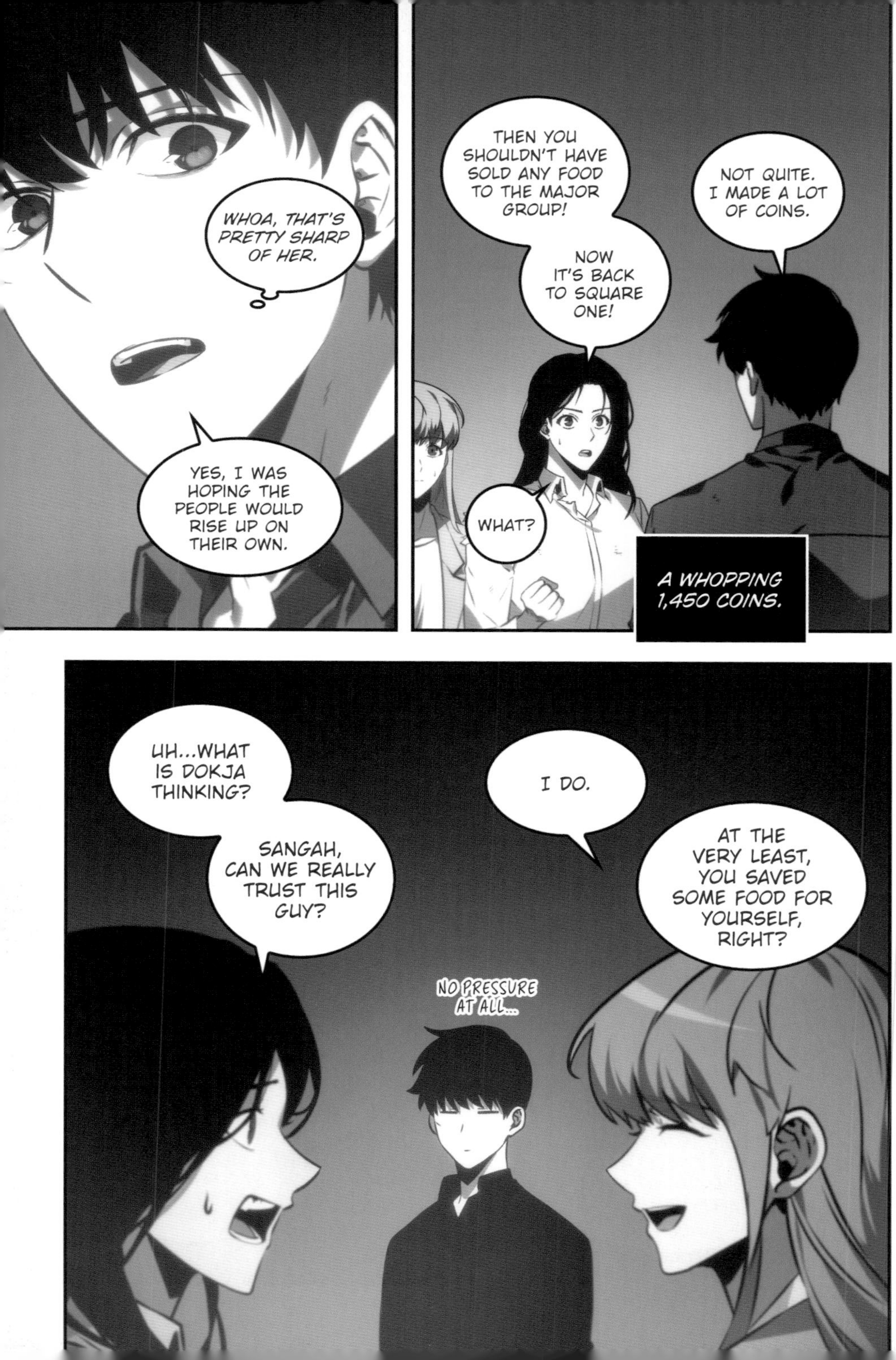
WHOA, THAT'S PRETTY SHARP OF HER.
YES, I WAS HOPING THE PEOPLE WOULD RISE UP ON THEIR OWN.
THEN YOU SHOULDN'T HAVE SOLD ANY FOOD TO THE MAJOR GROUP!
NOW IT'S BACK TO SQUARE ONE!
NOT QUITE. I MADE A LOT OF COINS.
WHAT?
A WHOPPING 1,450 COINS.
UH...WHAT IS DOKJA THINKING?
SANGAH, CAN WE REALLY TRUST THIS GUY?
I DO.
AT THE VERY LEAST, YOU SAVED SOME FOOD FOR YOURSELF, RIGHT?
NO PRESSURE AT ALL...

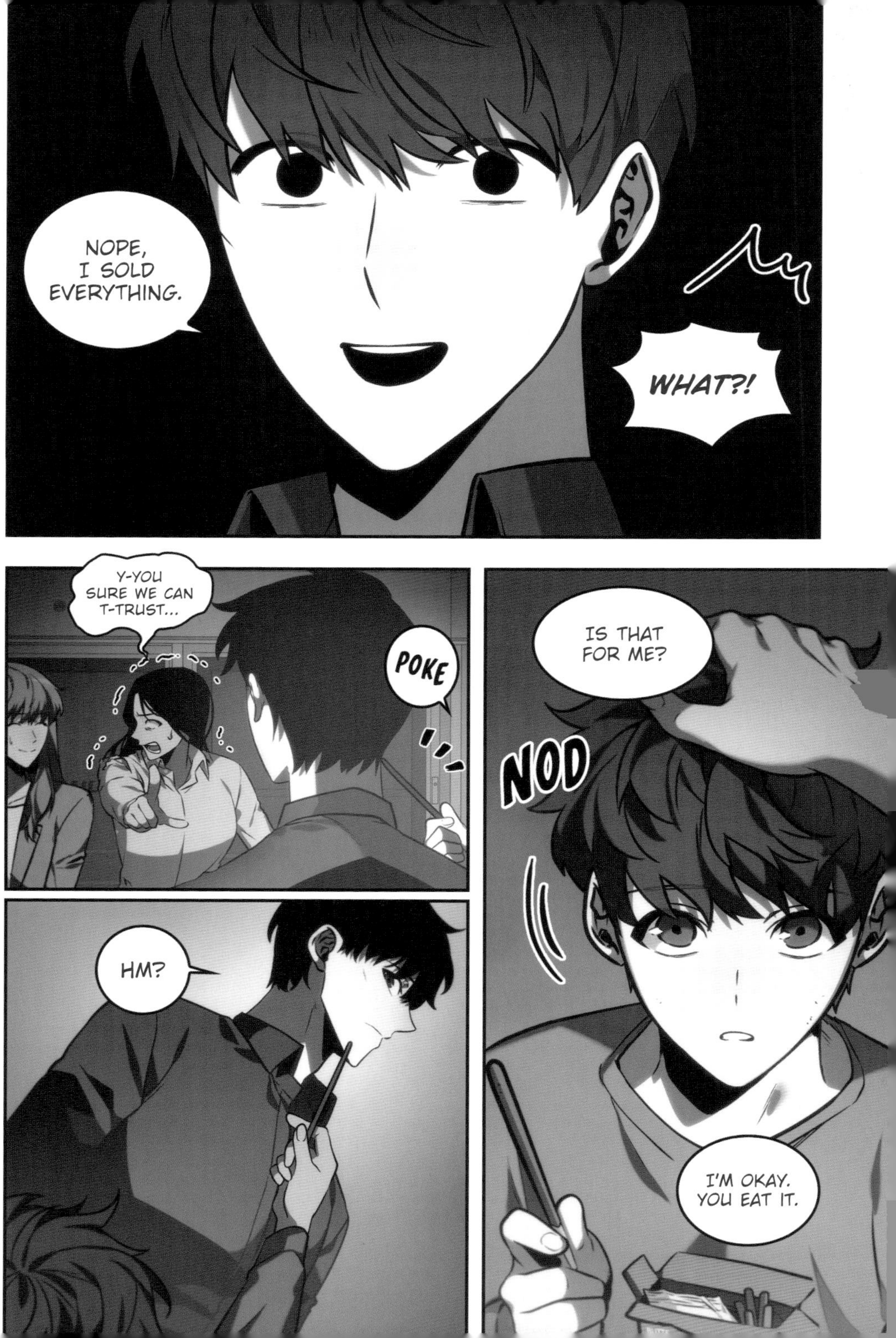
NOPE, I SOLD EVERYTHING.
WHAT?!
Y-YOU SURE WE CAN T-TRUST...
POKE
HM?
IS THAT FOR ME?
NOD
I'M OKAY. YOU EAT IT.

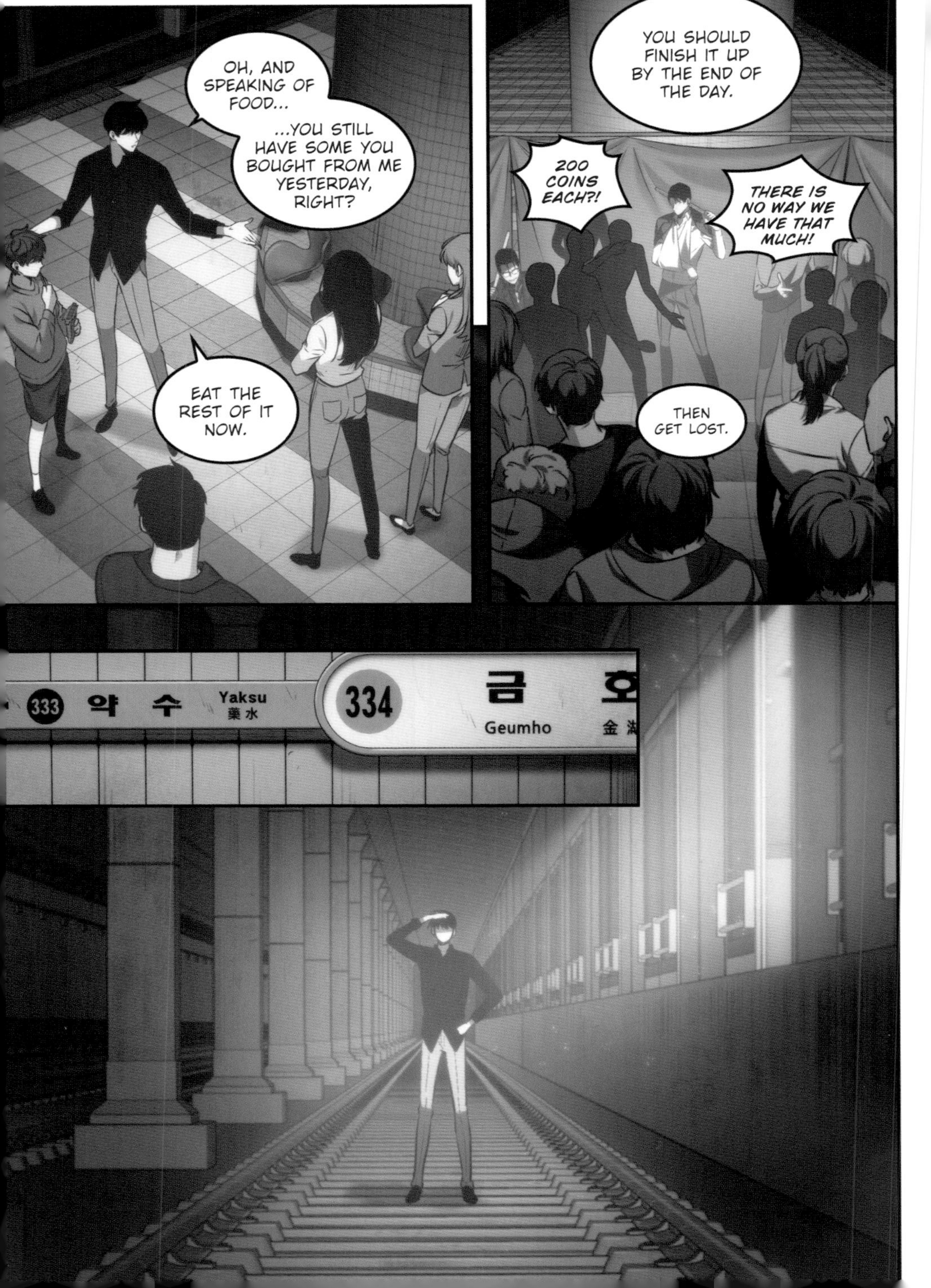
OH, AND SPEAKING OF FOOD...
...YOU STILL HAVE SOME YOU BOUGHT FROM ME YESTERDAY, RIGHT?
EAT THE REST OF IT NOW.
YOU SHOULD FINISH IT UP BY THE END OF THE DAY.
200 COINS EACH?!
THERE IS NO WAY WE HAVE THAT MUCH!
THEN GET LOST.
333 약 수 Yaksu 藥水
334 금 호 Geumho

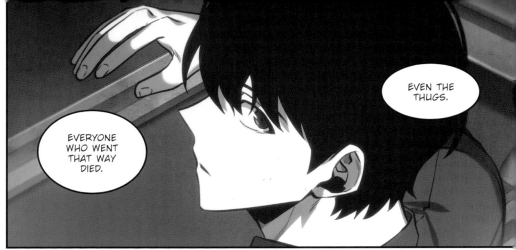

EVEN THE THUGS.

EVERYONE WHO WENT THAT WAY DIED.

YOU'RE NOT THINKING OF GOING THERE, ARE YOU?

DID I THANK YOU YESTERDAY?

I THINK SO.

WELL, I'LL SAY IT AGAIN. THANKS.

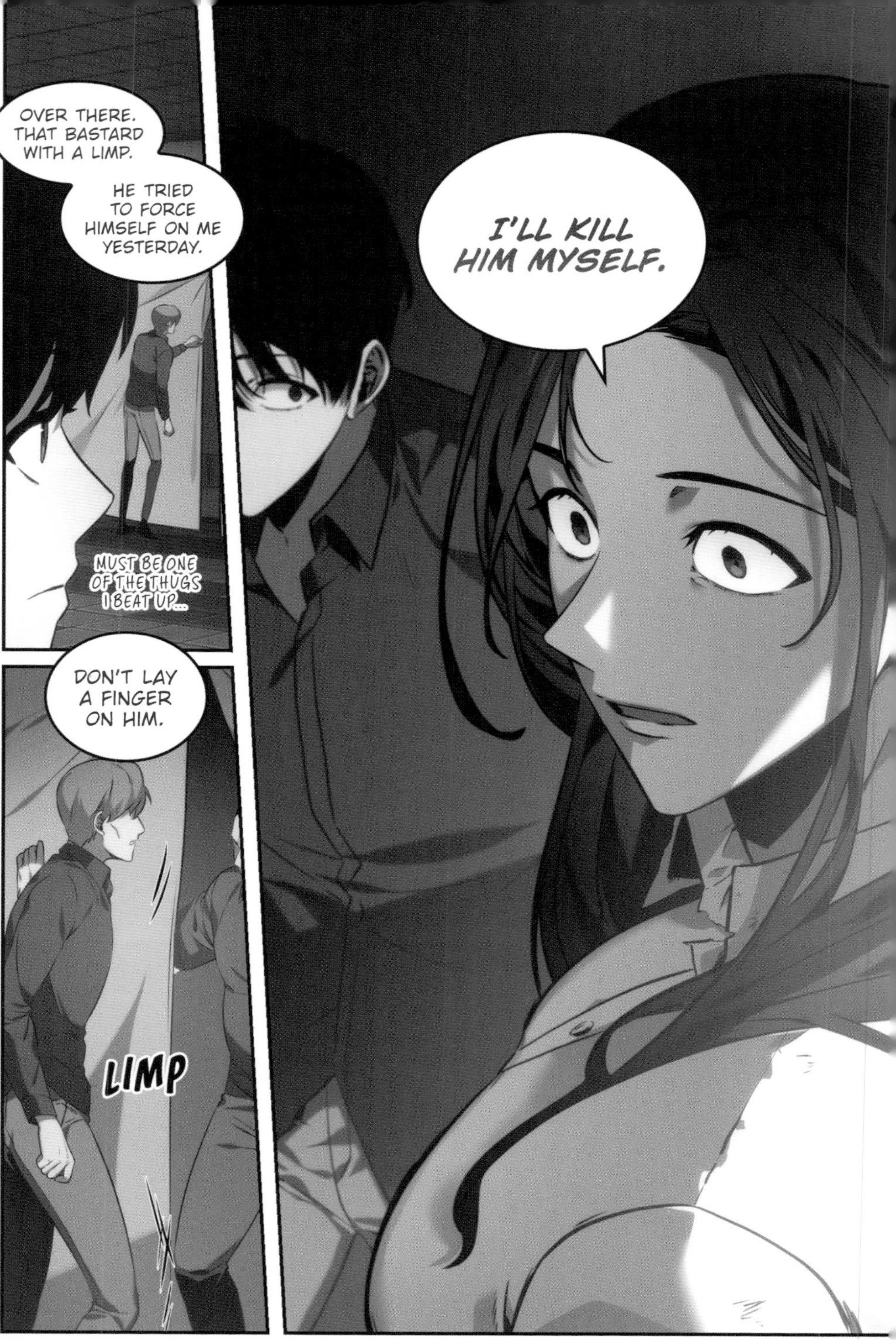
OVER THERE. THAT BASTARD WITH A LIMP.
HE TRIED TO FORCE HIMSELF ON ME YESTERDAY.
MUST BE ONE OF THE THUGS I BEAT UP...
I'LL KILL HIM MYSELF.
DON'T LAY A FINGER ON HIM.
LIMP

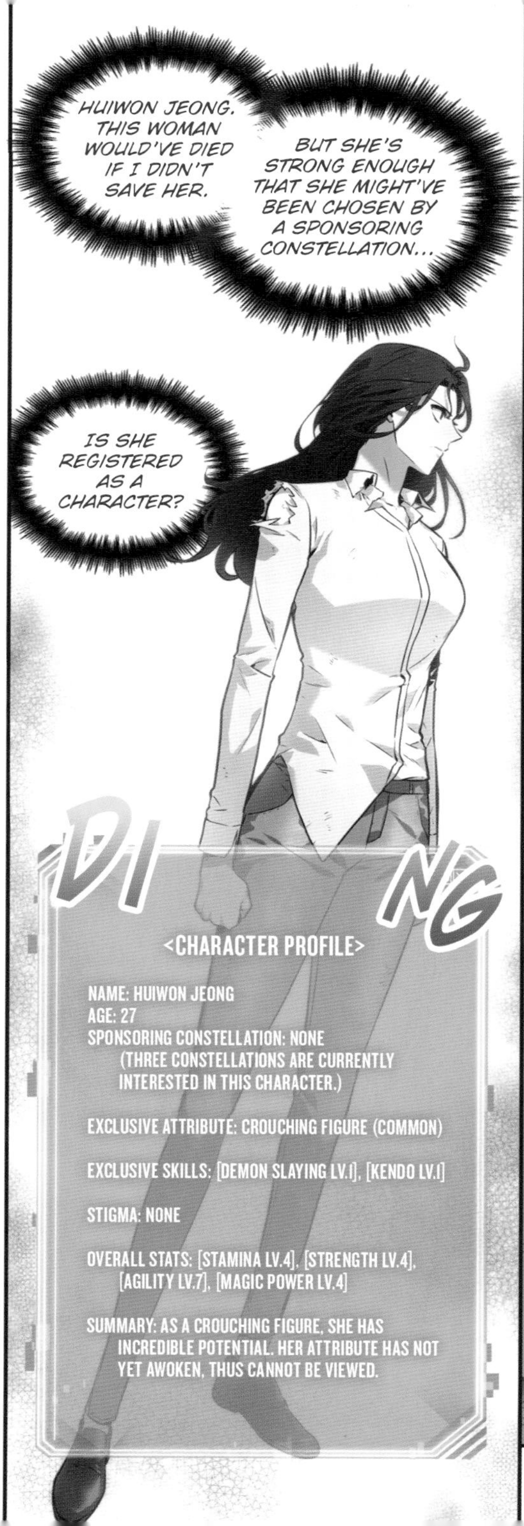
HUIWON JEONG. THIS WOMAN WOULD'VE DIED IF I DIDN'T SAVE HER.
BUT SHE'S STRONG ENOUGH THAT SHE MIGHT'VE BEEN CHOSEN BY A SPONSORING CONSTELLATION...
IS SHE REGISTERED AS A CHARACTER?
DING
<CHARACTER PROFILE>
NAME: HUIWON JEONG
AGE: 27
SPONSORING CONSTELLATION: NONE
(THREE CONSTELLATIONS ARE CURRENTLY INTERESTED IN THIS CHARACTER.)
EXCLUSIVE ATTRIBUTE: CROUCHING FIGURE (COMMON)
EXCLUSIVE SKILLS: [DEMON SLAYING LV.1], [KENDO LV.1]
STIGMA: NONE
OVERALL STATS: [STAMINA LV.4], [STRENGTH LV.4], [AGILITY LV.7], [MAGIC POWER LV.4]
SUMMARY: AS A CROUCHING FIGURE, SHE HAS INCREDIBLE POTENTIAL. HER ATTRIBUTE HAS NOT YET AWOKEN, THUS CANNOT BE VIEWED.

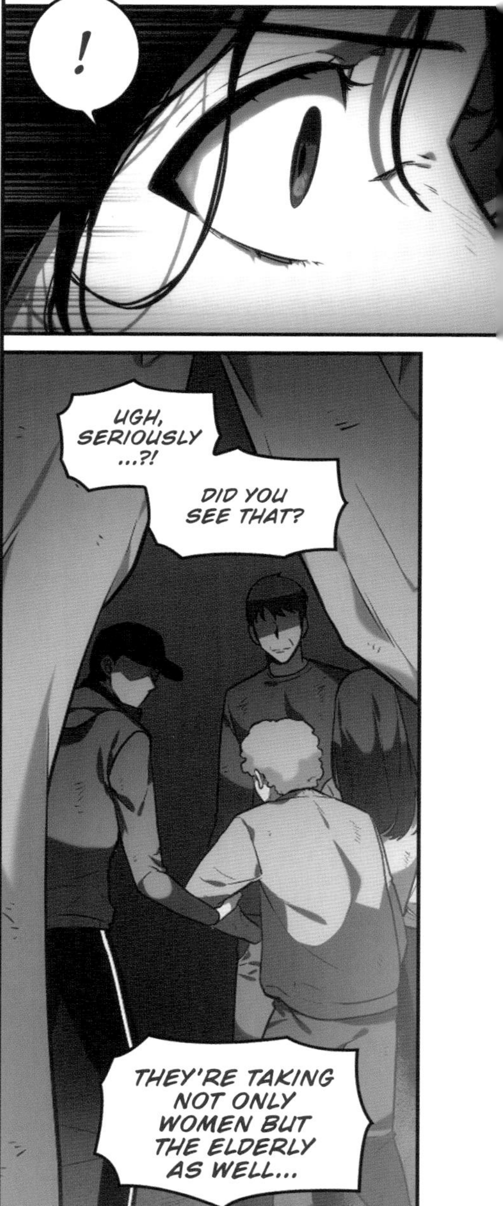
!
UGH, SERIOUSLY ...?!
DID YOU SEE THAT?
THEY'RE TAKING NOT ONLY WOMEN BUT THE ELDERLY AS WELL...

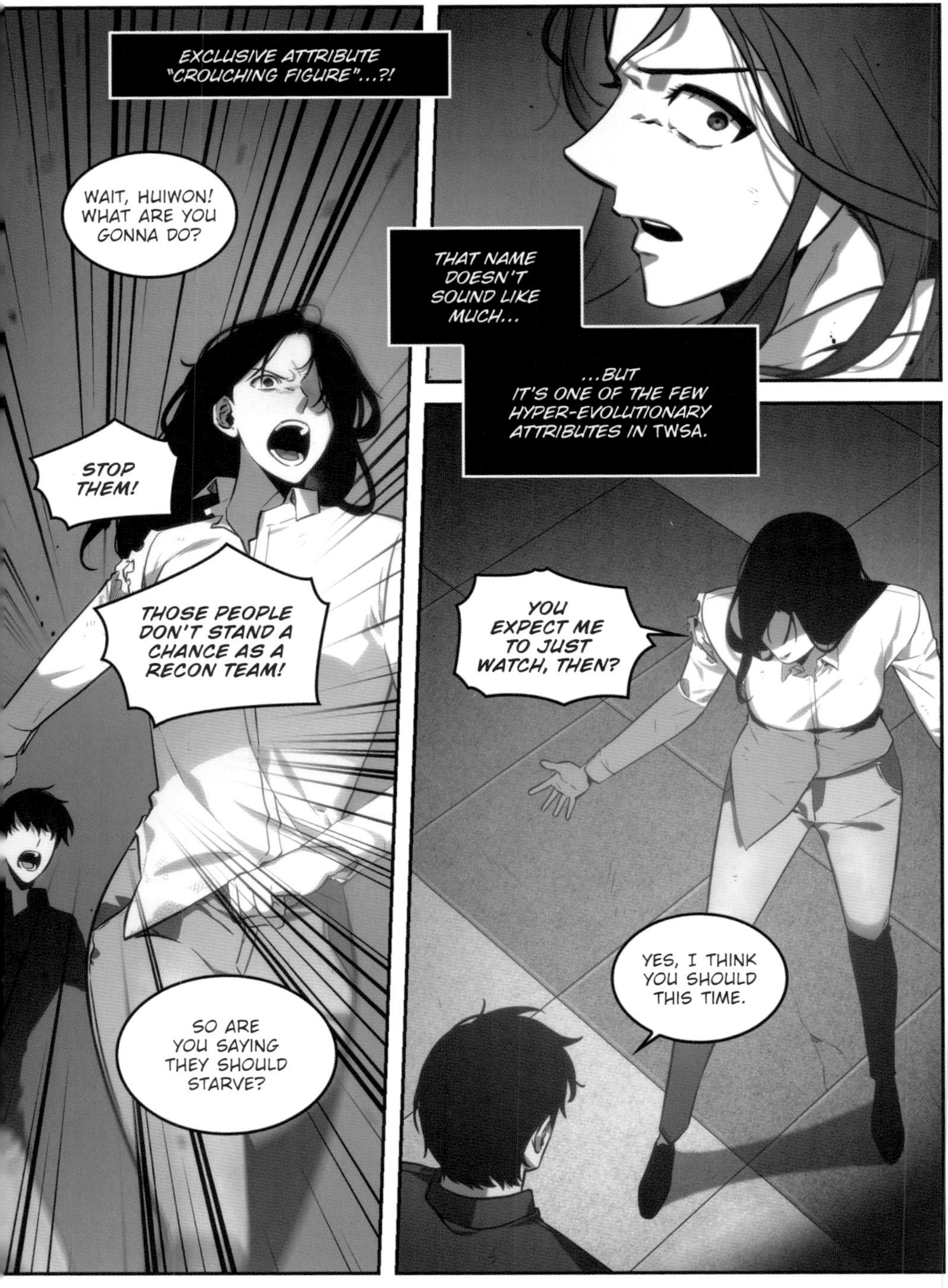
EXCLUSIVE ATTRIBUTE "CROUCHING FIGURE"...?!
WAIT, HUIWON! WHAT ARE YOU GONNA DO?
STOP THEM!
THOSE PEOPLE DON'T STAND A CHANCE AS A RECON TEAM!
SO ARE YOU SAYING THEY SHOULD STARVE?
THAT NAME DOESN'T SOUND LIKE MUCH...
...BUT IT'S ONE OF THE FEW HYPER-EVOLUTIONARY ATTRIBUTES IN TWSA.
YOU EXPECT ME TO JUST WATCH, THEN?
YES, I THINK YOU SHOULD THIS TIME.

...WHAT DO YOU MEAN?

I'M SAYING, YOU STOPPING THEM NOW WON'T SOLVE THE PROBLEM.

CROUCHING FIGURE IS A COMMON-GRADE ATTRIBUTE, BUT DEPENDING ON THE CIRCUMSTANCE OF ITS AWAKENING...

...IT CAN EVOLVE INTO A *RARE* OR EVEN A *LEGENDARY* ATTRIBUTE.

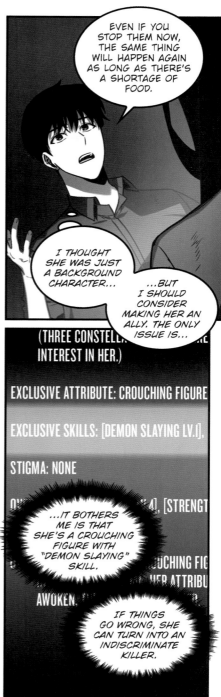

EVEN IF YOU STOP THEM NOW, THE SAME THING WILL HAPPEN AGAIN AS LONG AS THERE'S A SHORTAGE OF FOOD.

I THOUGHT SHE WAS JUST A BACKGROUND CHARACTER...

...BUT I SHOULD CONSIDER MAKING HER AN ALLY. THE ONLY ISSUE IS...

(THREE CONSTELL... ...RE INTEREST IN HER.)

EXCLUSIVE ATTRIBUTE: CROUCHING FIGURE

EXCLUSIVE SKILLS: [DEMON SLAYING LV.1],

STIGMA: NONE

...IT BOTHERS ME IS THAT SHE'S A CROUCHING FIGURE WITH "DEMON SLAYING" SKILL.

IF THINGS GO WRONG, SHE CAN TURN INTO AN INDISCRIMINATE KILLER.

AWOKEN.

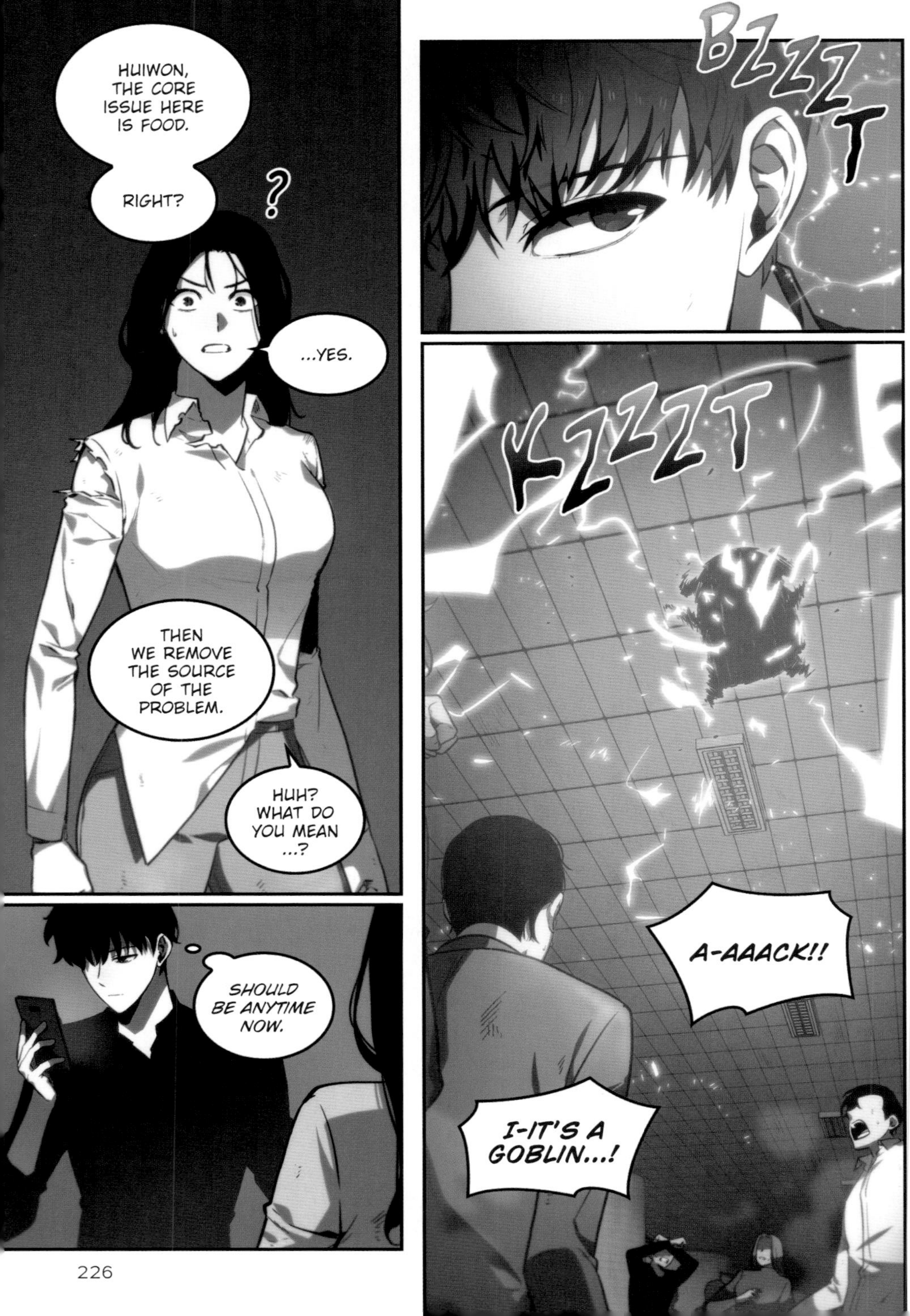
HUIWON, THE CORE ISSUE HERE IS FOOD.
RIGHT?
?
...YES.
THEN WE REMOVE THE SOURCE OF THE PROBLEM.
HUH? WHAT DO YOU MEAN ...?
SHOULD BE ANYTIME NOW.
BZZZZT
KZZZZT
A-AAACK!!
I-IT'S A GOBLIN...!

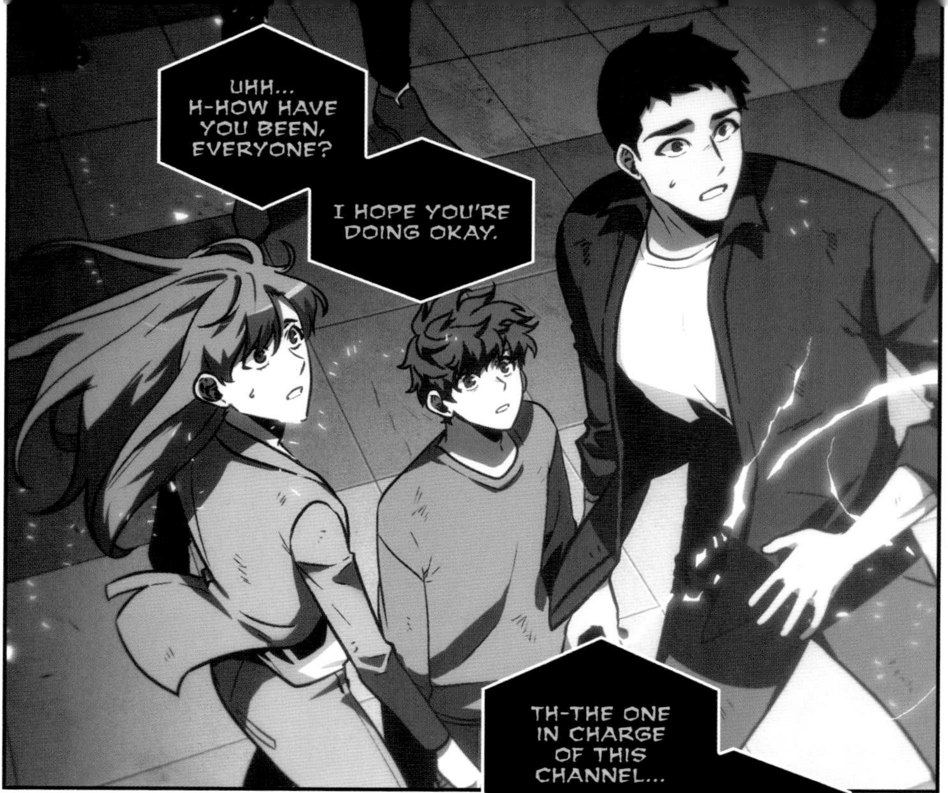
UHH... H-HOW HAVE YOU BEEN, EVERYONE?
I HOPE YOU'RE DOING OKAY.
TH-THE ONE IN CHARGE OF THIS CHANNEL...
...HAS BEEN DISCIPLINED...

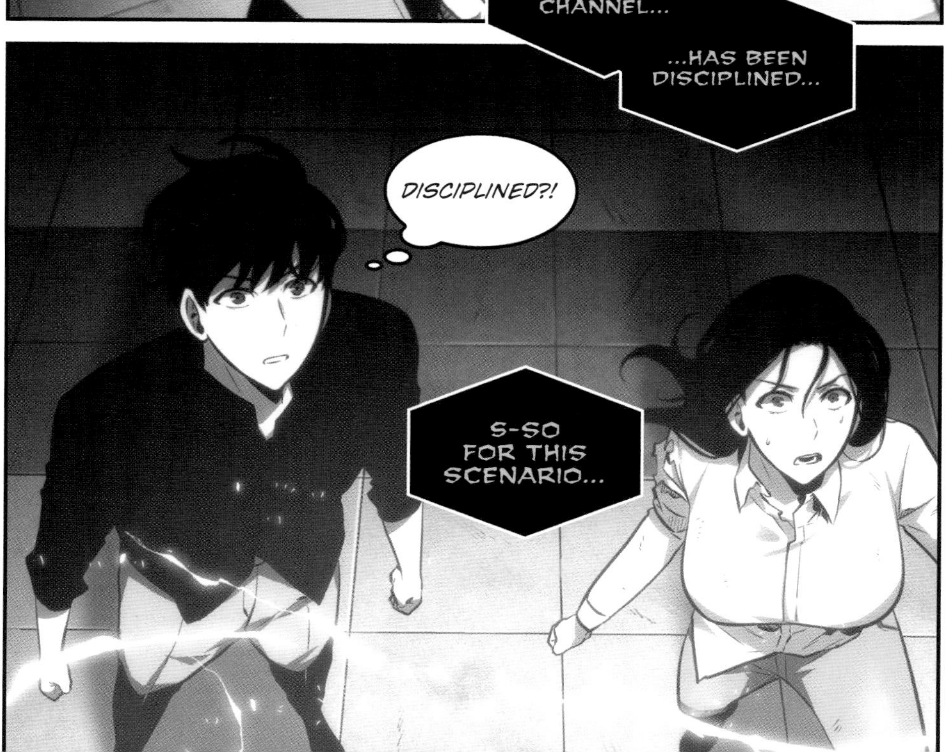
DISCIPLINED?!
S-SO FOR THIS SCENARIO...

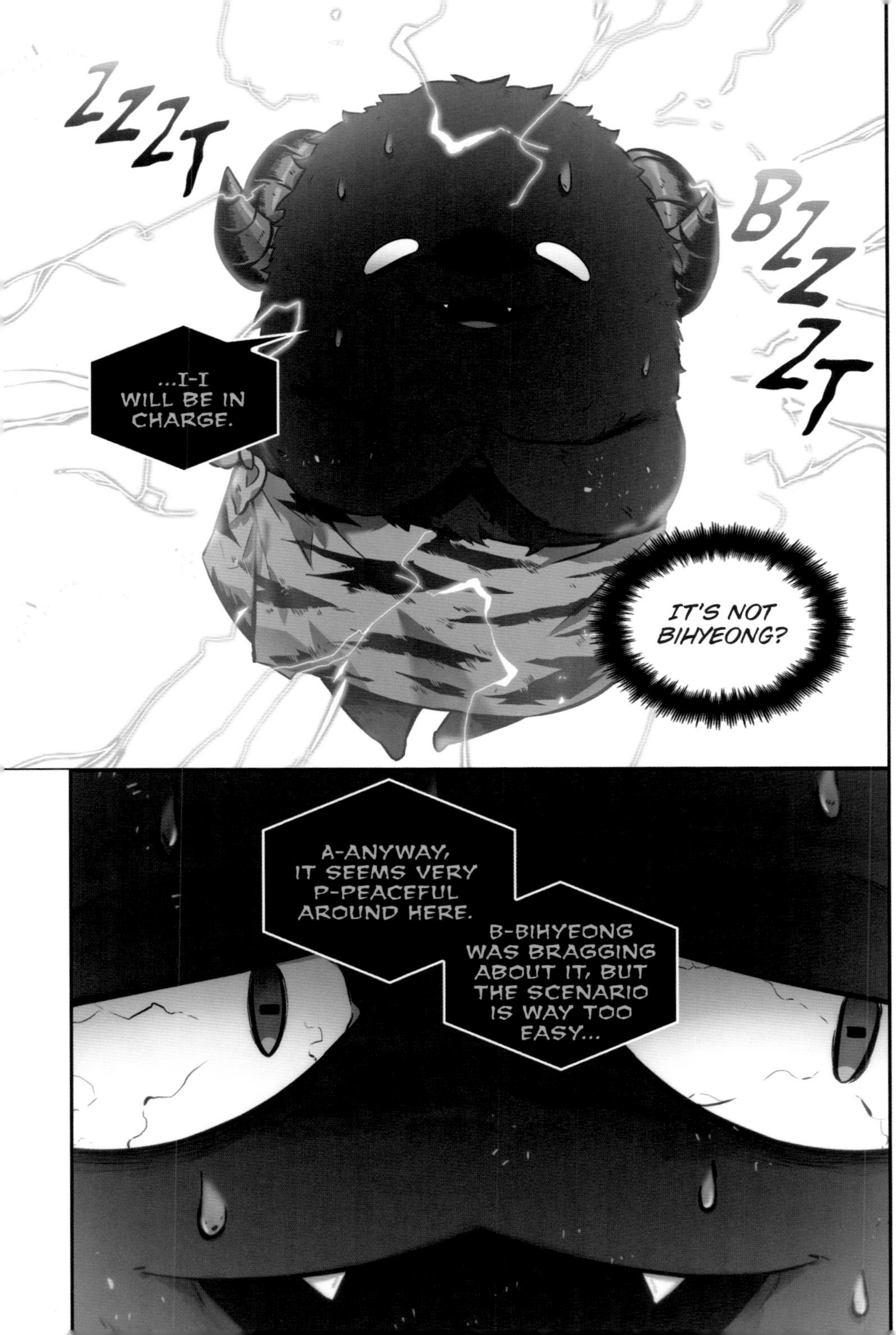

ZZZT
BZZZT
...I-I WILL BE IN CHARGE.
IT'S NOT BIHYEONG?
A-ANYWAY, IT SEEMS VERY P-PEACEFUL AROUND HERE.
B-BIHYEONG WAS BRAGGING ABOUT IT, BUT THE SCENARIO IS WAY TOO EASY...

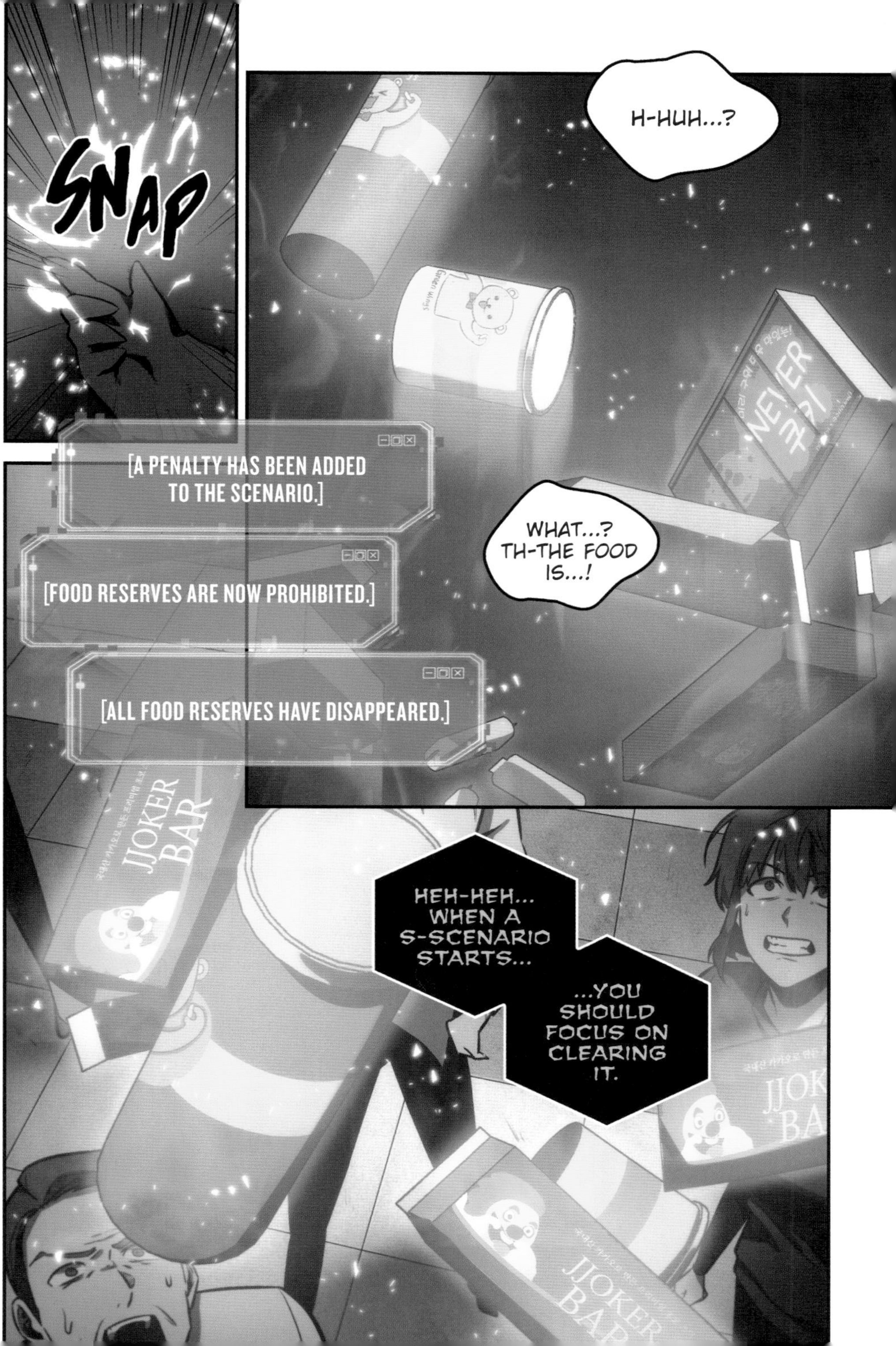
SNAP
H-HUH...?
WHAT...? TH-THE FOOD IS...!
[A PENALTY HAS BEEN ADDED TO THE SCENARIO.]
[FOOD RESERVES ARE NOW PROHIBITED.]
[ALL FOOD RESERVES HAVE DISAPPEARED.]
NEVER
JJOKER BAR
HEH-HEH... WHEN A S-SCENARIO STARTS...
...YOU SHOULD FOCUS ON CLEARING IT.
JJOKER BAR

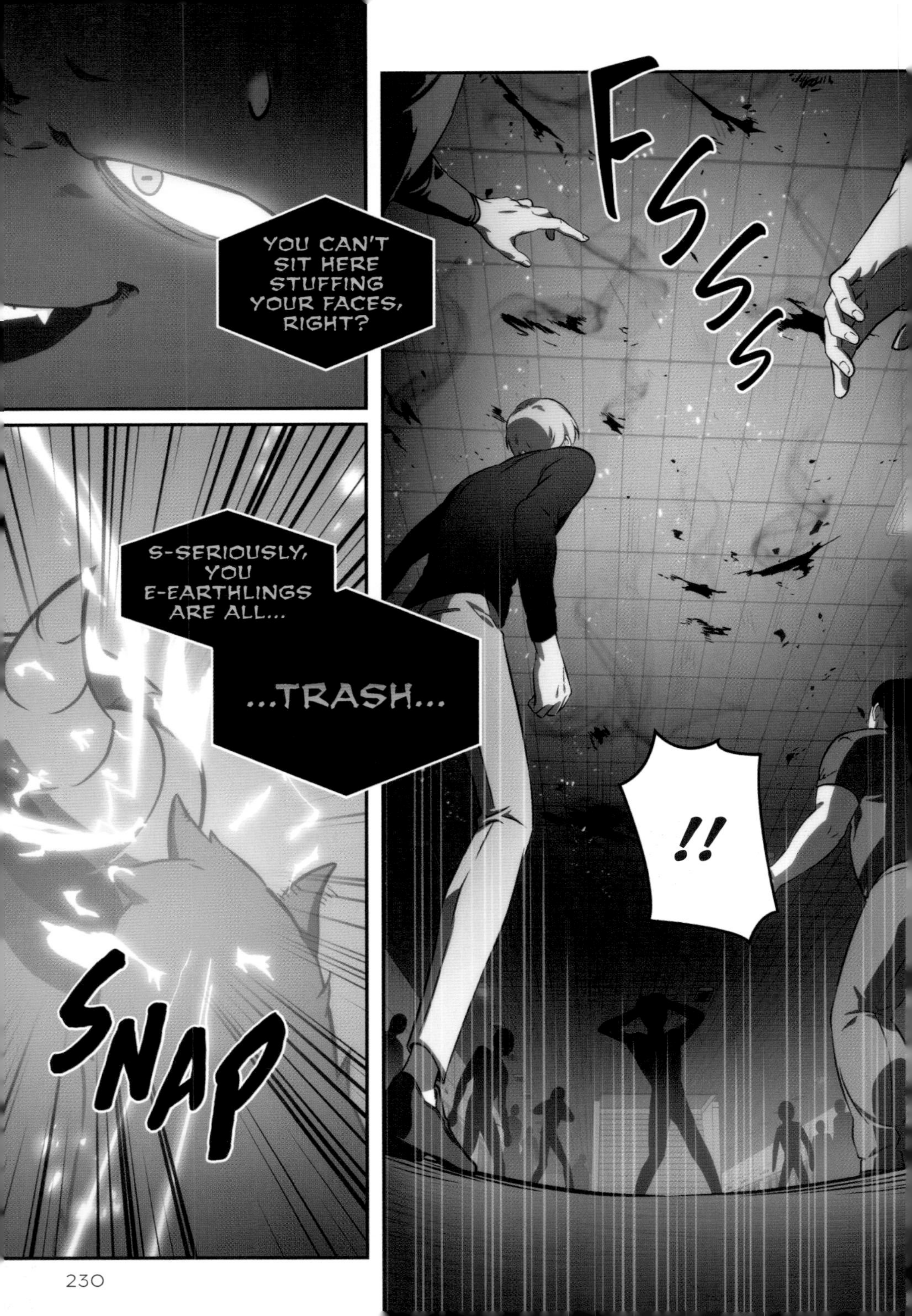
YOU CAN'T SIT HERE STUFFING YOUR FACES, RIGHT?
S-SERIOUSLY, YOU E-EARTHLINGS ARE ALL...
...TRASH...
SNAP
FSSS
!!

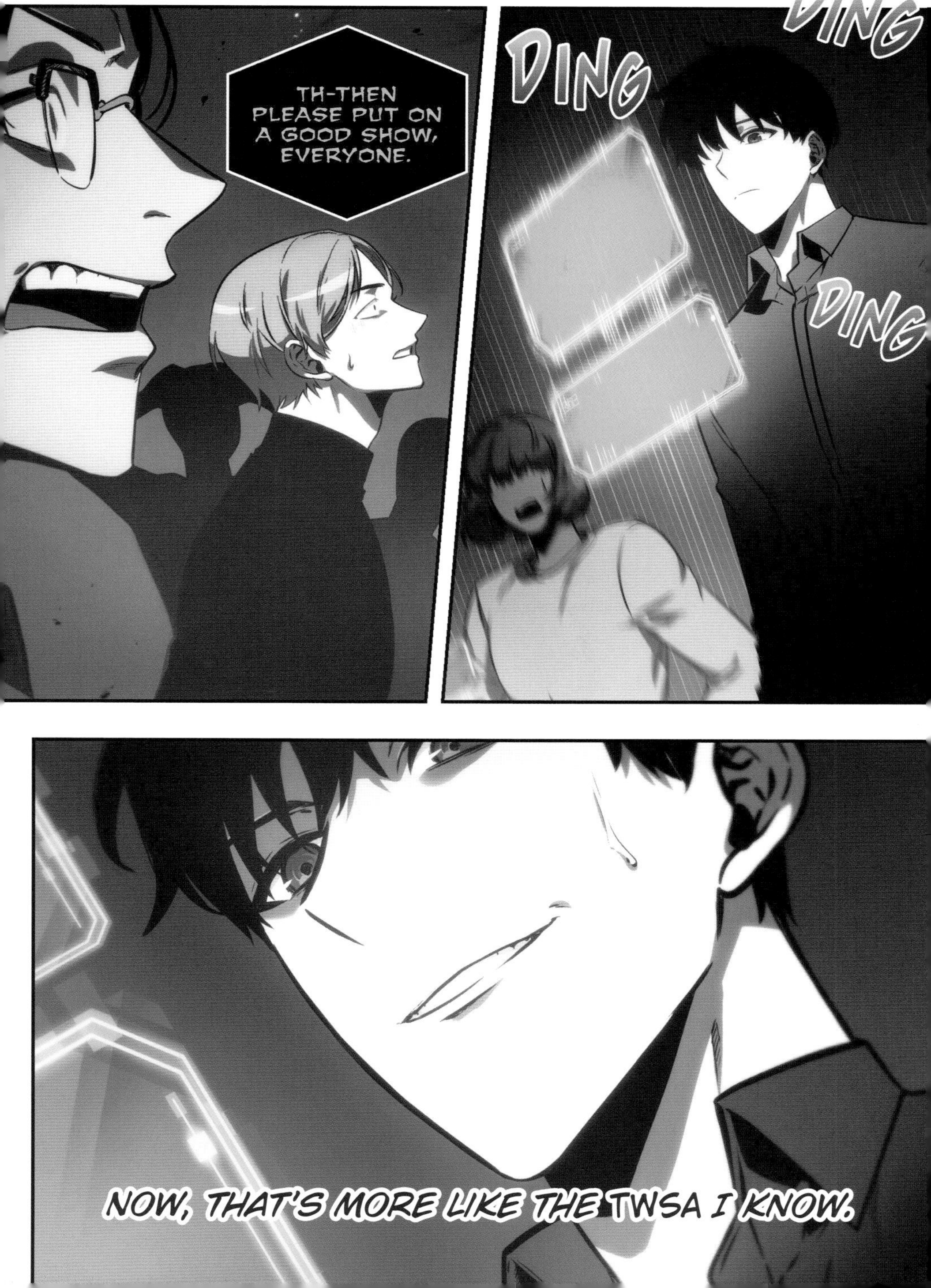
TH-THEN PLEASE PUT ON A GOOD SHOW, EVERYONE.
DING
DING
DING
NOW, THAT'S MORE LIKE THE TWSA I KNOW.

[A PENALTY HAS BEEN ADDED
TO THE SCENARIO.]

[A NEW CONDITION,
SURVIVAL FEE, HAS BEEN ADDED.]

[FROM NOW ON, A SURVIVAL FEE OF
100 COINS WILL AUTOMATICALLY BE
WITHDRAWN EVERY DAY AT MIDNIGHT.

YOU WILL DIE IF YOU CAN'T PAY
THE SURVIVAL FEE.]

[THE SURVIVAL FEE IS IN EFFECT
UNTIL THE SECOND MAIN SCENARIO
IS CLEARED.]

[YOU ARE CURRENTLY IN THE
SECOND SCENARIO ZONE.

FIND AND MOVE TO THE LOCATION
WHERE THE SCENARIO WILL BEGIN.]

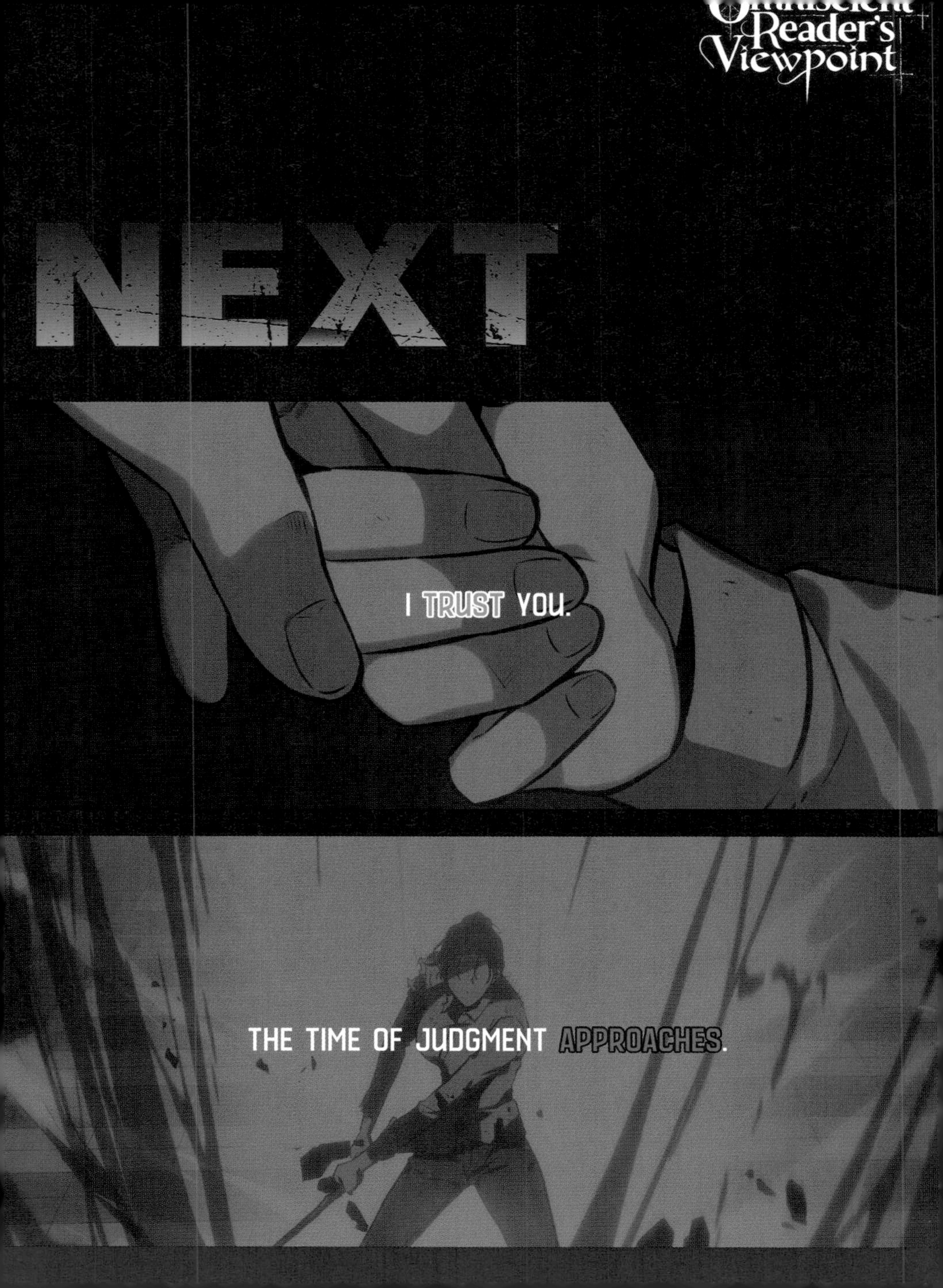
NEXT
I TRUST YOU.
THE TIME OF JUDGMENT APPROACHES.

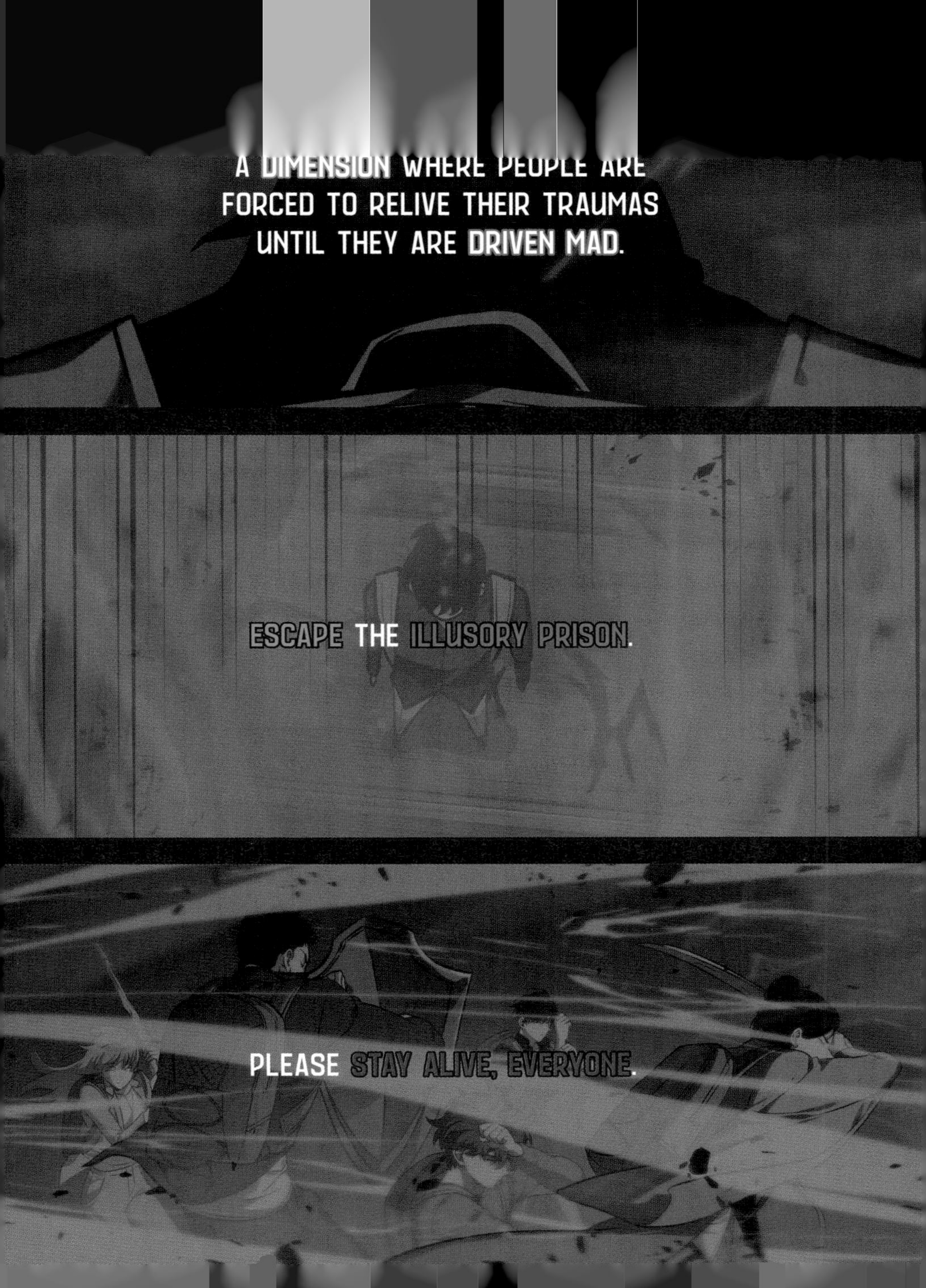
A DIMENSION WHERE PEOPLE ARE FORCED TO RELIVE THEIR TRAUMAS UNTIL THEY ARE DRIVEN MAD.
ESCAPE THE ILLUSORY PRISON.
PLEASE STAY ALIVE, EVERYONE.

PAGE 96 BIHYEONG

Bihyeong is a figure appearing in the *Overlooked Historical Records of the Three Korean Kingdoms*, a compilation of ancient Korean history and folklore written in the thirteenth century. According to these records, Bihyeong was born to the spirit of the deceased King Jinji of Silla and a commoner woman named Dohwanyeo. Perhaps due to the extraordinary circumstances of his birth, he is said to have possessed the ability to control ghosts and goblins.

PAGE 99 DOKGAK

Dokgak is likely named after *dokgakgwi*, a type of goblin appearing in Korean folklore. It is described as having one leg and giving off a nasty odor.

PAGE 99 GILDAL

Gildal is a figure appearing in the *Overlooked Historical Records of the Three Korean Kingdoms*. He was a goblin——or a ghost, depending on the source——in the service of Bihyeong. Eventually he was recommended to work in the royal court of Silla and turned out to be a capable aide for the king.

PAGE 137 CONTRACTS

Various contracts in Korea, such as employer-employee or lender-lendee agreements, often designate which party is *gap* (Party A) or *eul* (Party B), with the former holding a clearly advantageous position over the latter. Because of this, who gets to be which on the contract can become a major point of dispute.

PAGE 141 BAKING COOKIES

The constellation *Eyes Waiting for Tuesday Nights* refers to the readers of *Omniscient Reader's Viewpoint* webcomic, which has new episodes uploaded to Naver Webtoon every Tuesday evening. The currency used on this platform to view webcomics is called "cookies," and users jokingly refer to the act of paying for episodes as "baking cookies."

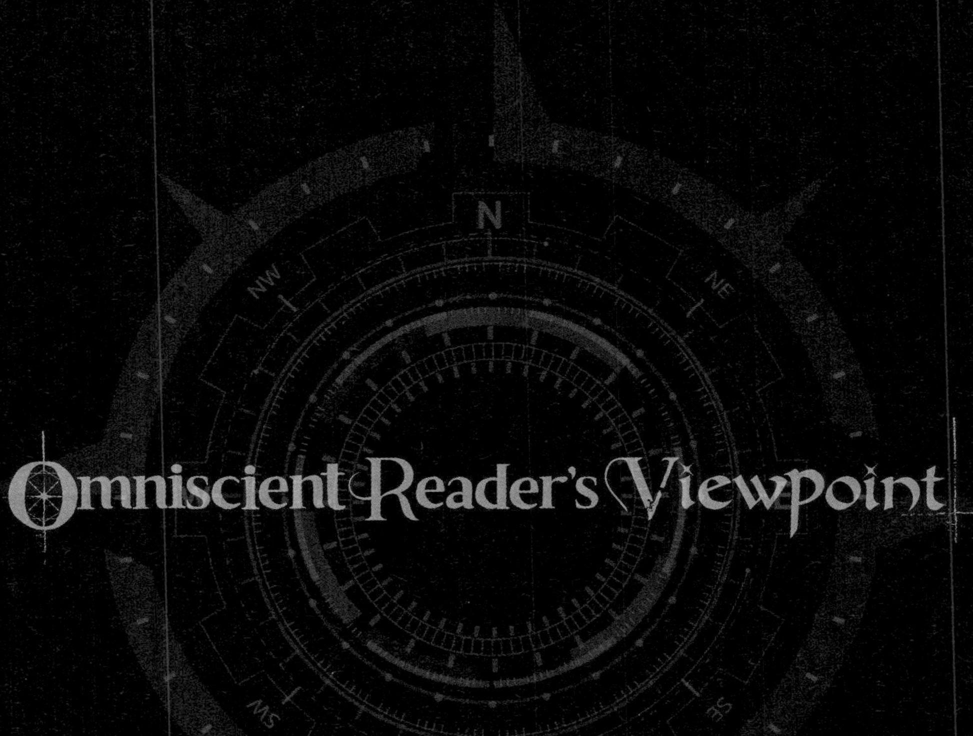

Omniscient Reader's Viewpoint
N
NE
SE
S
SW
NW

AUTHOR'S NOTE

CONGRATULATORY WORDS FROM SUNG-RAK JANG(DUBU:REDICE STUDIO)

Greetings.

This is DUBU, the artist of *Solo Leveling*.

Omniscient Reader's Viewpoint is an amazing work,

and I offer sincere contragulations

on the publication of the print edition.

I'm rooting for you, as a reader.

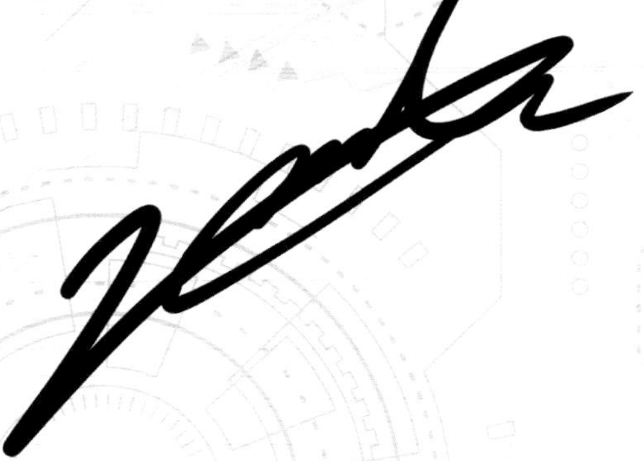

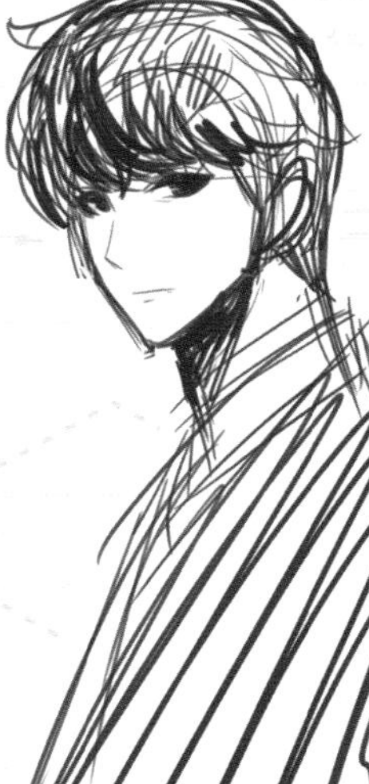

Omniscient Reader's Viewpoint

02

Translation:
HYE YOUNG IM

Rewrite:
J. TORRES

Lettering:
ADNAZEER
MACALANGCOM

Art by **Sleepy-C** ❖ Adapted by **UMI** (REDICE STUDIO)
Original story by **singNsong**

Omniscient Reader's Viewpoint, Vol. 2
©Sleepy-C, UMI (REDICE STUDIO), singNsong 2020/
REDICE STUDIO
All rights reserved.
English edition published by arrangement with
REDICE STUDIO through RIVERSE Inc.

English translation © 2024 Ize Press

Ize Press
150 West 30th Street, 19th Floor
New York, NY 10001

Visit us at izepress.com ✶ facebook.com/izepress ✶ twitter.com/izepress ✶ instagram.com/izepress

First Ize Press Edition: March 2024
Edited by Ize Press Editorial: Stephen Kim, JuYoun Lee
Designed by Ize Press Design: Wendy Chan

Library of Congress Control Number: 2023942811

ISBN: 979-8-4009-0129-4

10 9 8 7 6 5 4 3 2 1

TPA

Printed in South Korea